I0815168

Noguchi's Gardens

Noguchi's Gardens: Landscape as Sculpture

Marc Treib

ORO EDITIONS

The publication of this book has been supported in part by a generous subvention from the Hubbard Educational Trust.

Unless otherwise specified, all works illustrated in this book are by Isamu Noguchi.

All photos without credit are by Marc Treib.

Considerable effort has been made to determine the source of every image and its maker. Please contact the publisher concerning any oversight that should be corrected in subsequent printings.

Book Design: Marc Treib
ORO Project Coordinator: Jake Anderson

First Edition
Library of Congress data available upon request.
ISBN: 978-1-957183-99-2
International Distribution: www.oroeditions.com/distribution
10 9 8 7 6 5 4 3 2 First edition
World Rights: Available
Color Separations and Printing: ORO Editions Inc.
Printed in China

For

Peter Walker

and

Jane Gillette

>> CONTENTS

> 1.

A Broad Practice

While sculpture always remained central to his artistic practice, Isamu Noguchi's (1904–1988) interests and production spanned exceptionally broad terrain, arguably more diverse in type, material, and range of scales than those of any other sculptor active in the twentieth century [1-1]. In addition to object sculptures, whose production continued throughout his lifetime, Noguchi designed stage sets for dance; plazas, courtyards, and gardens; and furniture and lamps that have enjoyed extensive and continuous production. For some critics the scope of his creative endeavors, some of them commercial, diminished their respect for Noguchi as an artist; these writers conveyed difficulty in recognizing the possibility of excelling in more than one arena, even over time.[1] In his thinking Noguchi made no distinction between design, craft, and the so-called fine arts, and thus evinced values traditional to Japan. In his view ceramics, furniture and light design, theater sets, and gardens, could all be art should their aesthetic qualities sufficiently transcend those generated by the simple address of need. According to Noguchi, his Akari were not so much utilitarian objects to provide illumination as sculptures with light as their medium [1-2].

Although his gardens include several of the twentieth century's most iconic landscape designs and have received almost universal praise, Noguchi nonetheless occupies a place removed from the normal practice of landscape architecture. He did not design landscapes whose primary mission was to address a functional program through systematic study, nor to manifest or adhere to ecological principles or social codes. As an artist Noguchi relied more on intuition, bolstered by focused study where needed, than on objective analysis, and he shaped his landscapes as sculptures employing space as their primary vehicle. Without question, Noguchi also addressed the programmatic and cultural conditions of each commission, but his rankings of these concerns often diverged from those more characteristic of the landscape architecture profession. Instead, Noguchi approached landscape design as a spatial and formal art, and from his earliest environmental projects in the 1930s to the works of his later maturity, he succeeded in conceiving and constructing a series of remarkable places.

1-1
Isamu Noguchi with
Lessons of Musokokushi, 1962.
[© Niki Ekstrom,
© The Isamu Noguchi Foundation
and Garden Museum / Artists
Rights Society (hereafter
The Noguchi Museum/ARS]

>> ART AND/OR DESIGN

In his introduction to *An Outline of European Architecture*, British architectural historian Nikolaus Pevsner famously claims that "A bicycle shed is a building, Lincoln Cathedral is a piece of architecture."[2] Behind this now-celebrated—and today usually derided—aphorism is the belief that some ineffable attribute distinguishes building—i.e., construction without a conscious emphasis on form, space, aesthetics, or civic representation—from architecture as a class of buildings that values and embodies just those qualities. Since the book's original publication in 1942, the visions and values of architectural historians and their accepted definitions of architecture have broadened considerably, today often assigning equal merit to vernacular buildings and those of a more "polite" strain. Yet despite this egalitarian stance advocated by many historians, distinct differences that separate the two modes of construction nonetheless linger. Although possibly colored by the goal of creating a distinctive and attractive bicycle shed, the first approach works pragmatically within established and conventional patterns; the second aims more squarely at personal expression and, at times, at the realization of beauty. This question of quality—that elusive property or aura that transcends functional and pragmatic demands—underlies the discussion of Noguchi's spatial works, whether we choose to call them gardens, as he preferred, or landscapes.

In many cultures the garden has historically been regarded, at least potentially, as a work of art. So shall we. Not any garden qualifies; only those whose spaces, hues, use of plants, water, or other components elevate the level of its spatial, experiential, or horticultural achievement well above the ordinary. A vegetable garden or an agricultural field rarely receives designation as an artwork, but for many people considerable delight results when walking at a regular cadence through a geometrically planted orchard or passing endless rows of brilliantly colored flowers. At some point these productive fields become valued less as *agri*-culture and simply as culture, at its best rivaling or equaling the experience derived from the "fine arts." The Potager du Roi at Versailles, the famous kitchen garden Jean-Baptiste de la Quintinie (1626–1688) tended for Louis XIV, achieves this heightened aesthetic from its paradisical walled enclosure, endless rows of espaliered fruits, and the basic geometric disposition of its terraces and plantings. The Potager may be the Lincoln Cathedral of kitchen gardens; there are certain to be many others.

Gardens as art may take many forms, although their designation as such may follow rather than lead their making. In the same way that a functional object from centuries past—a glass tumbler or a ceramic plate, for example—may today be viewed as a work of art warranting inclusion in a museum collection, so too landscapes instigated by religious or political impulses may be judged as art. The dry garden at the Zen Buddhist temple Ryôan-ji in Kyoto (c. 1500) serves as a prime example of the first type; Versailles, the paramount exemplar of the second [1-3, 1-4].

A nagging question remains, however. What grants these gardens valuation as artworks, and is it actually possible to initiate garden making by intending to create a true work of art?[3] Should any landscape made by a person identified as an artist unquestioningly be deemed a work of art? To some, the delight or edification derived on-site may be insufficient to merit such reward; to others who use the garden, personal pleasure may alone provide the basis of appreciation. Noguchi clearly intended his gardens and plazas as works of art, not only because he himself identified as an artist, but also because he regarded art as an expression greater than that of the individual artist. His reason for making gardens originally stemmed from a desire to reduce, if not completely eradicate, the estrangement of the artwork from the public, the separation underlying the common view of the art museum as an institution with restricted access. "I do architectural things," Noguchi once told his assistant Gene Owens, "because they are not in anyone's possession really. They belong to the whole public."[4]

Despite Noguchi's lofty aspiration the open hours of most museums are limited, and most if, not all charge a fee for admission. Plazas or gardens, at least those in the public realm, are available to all at any time, and thus offer the public artworks uninterrupted by closure. Or so Noguchi argued. In some cases, this was wishful thinking on the sculptor's part: art-museum sculpture gardens control access, as do public institutions such as UNESCO in Paris. In addition, many public spaces today are public in name only, privately owned and managed, open only during certain hours, and patrolled by private security.[5] Yet despite these realities, there was a goal on Noguchi's part to bring art to the people—and to create habitable and moving spaces in the process.

1-2
Akari light sculptures.

1-3
Ryôan-ji.
Kyoto, Japan, c. 1500.

1-4
André Le Nôtre.
Jardins du Château de
Versailles, France, 1661+.

1-5
Assembled sculptures (details).
1940s.
[Marc Treib, © The Noguchi
Museum/ARS]

Any evaluation of designed spaces must establish and evaluate the differences between intention and perception. What the maker intends, proposes, and constructs rarely matches how visitors experience, interpret, and ultimately evaluate them. In discussing several of his gardens, Noguchi described them as places marked by quiet and intended for tranquil meditation. To him the garden was a place "where the human heart can come into direct, pure contact with the world of plants and flowers ... a space in which art itself is so artless as to be totally unapparent."[6] Yet for many visitors to his gardens an examination of their spaces, objects, and plants—or even the enjoyment of a smoke within them—may outweigh any urge for contemplation. In a similar way a landscape conceived as a place of rest and meditation may be interpreted in a far different way, perhaps as a locus of horticultural experiment, as a belvedere from which to enjoy the view over the city or the land, or for its display of sculpture. Neither the appreciation of plants nor a spectacular view is antithetical to contemplation, of course, and either may foster a calmer mental state. But response, interpretation, and meaning are ultimately the province of the individual and do not reside with the maker of the place or in the place itself.[7]

Habitable space distinguishes Noguchi's gardens from his object sculptures. The evolution of his art and production evolved from solid to spatial, from molding clay or shaping stone to assembling sculptures more open and fluid. Although he would continue to work with stone throughout his life—especially during his later years—these efforts paralleled formal investigations in which space played a greater role. In the early 1940s, Noguchi began to devise sculptures from thin slabs of marble cut into biomorphic shapes and assembled as if a game of interlocking playing cards [1-5]. Indeed, during his path to maturation he came to realize that space lay at the core of sculpture:

> *The essence of sculpture is for me the perception of space, the continuum of our existence. All dimensions are but measures of it, as in the relative perspective of our vision lie volume, line, point, giving shape, distance, proportion. Movement, light, and time itself are also qualities of space. Space is otherwise inconceivable.*[8]

And from these assembled sculptures he jumped in scale to produce habitable sculptures: stage sets for Martha Graham's dances were sized to accommodate—or, better put, serve—the human body in motion. And from there he moved outdoors. At the start of the 1950s he designed and realized his first garden. "I am not concerned here with monument or embellishment but with gardens," he admitted, "by which I mean that self-contained sculpturing of space with whatever medium, be it trees, water, rock, wire, or broken-down automobiles."[9] The mediums and elements were of less consequence than the spaces they defined between or among them. Space was the true nature of the stage set and the garden as well as the sculpture.

One could say simply that because Noguchi was known as an artist, we must regard his landscapes as works of art. That pronouncement, I feel, is a bit too accepting. Critically viewed, his many projects vary in their formal and spatial success; like his sculptures, some works may be judged "better" than others. For example, I would position *California Scenario* (1982) in Costa Mesa above the plaza for the Japanese American Cultural & Community Center (JACCC; 1983) in Los Angeles completed about a year later [1-6; see also chapter 9]. This is a personal evaluation, of course, based on what I as a design professional seek in the places I visit or use, and position in relation to my experience with others of the world's landscapes with which I am familiar. Such a conclusion is admittedly troubled by the imbalance of trying to equate apples and oranges. Noguchi treated *California Scenario* as a giant sculpture composed of distinct elements, while the JACCC plaza evinces a less emphatic sculptural presence, due in all probability to its having been designed as terrain whose primary purpose was hosting events [1-7].

In contrast to the high-rise towers and parking garages that bracket *California Scenario*, the plaza space in Los Angeles is more porous; its primary sculptural presence is limited to the two basalt stones of *To the Issei* set on a plinth at the plaza's core as its centerpiece [1-8, 1-9]. The linear constructions at the one-acre plaza's north and west edges are the most elaborately composed, each a complex relief of brick enlivened with steps, terraces, and depressions that articulate and enrich the composition. While both landscapes exude an aesthetic presence, *California Scenario* is more consciously sculptural, complex, and complete, with vegetation used in a more original manner. Given the significant differences in their program and design, can and should both be regarded as art? The facile answer is: "Yes, possibly, but to differing degrees."

1-6 *[opposite]*
California Scenario.
Costa Mesa, California, 1982.

1-7 *[above left]*
Japanese American Cultural & Community Center Plaza. Los Angeles, California, 1983. View from theater balcony.

1-8 *[above right]*
Japanese American Cultural & Community Center Plaza. The stage serves as the plinth for *To the Issei*, the work's central feature.

1-9 *[right]*
Japanese American Cultural & Community Center Plaza. Brickwork seating forms along the north edge of the plaza.

>> GARDEN AS ART

Even after completing my research, visiting the sites, and writing this text I am unable to offer any definitive word on just when, and how, a garden or other landscape becomes a work of art—or at least warrants its regard as such. We could retreat from any final judgment by merely saying that "Beauty is in the eye of the beholder." Or should we qualify that adage by adding "in the mind" of the beholder as well as the eye, since on-site we import and apply our prior experiences and aesthetic prejudices rather than simply unearth them during our visit. Could we then conclude that any garden made by any artist should also be taken as a work of art? In my experience—again, according to my personal bias—few landscapes actually achieve that rank, that unspecified or unspecifiable aesthetic, and the ultimately personal quality that elevates them well above the norm. For example, many visitors may regard Claude Monet's garden at Giverny as a work of art [1-10]. I would beg to differ, with the exception of the area encompassing the pond and its bridge that figure so prominently in many of Monet's paintings, especially his later series of water lilies. On my visit to Giverny some years ago, I experienced most of the garden as undifferentiated masses of floral color; pretty, yes, but not composed to a level that merits the status of art. Had Giverny not been the work of Claude Monet, the garden would probably be seen as just another colorful garden—again, aside from that beautiful area that surrounds the pond.

If we compare the plantings of flowers in Monet's garden with a truly outstanding garden by the British garden designer Gertrude Jekyll (1843–1942)—such as Hestercombe (1907) or the Manor House, Upton Grey (1908)—we can discern the difference between flowers as a potential subject for painting, and flowers used as a medium for a work of art [1-11]. In the designs for the herbaceous borders for which she is best known, Jekyll mixed and composed flowers and woody plants to their greatest artistic effect. Applying color theory—not in paintings *of* the garden, but *in* the garden itself—Jekyll used flower and leaf as Monet used paint and brush. Therein lies the difference between art as a practice and art as a manifestation.

Noguchi referred to most of his spatial works as gardens. I prefer the more comprehensive term "landscape" because it encompasses a broader range of sizes and types and suggests more diverse interpretations

1-10
Claude Monet.
Monet garden.
Giverny, France,
late nineteenth–early
twentieth century.

—including interior spaces devoid of plants, spaces such as *Tengoku* (1977), the sculptural installation that fills the ground-floor lobby of the Sôgetsu flower-arranging school in Tokyo. Both terms, "garden" and "landscape," will be used somewhat interchangeably in this book, however; "landscape" will be employed both literally, as it is more commonly known, but also to some degree analogically or even metaphorically. Sculptures representing landscapes or those that can be read as small landscapes, inform Noguchi's conception of habitable garden spaces, although admittedly in some works the connection might be tangential. The cast-bronze forms of the floor piece *Lessons of Musokokushi* [see 1-0], for example, are easily interpreted as rocks set deep in the ground, while *Young Mountain* (1970) can be read as both a compact stone form and a mountain in miniature [1-12]. Scale is fluid. Other works less literal or identifiable as natural surrogates will not be so regarded.

1-11
Gertrude Jekyll.
Hestercombe.
Taunton, England, 1907.
Dutch garden.

>> BOOK STRUCTURE

This book focuses on the landscapes, both exterior and interior, both literal and metaphorical, designed by Isamu Noguchi between 1933 and his death in 1988. It is structured thematically rather than rigorously chronologically, with each chapter exploring the artist's intentions and approaches as well as the realized forms of the work. Interwoven with chapters discussing such themes as landform or water are chapters that discuss in greater detail what I believe to be Noguchi's most significant landscapes: the UNESCO garden in Paris (1958), the Billy Rose Art Garden in Jerusalem (1965), *California Scenario* in Southern California, and the problematic—because posthumous—Moerenuma Park (1998; 2005) in Sapporo, Japan. The selection of projects is admittedly subjective, focused on those works that I have visited in person, and that I believe represent similar sites or solutions. Over his lifetime Noguchi produced an enormous body of work at both object and landscape scales, and to include them all would have doubled the number of pages.[10] Therefore, *Noguchi's Gardens* is not intended as an exhaustive catalog of all the sculptor's spatial works; Ana Maria Torres's *Isamu Noguchi: A Study of Space* fulfilled that role admirably some years ago, although additional works have come to light since its publication in 2000.[11]

Biography is mentioned only in relation to the conception or realization of the particular garden in which it might have played an active role or if it leads to a greater understanding of the design. Biographies by Dore Ashton, Masayo Duus, and Hayden Herrera trace in detail the story of Noguchi's mixed parentage and heritage, his artistic development, exhibition record, travels, and the formulation and progression of his aesthetic and philosophical ideas.[12] I make no attempt to repeat their considerable achievements. Being neither an art historian nor a biographer, I view these spatial works by Noguchi as a landscape and architectural historian. Where appropriate—in addition to issues of materials, vegetation, space, and form—the discussion addresses aspects of a project such as client relations, program, or the design's relation to the surrounding landscape or to contemporary works of art and landscape architecture by others. Any appraisal of success judged by function and aesthetic merit follows thereafter; needless to say, those with other interests or values may judge a landscape by applying other criteria and reach a different conclusion.

Some in the landscape-architecture profession have questioned—or even rejected—the merit of Noguchi's landscapes, citing their at-times less than functional aspects, their isolation from the environmental context beyond their limits, or their curious use of materials (see chapter 9). Much of the time Noguchi considered or created gardens in a manner different from a landscape architect. As an artist he considered his landscapes as spatial sculpture, as works of art. This is not to say that he was unconcerned about people and how they might use and enjoy the gardens. Although his values occasionally stood in oblique relation to those of the design professions, I feel there are important lessons—both syntactic and semantic—to be learned for those in the design fields by studying these landscapes. Syntactic lessons include those derived from Noguchi's explorations of new ways of using established materials or new solutions employing advanced technology—for example, in the fountains for Osaka Expo '70 (1970) or the Dodge Fountain (1975) in Detroit that followed several years later. These are practical lessons applicable to all landscape design. At the same time, Noguchi's gardens also offer us lessons positioned along a semantic scale—lessons drawn from the belief that a landscape can stimulate perceptions and interpretations that transcend the common ways in which we normally consider designed environments.[13] These two axes—of syntax and semantics, concerning vocabulary and meaning—supply the immediate lessons that Noguchi's landscapes may teach us. Beyond those, however, in his best works lies a world of beauty and intrigue that stimulates and elevates thought and feeling, a world where we forget what was done, and why, and dwell instead on its presence, affect, and beauty.

1-12
Young Mountain, 1970.
[© The Noguchi Museum/ARS]

> 2.

Object to Space

Throughout six decades of active practice, Isamu Noguchi ceaselessly produced original forms and spaces by treating old materials in new ways and introducing new materials and fabrication processes.[1] Noguchi's early production focused on objects readily identified as sculpture; the design of spaces he termed "gardens" would come only many years later. These landscapes, proposed or produced between roughly 1933 and his death in 1988, occupy the larger end of the scale and rank among his most engaging and impressive works; an interesting story lies behind most of them.

>> FORMATION

Isamu Noguchi was born in Los Angeles in 1904 to an Irish-American mother, Léonie Gilmour (1873–1933), and a Japanese father, Yonejirô Noguchi (1875–1947), known as Yone, a poet who had lived in the United States for over a decade.[2] Isamu's mother had answered Yone's newspaper advertisement for an English-speaking editor and initially served in that capacity; as the years passed, however, she became his confidant, muse, and wife, although they were not formally married. Noguchi *père* returned to Japan shortly after the birth of his son in Los Angeles. Despite this rupture, Gilmour maintained correspondence with Yone thereafter and even continued to edit works of his in English. In 1907 she traveled to Japan to renew her relationship with Yone and introduce him to the son he had never met. Unfortunately, the poet's response to their arrival was less than enthusiastic, having already married and established a Japanese family; nonetheless, he provided his American family with a separate household that he would visit periodically. Gilmour, Isamu, and eventually his sister Ailes remained in Japan, although the distance between Yone and the family only increased over time. Acquiring a piece of land in Chigasaki, Gilmour decided to build a house for the family, to be erected by a carpenter with whom the ten-year-old Isamu would train [2-1].

From this brief apprenticeship Noguchi gained not only knowledge and skills in carpentry and construction but also a sensitivity to materials and his first experience in garden making. Given the opportunity to plant and tend a garden for the new house, he learned about flowers and vegetables, and the resources and care required to sustain them. The boy became devoted to the garden: "The peach trees were not mine, but

2-0
A World I Did Not Make (detail), 1952.
[Kevin Noble, © The Noguchi Museum/ARS]

the flowers were. One of my mother's pupils named Iwasaki worked in a horticultural station nearby, and I used to go there all the time to beg for rose clippings, with the result that I had about fifty rose bushes."[3] This childhood exposure to materials, tools, and construction could be regarded as foundational for a career that would span more than half a century, an artistic practice that included small sculptures at one end and habitable environments like theater sets and gardens at the other.

Concerned that Isamu might be limited by his isolation in Japan, in 1918 Gilmour sent her thirteen-year-old son back to the United States to attend the Interlaken School in La Porte, Indiana. The school's curriculum was progressive. Influenced to some degree by the pragmatism promulgated by the philosopher John Dewey, time in the field and workshop shared equal status with learning from books and in the classroom. The background of the school's director, Edward A. Rumley, undoubtedly informed the curriculum; as Masayo Duus explains, Rumley was heir to a tractor-manufacturing company; his grandfather had emigrated from Germany and made a fortune manufacturing agricultural machinery."[4] Rumley took a particular interest in his young ward, and even after Noguchi left Indiana he would support Noguchi's studies and development.

Noguchi's experience at the school was short-lived, as the outbreak of the First World War in 1914 led to the commandeering of the school and its grounds for military purposes. Abandoned, and adrift without a home, he was taken in by a kindly couple in La Porte, where he attended high school before moving to New York in 1922 for premed studies at Columbia University. His academic interests there ended abruptly upon Noguchi's realization that medicine was not his calling. In 1924 he decided to change his focus to art, which led to art classes at the Da Vinci School, then directed by Onorio Ruotolo, who quickly recognized his young student's facility in modeling figurative sculpture [2-2]. With relatively little study and production to date, at age twenty-three Noguchi was awarded a Guggenheim Fellowship to support travel and study in France and lands beyond.

Shortly after arriving in Paris he was fortuitously accepted as studio assistant by the sculptor Constantin Brancusi (1876–1957), in which capacity he would serve for about six months [2-3]. From Brancusi, who stressed that art must condense and eliminate the extraneous, he learned the craft of carving, but, perhaps more important, that the sculptor should search for the essence of the artwork within each block of wood or stone. From the master the apprentice also acquired practical knowledge such as "how to correctly cut and true the edges and then by cutting grooves to level the space between, then on to squaring the cube."[5] Carving—whose "tricks," as he called them, he had quickly learned—differed completely from Noguchi's prior work modeling clay. Brancusi was primarily a carver, although pieces such as the series of sculptures *Bird in Flight* were executed in both marble and polished bronze.[6] Brancusi steadfastly held that each material was distinguished by particular inherent qualities, qualities that the sculptor must identify and then grasp. "Each material has its own life," Brancusi explained, "and one cannot without punishment destroy a living material to make a dumb, senseless thing."[7] One must find that life, and from it create art.[8]

Even early on it became obvious that Noguchi possessed multifaceted talents, with a skill set that well served his aesthetically peripatetic nature. Among these numerous talents was portraiture, and after his return to the United States from his truncated Guggenheim travels he earned his living during the Depression years by sculpting portrait heads. Following the initial from-life modeling in clay, Noguchi vitrified each piece through firing or casting in bronze. Beyond accurately rendering their subjects' facial features, Noguchi's portrait heads captured their character through abstraction. His approach is evident in the portrait of engineer, futurist, and close friend Buckminster Fuller (1932), which was ultimately cast in bronze, chrome-plated, and finely polished to heighten the reflections upon its surface [2-4].[9] Other works from that period, such as *Miss Expanding Universe* (1932), intertwine biomorphic shapes with a tinge of historical Japanese forms, such as those characteristic of the terracotta tomb sculptures known as *haniwa*, for which Noguchi had great appreciation [2-5]. Although the modeled and carved works of the 1930s are graced with a certain fluidity, space played only a minor role in their execution—despite Noguchi's evolving belief in space as the very basis of sculpture, prompted by his visits to gardens in Japan.

Although a gap almost always exists between aesthetic values and artistic action, the realization that space embodied the essence of sculpture profoundly affected not only Noguchi's object sculptures, but

2-1 *[above left]*
Noguchi, age seven,
in Kendô gear.
Japan, 1911.
[© The Noguchi Museum/ARS]

2-2 *[above right]*
Noguchi with Study of
Abraham Lincoln, 1922.
[M. I. Boris, © The Noguchi
Museum/ARS]

2-3 *[right]*
Noguchi in his studio.
Gentilly, France, 1927.
[© The Noguchi Museum/ARS]

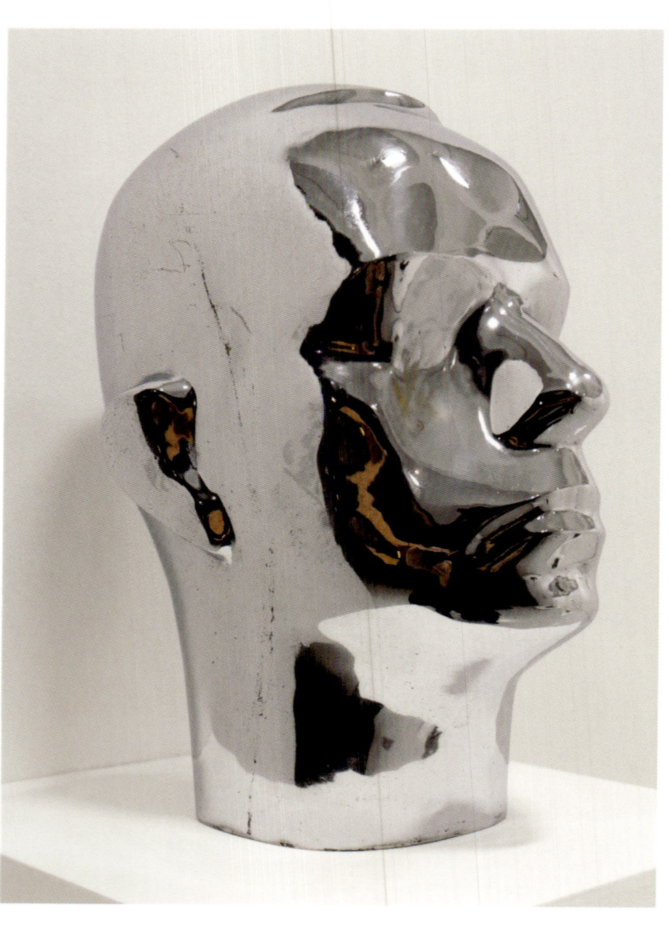

2-4
Buckminster Fuller,
1932.
[Samuel and Alexandra Snyder May; © The Noguchi Museum /ARS]

2-5
Miss Expanding Universe, 1932.
[F.S. Lincoln; Special Collections, Pennsylvania State University Libraries]

also conditioned his eventual transition into the expanded arena of interior spaces and landscapes: both those imaginary, as well as those enacted in earth, stone, and water. But that would be years in the future. In the series of sculptures fashioned from flat materials in the 1940s—drawn, cut, and thereafter assembled—space began to play a more prominent role. Transposing flat surfaces into interlocking assemblies, Noguchi outlined spaces within and around the sculpture. The process began with shapes initially drawn on graph paper, which provided an expedient medium for their later enlargement to full scale. When satisfied with the shapes and relations among the elements, Noguchi cut the shapes from stiff black-card stock and assembled them as a maquette [2-6].

The materials of the executed sculptures varied, with their selection based to some degree on availability. Around 1944 Noguchi realized that "the most available form of marble in New York was in slabs, since most of it is cut for the surfacing of buildings."[10] A stone yard not far from his studio was then in decline, and thin pieces of discarded marble could be purchased there at low cost. Using these slabs, he continued his "research into space, plus plane, plus void, using marble."[11] Unlike materials such as metal or wood, stone offered no temptation to join the pieces with an adhesive or by welding. Noguchi appreciated the crystalline surface of the stone but admitted that the marble's fragility demanded particular care when cut or shaped [2-7].[12] The sharp edges left by cutting were softened by rounding and shaping, with holes drilled into selected planes to increase their lightness and visual permeability. When constructed, the flat constituent parts were transformed into a composition of planes in space that congealed as a single form.

Constructive practices such as these led to sculptures whose elements became thin and attenuated, sculptures that breached their mass to gather in the surrounding space. "Giving the basic definition of volume (like a three-dimensional cartoon) each sculpture had only to be completed in the eye of the spectator," he claimed.[13] Perhaps drawing on his involvement with the assembled pieces, Noguchi centered on space in his artist's statement for the catalog accompanying the Museum of Modern Art's *Fourteen Americans* exhibition of 1946:

> *The essence of sculpture is for me the perception of space, the continuum of our existence... Movement, light, and time itself are*

2-6
Untitled.
1945.
Drawing for an assembled sculpture.
[Kevin Noble, © The Noguchi Museum/ARS]

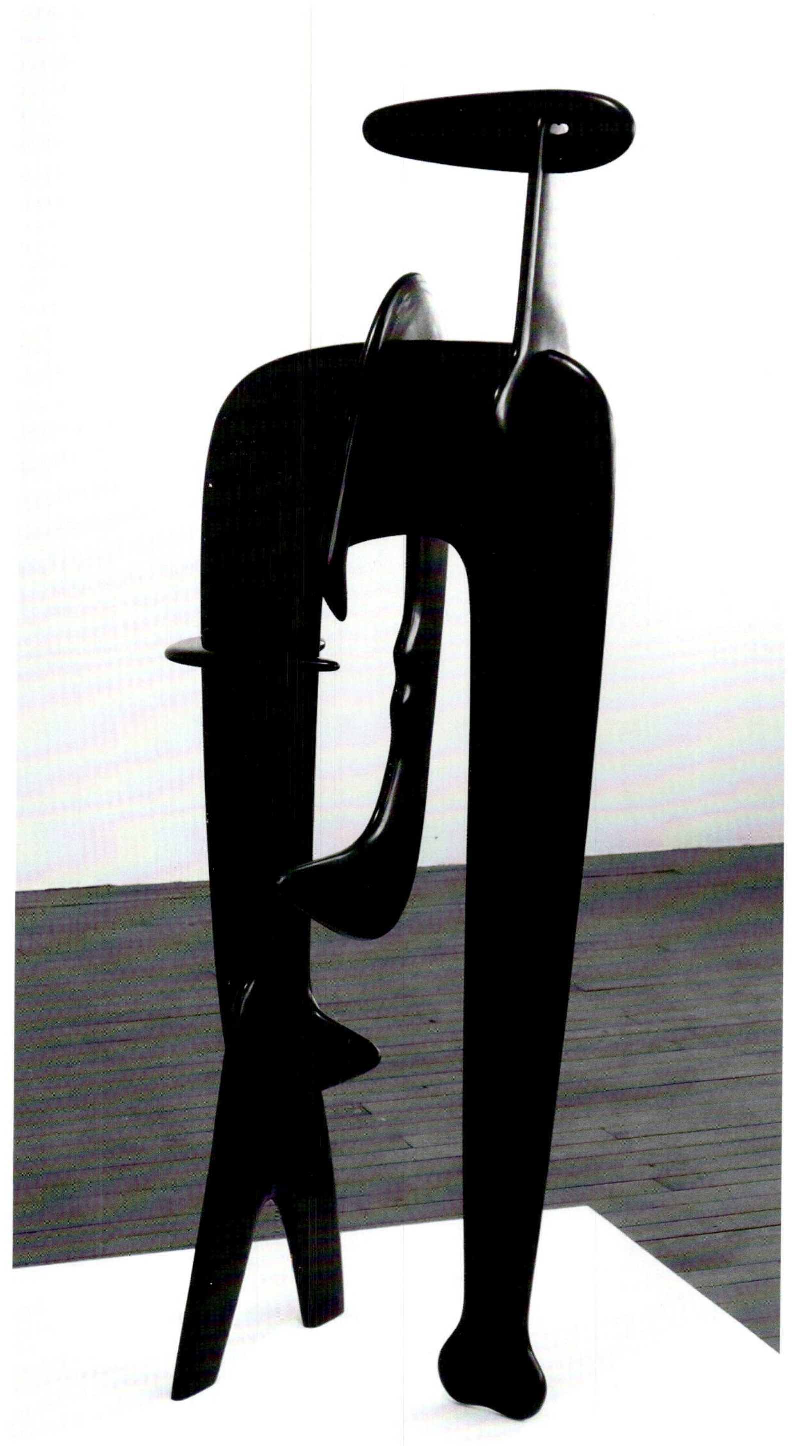

2-7
Figure,
1945.
[Marc Treib, © The Noguchi Museum/ARS]

2-8
Noh Musicians,
1958; 1974.
[Marc Treib, © The Noguchi Museum/ARS]

qualities of space. Space is otherwise inconceivable. These are the essence of sculpture and as our concepts of them change, so must our sculpture change.[4]

In his constant search for new materials and forms, Noguchi later added aluminum to his palette of mediums. The resulting works achieved a lightness that imbued the sculpture with an air of modernity that upended the traditional readings associated with stone, especially marble [2-8].

>> TABLE AND FLOOR PIECES

Among the vast number of works produced over Noguchi's many active years were "table sculptures" whose features and horizontal orientation suggest landscapes in miniature. These were never intended as representations of any larger work, however; on the contrary, they were to be read as sculptures independent of any attachment to a landscape of greater dimensions. Noguchi's floor pieces, in turn, explored the materials, forms, and references beyond the sculpture—landscapes and anatomy among them. To some extent Noguchi shared this interpretation. "My works in this vein are landscapes really," he wrote, "a sculpture of the whole, not an assemblage of parts or props, as with the theater. High, low, horizontal, or vertical, they are a landscape of the mind."[15]

Flat and nearly lacking in vertical elements, the terracotta plate *A World I Did Not Make* (1953) could easily be interpreted as a landscape: its horizontally set wedges prefigure the walls of the Cullen Sculpture Garden in Houston (1985), while its incised lines reappear in the marble flooring of the Beinecke Rare Book Library courtyard at Yale University (1963) [2-9, see 6-26, 6-27]. The dominant horizontal ground planes of other works suggest the term "table pieces," a name not far from Noguchi's view:

> *If my tables now suggest landscape, you must be aware that every garden is a landscape and every garden can be considered a table, too, especially Zen gardens. Some of them we call* kare sansui, *which means "dry riverbed," because they use conventions of gravel and rocks. . . . In my tables I don't use gravel or sand, but I use a flat area of stone which is more or less their equivalent. You can say every garden in Japan is an altar, in a sense, but an altar is a kind of table, too.*[16]

The teeth-like elements of white marble that support *The Field* (1948) penetrate its ground plane of cocobolo wood to emerge as vertical eruptions that articulate and enrich its surface (see 2-12).[17] Clued by the title of the work, associations with agricultural landscapes are as inevitable as they are appropriate: the lines chiseled into the wooden ground are easily interpreted as furrows, while the vertical elements evoke surrogates for the roots and shoots of the crops. Several forms rise from the base plane of *Night Land* (1947), "an image of people in bed," which is tilted around its two axes [2-10].[18] The truncated cone rising from its surface recalls in marble a similar figure of compacted sand in the fifteenth-century garden of Ginkaku-ji in Kyoto that Noguchi much admired [2-11]. The cone would resurface at a colossal scale as Mt. Moere in Moerenuma Park (see chapter 12), designed in 1988 at the very end of the sculptor's life; the divided dome would be reborn as the park's band shell. The pyramid first appeared as the principal form of two works proposed a decade and a half earlier, *Monument to the Plough* (1933) and *Play Mountain* (1933), and would recur in many reiterations in the years that followed.

Over the decades, even after he had begun to produce true landscapes, Noguchi continued to create table works. In *Whet Stone* (1970), a reference to the stones used to grind charcoal to make ink, a rising form appears only in one corner of the reshaped black granite slab, whose subtle form suggests a mesa or an outwash plain [2-13]. Although the edges of these slabs were commonly left irregular and jagged, their horizontal surfaces were usually smoothed and polished. The series continued into the 1980s, in such works as *Galaxy Calligraphy* (1984), whose carved forms rise from the rough-edged slab of black granite elevated on wooden blocks [2-14]. A shallow dome, highly honed and polished, counterbalances an irregular depression scooped from the ground plane.

Despite any correspondence with actual landscapes, the table pieces were intended solely as sculptures. Unlike landscapes that reshape terrain and manage planting, the sculptures rely on a formal continuity engendered by a homogeneity of material, whether stone, clay, or wood. At best, these sculptures might serve as metaphors for landscapes rather than analogs and be regarded as independent entities instead of representations of something at greater scale.

2-9 *[above left]*
A World I Did Not Make,
1952.
[© The Noguchi Museum/ARS]

2-10 *[above right]*
Night Land,
1947.
[© The Noguchi Museum/ARS]

2-11 *[below left]*
Ashikaga Yoshimasa.
Ginkaku-ji (Temple of
the Silver Pavilion).
Kyoto, c. 1480s.
Moon Viewing Platform
and Sea of Silver Sand.

2-12
The Field,
1948.
[© The Noguchi Museum/ARS]

2-13
Whet Stone,
1970.
[Kevin Noble, © The Noguchi Museum/ARS]

2-14
Galaxy Calligraphy,
1984.

Whereas the table pieces evoke impressions of larger terrain, Noguchi's floor pieces are literally grounded in reality and share relationships with elements found in the garden. Unlike the table pieces, whose shallow reliefs barely enter the third dimension, the floor pieces emerge more completely from the ground plane as independent volumes that define spaces among their parts. As in Noguchi's realized landscapes, the resulting interactions of form and ground, and form and space, are key to their interest and beauty. *Practice Rocks in Placement* (1983) distributes a group of stones—"pointed by apprentices but positioned by [Noguchi]"—and suggests sculpture as the trace of thought and intervention [2-15]. As Noguchi described it: "In an exercise in the placement of rocks, improvisation at its peak comes only once. . . . Impersonal parts that became a whole, like beads that make a necklace."[19] In his estimation, the whole—masses, spaces, and their shared synergy—yielded an artwork greater than the sum of its parts.

Lacking the props and horizontal surfaces of the table pieces, these floor sculptures are more fully integrated with their ground, instigating an innovative reading. "By placing the almost inert shapes on the floor," Dore Ashton concludes, "Noguchi forced his viewers to assume, as do the Japanese, that the floor is essential, the very ground of our living space and, therefore, of our being."[20] While at the American Academy in Rome in 1962, Noguchi used his feet rather than his hands to model an early floor work, *This Earth, This Passage*, as a shallow ring of clay.[21] The rough surface of the sculpture, later cast in bronze, retains the signs of its making [2-16]. Given these properties, and its coddling of the hollow at its core, the sculpture simultaneously reads as an independent object and a part of both floor and room.[22] In contrast to the rough demeanor of *This Earth, This Passage*, the elements of *Floor Frame* (1962) are more architectonic, freer in composition, and more complex in their mix of elements, materials, and finishes [2-17]. Consisting of bars set obliquely to the ground plane, the sculpture appears to intersect with, and then continue beneath, the floor, reemerging at some distance as if the ossified form of some geometric sea creature. While *This Earth, This Passage* may be read as an atoll whose brutish crown surges above the swell of the sea, *Floor Frame* more fully fuses with its base as a subsurface extension without limits. In its use of geometric forms, *Floor Frame* shares affinities with works by Robert Morris and Joel Shapiro, both of whom used bars or tubes, either straight or angled, although their sculptures did not engage the gallery floor to an equal degree.[23]

Closer relationships among elements are evident in three works that more attentively emulate natural forms, sculptures that could again be considered gardens in miniature. *Seen and Unseen* (1962) pairs a flatter, irregular dome with a more vertical counterpoint. Could the lower form be read as emerging, and the taller one as having emerged? The two parts of the sculpture share the same material and aspect, yet each is posed in soft opposition to the other. Together, the aesthetic presence derives from their shared relation to the floor.[24] Executed the following year, *Garden Elements* composed two rocks and one elongated stone in a way easily viewed as a natural stone cluster or a path in a Japanese garden, as its name suggests. The link between sculpture and garden is even more obvious in *Lessons of Musokokushi* (1963), both in its number of parts and in their rocklike modeling in bronze [2-18]. As in *Practice Rocks in Placement*, the spaces separating/joining the elements and the relation of the complete cluster to the floor and room are key.

Musô Kokushi, a fourteenth-century Buddhist monk, was responsible for the creation of the garden at the temple of Saihô-ji around 1338.[25] By transforming the ponds and banks of an existing paradise garden in the southwest corner of Kyoto, Musô brought the landscape into closer alignment with the Zen Buddhist practice of using the garden as a vehicle for thoughtful reflection. Over the centuries, nearly fifty species of moss have come to blanket the contours of the temple grounds and have become its dominant feature [2-19]. Noguchi's reference is found not in the lower pond garden, however, but in an uphill location accessed through a roofed gate and a stair of rough-cut stone. In this upper garden, large stones have been arranged to suggest the presence of a stream or a small river, possibly as a vehicle for contemplation [2-20]. Known as the "Dry Cascade," the composition of rocks is set deep in the clay soil, but only with rain does even a mild flow of water coat its surfaces. In "Poem on Dry Mountain," Musô writes: "A high mountain /soars without/a grain of dust/a waterfall/plunges without / a drop of water."[26]

The rocks serve as a vehicle for achieving a greater understanding of existence and perhaps, ultimately, for attaining enlightenment. Explaining his piece, Noguchi states: "The five elements recall rocks

2-15
Practice Rocks in Placement, 1983.
[Marc Treib, © The Noguchi Museum/ARS]

2-16
This Earth, This Passage, 1962.
[Kevin Noble, © The Noguchi Museum/ARS]

2-17
Floor Frame,
1962.
[© The Noguchi Museum/ARS]

2-18
Lessons of Musokukoshi,
1963.
[Bill Jacobson, © The Noguchi Museum/ARS]

2-19 *[below left]*
Musô Kokushi.
Saihô-ji.
Lower pond garden.
Kyoto, Japan, c. 1338.

2-20 *[below right]*
Musô Kokushi.
Saihô-ji.
Dry Cascade.

in some hidden garden in Japan. I was thinking of Muso Kokushi, the legendary master of Zen whose stone arrangements are the most esteemed."[27] Although the artist does not elaborate on the nature of Musô's lessons, the use of rock-like forms with a seemingly loose arrangement suggests that he had the Dry Cascade in mind when naming, and possibly even creating, the work.

The elements of the floor pieces do not only rest on the floor; they occupy it, while also suggesting a depth below. Wallace Stevens's poem "Anecdote of the Jar" (1919) begins: "I placed a jar in Tennessee, / And round it was, upon a hill. / It made the slovenly wilderness / surround that hill."[28] Like the jar, the floor pieces color the reading of the spaces in which they are presented, their affect dependent on the size of the display space, the material of the floor, and the number of other features in the room. Their forms suggest depths beyond their own, as if the bulk of their mass lies buried beneath the ground. Traditional Japanese gardening practice dictates that a true aesthetic or spiritual presence and aura of venerability emerges only when two-thirds of each stone rests below ground—like an iceberg afloat at sea—with only one-third exposed to view. We know, of course, that these sculptures of cast bronze are neither natural nor extend beneath the floor, yet they nonetheless evoke that impression. In their engagement with the ground plane, their interdependence of elements, and their command of space, the floor and table pieces prefigure Noguchi's works at large scale, works he referred to as gardens.

>> SPACE AND MOVEMENT

With Martha Graham's (1894–1991) invitation to design sets for her innovative dance work, Noguchi greatly expanded the measure of his practice with sculptures that directly engaged the human body. This opportunity to design for the theater was warmly welcomed, as Noguchi later told Dore Ashton: "I always wanted to go beyond art objects. I wanted to reach what may be defined as a way of life, a space of life, or even a ghetto closed and defended from the world. Or some monadic theater, a world that exists, grows and changes from its own force."[29] While still in his twenties, Noguchi had created masks for the dancer Michio Ito and had maintained a continued fondness for dance thereafter.[30] Through Ito, Noguchi met Martha Graham. Unlike his earlier association with Ito, Noguchi's collaborations with Graham—which extended over decades—would be more as equals, a relationship the dancer termed "distant closeness."[31]

Noguchi made no claim that his sets influenced the expression or merit of the dance; instead, his purpose was to strengthen the emotional intensity of the choreography and enhance the audience's psychological engagement with the performance. Yet in some instances, the sets did bolster Graham's confidence as she developed a work.[32] Although now afforded an enlarged aesthetic arena in which to create, Noguchi was nevertheless constrained by the dimensions of the stage and the realization that modern dance may not require any sets at all. In works prior to meeting Noguchi, Graham had already dismissed the traditional backdrop and décor as unnecessary. Noguchi's charge was to augment the atmosphere of the performance with sculptural elements that shaped the spaces in which the dancers moved and, in some cases, with which they interacted. In his words, "To me, dance is an extension of a sculptural air—the air we happen to sit around in. Merely to say that dance is another form of art is not enough. Art is more than what one happens to be looking at."[33] Here, art intertwined stationary objects with bodies in motion.

Practical concerns also constrained the nature and disposition of the sets. The pieces could be neither intrusive nor hazardous to the dancers; they should be minimal in size and complexity, and complement rather than compete with the performance. At the start of work on *Appalachian Spring* (1944), Graham brought Noguchi to the Museum of Modern Art to see Alberto Giacometti's (1901–1966) sculpture *The Palace at 4 a.m.* (1932), to suggest the aesthetic she had in mind [2-21]. Noguchi grasped her intentions immediately. Giacometti's palace is a spindly work, an abstraction of a building of a single floor. Four elements inhabit the interior of its tight cage: a human figure, what appears to be a pea in a pod, an abstracted vertebra, and the skeleton of a bird—or possibly a pterodactyl? Art historian David Sylvester describes the sculpture in this way:

> *Its forms are light, lifted off the ground, and brittle as skeletons—thus, insubstantial. At the same time they are perfectly smoothly finished, as if denying change, whether growth or decay. The scene is set for action, but action is suspended. Time is arrested, only the spell is fragile, itself transitory.*[34]

2-21
Alberto Giacometti.
The Palace at 4 am,
1932.
[Museum of Modern Art/ARS]

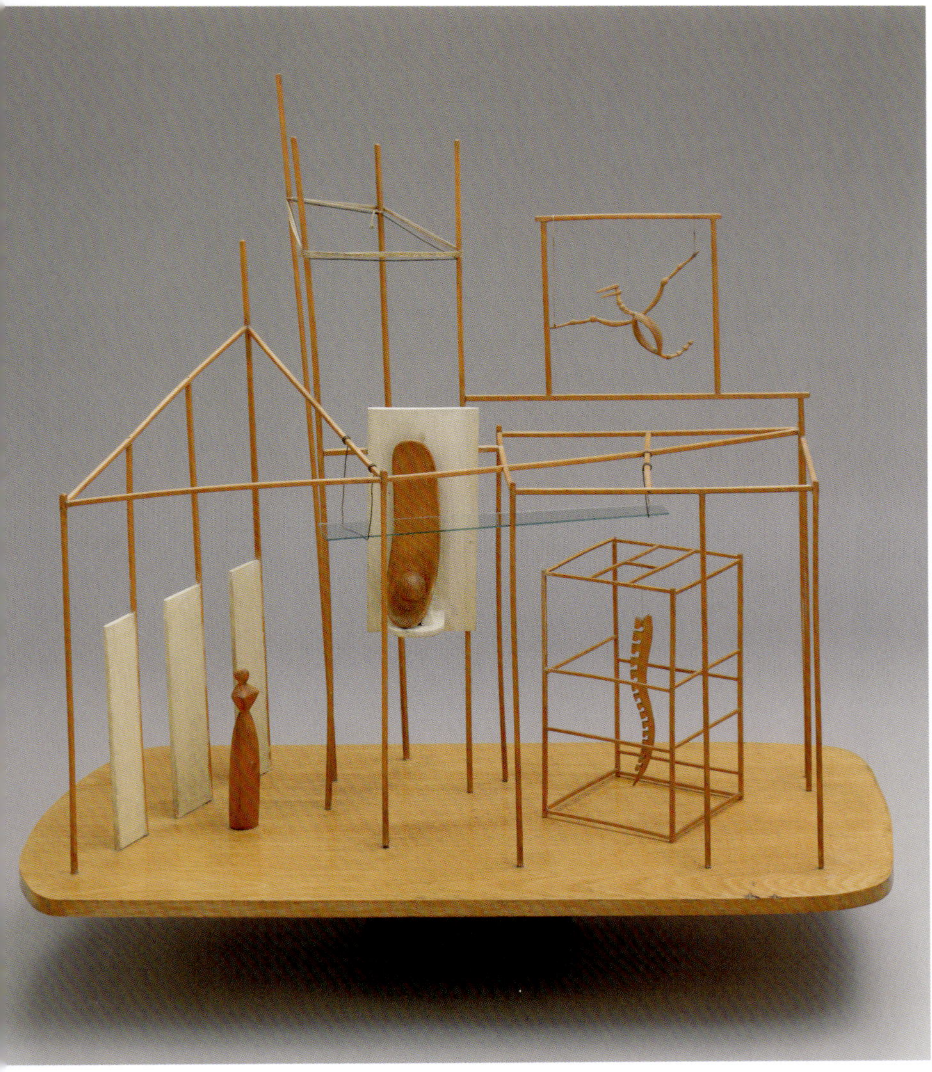

Years later, Noguchi acknowledged the influence of the Swiss sculptor on his thinking: "I don't deny that Giacometti may have influenced me. Surrealism was in the air in the thirties and forties, a definite force."[35] He also cited Brancusi's *Table of Silence* (1938) in Târgu Jiu, Romania, whose visual echoes could be seen in Paris more than two decades later in Noguchi's seats for the UNESCO garden [see 5-2].

Noguchi's spaces also relied on a minimal number of elements, arranged to be effortlessly navigated by the dancers. "The only thing I . . . demanded," Graham recalled, "is that the sets, whatever we had, were to be used. They had to be mobile; in other words they were to be in action. They were characters in this drama and as essential to me as the people. I [didn't] want anything decorative, because I [felt] that's death."[36] While Graham and Noguchi operated in independent spheres, the design of the sets resulted from an amalgamation of sensibilities. "Isamu decided where to place these things on stage—as far as feet and inches were concerned—then I arranged diagrams in the studio. No change is ever made in his concept of space."[37] The sculptor and choreographer's collaboration appears to have been nearly ideal.

Most of the sets Noguchi designed over the years featured few vertical elements, relying instead on inclined, flat platforms. The sets evinced a sense of lightness that paradoxically yielded a density of subject, with designs that depended on suggestion rather than the statement characteristic of Giacometti's early sculpture. The latter's *Model for a Square* (1932), for example, assembled on a flat plane an obelisk, a depression, a half eggshell, and a recumbent folded form. In some ways this sculpture could be read as a precedent for many of the gardens and spatial works Noguchi would design in the future, each assembling and composing natural and designed elements, often within a bounding frame. With Giacometti, Noguchi also shared a fundamental embrace of abstraction; in the set for *Appalachian Spring*, for example, the resemblance to the world beyond the theater is obvious only perhaps in the evocation of the farmhouse and its porch [2-22]. In several dance works, Noguchi applied the logic behind his assembled sculptures to the design of his sets, as in the 1944 production of *Herodiade* [2-23]. It made sense. Because Graham's troupe toured and performed in several cities, the sets had to be quickly erected and struck, a requirement easily met by the use of slotted pieces in the interlocking sculptures. In addition, their transparency and loose spatiality resonated with the dance forms that Graham envisaged.

Noguchi's first set for Graham, *Frontier*, was also his most protean [2-24].[38] Even in this initial design for the stage, he understood that the challenge was to define space as well as fashion objects to be viewed: "If sculpture is the rock, it is also the space between the rocks and between the rock and the man, and the communication and contemplation between."[39] "Isamu brought me this very simple, elegant thing," Graham recalled, "just ropes individuating the distance, the trail and the tracks of the railroad train, and the inevitable fence that gets built as soon as the pioneers take over."[40] Evidently, there was no question that the design was elegant, economical, and most of all, appropriate and effective.

The set for *Frontier* comprised only a handful of elements set against a barren stage reminiscent of the austerity of the Japanese Noh theater. Sawhorses supporting two roughly finished horizontal poles served as the surrogate for a rural fence. The looped rope that fell from the ceiling as a great catenary curve demarcated the edge of the titular frontier. In the first section of the dance—a work only six-and-a-half minutes long—the dancer used the fence as support, playing the paired objects and human form against the spaces defined by the rope. Like a line in space, the rope suggested a front and a back, a here and a there, that effaced the division between performer and audience. For Noguchi,

> *It's not a rope that* [is] *the sculpture, but it is the space which it creates that is the sculpture. I used the space of the stage and the whole space above it, which was an innovation. It is an illusion of space. It is not flat like a painting used as a backdrop—it is a three-dimensional perspective. It bisects the theater space; therefore it creates the whole box into a spatial concept.*[41]

A simple but effective device, the rope resembled the annually renewed Japanese rice-straw *shimenawa* strung above the thresholds of houses or across the posts of a *torii* at Shinto shrines [2-25]. Through the use of the rope, Noguchi claimed, he "was able to create within the void of the stage a vastness of the frontier."[42]

Appalachian Spring, which premiered at the Library of Congress in Washington, DC, in 1944 arguably remains Graham's best-known work, largely due to the success and subsequent popularity of the Aaron

2-22
Appalachian Spring.
1944.
Dance set.
[Lydia Joel, © The Noguchi Museum/ARS]

2-23
Herodiade.
1944.
Element from dance set.
[© The Noguchi Museum/ARS]

2-24
Frontier.
Dance set, 1935.
[Barbara Morgan, © Library Special Collections, Charles E. Young Research Library, UCLA]

Copeland score. The dance scenario describes the building of a farmhouse in rural Pennsylvania by a young newlywed couple—the Wife, first danced by Graham herself, and the Husband. These principals were supported by the Preacher, Believers, and an older Pioneer Woman. As one melody for his score Copeland adopted the Shaker hymn "Simple Gifts," and Noguchi's set for the dance displays something of the restraint and beauty typical of Shaker architecture and aesthetics. The narrow, abstracted condensation of the rocking chair on the porch, for example, shares the simplicity of Shaker furniture, if not their actual forms [2-26]. Similar to *The Palace at 4 a.m.*, Noguchi constructed the house of linear wooden elements, defining the wall planes in outline and thus rendering them transparent. The softly tilted platform, a common element in his later sets, elevates the Preacher when required by the scenario.

Noguchi again collaborated with Graham on *Embattled Garden* in 1958. The dance occupies the Garden of Eden, where a bite of the forbidden fruit forever changed the relationship of humans to landscape—a theme that undoubtedly held great appeal for the sculptor. Noguchi's set featured an inclined platform painted orange, red, and green, colors abstracted from those of an apple skin [2-27, 2-28].[43] The central platform was pierced by a gaggle of branches abstracted as thin metal rods, calling to mind the musical instruments fashioned by the sculptor Harry Bertoia around that time. Activated as the dancers moved around and through them, the rods energized the otherwise static set, which pitted the immobility of the décor against the shuffling of bodies.

From his sets for Graham, Noguchi extracted a group of objects later treated as independent sculptures. The rocking chair from *Appalachian Spring*, the archaically tinged objects from *Night Journey* (1947), and the tent of Holofernes from *Judith* (1950) all attest that while the design of a complete and integrated setting was Noguchi's primary objective, he regarded selected elements as independent sculptures in and of themselves. Unlike the lightweight wood pieces needed for a performance, these pieces were cast in more durable bronze. That they could become independent artworks appreciated as sculpture reveals that Noguchi's designs for the theater did not replace, or even displace, his engagement with sculpture, but that the two were interrelated. Noguchi told Robert Tracy that he never spent more than two weeks on the making of these sets, and that there "was

2-25
Shimenawa.
Izumi shrine, Kumamoto, Japan.

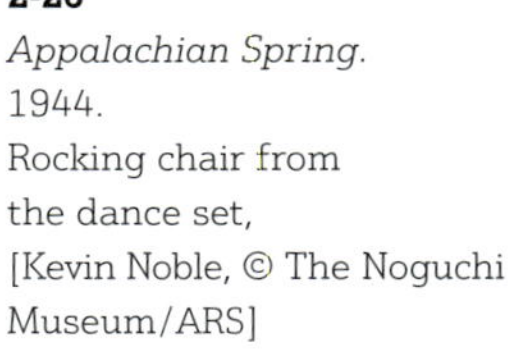

2-26
Appalachian Spring.
1944.
Rocking chair from the dance set,
[Kevin Noble, © The Noguchi Museum/ARS]

2-27
Embattled Garden.
Dance set, 1958.
Central element.
[Kevin Noble,© The Noguchi Museum/AR S]

2-28
Embattled Garden.
Dance set element.
[Kevin Noble,© The Noguchi Museum/ARS]

a constant correlation of what I did in and out of the theater and my work never went too far away from what I was doing anyway."[44]

The assembly of flat elements applied to the dance sets finds parallels in coeval Noguchi sculptures such as *Avatar* (1947) and *Figure* (1945) [see 1-6, 2-7]. Their transposition of flat profiles into interlocking, space-defining planes represented an approach particularly applicable to the portable theater sets required by the Graham troupe. The sculpture and architecture of the Dutch De Stijl group, whose members included artists such as Theo van Doesberg and architects like Gerrit Rietveld, present evocative precedents for these Noguchi planar works.[45] Van Doesberg and Cornelius van Eesteren's *Contra-Construction Project* (1923) used planes and colors to articulate open spatial compositions rather than rooms defined by four walls, ceiling, and floor. Similar in concept was Van Doesburg's 1927 design for Café l'Aubette in Strasbourg, France, whose panels were painted in primary and secondary colors that unified walls and ceiling in a life-size De Stijl architectonic construction [2-29].

In 1924 Rietveld had already used planar construction for his Schröder house in Utrecht, whose walls were left to bypass one another or to remain open at their corners. These designs continued Frank Lloyd Wright's initial venture to "destroy the box": to open and connect historically bounded rooms or link them to the exterior in a continuous and fluid spatial flow.[46] Planar construction was basic to Japanese architecture and well represented by the translucent or opaque sliding screens that infilled a building's structural wooden frame [2-30]. While Noguchi may or may not have been aware of De Stijl projects in the Netherlands, he was certainly familiar with Japanese architecture.

Noguchi's final collaboration with Graham was *Clytemnestra* (1958), after which Graham noted, "Isamu stopped working with me as he was more interested in gardens and playgrounds and pure sculpture—I've tried to woo him back into doing sets for me, but he isn't interested anymore."[47] Although the work for theater would continue for years to come, in 1950 Noguchi accepted an offer to design his first true garden, for the grounds for the new *Reader's Digest* offices in Tokyo. His work outdoors may have been predestined. "As time passed," Dore Ashton apply summarized, "this need to create an environment, a place in which things came together, grew in his imagination beyond the literal theater into a theater of the world a *theatrum mundi*."[48] Or, as Noguchi himself reflected:

> *When the time came for me to work with larger spaces, I conceived them as gardens, not as sites with objects but as relationships to a whole. I would say this came from my knowledge of the dance theater, where there is evidently a totality of experience by the audience.*[49]

Noguchi's position resonates today with some recent philosophies of art, among them Nicolas Bourriaud's, who claims that: "the role of artworks is no longer to form imaginary and utopian realities, but to actually be ways of living and models of action with the existing real, whatever the scale chosen by the artist."[50] Yet Noguchi declined to go so far as directing the activities to take place within the settings he created. Providing the settings to support the experience of the individual, and possibly even inspire, were sufficient.

2-29
Theo Van Doesburg.
Café l'Aubette.
Strasbourg, France, 1927.

2-30
Kusakabe house.
Hida-Takayama, Japan,
c. 1879.
Space defined by planes.

> 3.

Landform

Although Noguchi's designs for the theater elevated the scale of his practice from object to habitable space, they remained confined within walls. His theatrical interventions had produced sculptural objects, explored their interrelationships, and shaped the spaces among them. Ultimately, however, Noguchi found that in the theater, "everything is . . . illusion: bigness as such is merely a matter of let's say perspective and relationship. The only thing that tends to question this matter of scale are the people who perform."[1] In a true landscape, the elements are actual size with movement unscripted.

Noguchi's entry into the realm of landscapes was also inspired by a growing social conscience that sought an increased relevance for art in daily life. Early in the 1930s Noguchi proposed several artworks of vast magnitude, exterior sculptures upon which to move and even play, or landscapes by which to commemorate. Although function at times demanded the addition of furniture, play equipment, or figurative elements, topography—the shaping of the land—led their realization. That is to say, in these works soil and its reformation propelled the idea. Projects at this grand scale surpassed the ability of the sculptor to work independently and required the calculations of the civil engineer and the skill of the machine operator. The artist would instigate, create, and determine the designs, but their realization rested in the hands of others. The particular methods and materials by which the actual landscapes would be constructed might vary, but they were always intended to be regarded as works of art.

Excavation, grading, and deposition are acts basic to the making of landscapes. Whether by leveling a slope, terracing a hillside, mounding soil on a level prairie, or excavating a mine, the reconfiguration of terrain is consequential [3-1]. In folk societies, necessity commonly directs the reshaping of the land, whether for cultivation, defense, or the demarcation of sacred ground. Societies with more centralized authority and political ambition used their power to undertake projects of greater consequence, as seen in the perimeter mounds at Avebury in England or heroically dimensioned water features such as the Grand Canal at Versailles. Whether to create ground conducive to planting, movement, recreation, or vista, remodeling the land through addition and subtraction has shaped landscape architecture at both the folk and polite levels. Soil played a similar role in the making of the Noguchi landscape

3-0
Play Mountain (detail),
1933.
[© The Noguchi Museum /ARS]

Noguchi's design for the sacred site of Kukaniloko (1976), the locus of royal Hawai'ian births, appropriated the earthen-ring configuration early societies commonly utilized for defense and spatial demarcation. Unsurprisingly, his treatment of this circular embankment on Oahu employed greater refinement than its vernacular predecessors [3-2]. By subtly grading the height of the circumferential berm into higher and lower sections, Noguchi increased the formal interest while facilitating physical access to the sacred rocks standing within the ring. Sadly, nothing became of the project, although, given Noguchi's tendency to never let a good idea go unused, the ring reappeared, set horizontally or vertically, in later landscapes.

>> LAND ART

3-1
Bingham Canyon Mine.
Salt Lake County, Utah;
begun 1906; photo: 2006.

At the close of the 1960s, a handful of sculptors, mostly American, rejected the confines of the city and the gallery and turned to the abundant desert terrain of the American Southwest as the sites for their sculptures. Several early works, essentially drawings executed by displacing or removing soil, resulted from incisions made into the crust of the arid soil. These include *Circular Surface Planar Displacement* (1970) in Dry Lake, Nevada, which Michael Heizer "drew" by repeatedly driving a motorcycle in a fixed pattern. The titles of these works often derived from the actions or measures by which they had been conceived and created; for example, in California's Mojave Desert, Walter De Maria's *Mile Long Drawing* (1968) resulted from trailing two parallel lines of chalk for just that distance.

As more land and increased funding became available to the artists, their ambitions increased accordingly. Robert Smithson's *Spiral Jetty* (1970) and *Amarillo Ramp* (1973) were both shaped by the process of deposition, the former by dumping tons of basalt rock into the Great Salt Lake in the figure of a spiral; the second, by depositing and shaping earth and rock on a site in west Texas [3-3]. In contrast, Heizer's early works subtracted from the existing conditions. In making *Double Negative* (1970), a bulldozer scraped two opposing voids into the side of a mesa near Overton, Nevada [3-4]. In their number and alignment, the voids comprised a "double negative," with the spoil from the cuts spilling and collecting naturally in the intervening gap. The resulting artwork not only opposed a geometrically configured void against the irregular edge of the mesa, but through displace-

3-2
Landscape for Kukaniloko,
sacred site of royal births.
Oahu, Hawai'i, 1976.
[© The Noguchi Museum/ARS]

ment also created spaces in which to descend from the mesa top. For their scale and use of earth as their material, the earthworks were regarded as a refutation of the gallery system and the idea of the artwork as a commodity.[2] Although these projects benefited from their realization in the open landscape, proposals by Isamu Noguchi had actually preceded them by more than thirty years, in his own unrealized schemes for land art: two intended as monuments, two as sites for play.

>> A MONUMENT IN THE HEARTLAND

During the Depression years Noguchi suffered through trying times, surviving on a meager income. To a large degree, his livelihood at that time derived from his production of the portrait heads described in the previous chapter, commissions that remained popular among those who could afford having their likeness modeled. To create independent work of greater originality he enrolled in the Depression-era public Works Progress Administration (WPA) program, although his art never fit comfortably within its mandate.

In 1933, on his own initiative, he conceived the *Monument to the Plough*, a giant pyramid of earth to be constructed "in the middle Western prairie on land affected by the wheat crop curtailment program"—the precise location of the site was not specified.[3] The project was prompted by the artist's growing social concern, deepened by the ruin and despair then sweeping across the American heartland. These hardships were particularly severe in Oklahoma, Texas, and Kansas, states later known collectively, and derisively, as the Dust Bowl. Decades of poor agricultural practices had broken the crust of the plains and uprooted the grasses and other vegetation that had once stabilized the topsoil while trapping the scant moisture collected beneath its surface. Paired with a significant drop in crop production due to long-term drought, the depleted soil gave rise to widespread foreclosures and the displacement of multitudes of farm families from their limited holdings. Caravans of uprooted families moved westward, with California as their destination. There, the Okies and Arkies sought at least seasonal employment to keep their families intact and maintain any remnant of hope for a better future.

Their woeful story was told to the nation and the world by John Steinbeck in *The Grapes of Wrath* (1939) and by Pare Lorentz in his

3-3 *[above]*
Robert Smithson.
Spiral Jetty.
Rozel Point, Utah, 1970.

3-4 *[below]*
Michael Heizer.
Double Negative.
Mormon Mesa, Nevada, 1970.

documentary *The Plow That Broke the Plains* (1936), with a score by Virgil Thomson.[4] The soil, drought, and independence became prominent subjects for the era's painting and sculpture, sociological and economic studies—and even architecture. In 1934 Frank Lloyd Wright designed a chapel for the Newmann family as a *Memorial to the Soil*, projected for Cooksville, in the southern Wisconsin landscape he had experienced during his childhood.[5]

In part a response to the dire conditions of the decade, in part due to governmental support, local and regional subjects held particular sway in American art at that time, especially outside the major seaboard cities. Painters such as Thomas Hart Benton, John Steuart Curry, and Grant Wood produced scenes of rural life in a style that intertwined expressionism with illustration, ecumenically depicting scenes from the lower strata as well as the middle class, the farmer as well as the city dweller. In his series of paintings of the devastation wrought by drought, Alexander Hogue captured the bleakness shared by the soil and those who farmed it [3-5]. Although influenced by time spent in Europe on his several visits, Grant Wood saw regionalism, as the style became known, "as an elaboration of the general proposition that art, although potentially universal in significance, is always more or less local in inception" [3-6].[6] One might likewise regard Noguchi's idea for the *Monument to the Plough* in just this way.

At this time, American artists shared the economic vulnerability of the farmer, perhaps even more so given that few perceived art as a necessity. Supported by the WPA and the Federal Arts Project (FAP), artists received commissions to paint murals in new post offices, housing projects, railroad stations, and perhaps an airport, as well as support for individual projects. In general, the subjects were local or regional, and the rendering realistic. Art was intended to bolster a feeling of hope, security, and a sense of place, if outright optimism was too much to hope for. In programs such as these there was little room for a fantastic project like Noguchi's *Monument to the Plough*: essentially a design for a piece of proto-land art of dimensions never proposed in modern times, much less realized.

In addition to responding to the economic situation, during the 1930s Noguchi's purview turned from personal expression and portraiture toward an art more closely connected to everyday life, "more socially aware and communicative, an art humanly meaningful without being realistic, at

3-5 *[above]*
Alexander Hogue.
Dust Bowl, 1933.
[Smithsonian American Art Museum]

3-6 *[below]*
Grant Wood.
Fall Plowing, 1931.
[Wikiart]

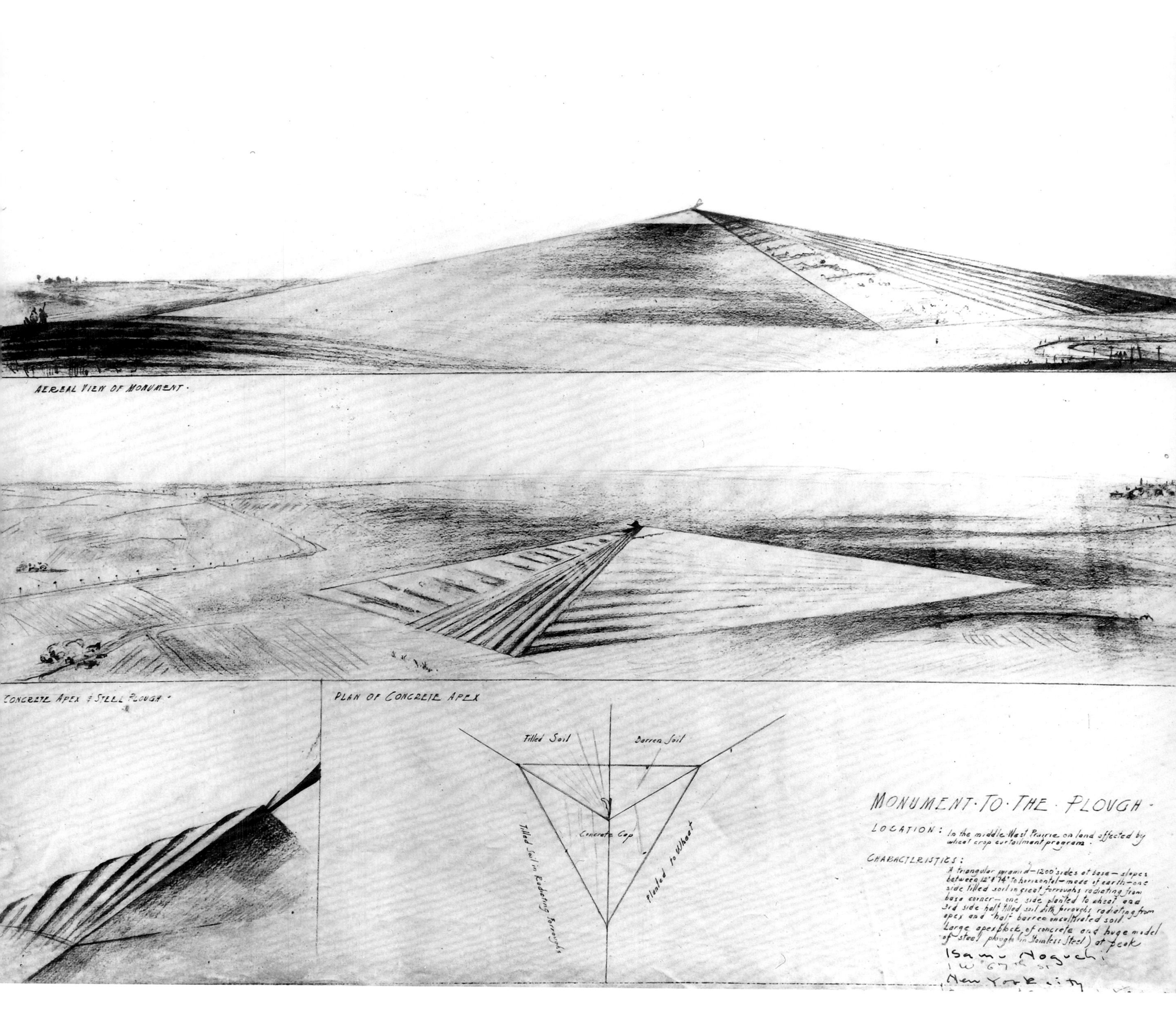
AERIAL VIEW OF MONUMENT·
CONCRETE APEX & STEEL PLOUGH·
PLAN OF CONCRETE APEX
Tilled Soil
Barren Soil
Concrete Cap
Tilled Soil in Radiating Furroughs
Planted to Wheat
MONUMENT·TO·THE·PLOUGH·
LOCATION: In the middle West Prairie on land affected by wheat crop curtailment program.
CHARACTERISTICS:
A triangular pyramid—1200' sides at base—slopes between 12° & 14° to horizontal—made of earth—one side tilled soil in great furroughs radiating from base corner—one side planted to wheat and 3rd side half tilled soil with furroughs radiating from apex and half barren uncultivated soil.
Large apex block of concrete and huge model of steel plough (in Stainless Steel) at peak
Isamu Noguchi
1 W 67th St
New York City

3-7 *[opposite]*
Monument to the Plough,
1933.
Perspective drawing
with notes.
[© The Noguchi Museum/ARS]

3-8
Monument to the Plough.
Model.
[Berenice Abbott, © The Noguchi Museum/ARS]

once abstract and socially relevant."[7] He claimed that in the winter of 1933–34 he had a "vision" of the "earth as a sculpture" and that "the sculpture of the future might be [of] the earth."[8] The result of this vision was an earthen pyramid capped by an oversized stylization of the iron plow, a work Noguchi characterized as "a monument to the American beginning."[9]

Unlike the land art of the 1970s described above, Noguchi's project was driven by a narrative rather than a concern for process or form. It was to be a memorial to the tool that made agriculture in the Great Plains productive but hastened the concomitant denuding of the land [3-7].[10] Each side of the softly sloping pyramid—measuring twelve thousand feet at its base—would be planted using strip cropping and other erosion-countering techniques promulgated by the Soil Erosion Commission for the US Department of Agriculture. These techniques, which included the rotation of crop species as well as the reconfiguring of the land, were intended to right the wrongs generated by decades of detrimental farming practices and to thwart their return in the future. The plow was the means by which furrows were cut for the seeding that followed.

The envisaged monument would celebrate the production of the steel-tipped plow—reputedly first proposed in correspondence between Benjamin Franklin and Thomas Jefferson but realized by John Deere only in 1837. The soils of the Midwest were said to be harder and more resistant to plowing than those in the South and the East, and the wooden plow had proved unequal to the task.[11] The addition of the steel blade rendered the land arable by digging deeply into the soils of the grassland. Supported by the effects of years of extended drought, however, the steel plow played a prominent role in creating the catastrophic conditions of the Dust Bowl.[12]

Why a pyramid? Noguchi provided no explanation for the form, but four possible reasons seem plausible. For one, the pyramid is a figure historically associated with remembrance, especially funerary commemoration, as with the Great Pyramids at Giza.[13] In addition, the pyramid is a structurally stable form, at least if its profile follows the material's natural angle of repose. Under those conditions, no constructed support is needed. Third, the pyramid produces an apex, an appropriate site for the installation of a sculpture. And lastly, the flat sides of a pyramid could support the recommended planting techniques. Noguchi specified that one side of the pyramid would be "tilled in great furrows radiating from the base corner; one side planted to wheat; 3rd side half-tilled soil with furrows radiating from apex and half-barren uncultivated soil."[14] At the apex of the pyramid, a concrete cap would check erosion and support an oversize stainless-steel rendition of the first steel plow. Although included in the drawing, neither the cap nor the planting appears in a model—which is possibly from a later date—with the plow rendered as an abstract sculpture [3-8].

Despite Noguchi's good intentions, had the monument been built as portrayed in the drawing, it would probably have endured for only a short period. Clearly, the artist understood neither the causes of soil erosion nor the means by which it could be prevented. The face of the pyramid shown in Noguchi's sketch—a photographic reproduction of which remains the project's sole documentation—appears to be entirely given to wheat, presumably planted in horizontal rows to stabilize the soil and retard the flow of water downward from the peak. On a second face, the furrows radiating from one corner of its base would probably have hastened the erosive effect of rainfall. The third side—one half of which is left as raw earth to illustrate crop rotation—would almost certainly have fared no better. Thus, the lifespan of the monument, as originally envisioned, would likely have been brief.[15]

However naïve Noguchi may have been in respect to strip cropping, he was hardly a foolish person. Had the project progressed, one can assume that he would have consulted agronomists on the proper manner by which to plant and plow the faces of the pyramid and select the appropriate crops to be propagated. The drawing, then, should be regarded as a preliminary representation to be developed with greater insight as the project moved toward realization. In any event, the venture was soundly rejected by the WPA as beyond the orbit supported by the agency—scarcely a surprise considering that an artwork of this magnitude had never been attempted by an artist in the modern period.[16]

Conceived the same year as the *Monument to the Plough*, *Play Mountain* (1933) represents Noguchi's second audacious attempt to depart from the traditional scale and purpose of sculpture. Rather than celebrating an agricultural instrument, he conceived the playground as a landform modeled to accommodate multiple types of activity [3-9]. Again employing

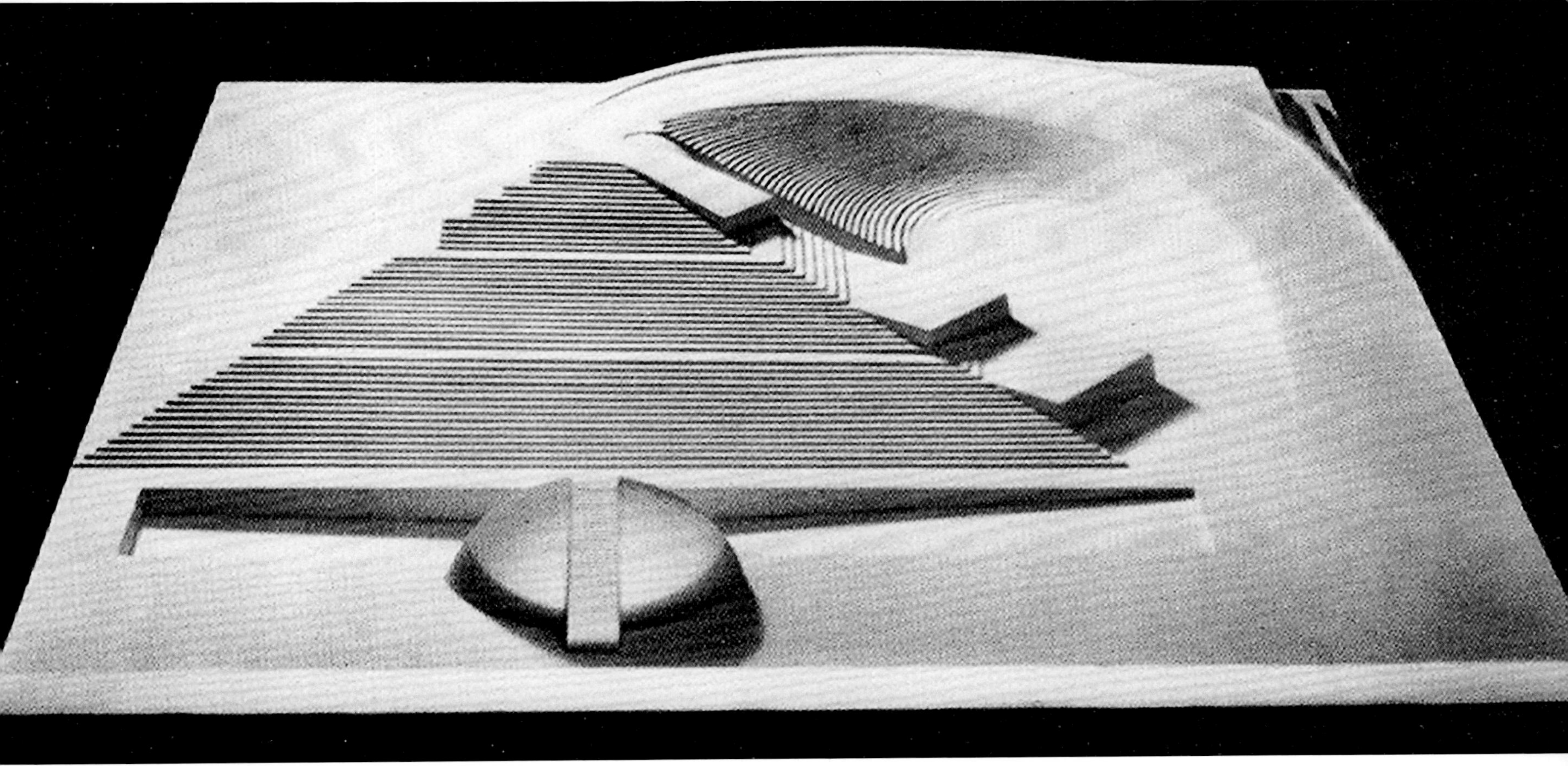

3-9
Play Mountain, 1933.
[© The Noguchi Museum/ARS]

the shape of the pyramid, Noguchi offered a terrain on and within which to play, using the internal and external spaces of the shape. The form of its terrain, he claimed, responded to a long-held memory of the fear invoked by a "desolate playground on a cliff near Tokyo."[17] He gave no specific location for the playground, identifying it only as somewhere in New York City.

In contrast to the *Monument to the Plough*, the surface of the pyramid in *Play Mountain* is stepped; some zones are graded more dramatically into three terraces, while the remaining surfaces are softly modeled as a bowl destined for wet sliding in summer and sledding in winter [3-10]. In place of the standard collection of swings, carousels, and steel-pipe jungle gyms set on a desert of asphalt, Noguchi fashioned the entire site as a sculptural ground upon which creative play would be a mental as well as physical activity. The specifics explaining context, materials, and even activities are missing, leading to potential criticism as to their ability to truly support play.

Yet if we judge these two projects as sculpture, as highly innovative works of art, any function-based criticisms such as these become less consequential. The beauty and achievement of *Play Mountain* and *Monument to the Plough* lie not in function but in their investigation of shaped terrain as a sculpture for commemoration or enjoyment. Sculpture was Noguchi's purview and métier, not the address of construction demands or building codes required to achieve public works. Or, as his colleague Shoji Sadao noted, Noguchi was not interested in following schedules and working within budgets.[18]

>> SOCIAL ACTIVISM AND INTERNMENT

On 18 March 1942, in the wake of the 7 December 1941 Japanese attack on Pearl Harbor, President Franklin Delano Roosevelt issued Executive Order 9066, which illegally mandated the internment of all Japanese non-citizens and American citizens of Japanese ancestry in camps set inland from the 100-mile-wide security zone established along the Pacific coast. Being a resident of New York, Noguchi was exempt from internment, but he was nevertheless outraged by the "voluntary evacuation" demanded by the executive order. In response, he joined in the struggle to demonstrate the patriotism of Japanese-American citizens being so unjustly treated.

3-10
Play Mountain, 1933.
[© The Noguchi Museum/ARS]

His involvement took several forms. He wrote for the mainstream press, passionately arguing against the intolerable conditions in the internment camps and the widespread misconceptions held by the American people about those citizens of Japanese ancestry.[19] Noguchi also played an instrumental role in founding the Nisei Writers and Artists Mobilization for Democracy, whose goal was to create an effective communication network among the various "relocation" camps; "Nisei" refers to second-generation Japanese Americans. [20] The organization's statement of purpose called for "a government sponsored vernacular press to help the people of Japanese descent to realize the identity of their interest with that of the United States." Despite the group's brief existence—it faltered and faded within a relatively short period—and its ultimate ineffectiveness in conveying its message to the broader public, it did have some positive effects on the members of the organization and perhaps on portions of the greater Nisei population as well.

Morally motivated, Noguchi believed that arts instruction in the camps could improve the daily lives of their internees as well as the environmental quality of the camp landscape. As he explained, "I wondered whether the Nisei might not gain through the arts the self-confidence they so need." [21] This belief prompted his voluntarily joining the incarcerated Japanese Americans at the Colorado River War Relocation Camp in Poston, Arizona. The camp was located ten miles east of the California state line and ninety miles north of the Mexican border; the nearest town was Parker, seventeen miles away.[22]

The physical conditions in the Sonoran Desert site were brutal, with summer temperatures averaging well above 100 degrees Fahrenheit on a nearly daily basis; the area saw only four inches of rainfall annually, all occurring on average within a single eleven-day period. The Poston camp occupied 71,000 acres of land appropriated from the Colorado River Indian Reservation with the assurance that after the war and the subsequent vacating of the site, the land would be returned to its original state.[23] Over time Poston would become the largest of the internment camps, at its peak incarcerating over 17,000 people, most of whom were American citizens.[24] This was ethically among the darkest hours in American history, an intolerable action propelled by racism and land grab, fueled by the general terror that followed in the aftermath of Pearl Harbor.

Just why Noguchi selected Poston is not known; as it was the largest of the camps, he may have felt it was there he could do the most good. As noted above, he believed that instruction in arts, crafts, woodworking, and building construction would benefit the internees, not only by keeping their minds and hands active, but also by producing products and furnishings needed by those in the camp who could leave only with special permission. His mission was grand and ultimately quixotic: that he "might contribute toward a rebirth of handicraft and the arts which the Niseis have so largely lost in the process of Americanization."[25] In Noguchi's eyes this loss of ability to create, coupled with their removal from the land, was a characteristic shortcoming of the Nisei—as opposed to their parents, who even after emigration maintained a connection with the land, typically as farmers or nursery people. His program at Poston, he hoped, would become a model to be adopted by other internment camps in communication with one another.

Noguchi's vision for Poston was comprehensive and detailed. In a memo written in 1942, presumably soon after arriving in Arizona in April of that year, Noguchi proposed the construction of a recreation center to house several workshops and even sawmill facilities. His proposal lists "ceramics, music, painting, sculpture, a small museum and store, as well as the buildings of the recreation department where will be located the headquarters for all phases of athletics from sumo and judo, to baseball, football, tennis and so forth." Recognizing the grandeur of his vision, he qualified his request by noting that these would be constructed and implemented only over time. He also stressed the need to raise money outside the camp, as his efforts to secure funding through governmental channels had been completely unproductive.[26] As with the response to all his prior requests for supporting public projects, no money was forthcoming. In "I Become a Nisei," an unpublished article intended for *Reader's Digest*, Noguchi narrates how life in the camp was evolving:

> *We plan a city and look for nails. Some lose courage and think only of getting out.... Here in Poston we are making one million adobe bricks with which to build our own school houses for over a thousand pupils. We are trying to get a saw mill to make our own lumber....We must find kilns with which to supplement our fast-diminishing supply of chinaware by using [the] plentiful clay.*[27]

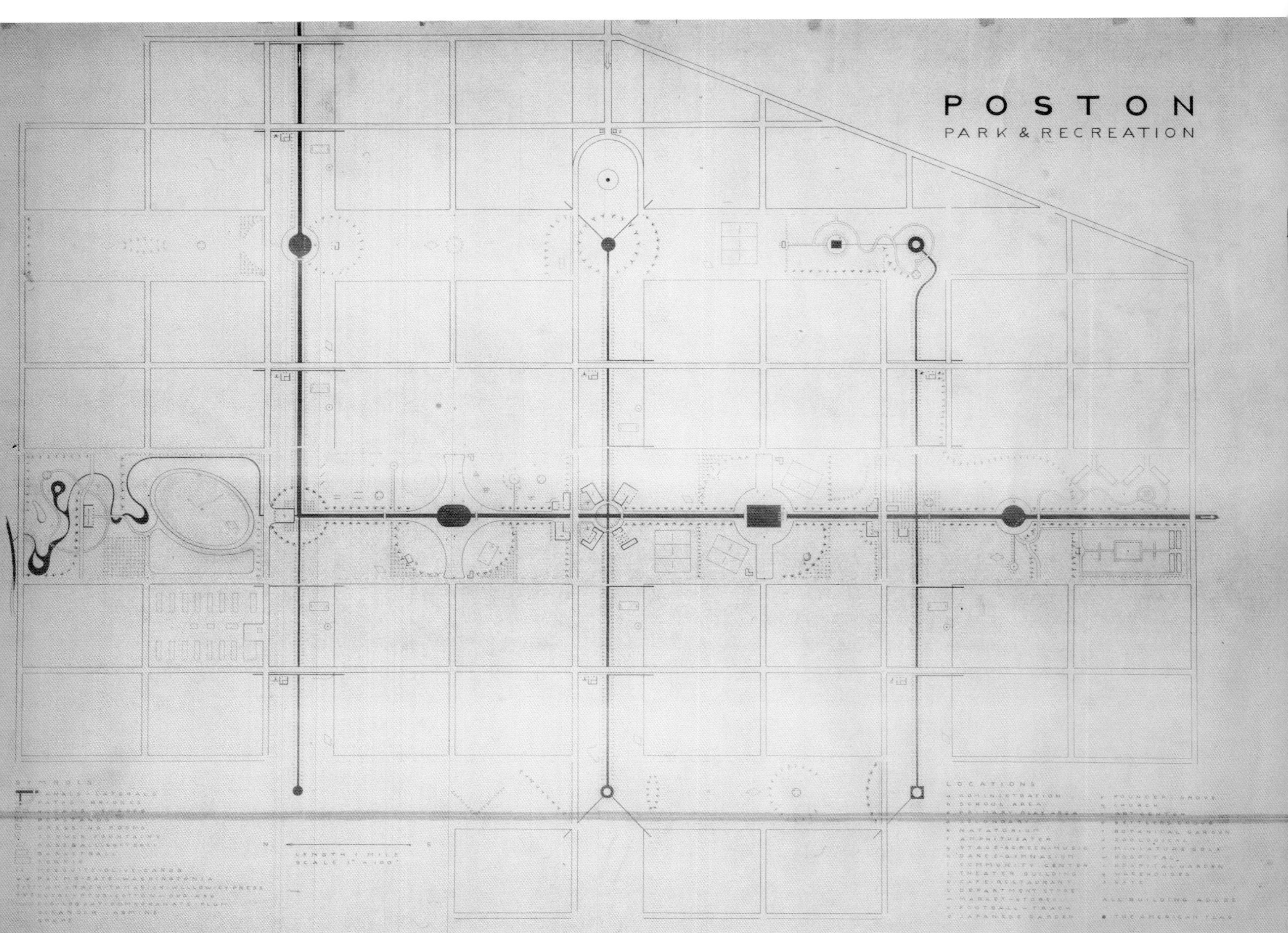
POSTON
PARK & RECREATION
SYMBOLS
PATHS - BRIDGES
DRESSING ROOMS
BASKETBALL
TENNIS
MESQUITE-OLIVE-CAROB
PALMS-DATE-WASHINGTONIA
OLEANDER - JASMINE
GRAPE
N
S
LENGTH 1 MILE
SCALE 1" = 100'
LOCATIONS
ADMINISTRATION
SCHOOL AREA
NATATORIUM
AMPHITHEATER
STAGE-SCREEN-MUSIC
DANCE-GYMNASIUM
COMMUNITY CENTER
THEATER BUILDING
CAFE-RESTAURANT
DEPARTMENT STORE
MARKET-STORES
FOOTBALL - TRACK
JAPANESE GARDEN
FOUNDERS GROVE
CHURCH
SETTLERS GROVE
BOTANICAL GARDEN
ZOOLOGICAL
MINIATURE GOLF
HOSPITAL
HOSPITAL GARDEN
WAREHOUSES
GATE
ALL BUILDING ADOBE
THE AMERICAN FLAG

3-11 *[opposite]*
Poston Relocation Camp,
Arizona, 1942.
Site improvements.
[Kevin Noble, © The Noguchi
Museum/ARS]

3-12
"Landscape done by
evacuees. Pond for
miniature boats with
model houses."
Poston Relocation Camp #1,
Arizona, 1942.
[Stewart Francis,
Library of Congress]

3-13 *[below]*
Poston Relocation Camp.
Site improvements (detail).
Ornamental and Japanese
gardens are on the left.
[Kevin Noble, © The Noguchi
Museum/ARS]

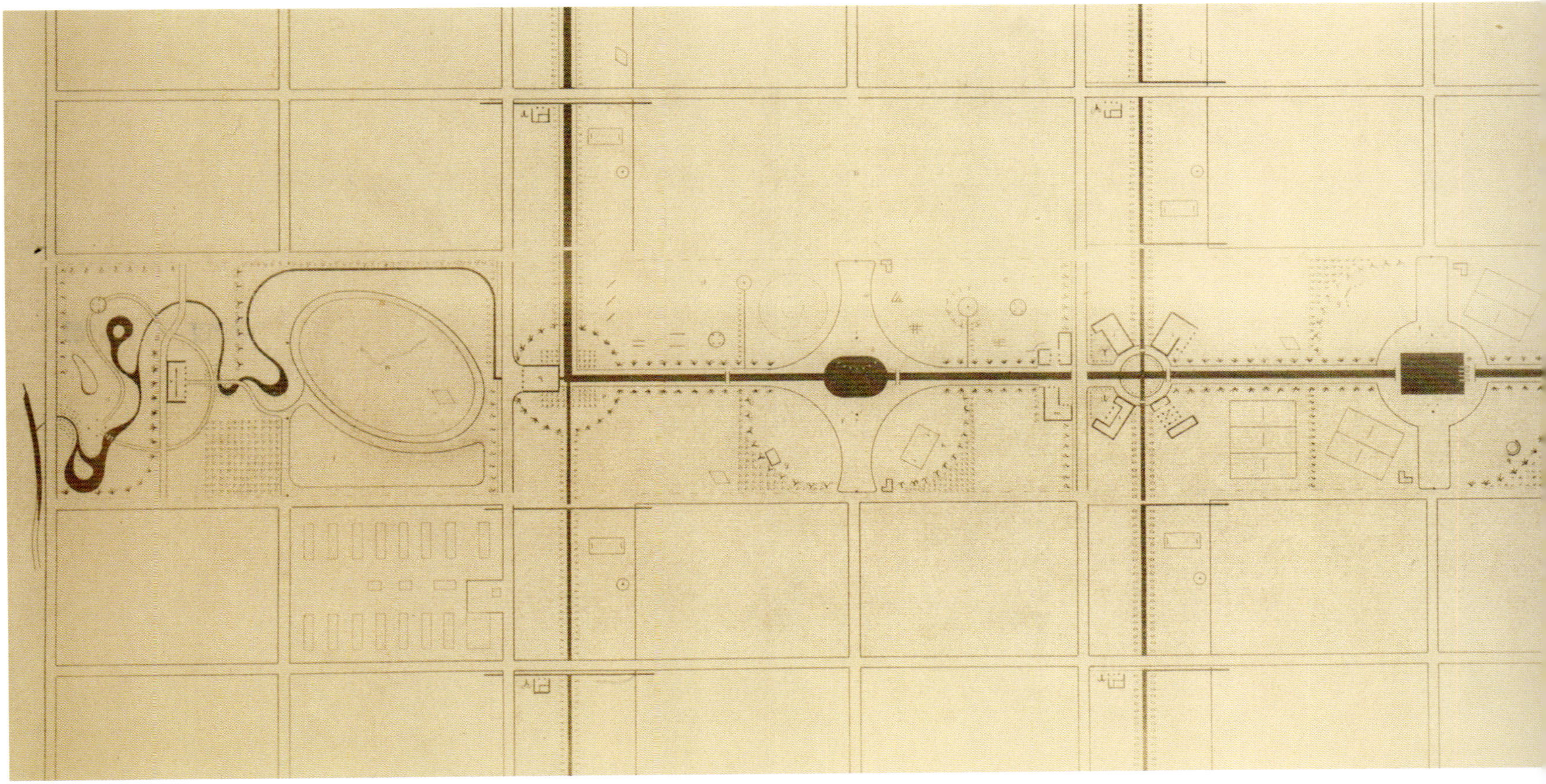

Poston actually comprised three separate camps arranged in a chain from north to south, each situated about three miles apart from one another. Given the pitiless conditions at the sites, the internees sarcastically nicknamed the camps Roasten, Toastin, and Dustin.[28] As in numerous projects undertaken in the following decades, Noguchi's original vision soon expanded beyond the scale of the craft object and even the single building. One can only speculate as to the reasons why he embarked on this major undertaking to replan the camp and why he felt qualified to do so, given that he had no specific training in architecture, site planning, or landscape design. Perhaps he rightly believed that by treating the piece rather than the complete parcel, only limited improvements would ever materialize. Or perhaps he truly sought a vehicle by which to render incarceration under inhuman conditions just a bit more bearable.

Two drawings of Noguchi's proposals remain in the archives: a large site plan for one of the Poston camps drawn at a scale of 1"=100', and a second on which are drawn a plan and an isometric projection of the proposed cemetery; no scale is given. Titled "Poston: Park & Recreation," the site plan developed and enhanced the camp's blocks of barracks—still being constructed by Del Webb's firm—using water, vegetation, and architecture [3-11].[29] With the Colorado River as source, irrigation channels brought limited amounts of water to the Native American reservation in quantities barely sufficient to make life and farming possible. The large population of inmates planned for Poston, however, would require vastly increased acre-feet of water to meet domestic and agricultural needs. In October 1942 the canals were still incomplete, but in time water was diverted into the camp from the newly built Parker Dam, where it was used primarily for agriculture. But "along its route, the young men had scooped out three huge basins in the earth. When filled with water, they became Poston's swimming pools" [3-12].[30]

Noguchi had a grander vision for modeling the water, however. In the proposed site plan the principal canal irrigates a central green space that extends from north to south—displacing blocks presumably assigned to additional barracks; branch canals running east-west expand the system to bring water deep into the camp. In a manner distantly recalling the plans of André Le Nôtre—who, albeit, worked in a very different economic and political context—Noguchi expanded the thin channels at intervals at key points to become basins and swimming pools. Three of these are shaped as a circle, a rectangle, and an oblong with rounded corners, and drawn in greater detail on the right margin of the plan [3-13]. At the western terminus the channel skirts an elliptical play field and terminates in a meandering stream, perhaps to add a naturalistic landscape more familiar and comfortable for the internees. While both a botanical garden and a garden in the Japanese manner were planned, determining their specific locations has been elusive. Perhaps this area was intended as the location of one or both of them.

The basic idea for the park and the metamorphoses of the functional channels into water features is impressive, as are its spatial shaping and complexity. While by that time Noguchi had already displayed accomplishments as a sculptor and an agile designer, evidence of his ability to design landscapes at large scale was lacking. As a result, one wonders whether Noguchi drew the plan himself or whether it was made by some other interned draftsman. In addition, it is doubtful—though of course still possible—that Noguchi would have had his own equipment for drafting plans with such precision; perhaps there was a drafting office for the camp. As a voluntary internee whose stay was supported by the government, he could have had access to these tools assuming such existed. There is another explanation, however, one perhaps more plausible.

Quoting a government report of 9 June 1942, Amy Lyford, in her excellent study of Noguchi's art and politics, writes that "Noguchi and a certain Mr. Kinoshita were designing a chapel, columbarium, and crematory and had made plans for plotting out individual graves."[31] The Mr. Kinoshita in question was possibly Robert Kinoshita (1914–2014), who in 1940 had graduated with a degree in architecture from the University of Southern California.[32] Kinoshita would probably have possessed greater architectural drafting skills than what might have been available at the camp, and possibly the drafting tools as well, and would have been more informed about recent ideas concerning site planning. In any event, by whosever hand it was drawn, the plan reveals a wealth of detail and refinement in the overall structuring of the site as well as in the conception and detailing of its landscape.

3-14
Garrett Eckbo.
Community Park,
Central Valley, California,
mid-1930s.
[Environmental Design Archives, University of California, Berkeley, hereafter EDA/UCB]

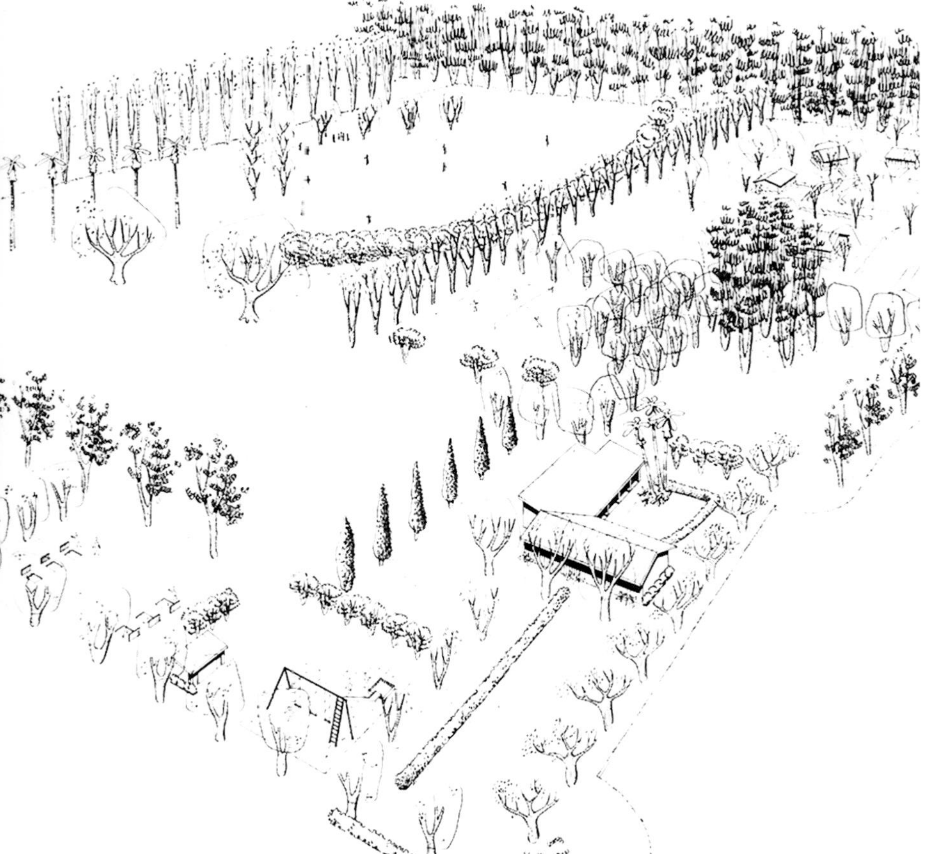

The plan's legend identifies the primary species of trees, shrubs, and vines to be planted: mesquite, olive, carob, date , tamarisk, willow, Washingtonia palms, and cypress; eucalyptus, cottonwood, ash; fig, loquat, pomegranate, plum; oleander and jasmine; and grape. Hardly comprising a random list, the plants are grouped by height, mass, flowering, and fruit, suggesting their role in providing shade and other amenities and for defining and enriching the building sites along the central greenway. The sole vine noted is the grape, perhaps to cover pergolas and other shade structures, and possibly for making wine. In addition to their provision of shade and ornamentation, trees and shrubs were used "structurally" to demarcate the zones of the camp. Squat date palms would be planted along several channels to mark the presence of water. In other areas, taller trees like ash and eucalyptus would draw tall silver-green lines along the central greenway and cross axes.

At the western terminus of one cross canal, for example, the larger channel forks into two prongs. This splayed shape would be lined with tall trees like cottonwoods or ash, accompanied by fruit trees of lower height that afforded nourishment as well as color and scent in the spring. Both the use of particular species and their configuration suggest parallels with then-recent developments in modern landscape architecture such as Garrett Eckbo's 1930s camps and parks for agricultural workers in California's Central Valley under the auspices of the Farm Security Administration (FSA). These designs further support speculation that some nurseryman, landscape architect, or architect contributed to Noguchi's scheme [3-14]. Inexplicably absent from the landscape plan, however, are dense windbreaks to stifle the flows of sand, soil, and other airborne particles that plagued life in the camp.

Although Noguchi was born in Los Angeles and had visited the city shortly before incarceration, it is doubtful he would have possessed the expertise in desert species demonstrated by the plan. No doubt, the Nisei (and Issei, first-generation Japanese Americans) interned in the camp included farmers and nurserymen, as these were common vocations for Japanese Americans. Therefore, one can speculate with a reasonable degree of certainty that Noguchi relied on their experience in determining the selection of plants. There were also those holding architecture degrees, for example, George Matsumoto (1922–2016), who had recently graduated from the University of California, Berkeley. It is also tempting to speculate as to the possible role of Hideo Sasaki (1919–2000), who went on to achieve fame as landscape architect and professor at Harvard University, whose landscape-architecture department in the Graduate School of Design he would chair for many years in the postwar period. Although Sasaki had not yet completed his degree and was later allowed to work outside the camp as a farmer in Colorado, he may have also aided in developing the plan. While others may have contributed to Noguchi's design thinking more broadly, or helped guide specialized interventions like plant selection, we can nevertheless credit Noguchi with the design ideas represented in the site plan.

Unfortunately, the size and partial illegibility of the text in reproductions of the existing drawing hampers the ability to determine the precise disposition of the various buildings and the species of trees employed in each sector of the camp. The list of proposed structures and gardens was highly optimistic given the camp's status as a temporary measure for which funding was spare. Among those structures listed in the legend are an administration building, a school, a theater, a play area, a swimming hall, an amphitheater, a gymnasium, a church, an art center, a hospital, a department store, a market, a botanical garden, a miniature golf course, and a Japanese garden. Noguchi proposed that all buildings would be constructed of adobe blocks; a precedent for this decision was set by the FSA's Cooperative Farm and Workers' Housing in Chandler, Arizona, designed by Burton D. Cairns and Vernon DeMars and occupied in 1937. Supported by the adobe walls enclosing the ground-floor spaces, the second-floor rooms of wood construction were planned as more flexible spaces to allow increased cross-ventilation.

That Noguchi's most detailed effort tackled the design of the camp's cemetery suggests that his belief that Poston would be a short-term venture was not entirely optimistic. Destined for a capacity of 1,500 burials, the cemetery provided land for both urn and earth burials. As shown in the isometric drawing and the accompanying plan, the columbarium was to be defined by walls arranged as three parallel Ls. Facing them across the central area is a second set of walls appearing almost as their reflection; a figurative statue stood at its center [3-15]. A chapel and two service buildings complete the funerary precinct.[33] The most notable omission from the design is the chimney that any crematorium would have required.

As Poston was known to be the hottest and driest of all the concentration camps, the Noguchi plan is incontrovertibly visionary, utopian, and in the end unrealistic. Of the proposals, nothing was ever realized: no comprehensive planting was ever installed; no formal cemetery or chapel was constructed. But somehow a copy of the drawing(s) reached the attention of Nicolas Ciriano, resident engineer with the Western Division of the FSA, who had constructed Depression-era migrant-worker camps in collaboration with designers such as landscape architect Garrett Eckbo and architects Vernon DeMars and Burton Cairns. Ciriano was intrigued by Noguchi's design and requested further information, inquiring as to whether any of its many ideas could be adapted to the agricultural-worker camps or defense-worker housing in California then on the drawing boards.[34]

Noguchi began to realize that he had virtually nothing in common with the incarcerated Issei and Nisei, and that he was even regarded with some suspicion as being on the side of the camp administration—or worse, an informant—factors that increased the distance he had sought to reduce between himself and those he had intended to help. He wanted out. "Inwardly," noted historian Paul Bailey, "the people were crying for someone other than management or experts. They desperately needed souls they could trust, who could talk in their behalf."[35] Unfortunately, given the wariness already directed toward the artist, Noguchi could not play that role. And in less than six months he recognized that staying at Poston was futile, as the interests of the War Relocation Authority (WRA) were "hopelessly at odds with that ideal cooperative community pictured by Mr. [John] Collier [director of the Bureau of Indian Affairs]. They wanted nothing permanent nor pleasant. My presence became pointless."[36]

He also wrote friend and fellow artist Man Ray about his disillusionment: "This is the weirdest, most unreal situation—like in a dream—I wish I were out. Outside, it seems from the inside, history is taking flight and passes forever. Here time has stopped, and nothing is of any consequence, nothing of value, neither of our time or our skill."[37] Bureaucratic wheels turn slowly, however, especially in wartime and in a place so far removed from Washington, DC, and it required time and the support of notables such as Frank Lloyd Wright and John Collier to help the artist escape the heat and oppression of the Arizona desert and return to the density and bustle of the East Coast. On 12 November 1942 Noguchi drove out of Poston and headed

3-15
Chapel, crematorium, and cemetery.
Poston Relocation Camp, Arizona, 1942.
Plan and isometric drawing.
[Kevin Noble, © The Noguchi Museum/ARS]

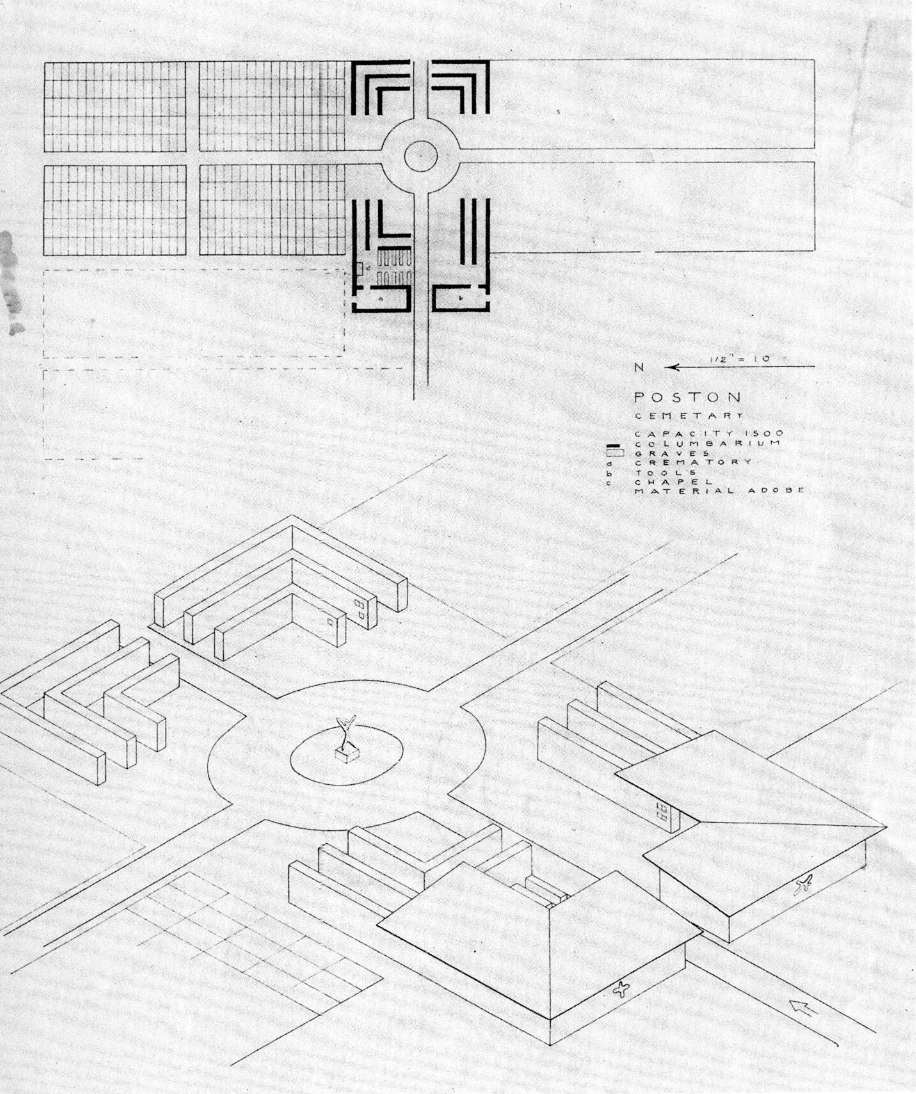

back to New York, having been granted a temporary leave. He never returned. The sum total of his efforts to reshape the Poston camp landscape and improve the lives of those incarcerated within its barbed-wire fences remained on paper.

>> LANDSCAPE AS METAPHOR

It would be some years before Noguchi returned to projects involving landform at a scale to be occupied and used. His sculptures, however, further explored the modeling of surfaces that, like the table and floor pieces, could be read as studies for subsequent landscapes. A year after his exit from Poston, Noguchi created *My Arizona* (1943), a square relief divided into four zones, two corners of which are rounded and the other two of which are left as right angles [3-16]. In one quadrant a cone with a void suggests a volcano; in the second the shallow pyramid first introduced in the *Monument to the Plough* occupies a corresponding quarter. In the third quadrant an ominous hook protrudes from a shallow hill, and over the fourth corner of the relief a square of pink Plexiglas hovers above a softly contoured hill. The interpretation of these forms is left open. Modeled in magnesite, the surface of *My Arizona* suggests a landscape, perhaps a nagging memory of Noguchi's incarceration at Poston.[38]

Although in form the sculpture suggests terrain, *Lunar Landscape* (ca. 1944) was installed vertically on the wall, with lines of string and spheres of cork suspended above its surface. *Lunar Landscape* is the initial relief of the series Noguchi termed Lunars, consisting of softly contoured magnesite surfaces integrating electric lights tinted by sheets of colored acetate [3-17]. Red, yellow, and blue lights shine from within the relief, complemented by the gently protruding form in the lower left portion of the relief that conceals a lamp emitting soft yellow light. The forms of these works share a vocabulary with Noguchi's assembled sculptures and with surrealism—a resonance that, as he himself explained, was understandable: "Surrealism was in the air in the thirties and forties, a definite force."[39] While conceived as coherent sculptures, the Lunars could also be read as groups of elements unified by a single contoured surface—an arrangement that would later appear frequently in Noguchi's built landscapes.

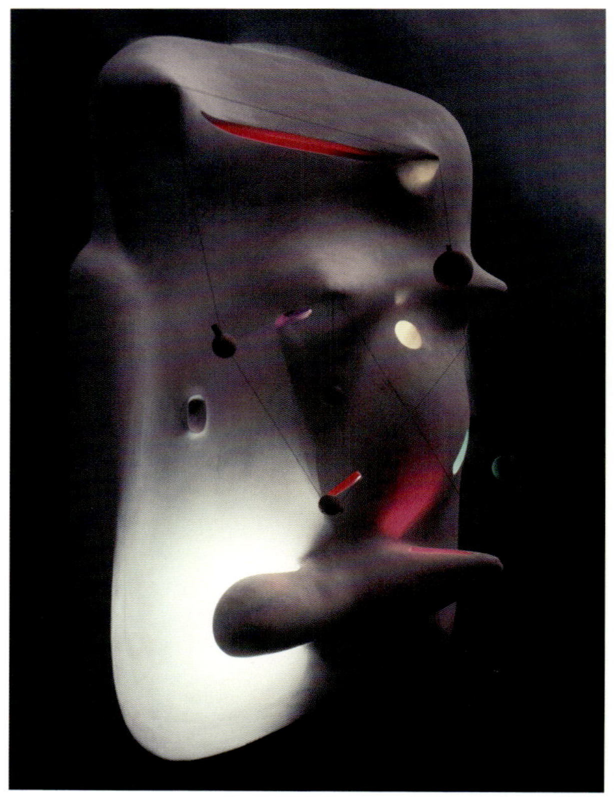

3-16
My Arizona, 1943.
[Kevin Noble, © The Noguchi Museum/ARS]

3-17
Lunar Landscape, ca. 1944.
[© The Noguchi Museum/ARS]

>> SHAPING THE SITE

In fact, the origins of the Lunars may be found in landform on this planet. In 1941 Noguchi returned to the subject of children's play and produced *Contoured Playground*, to be discussed more fully in the following chapter [see 4-2, 4-3]. Unlike *Play Mountain*, the design language is completely biomorphic. Countering the criticism leveled against *Play Mountain*, Noguchi defended his design by noting that there were no hard edges that could injure a child at play. *Contoured Playground* is clearly a sculptural relief, however, whose shapes and forms flow into one another, with the Platonic geometry of the circular zones stiffening the soft contours of the playground's earthen surfaces.[40] Despite the beauty of *Contoured Playground* as a sculpture, the critique of *Play Mountain* on functional grounds could also apply. Perhaps the design was never meant to be realized but only to serve as a sculptural metaphor—a mental playground in which the eye ably traces the surfaces of the relief in a manner impossible for a body experiencing the contours at full scale.

As Noguchi had been recently released from the Poston War Relocation Camp, the effects of war on the civilian populations and the land upon which they lived must have weighed heavily on his consciousness. A photograph of a North African landscape heavily scarred by aerial bombing instigated the making of *This Tortured Earth* (1943), which he regarded as a potential memorial to "the tragedy of war" by its evoking a sense of human agony [3-18].[41] Although the formal vocabulary bears resemblances to the Lunar wall reliefs, their benign, softly sculpted topography has been violently rent, twisted, and stretched as if a piece of fabric. Whether in complete seriousness or not, Noguchi suggested that the full-scale realization of the design could be achieved by aerial bombardment. "The war machine, [he] thought, would be excellent equipment for sculpture, to bomb it into existence."[42] Unlike the vertically mounted Lunars, *This Tortured Earth* was intended to be displayed horizontally, an aspect reinforcing the possibility of its construction at larger scale.[43]

The horrors of war became even more terrifying with the release of the atomic bombs on the cities of Hiroshima and Nagasaki on 6 and 9 August 1945. Incendiary and carpet bombardment throughout the later years of the war had leveled cities and destroyed untold numbers of dwellings in countries across the world, but in the wake of the atomic bombs

3-18
This Tortured Earth, 1943.
[Kevin Noble, © The Noguchi Museum/ARS]

suffering and devastation increased exponentially. In the early 1950s Noguchi designed an unexecuted memorial cenotaph and realized two bridge railings for the Peace Memorial Park in Hiroshima designed by architect Kenzô Tange. Prior to his visit to the site, Noguchi had reflected on the fear of nuclear cataclysm, as did Akira Kurosawa in his 1955 film *I Live in Fear* (*Record of a Living Being*). In the film, Toshiro Mifune plays Kiichi Nakajima, a major industrialist and patriarch so gripped by the terror of nuclear holocaust that he plans an escape to Brazil, where he thinks he and his family will be safe. The turmoil to the lives of his extended family—who believe Nakajima to be insane—caused by the threat of leaving Japan occupies the core of the film. Paired with this desire to leave is the distressing uncertainty that moving to South America will not provide the escape from what had become a global threat.

Sculpture to Be Seen from Mars (1947) offers a record to be read in the aftermath of such a nuclear catastrophe [3-19]. For those who survived extinction by escaping to Mars, Noguchi's monument would commemorate those who had perished: a memory of a civilization on an Earth eradicated by nuclear holocaust. Its alternate title, *Pyramidal Memorial to Man to Be Visible from Mars*, clarifies the sculptor's intentions.[44] Curator Martin Friedman describes the work as a memorial to humankind, which would have become a "vanished species."[45] At first glance, the sculpture appears to be an unremarkable geometric rendering of a human face. Only after reading Noguchi's explanation that the nose itself was to measure a mile on its long side do we realize the colossal scale of the projected undertaking. In tandem with the elongated tetrahedron that forms the nose—once again a pyramid—stand two hemispherical mounds that form the eyes; the mouth suggests a sports stadium, or perhaps some Mesoamerican ball court. Largest of all is the forehead, shaped as a massive ovular mesa with sloping sides. The original piece, made of sand on Masonite, was little more than a foot square, almost literally a world contained in grains of sand. Unlike *Play Mountain* or *Contoured Playground*, however, the *Sculpture to Be Seen from Mars* was a conceptual landscape never intended to have been constructed at true size.

>> JEFFERSON NATIONAL EXPANSION MEMORIAL

The year *Sculpture to Be Seen from Mars* was conceived, 1947, was also the submission date for entries to the competition for the Jefferson National Expansion Memorial, a monument celebrating the westward expansion that followed the 1803 Louisiana Purchase during the presidency of Thomas Jefferson. The idea for the memorial, to be erected in St. Louis, originated in 1935 during the administration of Franklin Delano Roosevelt, but several factors—first bureaucracy and then war—postponed the competition for its design until 1946.[46] Another stimulus was the contentious urban-renewal project to remove the blight of "slums" on the site while rejoining St. Louis's downtown with the Mississippi River.

By late 1942 several blocks of nineteenth-century commercial structures had already been demolished through eminent domain, in the firm belief that work on the memorial was certain to proceed immediately upon the return of peace.[47] The competition opened in May 1947; the year before, Philadelphia architect George Howe had been named professional adviser. His choice of jurors tilted the outcome of the competition in favor of a more modern solution, the antithesis of John Russell Pope's Pantheon-like Jefferson Memorial (1941) in Washington, DC, erected six years prior.[48] The competitors were given only three months to prepare their entries; the deadline was 1 September 1947.

The riverfront site constituted ninety-one acres and required the demolition of some forty city blocks. Given the celebrity of the project, the recovering postwar economy, and the number of architects among the flood of returning veterans, the competition received numerous submissions: 178. The revised program for the memorial was relatively simple, calling for a monument of an unspecified type, a visitor center with display spaces, and structures for support services. An existing church on-site was to be retained. The competition brief outlined a vision that included:

> *(a) an architectural memorial or memorials to Jefferson; dealing with (b) the preservation of the site of Old St Louis—landscaping, provision of an open-air campfire theater, re-erection or reproduction of a few typical old buildings, provision of a museum interpreting the Westward movement; (c) a "living memorial" to Jefferson's "vision of greater opportunities for men of all races and creeds;"*

3-19
Sculpture to Be Seen from Mars, 1947.
[Soichi Sunami, © The Noguchi Museum/ARS]

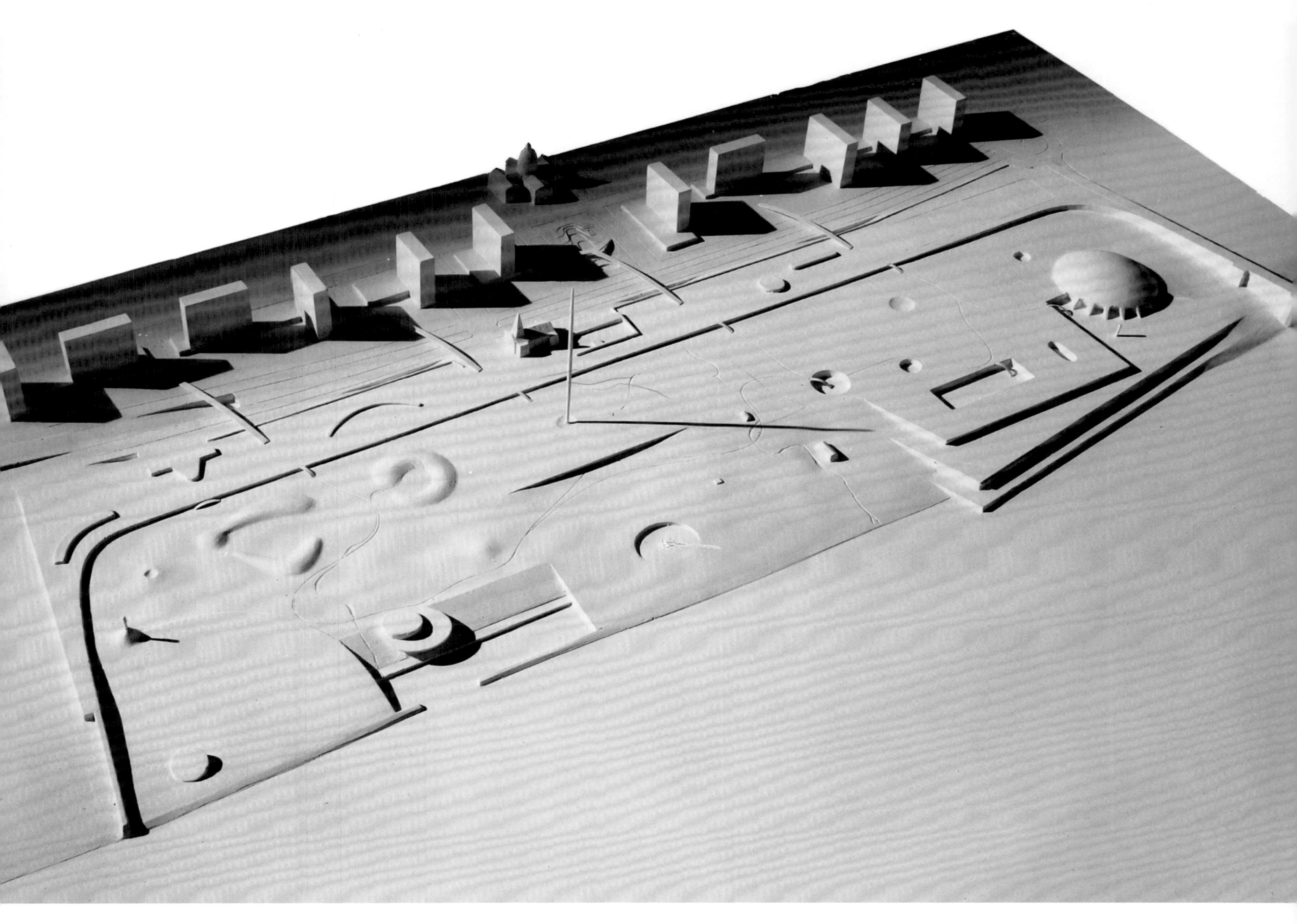

3-20
Isamu Noguchi and
Edward Durell Stone.
Jefferson National
Expansion Memorial.
St. Louis, Missouri, 1947.
Site model.
[Ezra Stoller / ESTO]

3-21 *[opposite above]*
Isamu Noguchi and
Edward Durell Stone.
Jefferson National
Expansion Memorial.
Aerial perspective.
[Arkansas Architectural
Archives]

3-22 *[opposite below]*
Isamu Noguchi and
Edward Durell Stone.
Jefferson National
Expansion Memorial.
Site plan.
[Arkansas Architectural
Archives]

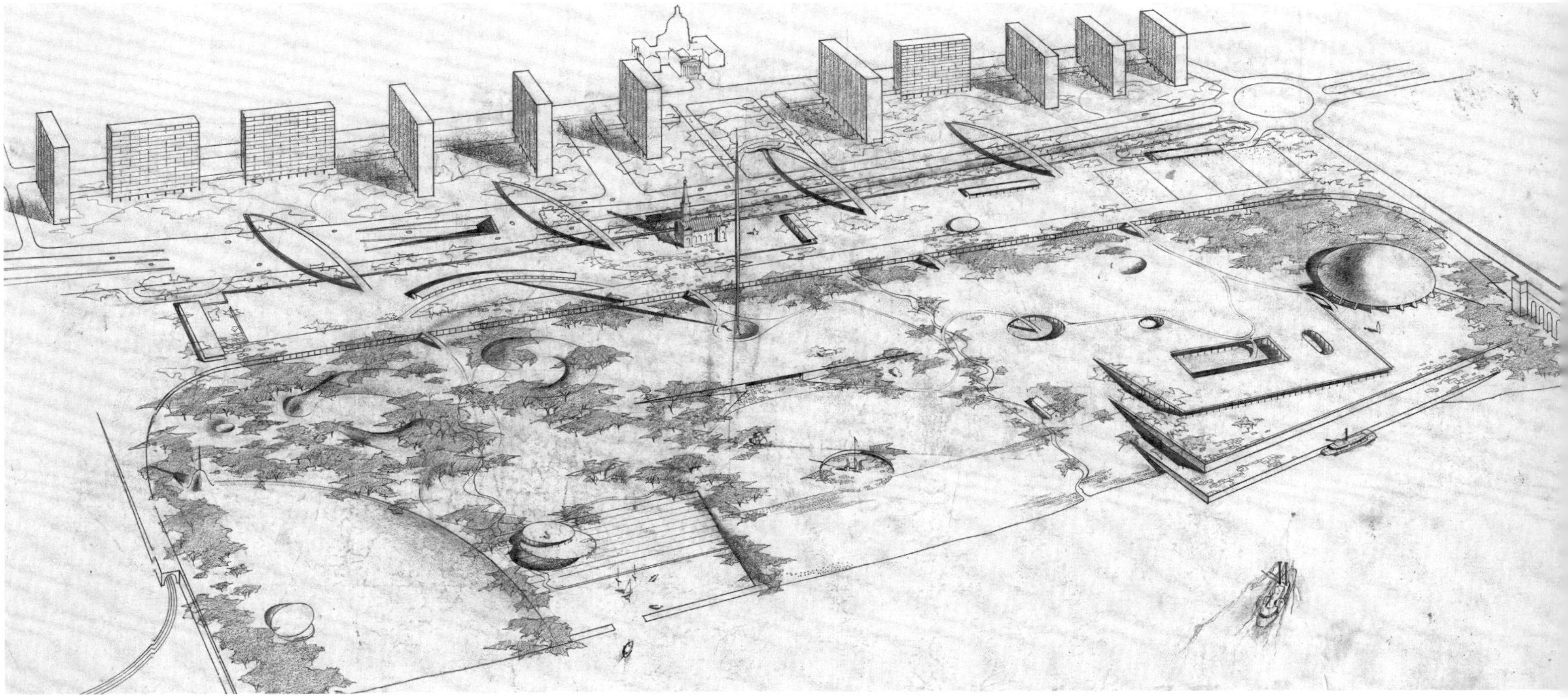

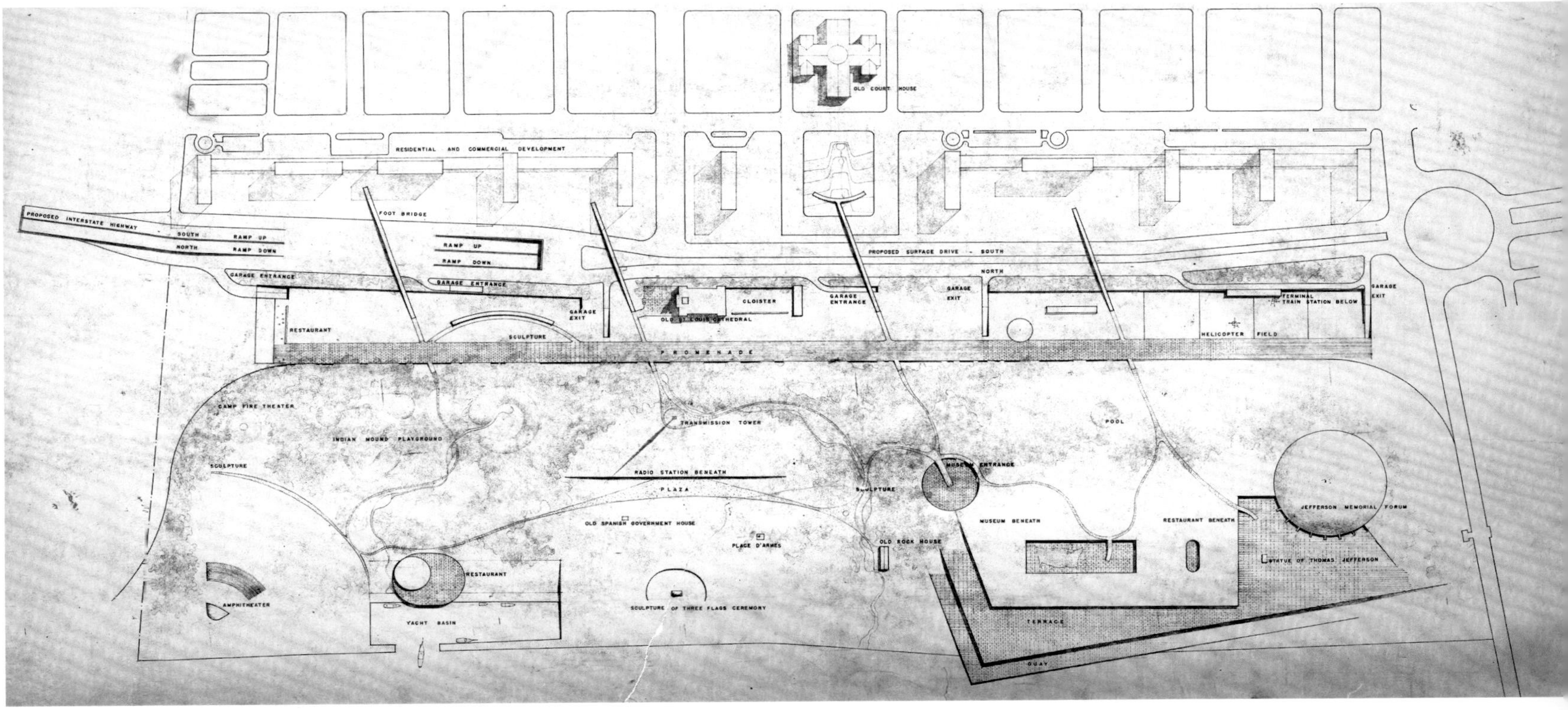

OLD COURT HOUSE
RESIDENTIAL AND COMMERCIAL DEVELOPMENT
PROPOSED INTERSTATE HIGHWAY
FOOT BRIDGE
SOUTH
RAMP UP
NORTH
RAMP DOWN
RAMP UP
RAMP DOWN
PROPOSED SURFACE DRIVE - SOUTH
NORTH
GARAGE ENTRANCE
GARAGE ENTRANCE
GARAGE EXIT
CLOISTER
OLD ST LOUIS CATHEDRAL
GARAGE ENTRANCE
GARAGE EXIT
TERMINAL TRAIN STATION BELOW
GARAGE EXIT
RESTAURANT
SCULPTURE
HELICOPTER FIELD
PROMENADE
CAMP FIRE THEATER
INDIAN MOUND PLAYGROUND
TRANSMISSION TOWER
POOL
SCULPTURE
RADIO STATION BENEATH
PLAZA
MUSEUM ENTRANCE
SCULPTURE
OLD SPANISH GOVERNMENT HOUSE
PLACE D'ARMES
OLD ROCK HOUSE
MUSEUM BENEATH
RESTAURANT BENEATH
JEFFERSON MEMORIAL FORUM
STATUE OF THOMAS JEFFERSON
RESTAURANT
AMPHITHEATER
YACHT BASIN
SCULPTURE OF THREE FLAGS CEREMONY
TERRACE
QUAY

(d) recreational facilities on both sides of the river; and (e) automotive access and parking facilities, the relocation of railroads, and the placement of a future interstate highway.[49]

On this project Noguchi collaborated with the then-modernist architect Edward Durell Stone (1902–1978). Their presentation model suggests that Stone contributed the rack of slab blocks on the eastern edge of the site—presumably housing—while Noguchi designed the sculptured landscape that prevailed [3-20; 3-21; 3-22]. Although the Lunars and the *Contoured Playground* may have informed his design, Noguchi himself cited the influence of the Serpent Mound (ca. 1000) and other Indigenous earthworks in Ohio he had recently visited [3-23]. The jump in scale necessitated by the memorial site provokes the question as to the suitability of a small-scale relief serving as the basis of a large-scale landscape, especially when the size of the human body experiencing both forms remains constant. Rejecting the ground-dominated Noguchi-Stone design, the commission instead selected Eero Saarinen's heroic arch, triangular in section and clad in stainless steel, accompanied by a heavily planted park designed by Daniel Kiley.[50]

Although unappreciated by the competition jury, Noguchi's vision for a landscape of this size demonstrates that his interests were continually growing and that the model for the project embodied his ideas concerning the relationship of building and landscape:

The spaces around buildings should be treated in such a way as to dramatize and make space meaningful....The sculpting of space—sculpture which defines space—may even be invisible as sculpture and still exist as sculptural space. The relationship of the architect to the sculptor should be reconsidered on that basis. The sculptor is not merely a decorator of buildings but a serious collaborator in the creation of significant space and of significant shapes which define this space.[51]

He would have to wait four more years for the opportunity to design and construct a true landscape.

>> READER'S DIGEST

That opportunity arrived in the form of an invitation to design the garden for the *Reader's Digest* building in Tokyo, scheduled to open in 1952 [3-24]. Founded in 1922 by DeWitt and Lila Acheson Wallace, the popular general-interest publication condensed books into articles that provided the basic content if not the complete texts of the original. An immediate success, the magazine had survived the Depression years and over the decades had begun to publish several foreign-language editions, leading to the establishment of editorial offices in several countries. The Japanese edition of the magazine first appeared in 1946, a year after peace was secured and the start of the American Occupation. Its quick success was largely due to the Japanese embrace of the culture of the occupiers and the hunger for new ideas and broader worldviews that followed the isolation and privations of the war years. In 1949 the Czech émigré architect Antonin Raymond (1888–1976) was commissioned to design the new office building in Tokyo for the Japanese edition.

Having maintained a thriving practice prior to the war, Raymond was the most likely candidate for the job. He had come to Japan around 1920 to serve as project architect for Frank Lloyd Wright's Imperial Hotel in Tokyo, which opened three years later. Wright returned to Wisconsin in the midst of construction, but Raymond stayed on to become one of the country's premier architects working in the modern manner. Recognized as arguably the most prominent architectural firm in Japan, the Raymond and Rado office became a training ground for young architects seeking knowledge of a more advanced and international perspective regarding modern architecture. These included Kunio Maekawa (1905–1986) and Junzô Yoshimura (1908–1997), each of whom would maintain a practice that achieved international recognition. When the clouds of war gathered in the late 1930s, Raymond returned to the United States, and in 1937 opened an office in New Hope, Pennsylvania, where he stayed until the end of hostilities. He and his wife, Noémi, an artist and designer, returned to Japan shortly after peace was established, in part bolstered by the commission for the *Reader's Digest* building.

The building site was located on the edge of the grounds of the Imperial Palace and, like all political issues concerning Emperor Hirohito, it came with restrictions. In deference to the palace, located just

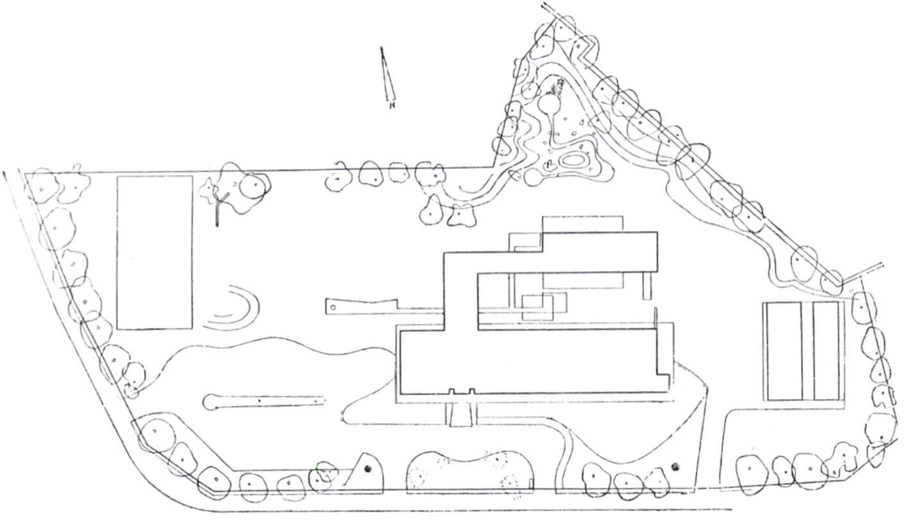

3-23
Serpent Mound.
near Locust Grove, Ohio,
ca. 1000 CE.

3-24
Antonin Raymond.
Reader's Digest Building.
Tokyo, Japan, 1952.
Site plan.
[*Shin Kenchiku*]

across the outer moat, the height of the *Reader's Digest* building was restricted to two stories, although the structure would be executed in an uncompromisingly modern style using reinforced concrete, steel, and glass. With the availability of building materials still governed by wartime restrictions, steel construction was an accomplishment in itself, and no doubt intended to serve as a positive demonstration of American prowess and an advertisement for the magazine. The interior arrangement of the bar-shaped office building, with the cafeteria appended as a separate block, was straightforward. Inside, a central aisle flanked by working stations extended along its length. Façades sheathed primarily in glass supported the visual connection between the workspaces and the surrounding gardens.

Raymond harbored no illusions that he could create an external complement to his building of commensurate distinction, and in a letter to Noguchi on 25 October 1950 he solicited the artist's participation. The letter was filled with considerable flattery and a proposition for creating a garden as the setting for this important structure. In a follow-up letter of 22 November to Noguchi, who probably had not yet accepted the commission, Raymond bemoaned the small budget that would limit the scope of the sculptor's contribution. Yet he was convinced that Noguchi was the only artist suitable for the undertaking: "I know that I could never hope to make the *Reader's Digest* site anywhere near as interesting alone, without you, as with you," he offered in closing. He himself had made similar studies for one of his projects, "and found it a lot of fun."[52]

In his autobiography, Raymond wrote that, "For the gardening, I asked Isamu Noguchi to come and help me, which he did. We built on only part of the ground instead of filling it up to the legal capacity, thereby hoping to set an example of unselfish utilization of the ground for the sake of good urban design." An "ample garden" would represent a more sympathetic use of the site.[53] Although, as noted above, funds were limited—the budget was a mere $1,500— Noguchi was intrigued by the building and the project; perhaps more importantly, the commission would facilitate his return to Japan. He later told an interviewer, "That's how I did it, it was for experience that I did it."[54] The agreement was signed by architect and artist on 30 January 1951; he would work on-site from 28 March to 5 July 1951.[55] Design could now begin.

3-25
Reader's Digest garden.
Tokyo, 1951.
Noguchi on site
during construction,
c. 1951
[© The Noguchi Museum/ARS]

3-26
Reader's Digest garden.
Landforms seen from
the cafeteria.
[Isamu Noguchi, © The Noguchi Museum/ARS]

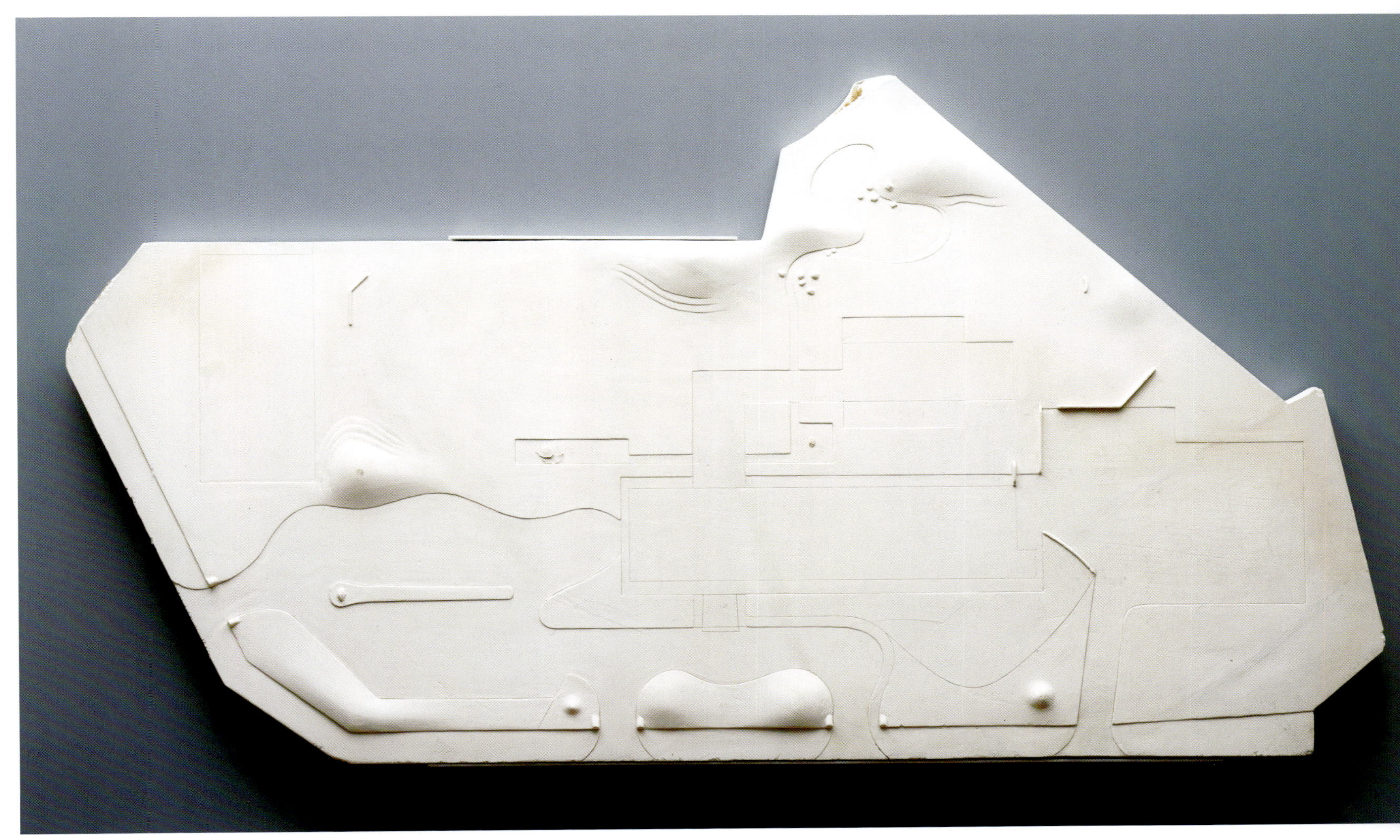

3-27
Reader's Digest garden.
Plaster relief of the landscape; the building footprint and parking are recessed.
[Kevin Noble, © The Noguchi Museum/ARS]

On his earlier stay, and even as a child in Japan, Noguchi had developed an interest in gardens that continued to develop in tandem with his interest in joining art and life, and sculpture with lived space. The garden became the embodiment of these goals. Soon after accepting Raymond's invitation, he began to formulate his ideas for the landscape as a one-acre relief that played rolling earthen mounds and pools against a rectangular parking area.[56] Wisely, Noguchi used the spoils from the building excavation and site work to enhance the contours of the essentially flat site [3-25]. In some areas changes to the prior terrain were minimal, but in others—behind the building, for example—the interplay of staged mounds was consequential, with softly sculpted hills whose height seems to have peaked at about ten feet. Along the road, the earth was reshaped as a linear, grass-covered hillock that buffered the offices from the adjacent city [3-26]. An initial study, produced as a plaster relief, presents the subtle modeling of the ground plane in and around the structure, which intermixed orthogonal geometry with biomorphic shapes [3-27].[57]

While difficult to determine with precision, Noguchi evidently initially proposed surrounding the building with a reflecting pool to increase its sense of lightness. In later stages of design, however, the amount of water was reduced, with the pool adjacent to the building treated as a canal that flowed beneath the corridor to ultimately join a sinuous stream that terminated in a round basin [3-28]. Here, Noguchi profited from the subsurface hot springs also used to heat the building.[58] In the more private zones to the rear of the building, its orthogonal geometry spread outward, ultimately melting into softly modeled mounds set at a distance. Accompanying the site work, Noguchi created three sculptures. A pair of granite figures, abstractions of the traditional *kokeshi* doll, for which the sculptures are named, was executed off-site. More impressive was a fountain set within a towering cage of iron sited at the end of the small canal, whose tumbling water served as the source for the pool [3-29].[59]

The *Reader's Digest* garden was a pivotal project in Noguchi's career, not only as his first realized landscape, but also as his first experience "working in the mud" with Japanese gardeners, from whom he learned "the rudiments of stone placing—using the stones we could find on the site." From them he also gained the insight that each stone possessed both "a live and dead side."[60] In photographs, however, many of the rocks appear almost superficially and randomly placed, resting on the ground rather than emerging from it in the preferred traditional manner. In Noguchi's mind, however, this was not the case. For him, the *Reader's Digest* project was transformative, with the setting of the stones an "almost ritual improvisation of placing them upon the earth with an exactitude that astonished me."[61] A Japanese gardener might hold a different opinion.

While the visual documentation of Noguchi's design for the *Reader's Digest* garden is now limited to black-and-white photographs and a plaster relief model, one can identify elements that returned in later landscapes, among them the courtyards for a corporate office building in Connecticut and a sculpture garden in Israel. To a greater degree than in his sculptures, Noguchi's making of landscapes was reiterative, frequently recasting earlier forms and spatial ideas in the new designs. Each served as a lesson or stepping stone in a progression toward the mature works that culminated in *California Scenario*, the subject of chapter 9.

3-28
Reader's Digest garden.
Tokyo, 1951.
Pool with sculpture.
[© The Noguchi Museum/ARS]

3-29
Sculpture/fountain from *Readers Digest* building (detail); today at Macalester College, St. Paul, Minnesota.

> 4.

Grounds for Play

Play, its equipment, and grounds were frequent subjects of Noguchi's designs, almost literally from his first to his last landscape project [4-1]. More than once in his writings and interviews he mentioned play in relation to art, citing Constantin Brancusi's maxim that when an artist stops being a child, she or he stops being an artist. Yet, more specific statements by Noguchi regarding the nature of play are limited, and those pertaining to the grounds on which it occurs are even more so. Rather than published or otherwise recorded statements on this subject, one must therefore look to the designs he proposed, designs that spanned nearly half a century.

>> THE NATURE AND NURTURE OF PLAY

The physical exercise accompanying play strengthens the body while developing cognitive, social, and emotional abilities. Toys, play equipment, and playgrounds support the acquisition of physical goals or appropriate behavior. An activity such as climbing to attain a greater height represents the first goal of play; enacting an afternoon tea party or playing astronaut more comfortably falls under the rubric of social integration. Most forms of play develop these benefits in combination, however. Play equipment may replicate at small scale objects in the "real world" or offer more abstract forms that rely on analogy or metaphor.[1] Although it is tempting to speculate that a landscape of abstract forms promotes child development more effectively than play equipment such as swings, slides, or a concrete bear, no conclusive evidence supports this hypothesis. It appears that whether creating a frigate from boxes of debris, or playing pirate on a miniature ship, children interact with equal verve and fantasy. Regardless of one's own stylistic preferences, however, most would agree with landscape architect M. Paul Friedberg that "play is the child's work.... Play is the research by which he explores himself and his relationship to the world."[2]

In *Designing the Creative Child*, Amy Ogata examines the origins of the post–World War II movement to design equipment and environments specifically to stimulate children's creativity.[3] At that time, there were (and currently still are) widely varying opinions concerning the ways in which exercise and equipment impact the development of intelligence and creativity. In the past most toys replicated, usually at reduced scale, the implements of adult life to support established identities and roles.

4-0
Contoured Playground (detail), 1941.
[Rudolph Burckhardt, © The Noguchi Museum/ARS]

Some fostered gendered behavior and social integration; others, vocational indoctrination; still others, creativity. Thus, one could hypothesize that by gathering and assembling some leaves, sticks, and boxes, children better imagine, construct, and inhabit their environment. So believed Dutch architect Aldo van Eyck (1918–1999), who built approximately seven hundred playgrounds in and around Amsterdam from the 1940s through the 1970s: "An aluminum elephant is not real, since an elephant is meant to move, and as an object in the street it is unnatural. A child can make anything out of a simple form."[4]

Norman Brosterman contends that early childhood exposure to abstraction leads to more complex thought processes and the fostering of sensitive and talented artists and designers. In *Inventing Kindergarten*, he links exposure to Friedrich Froebel's (1782–1852) creative exercises using color and geometric shapes—what the pioneering German educator termed "gifts"—to the nurturing of creativity, a connection well-known to anyone familiar with the writings of Frank Lloyd Wright.[5] "By explicitly equating ideas, symbols, and things," Brosterman writes, working with the Froebel blocks "encouraged abstract thinking, and, in its repetitive use of geometric forms as the building blocks of all design, it taught children a new and highly disciplined way of making art." More consequentially, "Simple linear thinking was superseded by a more sophisticated, genealogical approach to knowledge that valued relationships as much as answers."[6] I suspect that Noguchi would have agreed, at least with the premise that abstraction, rather than replication or miniaturization, was the better vehicle by which to enrich childhood experience and promote bodily, cognitive, and creative development.

>> PLAY GROUNDS

At almost the same moment in 1933 that Noguchi was proposing his *Monument to the Plough*, he was also imagining *Play Mountain*, his first interactive terrain for children [4-1; see also 3-9]. The origins of the work, which seems to have emerged *sui generis* with no established precedent, may be traced back to Noguchi's childhood in Japan, where he enjoyed some of his happiest days. Rather than spending time on school playgrounds detached from everyday life, the ten-year-old Noguchi helped build his family's house; his efforts to tend its garden nurtured his sense of well-being, self-confidence, and happiness.[7] Years later, while living in New York, he was troubled by the condition of the city's asphalted schoolyards. In reaction, he conceived a new type of playground—a "seasonal pyramid"—a playground considered sculpture, which he hoped would be funded by the Depression-era Works Progress Administration (WPA). This innovative terrain would embody a new world of play for New York's children, who had "nothing more than a cement area with a fence around it high enough so that they couldn't climb over it, in which they were left like birds in a cage or animals in a zoo."[8] Or perhaps, as Dore Ashton has suggested, the idea for a playground "had entered into [Noguchi's] own experience when he began to experiment with clay, and it was endemic to Japanese theories of art, particularly Zen, which regarded play as a vital aspect of existence and, with it as a concomitant humor."[9]

Unlike the playgrounds that preceded it, *Play Mountain* did not comprise a fenced yard furnished with play equipment from a catalog bolted into concrete or asphalt. Now the ground itself became the play structure: a single, integrated landscape that would occupy an entire city block. Its principal feature was a stepped mountain, which, like *Monument to the Plough*, was predominantly triangular in plan but rose in stages toward an overall pyramidal form: a "vision of a pyramid in Idaho, [brought] into the experience of people in the city where I lived . . . a mountain which would provide an enhanced terrain for children's play."[10] This play area would include an array of innovative aspects: hard and soft surfaces, water, geometry, and biomorphically contoured surfaces that in winter might accommodate hoards of children screaming with delight as they slid down the slopes or that in summer could encourage children to use cardboard skids if the grass were sufficiently wet. Although missing kinetic features like a rotating carousel or a seesaw, this cascade of textures and shapes would provide an endless panoply of stimuli for the young child. Noguchi's scheme does not specify the materials from which the elements of *Play Mountain* would be constructed nor the areas to which they would be assigned. Also absent from his proposal is information on such matters as the ways in which the steps and contours would be stabilized, how their forms would be maintained, and the ages of the children who would play in this space.[11]

As such, any readings of the playground's use can only be speculative. The landscape designer generally begins with analysis that

4-1
Play Mountain (detail).
New York, 1933.
[© The Noguchi Museum/ARS]

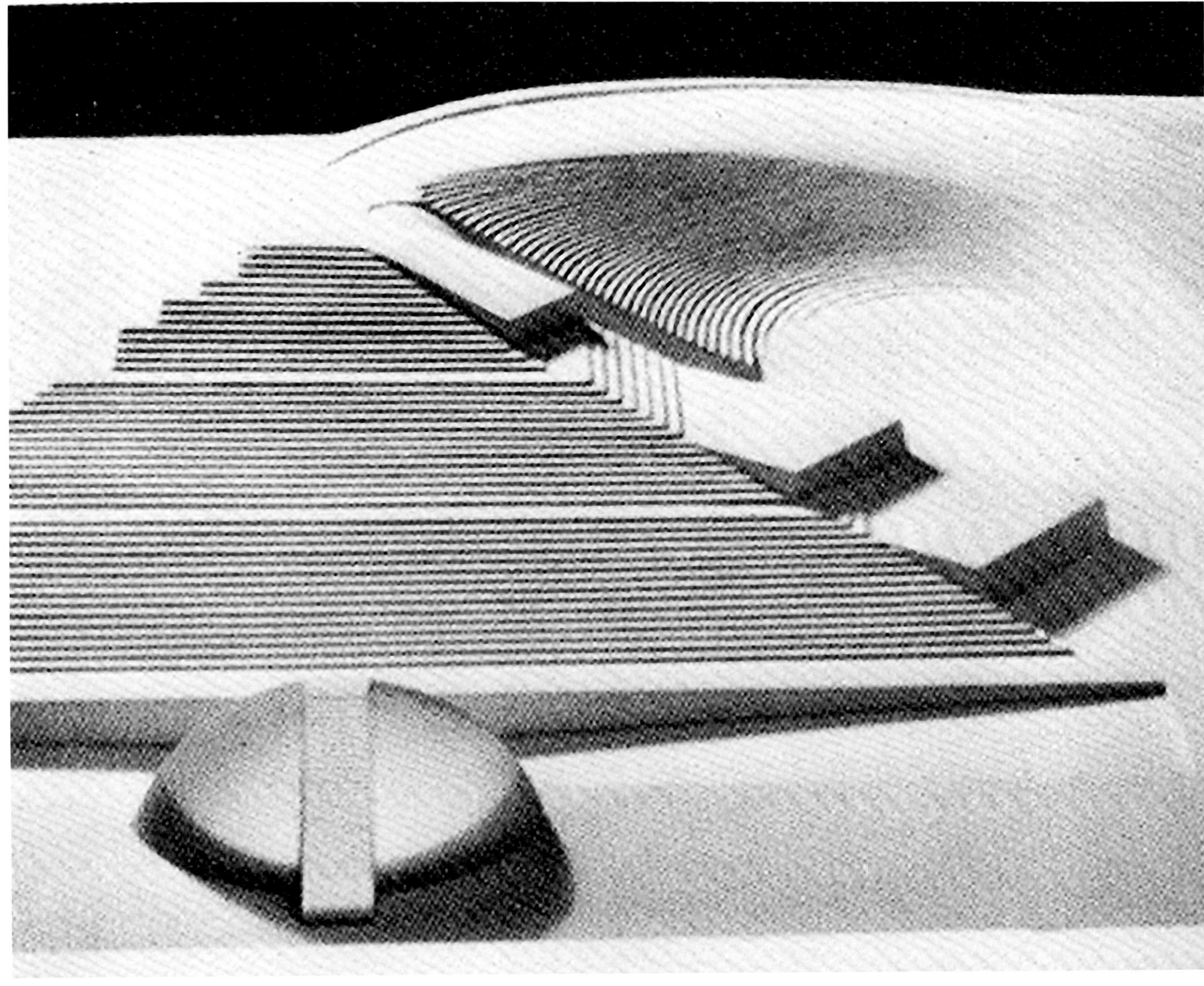

addresses the greater context, and thereafter focuses on the particulars of the site. In an almost opposite manner, Noguchi began from within, from feelings and ideas concerning the nature of play and its relationship to a sculptured ground. Therein lies the difference between the centripetal process of the landscape designer and the centrifugal approach of the sculptor. Neither is more valid, and criticism of Noguchi's project should not be taken as condemnation but offered only to establish the limits as well as achievements of his schemes. A playground of this type encourages and supports, rather than dictates the activities it will accommodate. As well as a work of art, his playground is thus perhaps best read as a manifesto regarding the importance and nature of play, a suggestion of what could, rather than what should, be.

Despite its radical concept—or, more likely, because of it—*Play Mountain*, like *Monument to the Plough*, was summarily rejected by the WPA review board. In fact, the agency was so put off by the two proposals that they dropped Noguchi from their rolls. On a more sympathetic note, however, they informed him that should he have any ideas for art of a more conventional scale and manner, he was welcome to reapply. Undeterred, through *New York Times* art critic Murdock Pemberton, Noguchi secured an interview with Robert Moses, Commissioner of the New York Parks Department, who for several decades reigned over the city's open spaces and motorways.[12] Alas, Moses was no more receptive than the WPA reviewers; he met Noguchi's playground proposal "with thorough sarcasm."[13] Noguchi recounted that "he just laughed his head off and more or less threw us out . . . I never had such a tough time. Mr. Moses took offense at me, thought I was trying to kill people, said a playground had to [use] tested equipment and that New York City could not afford to test my mountain."[14] In the end, both of Noguchi's radical works were left unrealized. And yet, as Noguchi looked back on his personal development many years later, he saw that "*Play Mountain* was the kernel out of which [grew] all [his] ideas relating sculpture to the earth. It [was] also the progenitor of playgrounds as sculptural landscapes in many locations around the world."[15]

Some eight years later, in 1941, shortly before his voluntary incarceration at the Poston internment camp, Noguchi proposed a second innovative ground for play. Responding to criticism that the sharp edges in *Play Mountain* could be dangerous for its young users, Noguchi sculptured a play *ground* of biomorphic forms titled *Contoured Playground* [4-2]. "This would be proof against any serious accidents," he argued, "being made up entirely of earth modulations. Exercise would be stimulated by running up and down the curved surfaces. There were various areas of interest, for hiding, for sliding, for games. Water would flow in summer."[16] Or, as Noguchi more succinctly put it, he believed the forms were "fail-proof for the simple reason that there was nothing to fall off."[17]

Contoured Playground provided a more comprehensive vision for children's play than his earlier project. The design offered a greater sense of a whole, an engaging composition, albeit as equally abstract and frustrating as *Play Mountain* in its lack of specificity regarding materials, location, and, to some degree, intention. To *Contoured Playground* we might reasonably apply much of the criticism leveled against its predecessor: its failure to relate certain forms to specific activities; its dismissal of context; and even the relation of its edges, heights, and depressions to the surrounding streets. Noguchi left us only with a relief that serves as a tantalizing and eloquent idea for a playground.

Most photographs of both playground reliefs were taken from above, where they are viewed as sculpture and grasped in their entirety. Rarely were any photographs or other depictions of the forms or projected experience made from eye level—much less through the eyes of a child [4-3]. Designers might judge this as a major shortcoming, as they are taught to imagine the experience within their landscapes rather than merely create their forms. But again, we need to understand that Noguchi was neither an architect nor a landscape architect but an artist, and that *Contoured Playground* was first and foremost conceived as a work of art large enough to inhabit, with only suggestions of the play it would host upon its surfaces.

In *Towards a New Architecture*, an early manifesto for architectural modernism, Le Corbusier (1887–1965) characterizes the plan as the generator of the building's design.[18] As a horizontal section taken above the principal window level, the plan portrays a synchronic projection that reveals the relations among the building's internal spaces—something almost impossible to discern through direct experience. Le Corbusier does not address the fact that plans are used differently by designers at different

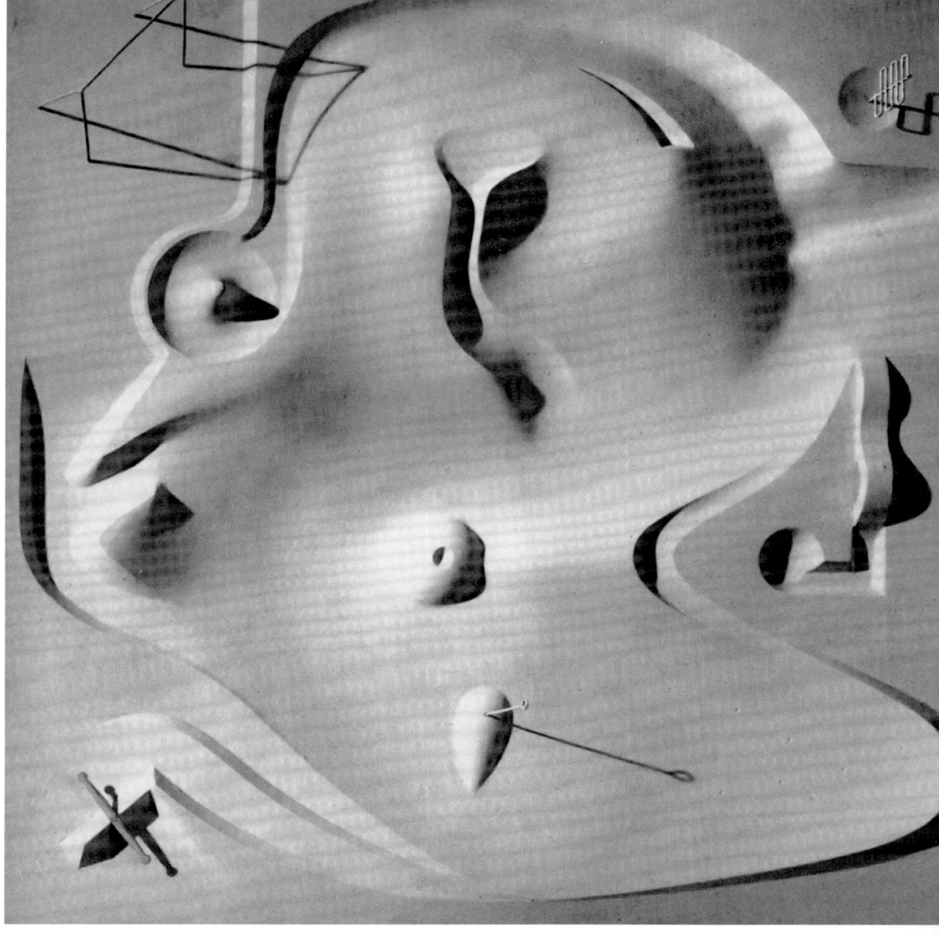

4-2
Contoured Playground,
1941.
[Rudolph Burckhardt, ©
The Noguchi Museum, ARS]

4-3
Contoured Playground.
Maquette with play equipment.
[F. S. Lincoln; Special Collections,
Pennsylvania State University
Libraries]

stages of the design process, as well as different stages of their professional development.[19] For the student and the inexperienced designer, the plan is usually determined first, and then extruded vertically to realize the spaces and the ultimate form of the building.[20] To an experienced architect like Le Corbusier, however, the plan serves as a shorthand condensation of a complete vision that, accompanied by perspectival sketches, pairs the proposed forms and spaces with their projected reading. Like the plan for Le Corbusier, I would imagine that the relief for Noguchi was a shallow, three-dimensional vision of the forms and experience he anticipated for the site; detailed development would follow. Or, at least, I will grant him that latitude.

In 1951 Noguchi received an invitation to design a playground near the United Nations compound in New York City on the northeast corner of a site whose title had been transferred to the city [4-4]. In contrast to his preceding hypothetical projects, this playground was an actual commission for a real site, sponsored by the United Nations Playground Association with the participation of the "residents of Beekman Place who had sacrificed their open space for [the United Nations] construction."[21] For the playground's design Noguchi would partner with the architect Julian Whittlesey (1905–1995), who had been selected based on his "understanding of the special considerations requisite in designing effective play areas for small children."[22] By August of that year a preliminary design had been prepared, already accompanied by concerns about Robert Moses's position on the nature of the proposal.

Once again, we are somewhat hampered in our understanding of the design by the dearth of information as to where, exactly, the playground would be located: its relation to First Avenue, the surrounding urban fabric, and the recently completed United Nations Secretariat and General Assembly buildings. In the maquette Noguchi again presents the design for the playground as a land unto itself. Like other of his landscapes—the courtyards of the IBM headquarters in Armonk, New York (ca. 1970), for example—the design assembles and composes independent elements on a contoured ground. Earth (or concrete?) forms elevate the land at the edge of the property (perhaps at the East River) to form a mound and a wall. In other parts of the play area the ground rises as a small hill, hollow at its core like a volcano to entice children to first climb over and then into it, and a rounded-arch form and metal climbing structure that might pique their interest. Thomas Hess, editor of *ARTnews*, reviewed the playground model, on display at the Museum of Modern Art (MoMA) soon after the design was made public. Impressed with its restatements of traditional forms, he noted: "Cleverly spotted hollows filled with sand replace the usual boxes; a jungle-gym is transformed into an enormous basket that encourages the most complex ascents and all but obviates falls."[23] A series of triangular steps converts the ground into a tesserated relief—another element that would return in several later Noguchi playgrounds. While the sculptured ground plane is the work's principal feature, the shapes and objects that rise from, or were dug into it, increase its formal complexity and spatial play.

In its generating concept, the United Nations playground proposal recalls Alberto Giacometti's *Model for a Square* (1932).[24] Upon a level ground Giacometti positioned two strong vertical elements against a circular depression and a hollowed hemisphere. Like Noguchi's use of triangles in New York, Giacometti counterposed a bench-like form, folded as a horizontal zigzag, to the more unitary figures of the tall menhir and its pointed, vertical counterpart.

When the model of the first iteration of the design was displayed at MoMA, an anonymous author cautioned that "the Museum makes it clear that the model is intended as a collection of ideas rather than a hard and fast specification. As either, it looks almost incapable of being opposed."[25] But sadly, it was. As with Noguchi's proposals for prior play landscapes, the project for the United Nations playground was ultimately vetoed by Robert Moses and representatives from other city agencies.[26] Evidently, the governing authorities were unable to comprehend a play landscape different from the installations of play equipment that had long been the norm. Of the roughly 400 playgrounds in New York City that opened during Moses's tenure from the mid-1930s through the late 1950s, Shaina Larrivee calculated that all relied on a "regularized design and mass produced equipment" that comprised "the S-es: swings, slides, sandboxes, seesaws and spray showers."[27] Beyond the client group and the artist himself there seems to have been little or no support, much less acceptance or appreciation for the notion that the landscape itself could be capable of stimulating cognitive and physical development—and even well-being. For a short time after the rejection of the proposal, rumors circulated that other

4-4
Isamu Noguchi and
Julian Whittlesey.
United Nations Playground.
New York, 1952.
Model.
[Charles Uht, © The Noguchi
Museum/ARS]

cities might be interested in hosting construction of the design.[28] Nothing resulted, however, and the project and its ideas remained only in the maquette stage.

>> PARALLELS AND INTERSECTIONS

As the homogeneity in the Moses-era playgrounds suggests, play landscapes in the United States had long remained ossified, making Noguchi's proposals appear all the more radical, and ultimately unacceptable, to governmental bureaucracies. A primarily urban institution, the playground often accompanied a school and was fortified by a chain-link fence, paved in asphalt, and furnished with the requisite slide, swings and jungle gym—perhaps also a sandbox and a carousel made of pipes and boards. The postwar baby boom and the accompanying widespread move to suburbia, however, spurred the construction of new and inventive park equipment and landscape types for the burgeoning population and their children. In Northern California, landscape architect Robert Royston (1918–2008) designed a series of suburban parks often sited adjacent to and integrated with the neighboring primary school.[29] Royston's ideas concerning children and play derived from personal observations as well as research into the latest sociological data and protocols, which assigned zones to specific ages and user groups, both adults as well as children [4-5]. Among his most inventive designs were the facilities for toddlers and small children, intended to delight and stimulate the mind and socialize the child through group play.

Royston's playgrounds combine figurative and abstract elements. For example, at Krusi Park in Oakland (1956), along with more conventional play structures, he created a freeway landscape in miniature, complete with peddle cars and the A-frame garages to house them [4-6]. Other landscapes, such as Mitchell Park in Palo Alto (also 1956), featured long pergolas that structured the zones of the park and provided shade for its visitors, and a biomorphically shaped play structure and wading pools for the youngsters. Royston called his concrete-shell forms "gopher holes," shallow vaults perforated with openings of sufficient diameter to permit the small child to enter, crawl around, and emerge [4-7]. Gopher holes became a staple of Royston's playgrounds in the San Francisco Bay Area. It is possible, though doubtful, that Royston was aware of Noguchi's unrealized playground designs, but it is intriguing to note that he designed and constructed forms quite similar to those proposed by the artist. Of course, by the late 1940s biomorphic shapes were ubiquitous, appearing on wallpaper, textiles, plates, furniture, and three-dimensionally as swimming pools and play structures.

Also in the Bay Area, landscape architect Douglas Baylis (1915–1971) produced a series of simple backyard play structures that could be built by parents with limited skills and available time. For ease of assembly, they were constructed of plywood; for ease of storage, the structure's parts could be stacked concentrically like a Russian doll [4-8]. By the 1950s primary colors had become the norm for children's play equipment, a tendency that Noguchi never accepted, instead preferring secondary and tertiary hues in a range of values.

The work of these landscape architects is cited here only to indicate that Noguchi was not alone in exploring the question of which types of designs were appropriate for the child at play. In Richard Dattner's (born 1936) urban playgrounds of the 1960s and 1970s one can discern echoes of the paths blazed by Noguchi, perhaps touched by a greater concern for managing groups of children. His playground for Central Park in New York (1967), for example, populated the play area with sculptural forms arranged as a ring with a void at its center, more or less in the manner of the ancient Roman circus.[30] Each element was graced by a certain mild drama, rather than their collectively producing a comprehensive spatial play [4-9].

In Europe related goals gave rise to the "adventure playground" movement that emerged from the rubble of World War II. Often credited to the Danish landscape architect Carl-Theodor Sørensen (1893–1979), the adventure playground challenged children to creatively use the debris left by shelling and bombing, or from the reconstruction that followed [4-10]. Tools, supplies, and limited supervision were provided to the child, who was encouraged to discover the possibilities in the materials at hand and use them accordingly. All efforts on-site, all constructions, were regarded as transitory; the lessons learned were deemed more significant than the resulting product. There could be an element of risk, even danger, on these playground sites, as there were risks and dangers in the city itself. That was the point; ideas explored and knowledge acquired on the playground related directly to the world beyond its enclosing fence.[31] In Britain, Marjory Allen (1897–1976),

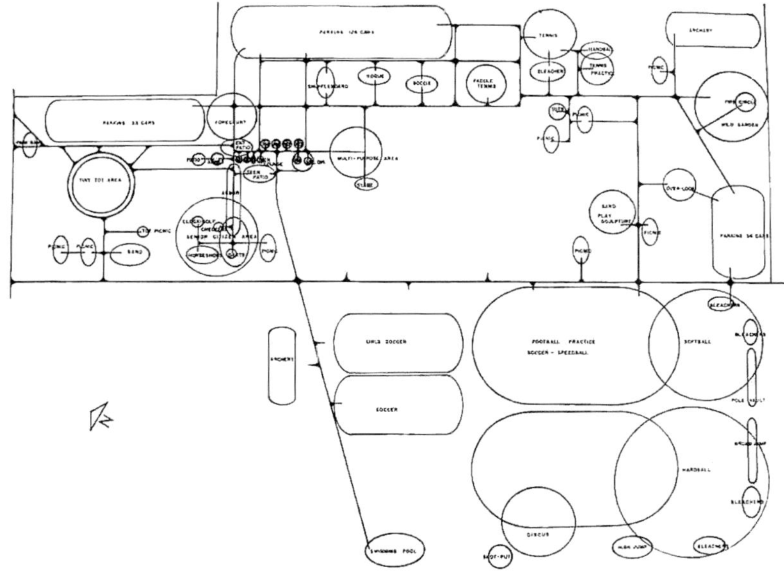

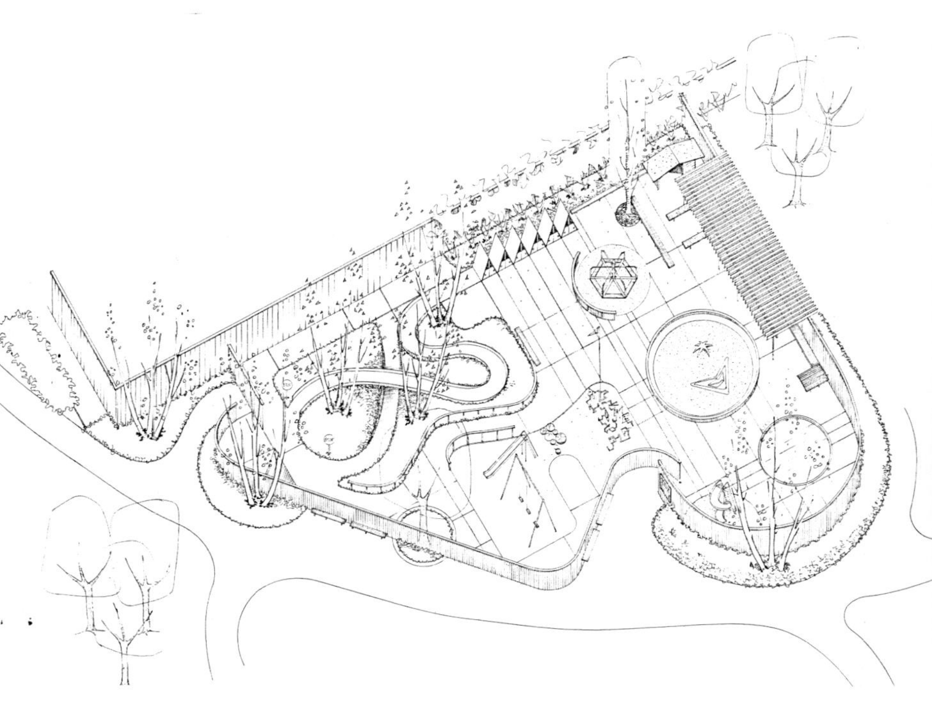

4-5 *[above left]*
Robert Royston.
Mitchell Park.
Palo Alto, California, 1953.
Social-use diagram.
[EDA/UCB]

4-6 *[above right]*
Robert Royston.
Krusi Park.
Oakland, California, 1953.
Axonometric.
Characteristics similar to the Noguchi playgrounds appeared in the designs of Californian landscape architects. Note the "freeway" to the left.
[EDA/UCB]

4-7 *[left]*
Robert Royston
Mitchell Park.
Palo Alto, California.
Gopher holes.
[EDA/UCB]

4-8
Douglas Baylis.
Plywood play equipment.
McCall's Magazine,
ca. 1958.

4-9 *[below]*
Richard Dattner.
Central Park Adventure
Playground.
New York, 1976.

4-10 *[bottom]*
Hillside Adventure
Playground.
London, 1960s.

aka Lady Allen of Hurtwood, championed the adventure playground with considerable success.[32] But the adventure playground never gained traction in the United States, where a litigious society frowned upon hazard, danger, and the hurt that the child might suffer as a result of potentially unsafe conditions—not to mention the lawsuits that might follow. This was one of the reasons why the designed playground resonated with the swelling population of young parents as they settled in their new suburban homes—and less frequently in the city. And even in the lands of its birth—Denmark and Great Britain—the adventure playground became more fixed and less adventurous over time and suffered waning popularity.

In Canada, Vancouver-based landscape architect Cornelia Hahn Oberlander (1921–2021) designed a series of play facilities related to, but somewhat distinct from, those of her American contemporaries. Her Children's Creative Centre at Expo 67 in Montreal interwove figurative and abstract features while relying on what landscape historian Susan Herrington terms "the basic elements of landscape—terrain, water, plants, and structures"; these were left "open to use and interpretation" by the child at play [4-11].[33] While seemingly focused on mental development through "imagination, challenge, and spontaneous exploration," the design also fostered physical improvement through curious features such as the "wobble walk," an old unstable dory purposely allowed to rock, challenging the child's sense of balance.[34] Although play within the landscape was supervised it was unstructured, and Oberlander's playground soon became a popular destination for the thousands of children visiting the fair.

Aldo van Eyck's vast number of playgrounds produced in and around Amsterdam between 1947 and 1978 represent yet another approach. For the most part, Van Eyck appropriated urban spaces with dimensions sufficient only to support the installation of a few play structures, usually of his design [4-12]. Rather than assigning play to a detached compound, the playground became integral to the city, a somewhat unique approach to play. In addition, Van Eyck regarded children as only one of several possible user groups. At night, after the kids had gone, a playground's brick or stone forms might provide seats for adults or support their conversation as they leaned against an inclined wall. Usually devoid of vegetation and constructed of masonry and concrete that matched the toughness of

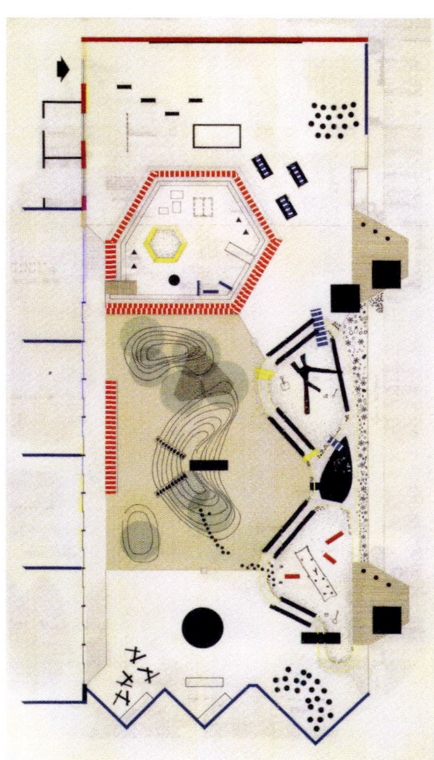

4-11
Cornelia Hahn Oberlander.
Children's Creative Centre.
Expo '67, Montreal, Quebec, Canada, 1967.
Plan.
[Canadian Centre for Architecture]

4-12
Aldo van Eyck.
Dijkstraat Playground.
Amsterdam, Netherlands, 1955.
[Stadsarchief Amsterdam]

the existing street, Van Eyck's playgrounds inspired use rather than offered comfort—for which they were roundly criticized. Fragments of the playgrounds still exist, although the demographics of their locations have significantly changed, as have their forms.

Nearly all of Noguchi's landscapes were destined for urban sites, where he thought they were needed most. "Playgrounds haven't changed since the invention of the swing and the sandbox," he claimed. "This one will free the child's imagination to create his own games . . . it's an adventure."[35] While sharing limited features with play areas designed by landscape architects and architects, Noguchi's grounds for play were a zebra of a far different stripe. Designers tend to begin with reality and focus on the site, the program, and the social constitution of the user group, whereas Noguchi began with a concept and a personal, somewhat abstract vision of play, as well as an idea of what forms would generate a positive response and potential interpretation.

>> RIVERSIDE DRIVE PLAYGROUND

Noguchi's most significant commission for a play space dates to the early 1960s, a complex landscape to be constructed on Riverside Drive in Manhattan. The commission came from Audrey Hess, who believed that a playground in this Upper West Side neighborhood on the Hudson River would serve as a fitting memorial to her aunt, philanthropist Adele Rosenwald Levy, to whom it would be dedicated.[36] She also believed that Noguchi would be the best person to create an innovative setting for play, a landscape that might rank as an artwork as well as a welcoming environment for children. Hess promised to be a powerful advocate for the park, as would her husband, Thomas Hess, then editor of *ARTnews*, who would later become the chief curator of twentieth-century art at the Metropolitan Museum of Art on the other side of Central Park.

The Upper West Side also had its share of influential and well-healed residents, however, who had no wish to see the project realized. As early as 1961 they had filed a suit against its implementation, revealing that resistance to the endeavor on both economic and social grounds existed from its earliest days.[37] Nor was the design well received within the municipal department that would manage it. On 13 November 1961 Newbold Morris, Commissioner of Parks, sent a memo to Stanley M. White, Director of Park Maintenance, claiming:

4-13
Louis I. Kahn.
Riverside Drive Playground.
New York, 1963.
Final design.
Sketch perspective.
[Architectural Archives,
University of Pennsylvania]

4-14
Isamu Noguchi and
Louis I. Kahn.
Riverside Drive Playground.
First design, 1961.
Model.
[Kevin Noble, © The Noguchi
Museum/ARS]

The proposal to reconstruct this section of Riverside Park . . . is certainly not warranted on the basis of cost . . . The duplication of existing facilities would present a very difficult control and operation problem and would require additional personnel service and other maintenance costs all out of proportion to the services rendered.[38]

Two days later White replied, asserting that the scheme was "massive in scope" and that the money needed for its construction would be better spent improving existing facilities. On 14 December and again on 20 February 1962, Morris restated that even if construction costs were covered by private funding, the proposed park would be too expensive to maintain, especially considering the small community it would serve. The "very imaginative design" —then in its earliest iterations—was deemed too costly to construct, too large for its needs, and too dramatic in its forms to be suitable for small children and their parents. The designers, Morris maintained, had,

permitted their talented imaginations to soar with the result that we were presented with the design for an unjustified architectural monument, which might draw attention from the tourist, the curious and the avant garde . . . but in our opinion is quite unsuitable.[39]

Although Noguchi approached the playground as a site for free play and unspecified activities, the program required sheltered facilities such as a nursery, a band shell, and a performance space. Considering these functional requirements, he thought it prudent to partner with an architect, at first considering Philip Johnson—whom he possibly knew through his associations with MoMA. In the end, for whatever reason, he chose the Philadelphia architect Louis I. Kahn (1901–1974).[40] In August 1961 Noguchi wrote to Kahn, outlining what he envisioned as their respective assignments:

As I see it our chief areas of collaboration are the nursery building and the music hall. In both the integration of structure and form—earth formed and monolithic. I presume my part will be more of the form, yours more the structure although it may be difficult to differentiate one from the other.[41]

Given Kahn's poetic leanings, one wonders how the architect responded to this rather stark division of labor and responsibilities. In his writings Kahn had once proposed two curricula for the study of environmental design: the first called Architecture and Land and the second, Land and Architecture—i.e., landscape architecture. The two are inherently intertwined, of course, and it is only in the weight given their respective concerns that distinguishes architecture from landscape architecture. Where sculpture fits within this dyad one can only guess; perhaps sculpture spans both building and land; perhaps it resides more in the realm of one than the other.[42] But in which one?

The Noguchi-Kahn collaboration spanned a period of five years and yielded an equal number of design iterations. Although in theory their respective roles as sculptor and architect were clearly defined at the outset, the two worked together principally in model form and over time their individual provinces tended to become conflated. The few known sketches for the project were solely by Kahn, however, executed in his characteristically loose-charcoal or soft-pencil hand [4-13; see also 4-21].

At the outset Noguchi defined the project in this way:

The purpose of the Adele Levy Playground is to establish an area for familiar relaxation and play rather than an area for any specific sport. We have attempted to supply a landscape where children of all ages, their parents, grandparents and other older people can mutually find enjoyment."[43]

When the team began its work, the site on Riverside Drive extended from 101st to 105th Streets. Laterally—that is from west to east, from the road to the river—the land fell precipitously; its topography suggested the use of the built structures to link the high land at the street to the lower levels adjacent to the water. Significant tree cover softened the dramatic fall of the terrain, although trees are missing from all the models, and only in Kahn's sketches is their presence ever acknowledged. In all the schemes that followed stairs or a long ramp provide the primary means of access to the playground and its services.

The first scheme, dating to 1961, established the basic grammar that would be maintained throughout all the subsequent proposals. In this design the roof of the nursery facility doubles as the ramp providing access to the eastern half of the site, which presumably would be left as earth and lawn [4-14]. Strung along the riverside promenade, a set of small spaces defined by benches and walls—straight or curved, alone or paired—modulate the flow of visitors; in their geometric play and variety they appear

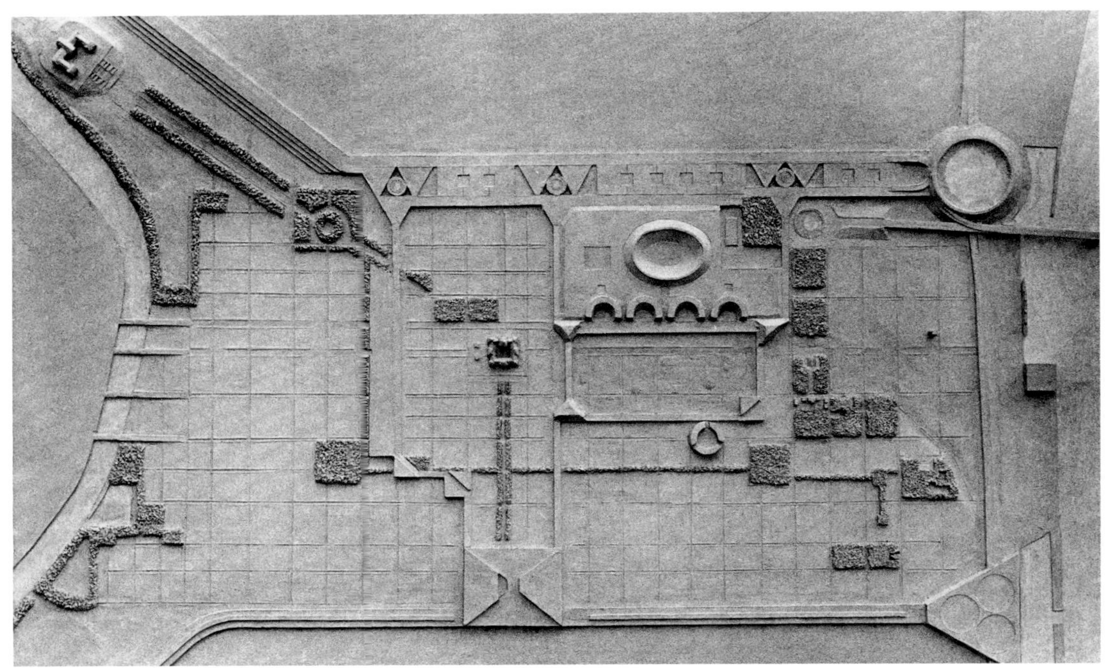

4-15
Louis I. Kahn.
Market Street East
Redevelopment.
Model.
Philadelphia, 1961+.
[Architectural Archives,
University of Pennsylvania]

4-16
Isamu Noguchi and
Louis I. Kahn.
Riverside Drive Playground.
New York.
Second scheme, ca. 1962.
Model. Looking east from
the Hudson River.
[Kevin Noble, © The Noguchi
Museum/ARS]

to be Kahn's contribution and echo forms used in his design for Market Street East in Philadelphia from around this same period (1961) [4-15]. In the architect's drawings, trees reinforce the limits of the play area, irregularly planted within an elongated arc on the urban edge of the site and configured as a rigid allée along the promenade. Within this green superstructure, the scheme's three principal zones flow north to south, augmented by two auxiliary play areas. The circle provides the guiding figure defining each of these areas.

Anchoring the northern limit of the playground is a curious form suggesting a maze patterned on fractal geometry or the structure of ice crystals, bounded by a curving wall, and surfaced with gravel and sand. Two additional subareas, also circular in plan, follow to the south; their use was left unspecified. A circular space ringed by battered walls serves as the central feature of the scheme. Although their profile far exceeds the natural angle of repose for soil, they were possibly still intended to be of earth rather than masonry. Within the circle an amphitheater, stepped down from the top of the wall, faces the concrete surface of the band shell. The amphitheater opens to a set of cubic steps that metamorphose into small, triangular terraces —Noguchi referred to them as a "play mountain"—retrieved from his proposal for the previous decade's United Nations playground [see 4-4]. This glacier of triangular steps flows downward toward the southwest portion of the site, disturbing a quarter of the boundary wall and undermining its rigor. Anchoring the south—while not at the precise limit of the allotted site—is a gentle hill into which are inscribed two pairs of slides, each of a different inclination. Within it were to be spaces to "crawl in and out of."[44] The encircling walkway bounded a semicircular area that marked the territory of the slide mountain and rehearsed in plan the sandbox/maze at the park's north end. Modeled as a continuity of surface and form, the zones of the playground appear autonomous and self-sufficient in relation to the existing park.

The following year, the surface area assigned to the project was reduced; in response, Noguchi and Kahn compressed the elements of their design.[45] Their planning strategy now concentrated development at the southern part of the site, near 101st Street [4-16]. The hill hosting the slides remained, but level play areas had now been cut into its slopes; other features from the first design were integrated into a single, sprawling complex, softly divided into two primary zones. Both a ramp and a staircase bring children and adults to an intermediate level faced on three sides by stepped seating derived from the original *Play Mountain*. The largest of these seating blocks faces west and offers a view of the Hudson River that, although grand and expansive, is partially obstructed by the seating facing it. Both the east and west echelons of the amphitheater appear to have embedded stones into their steps, a treatment perhaps intended to soften the purity of the geometry.

As a totality, the amphitheatrical portion of the scheme recalls the planning of a Mayan ball court, although the treatment of the seating areas on Riverside Drive offered far greater variety. Several of the facilities, unnamed, are now set below ground and given courtyards to provide air, light, and a view to the sky, their forms reflecting Kahn's designs for the National Assembly in Dhaka, Bangladesh (1961–82). The entire scheme has been contracted and no longer structured by a promenade; by accommodating all the programmatic units within only two zones, the design was far more coherent than the initial scheme.

In response to criticism of the second scheme, the design team revealed its third proposal in October 1963. The area of the site has been further compressed and its principal entrance shifted to 102nd Street. The suite of forms has now been completely amalgamated [4-17]. Only a lone slide remains, with its starting point atop the hillock anchored by a circular zone and a corresponding landing area at its base, also a circle. The amphitheater has returned as a single staircase facing south, with its steps reduced in prominence. The scheme appears to have flattened the topography to almost a single plane, effected by the use of retaining walls that would enfold the playground on two-and-a-half sides. Over the course of the two years since the first scheme, the design acquired greater concision and coherence, now occupying less land while achieving greater synergy. Over time, the site became less a surface *upon* which to build, than a material *with* which to build. Topography—whether above, upon, or under the ground —played its part, and thereafter directed the changes in the two revised designs that followed.

For the fourth design, dating from March–April 1964, there was no maquette; a sole drawing announces the adjustment to the forms and relationships rather than any major restructuring [4-18]. The amphitheater

4-17
Isamu Noguchi and
Louis I. Kahn.
Riverside Drive Playground.
New York.
Third scheme, ca. 1963.
Model.
[Kevin Noble, © The Noguchi Museum/ARS]

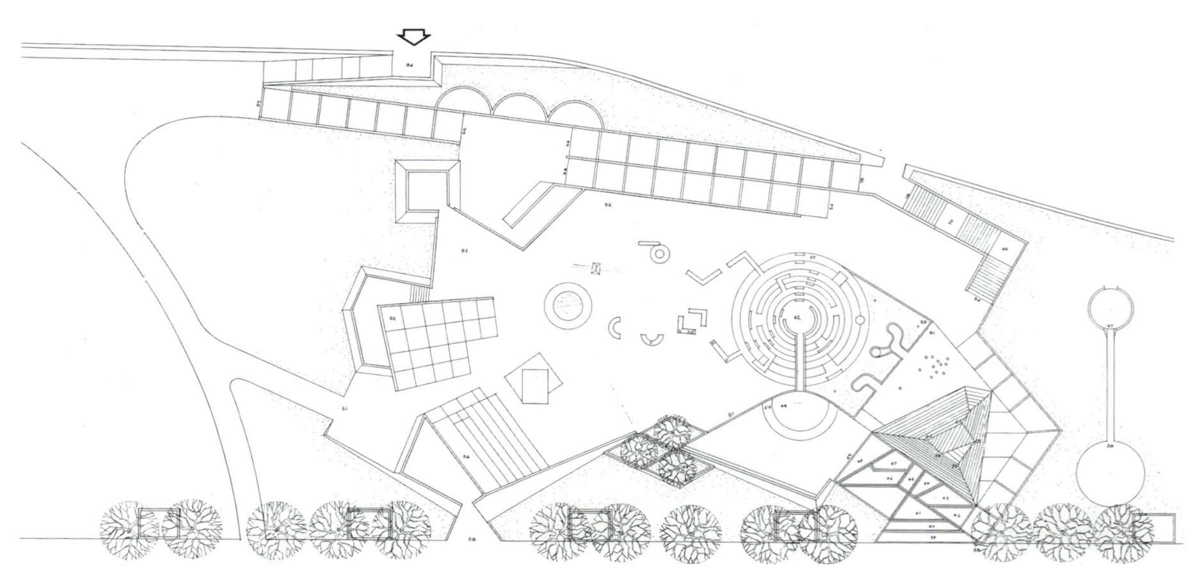

4-18 *[right]*
Isamu Noguchi and
Louis I. Kahn.
Riverside Drive Playground.
Fourth scheme, 1964.
[© The Noguchi Museum/ARS]

has been divided into two units, and, like the pyramid, the round hill accommodating the second slide has been serrated by the steps that replace the once-smooth slope. The reasons for these modifications are not recorded but they presumably addressed concerns by clients or critics as well as stemming from the aesthetic predilections of the designers.

The final iteration, dating from late 1964, further tweaks the elements of the previous two schemes and tightens the spatial relationships among the principal programmatic features. One slide hill has retained its original form, with circular areas at its crest and base; its sibling mound has disappeared, however. The amphitheater has become a single element, strengthening its identity.[46] By this point in the design process the division of labor had reached a stage that to some degree mirrored Noguchi's original assignments: Kahn became responsible for the playground's more architectonic elements like the ramp and habitable spaces, while Noguchi's efforts focused on play elements such as the crawling tunnel, the stepped pyramid, the sandbox, and the multipurpose central area [4-19, 4-20]. No materials were ever specified, and from the plaster maquette, or the bronze casting that followed, it is impossible to determine which surfaces would be hard, which ones soft, which were to be masonry, which were to be vegetation. As a result, one can judge the design only as sculpture.

For the play elements, however, Noguchi did have specifics in mind: he had discussed the selection of materials with Kahn and proposed covering their surfaces with brightly colored tile so that it would resemble a pinwheel. One must admit that the fifth and final scheme, although arguably the most coherent, is not necessarily the most engaging. While difficult to assess the relative sizes of the various features from a small-scale model, it appears that the open spaces surrounding the amphitheater and the ramps rise to heights far beyond those comfortable for children, and on two or three sides, the resulting space appears constrictive and unwelcoming.

Each iteration of the playground's design had its strengths, each its weaknesses, and these were discussed by those who reviewed the project at its various stages. The second design appears the most open, the design in which landscape has the greatest presence as a site for play, while the third scheme may have offered more architectural interest. Aspects of the later schemes understandably troubled reviewers of the designs. In response to a comment by one Mr. Jones, Noguchi replied: "My position is, of course, concerned with the play area. When you say, 'the site shows less conscious efforts to provide play spaces as such,' this is precisely the impression I get, that the architecture is now in ascendancy over the playground. I had hoped it would be the other way round, of course."[47]

Interestingly, Noguchi himself considered the final version of the playground "too architectural," perhaps feeling that he had lost control of his original vision. Kahn remarked that "Noguchi's design was overly concerned with details, and that the flaws in the design would affect children and their spontaneous playground activities."[48] This assessment conveys a certain irony, should we look to the rigorously geometric architecture associated with the mature Louis I. Kahn and his concern for materials and details at both a philosophical and a physical level. Yet despite the rigor, even rigidity, of his other projects then on the boards, Kahn nonetheless believed that "a thing is made to be incomplete for play. This incompleteness has to be affirmed," adding, "I'll have to speak to Noguchi; there are many things that need tremendous harsh criticism."[49]

As noted above, the presentations of the designs largely relied on models and somewhat dry drafted plans and sections. Whether Kahn's soft-pencil sketches were included in the presentations is not known, but his sketch for version five (1966) could be easily mistaken for a design for a monumental ceremonial complex rather than an intimate space where children enjoy play—an aspect not lost on journalist Joseph Lelyveld.[50] "At a glance the model looks like an amalgam of ancient civilizations," he wrote. "At one end there is an amphitheater; at the other, a pyramid. Nearby are a couple of mounds that could be Aztec or Indian."[51] At this point in his career, Kahn had adopted and abstracted lessons from Rome and other classical sources, but historians have suggested that his involvement with the playground influenced later projects such as his design for the Philadelphia College of Art (1965).[52] In Noguchi's own landscapes, especially those for play, architecture would never again appear so prominently.

Although the New York State Supreme Court had recently ruled that the Riverside Drive playground constituted an "improper use of park land," on 29 December 1965 a public ceremony featuring Mayor Robert Wagner celebrated the signing of the construction contract for the playground.

4-19 *[below]*
Isamu Noguchi and
Louis I. Kahn.
Riverside Drive Playground.
New York.
Final design, 1965.
Model.
[Bill Taylor, © The Noguchi
Museum/ARS]

4-20 *[opposite]*
Louis I. Kahn.
Riverside Drive Playground.
Final design, 1965.
Sketch perspective.
[Architectural Archives,
University of Pennsylvania]

In January 1966 the administration of the City of New York changed hands; John V. Lindsey became mayor and abruptly canceled the project.[53] By that single act five years of extensive discussions, criticism, design, and deliberation were all discarded, and the project pronounced dead.

Looking back, it seems that the project for the Adele R. Levy Playground was doomed from the start. For one thing, the project never had the support of New York City's Department of Parks and Recreation, which lacked any understanding or interest in a playground that departed from long-established norms. In addition, the aspirations and proposals of the designers had risen to a level far surpassing the needs or desires of their users. In addition, certain neighbors did not want a playground that might attract children from "other" (read: lower income) segments of the population who lived in bordering neighborhoods. Others feared that too much masonry and too many hard surfaces would replace existing areas of lawn and greenery. As a result, half a decade's worth of design studies ended with some sketches, drawings, and models as its record and testament. As with *Play Mountain* and *Contoured Playground*, Noguchi later cast the models in bronze and treated them as sculptures in themselves; perhaps this is the way he had regarded the project all along. Among the publications in which the Riverside Drive playground appears is Elizabeth Kassler's *Modern Gardens in the Landscape*, first published by MoMA in 1964, an influential book that underscores the project's significance and established its place in modern landscape history.[54]

Simultaneous with the later iterations of the Riverside Park project, Noguchi accepted a commission for another playground, this one thousands of miles away on a far larger site: the Kodomo-no-Kuni (Children's Land), in Yokohama, Japan. The project, which comprised some 240 acres, commemorated the royal marriage of Prince Akihito and Princess Michiko.[55] The architect would be Sachio Otani (1924–2013), whom Noguchi knew from his previous employment at Kenzô Tange's office and his participation in the Hiroshima Memorial Peace Park. Underlying his design was the intention to create a play area "evocative ... of [Japan's] prehistory" while also as "modern as science and yet retain[ing] the quality of nature; in other words, a children's world acceptable to children anywhere."[56] Noguchi's main contribution to the project was the comprehensive shaping of the

central zone of the park and the regrading of the terrain into gently rounded earth forms [4-21]. A series of linked triangular pavilions across the central area of the landscape would serve as the project's dominant structure. Near its center was a concrete dome in and over which the children could climb and a sandbox in which they could dig and pile [4-22]. Little of Noguchi's proposal was ever realized, and even less of it remains today.

>> EQUIPMENT AS SCULPTURE

In 1939 the Hawai'ian Pineapple Company invited Noguchi, along with artists such as Georgia O'Keeffe, to produce artworks that would bolster their collection and serve promotional purposes.[57] While there, Noguchi met Lester McCoy, "a progressive architect and park commissioner," who asked Noguchi if he would design play equipment for the oceanside Ala Moana Park in Honolulu. Unfortunately, McCoy died before Noguchi's designs could be implemented, and the possibility of producing the equipment died with him. The primary photograph of Noguchi's model is dramatic: high in contrast, with a play of shadows enhancing the visual qualities of the proposed swings and slides [4-23].

Noguchi's proposal was not a design for a complete play landscape but instead a series of new sculptural interpretations of established equipment. The swings, for instance, are supported by an inclined rather than horizontal support, and bolstered by two corresponding members to form a structural tripod. Perhaps the most interesting element is the basketball backboard, which Noguchi treated as a constructivist sculpture. The hoop terminates a long bar that passes through the backstop to connect with the support frame, strengthening its structural rigor.[58]

Never one to abandon a good idea, Noguchi resurrected selected elements of the Hawai'ian design in his scheme for the *Playscapes,* installed in Piedmont Park in Atlanta, Georgia, in 1976. The inception of the project began three years prior with a suggestion to the director of the High Museum of Art by one its volunteers, Frankie Cox, who proposed the creation of a playground as a fitting contribution to the city's celebration of the American bicentennial.[59] With financial support from the National Endowment of the Arts, the museum invited Noguchi to design the play area as an artistic as well as ludic terrain. The site on a knoll within the park was

4-21 *[opposite above]*
Isamu Noguchi
and Sachio Otani.
Kodomo-no-kuni.
Yokohama, Japan, 1965.
Site model.
[Osamu Morai, © The Noguchi Museum/ARS]

4-22 *[opposite below]*
Isamu Noguchi and
Sachio Otani.
Kodomo-no-kuni.
Pavilions and climbing mound.
[© The Noguchi Museum/ARS]

4-23 *[above]*
Ala Moana Playground.
Honolulu, Hawai'i, 1940.
Play equipment models.
[© The Noguchi Museum/ARS]

regraded prior to the installation of the play equipment, reworked from the earlier Hawai'ian commission and surfaced with wood chips thereafter. Curving walls delimited the play area but their low height, and distance from the center, were insufficient to effectively define the space [4-24, 4-25]. To the west a mound was created from the displaced soil, with its outer limit bounded by a segmented wall. The treatment of the ground was restrained although gently modeled to accommodate the various pieces of equipment and set them in an aesthetic symbiosis. No basketball courts were included, as the intended population was a younger cohort who would not be engaging in team sports.

Color plays a major role in Noguchi's design, with the swings—the dominant element of the playground—painted a bright vermilion, while features such as the orthogonal climbing blocks were colored in tones of lime green and royal blue [4-26; 4-27]. A slide wraps around the supporting cylindrical tube, whose spiral form appeared in a fountain for the Osaka Expo in 1970 and later as a slide in the black and white versions of *Slide Mantra* [4-28]. Perhaps the most innovative component is the double slide linked by a bridge whose complex form no doubt attracted children by the variety of experiences it offered [4-29]. Underfoot are earth and wood chips in place of the hard surfaces of Noguchi's urban courts and plazas, where lines scored in their paving unify the elements of the composition.[60] A small structure to the east housed services such as toilets; its pitched roof sheltered a terrace on top of the building from rain, or the sun in the warmer months. In all, despite their individual interest as forms, the elements are too few and too widely spaced to achieve the integrated composition proposed for the earlier playgrounds. On the other hand, the increased surface area has allowed larger groups of kids to play together within the greater landscape of the park, of which the playground is only a fragment.

Over the years the playground and its equipment fell victim to rust, corrosion, graffiti, and vandalism; maintenance had been minimal. In 2005 limited repairs were made but only in 2014 was a major renovation undertaken with funding from Herman Miller Cares.[61] At that time repair, replacement, and repainting injected new life into *Playscapes*, essentially restoring it to its original form, with modifications made only to bring the project up to the latest codes guiding children's safety.

>> COMPARISON AND COMPLETION

Noguchi's two playscapes were destined for clearings in the comfortable, natural settings of public parks—in stark contrast to the Van Eyck playgrounds discussed above, many of which were located in gritty urban sites. He condemned most catalog play equipment as not being "real" enough and thus unsuitable for public use. "Playground equipment," he held, "has to be real, just as a telephone box is real because you can phone in it and a bench is real because you can sit on it." Despite their formal and material differences van Eyck and Noguchi shared the idea that the child must discover, and that play forms for the child should be simple and elementary, while providing "the opportunity for what the child already does: tumbling, climbing, jumping."[62] Play as a creative and developmental act.

Play and recreation constituted a central concern in Noguchi's design for the Moerenuma Park in Sapporo, Japan, left in its early stages of design at the time of the artist's death in 1988. As discussed in a later chapter, the park was Noguchi's last as well as largest landscape and completed by others after his passing [see 11-18, 11-19, 11-20, 11-21, 11-23]. While the design team made every effort to remain true to the artist's original intent, this was challenging given Noguchi's predilection for making changes during the development and construction of any of his landscapes. That said, in his early designs, several areas were already assigned to play, mostly circular voids extracted from a forest of cherry trees and other species to be populated with play equipment of Noguchi's design [4-30]. There are octet forms with holes that encouraged climbing into and over; orthogonal blocks that the child might recast as mountains, buildings, or structures of even greater fantasy; and softly curving shapes attractive and sensual in contrast to those more purely geometric. The menu is extensive, with curves as well as straight lines; with solids and surfaces over which the child can scamper, climb, enter, and even hide. Rather than forms created for any specific physical or mental challenge, these are essentially sculptural forms with which children can physically interact, mentally engage, and develop their imagination. Which brings us back to the point raised at the beginning of this chapter: whether abstract or literal play forms better support childhood development. The jury seems to be taking its time in its deliberation. I'll await their decision before offering mine.

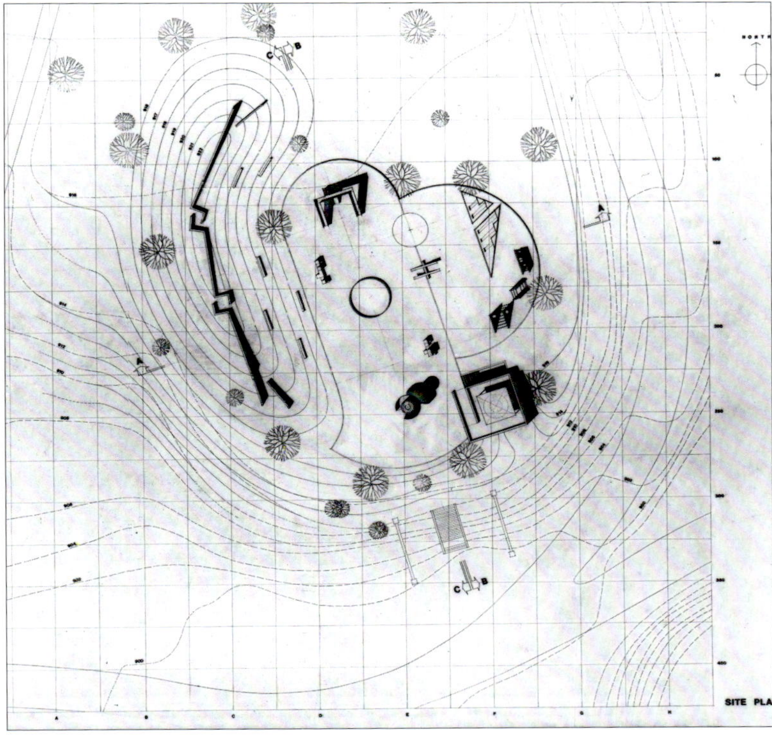

4-24
Playscapes.
Piedmont Park, Atlanta, 1976.
Site plan.
[© The Noguchi Museum/ARS]

4-25
Playscapes.
General view.

4-26
Playscapes.
Piedmont Park, Atlanta, 1976.
Climbing structures with spiral slide beyond.

4-27
Playscapes.
Retrieving the swings proposed for the proposed Ala Moana Playground.

4-28
Playscapes.
Piedmont Park, Atlanta.
Cubic climbing forms
painted in tertiary colors.

4-29
Moerenuma Park.
Sapporo, Japan, 2005.
Play equipment.

> 5.

Garden as Sculpture: Paris

The 1951 commission for the *Reader's Digest* landscape provided Noguchi with the opportunity to conceive a garden as art and guide it through construction. Looking back years later, he stressed the significance of the first garden he had realized in Tokyo and the opportunity to learn from experienced Japanese gardeners. His next landscape would be far larger and far more complex, involving collaboration with an international team of architects and interactions with functionaries on a project fraught with political, economic, and aesthetic conflicts.

Five years after the inauguration of the *Reader's Digest* garden, Noguchi was invited to create a sculpture for UNESCO House, the new seat of the United Nations Educational, Scientific, and Cultural Organization being planned for Paris [5-1].[1] The agency had been created in 1946, and the acronym UNESCO adopted for common usage. To distribute its influence and economic resources broadly while demonstrating its constitution as a truly international body, the United Nations located the seats of its various agencies in different countries, all in the Northern Hemisphere: the General Assembly and the Secretariat in New York City; the Food and Agriculture Organization in Rome; the World Health Organization in Geneva; and UNESCO in the City of Light. For the first decade of its existence, UNESCO occupied rented quarters on the Left Bank of the Seine. As the number of staff increased, working-space requirements expanded accordingly, and the need for a more appropriate headquarters—both symbolically and functionally—became more apparent.

A five-member architectural advisory panel was charged with selecting the building's architect(s). Chaired by Walter Gropius, its members included Eero Saarinen from the United States, Sven Markelius from Sweden, Lucio Costa from Brazil, Ernesto Rogers from Italy, and, later, Le Corbusier from France.[2] Their mission was to choose the designer for the new headquarters and its grounds. Upon concluding their deliberations the committee nominated an international troika of architects with resolutely modernist leanings: Marcel Breuer, Hungarian-born but long established in the United States, would serve as lead design architect; Bernard Zehrfuss, whose office in Paris would execute the construction documents and supervise construction; and the Rome-based engineer-architect Pier Luigi Nervi, who would provide structural expertise.[3] The building site on the Right Bank of the

5-0
UNESCO garden.
Paris, 1958.
The Delegates Patio with the source stone in the foreground.

5-1
UNESCO garden.
Paris, 1958.
The recently completed garden viewed from above. With trees in their juvenile form, the sculptural aspect of the ground plane was more evident at that time than it is today.
[© The Noguchi Museum/ARS]

Seine occupied one side of the Place de Fontenoy and faced the rear side of the École Militaire. The proposed eight-floor structure was configured as a Y to maximize daylight in the offices. The scheme derived to some degree from earlier office- and housing-tower proposals by Le Corbusier, who desperately sought to be a part of—if not control—the building's creation. Appended to the office tower on its south side was a grand auditorium for the meetings of the General Assembly. As an uncompromising Brutalist statement in mass, style, siting, and material—concrete cast in situ—UNESCO House stands detached from the street and rejects any relationship with the surrounding architectural milieu. At least in terms of its architecture, it forms a world apart, .

As part of the building program, a second advisory committee was assembled to select and commission artists to enrich the agency's environment, both indoors and out. The specific nature of those works had not been strictly defined by the original brief, however. As a result, from the very beginning of the selection process, a division existed between those who favored art acquired from each member nation, and those—including the architects—who believed that, like the building, its art program should reflect the world's most advanced work of that moment. They favored "blue-chip" (i.e., Western) artists whose inclusion would grace the premises with their prestige as well as their products. The debates over the nature of the art program were at times heated, with the representatives of various countries expressing widely diverging views. But in the end the art advisory board won out and selected an inaugural group of artists that included Henry Moore from Britain, Joan Miró from Spain, Jean Arp from France, and Isamu Noguchi, who—perhaps ironically—was chosen to represent Asia.[4]

>> INITIAL EFFORTS, DESIGN, AND FUNDING

Noguchi's original site was outdoors, on the Delegates Patio adjacent to the main lobby, which unfortunately had no direct access to the terrace; even the visual connections were restricted.[5] While his commission specified only a sculpture, Noguchi chose to magnify his contribution by adding a functional component to the work. In response, the sculpture took form as a series of skewed cubes and inverted truncated cones of concrete he characterized as embodying "a new and formal variation of the tea ceremony" [5-2].[6] In form the truncated cones recalled, if distantly, the seats at Constantin Brancusi's *Table of Silence* in Târgu-Jiu, Romania, from 1938. Complementing these sculptures—collectively a constellation of seats with skewed geometries—were clusters of natural stones and stone benches enlivened with compact insets of vegetation [5-3]. Partially extending beneath the south wing of the building elevated above terrace level on splayed, V-shaped columns, the sculptures gained more presence as a group than as independent works of art. As a whole, the terrace could be read metaphorically as the playing surface of a giant board game, with Noguchi's seating, stonework, and plantings appearing as deftly arranged objects set upon it beneath the hovering concrete mass of the architecture.

The scope and nature of Noguchi's project changed dramatically during the course of construction, when calculations determined that the square footage of the new building would be insufficient to meet the immediate needs of the agency; an annex would be required to accommodate its functions, even at the moment of inauguration. Would Noguchi consider designing a path to connect the Delegates Patio with the proposed annex? Yes, he would. In his mind Noguchi conceived the path as an interpretation of the *hanamichi* used in Japanese theater, the wooden catwalk by which actors enter and exit the stage [5-4]. In both the Kabuki and Noh theaters, the linear walkway is usually set askew; in Paris, however, it was predetermined that the walk would trace a straight line. This additional design task again proved inadequate to satisfy Noguchi's growing ambition, and he soon began to lobby for the opportunity to design a true garden on land below the Delegates Patio as yet unassigned to any specific use. UNESCO's governing body granted permission, contingent on the artist himself raising the money to pay for the garden, whose cost was estimated at $35,000.

From the time he was offered the commission to design the path, perhaps even from the time of the start of the work on the Delegates Patio, Noguchi had continually sought to increase the scope of his intervention. With the design for a far larger and more ambitious work, he could demonstrate that a garden could be a sculpture, and perhaps also conversely, that a sculpture could be used as a garden. The differences in elevation, paired with the boundaries defining the Delegates Patio and the annex below,

5-2 *[opposite]*
UNESCO garden.
Paris, 1958.
Cubic and conic forms on the Delegates Patio also serve as seating.

5-3
UNESCO garden.
Delegates Patio.
Compositions of seating, stones, and plants. The source stone is in the rear to the right.

[following page]:

5-4
Torii Kiyostune.
Interior of a Kabuki Theater, pre-1915.
The *hanamichi* is on the left.
[Library of Congress]

5-5
UNESCO garden.
First scheme.
Model.
[© The Noguchi Museum/ARS]

5-6
Katsura Imperial Villa.
Kyoto, seventeenth century.
The Ama-no-hashidate peninsula.

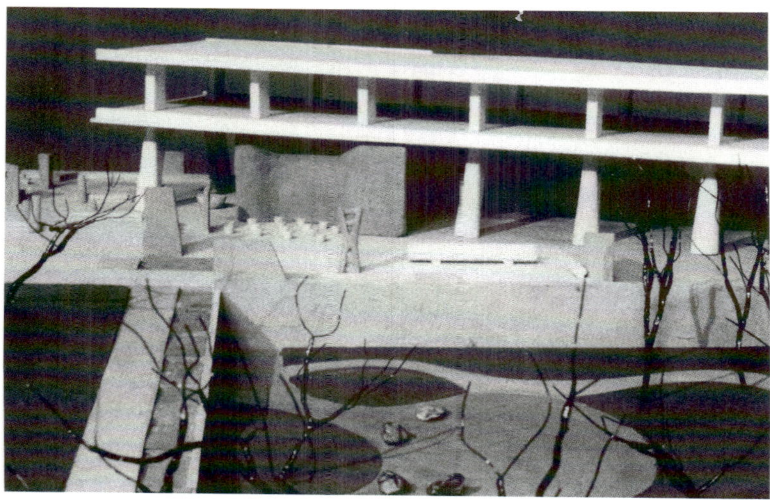

suggested a different concept for each area. Noguchi, as he explained,

> *gradually became more and more involved, ever more ambitious for* [the garden] *to be something exceptional. In the beginning I had hoped only to integrate the two levels by raising portions of the lower one containing greenery and trees. However, as I elaborated on the model it became apparent to me that it would be ideal if the area below should be transformed into a major sculptural effort through the introduction of rocks and so forth.*[7]

The issue, of course, was how to obtain the funding to finance the project; almost immediately he initiated a personal campaign to secure financial support from international sources with which and with whom he was acquainted. Soliciting the assistance of Contessa Pecci Blunt, Noguchi contacted potential sponsors, among them Toshikazu Kase, the Japanese ambassador to France. On 28 August 1956, the artist wrote UNESCO Cultural Division head Michel Dard, informing him that,

> *shortly before leaving Paris I met with Mr. Sojiro Ishibashi, powerful industrialist and patron of the arts in Japan, and took him to see the model I had made. He told me that he would like to help and could possibly do so through his being an adviser to the government on such matters.*[8]

Next followed contact with the Japanese ambassador to the United States, in which Noguchi capitalized on his father's nationality and heritage:

> [UNESCO] *wished from the first to have an Asian among the artists involved. I was apparently selected by an international committee of the arts partly with this in mind, a compromise, as someone whose efforts would be both modern and Japanese in feeling, which is what they wanted. A garden is, after all, a collaboration of architecture and the poetry of spaces.*[9]

Toru Hagiwara, posted in the Japanese embassy in Bern, strongly backed the project, but suspected that certain members of the Japanese Diet—the governmental body that would ultimately finance the undertaking—would be troubled by the differences in form and character between a traditional Japanese garden and the mass and modernist character of the building.[10] Despite the odds, a happy ending was forthcoming. A February 1957 governmental memo to Akira Matsui, the Japanese representative to the UNESCO Executive Board, announced as a gesture of goodwill a grant of $35,000, the minimum sum considered necessary to implement Noguchi's garden as designed.[11] In addition, the Japanese government would sponsor a team of gardeners from Kyoto to aid the sculptor's efforts on-site and, in all probability, the handling of the rockwork *à la japonaise*. From this successful campaign we can deduce that, in addition to his artistic abilities, Noguchi possessed considerable charm, and when required, the entrepreneurial skills needed to finance ambitions that, in many cases, far surpassed the purview of the original commission.

>> PROCESS

Noguchi conceived the UNESCO garden as a relief of sufficient size to enter, walk upon, traverse, and linger, with zones of stone, gravel, planting, and water shaped with a biomorphic vocabulary. His first proposal for the garden, which from the start included the idea and features of the final scheme, had been rejected by the art advisory committee. Although their reaction is unrecorded, given the abundance of elements in the first design they probably had found its composition restless and unresolved, overcrowded with disparate fragments and lacking a sense of repose [5-5]. Their judgment was accurate. Perhaps in his desire to create a significant work, perhaps due to the pressure placed upon him to make a "Japanese garden," Noguchi included more elements than he normally would have. As he saw it, a garden was something quite different from how it is popularly understood, not so much a collection of forms as a totality that coheres as a retreat or setting for contemplation. In response to the board's rejection of the initial scheme, possibly abetted by his personal dissatisfaction with the design, Noguchi whittled down the number of rocks and mounds, to produce a sculptural terrain in which topography rendered the other features subsidiary. Understanding that the experience of a garden unfolds by walking through it, Noguchi unconsciously positioned the UNESCO design within the tradition of the Japanese stroll garden so magnificently represented by the seventeenth-century imperial villas of Katsura and Shugaku-in in Kyoto [5-6].

When UNESCO House was initially planned the site was relatively, if not quite completely, flat; serious modifications resulted from the building's construction, however, as at least one floor would be subterranean. The Y plan of the main building was sited with one wing parallel to Avenue de Lowendal, its tip adjacent to Avenue de Saxe, along which the annex was also to be constructed. The Noguchi garden would occupy land at what was essentially the southeast corner of the site, with Avenue de Ségur to the south and Avenue de Saxe to the east. The annex filled the corner [5-7]. The only access to the garden came from the the building's lobby, by crossing the Delegates Patio and descending the path to the annex, entering the garden midway.

UNESCO landscape comprises three zones: the seating blocks, stone clusters, and plants that occupy the Delegates Patio; the walkway and waterway that link terrace and annex; and the lower garden itself, with its entrance at the path's midpoint. In early photographs, especially those taken from above, the biomorphically sculptured elevated plateau at the garden's center dominates the landscape [see 5-1]. "The raised paved area in the center of the lower garden," Noguchi believed, "recalls the upper patio. One arrives on it and departs from it again with time barriers of stepping stones between." He optimistically envisioned this area as a "land of voyage, the place for dancing and music which may be viewed from all around the garden and from all levels of the surrounding buildings."[12]

Sculptured and softly rolling, the surface of the plateau revisited formal ideas first broached in the early 1940s in *Contoured Playground*. Its freeform contours, however, are more apparent in plan than in either the maquette or in reality, especially today, when vegetation obscures the purity of its forms. While biomorphic curves define the central plateau, the profile of the pond, and the lines of the earth mounds, buried within each of them is the Platonic geometry of the circle. The path to the annex and the water channel that parallels it divide the first circle, inscribed in the paving at the entrance to the lower garden. As such, its identity as a circle is less easily discerned. A second circle, also expressed in a paving pattern, marks the center of the plateau; a third lies on the plateau's cusps and subtly inflects its stone-paved surface. Thus, within the design for the UNESCO landscape Noguchi interwove biomorphism with the circle and the straight line, using them to join the lower garden with the walkway that borders it, and the Delegates Patio standing some twelve feet above [5-8]. The great biomorphic

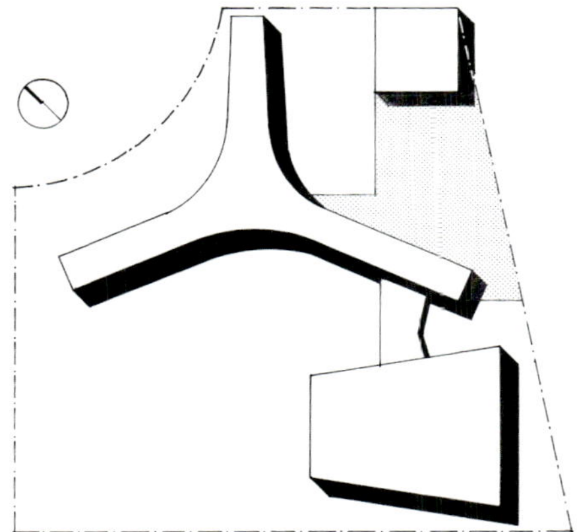

plateau at the garden's center stands as an object afloat within the rectangular site, as Noguchi never fully exploited the possibilities offered by the residual spaces that surround it [5-9].

Within the garden proper Noguchi suggested, rather than directed, the path of movement. On its descent from the plateau, the path crosses beds of grass and gravel, followed by a group of natural stones that allows visitors to cross the pond and conclude at a bench at the base of the retaining wall supporting the Delegates Patio. From here, one must turn and retrace one's path or perhaps discover an alternate route back to the entrance. Vegetation within the garden softens the solidity of the hard surfaces: cherry trees that bloom a brilliant pink in spring; plums with a blossom of softer hue; the dark, waxy leaves of the magnolias that create an appropriately forest-green background for their creamy yellow-white flowers. Pines, in contrast, are less transient in their effects; they are the constants, columns, remaining at their posts fully clothed throughout the year like dutiful sentinels. Nonetheless, it is difficult to unravel the logic behind Noguchi's selection and placement of trees and shrubs, and, in all honesty, as the plants and trees have grown they have diminished rather than enhanced the sculptural presence of the principal forms.

Water plays a central role in the UNESCO garden, as it had in the stroll gardens of seventeenth-century Japan, here flowing downward from its origins in a large slab of Mannari granite quarried near Okayama and shipped to France with the other stones. Set at the edge of the Delegates Patio, it serves as a lynchpin for the composition and a pivot between the upper and lower levels of the garden [see 5-11]. From a pipe embedded in the stone the flow begins, first filling the shallow pool at its base, then tumbling downward as a restrained cascade that follows the path to the annex.[13] The artist believed that the source, a single stone eight-feet tall, "might be read as 'man.'" It is today prized by UNESCO as a signature feature of the garden and is regarded as a Noguchi sculpture in and of itself. Into the coarse surface of the stone has been carved the Japanese ideograph for "peace" (*wa*)—but deliberately written backwards and elongated so as to be "generally illegible."[14] Exactly why the artist chose to do so he did not explain; perhaps to add an air of abstraction and intrigue to what otherwise would have been immediately intelligible, at least to Japanese visitors. A shallow, square pool lies at the foot

5-7 *[opposite above]*
UNESCO garden.
Paris, 1958.
Site plan.
[Dorothée Imbert]

5-8 *[opposite below]*
UNESCO garden.
In the lower garden Noguchi combined the straight line and the biomorphic curve, natural stone with the crafted stone bench.

5-9 *[below]*
UNESCO garden.
For the most part, the peripheral zone around the central plateau was left relatively undeveloped.

5-10 *[right]*
UNESCO garden.
Looking over the lower garden from the Delegates Patio.

5-11
UNESCO garden.
Paris, 1958.
The source stone inscribed with the stylized Japanese ideogram *wa*, meaning "peace."

5-12
UNESCO garden.
The pool at the base of the source stone.

5-13
UNESCO garden.
Garden plan.
[© The Noguchi Museum/ARS]

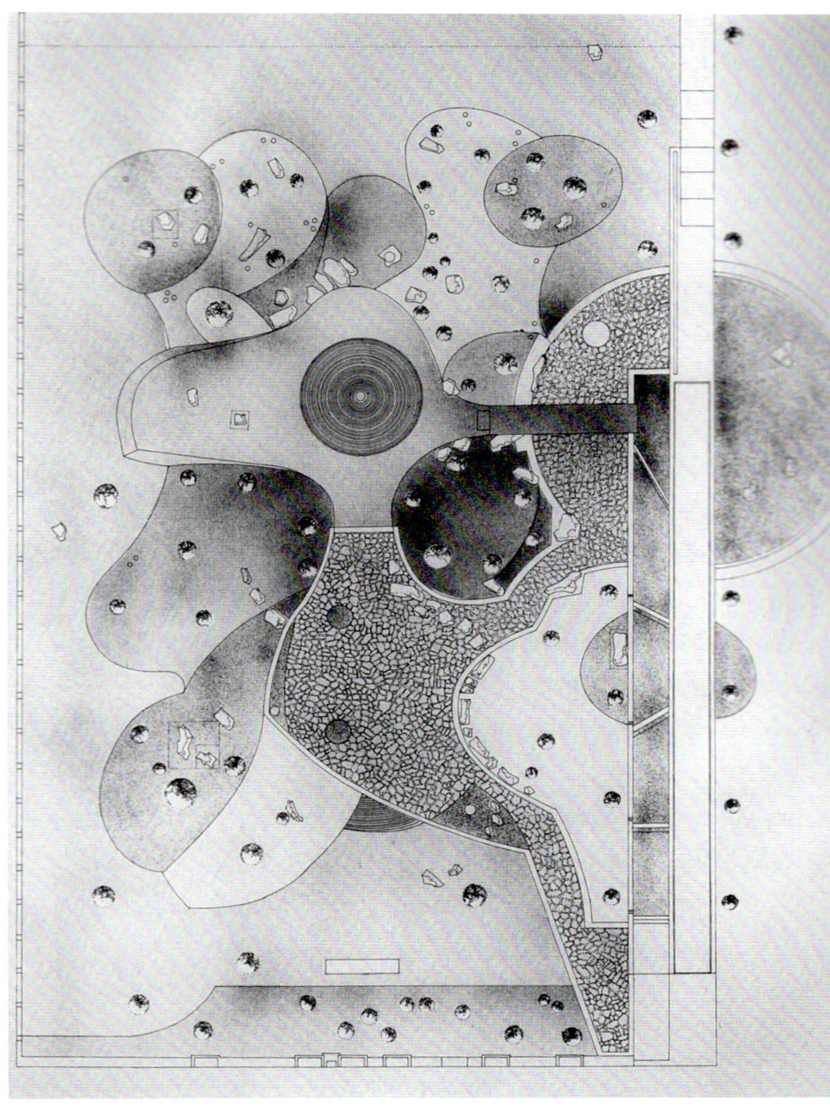

5-14
UNESCO garden.
The entry path, water channel, and a row of cherry trees in autumn.

of this source stone; rectangular stepping stones in the pool are arranged to allow passage across the water without impeding the flow of water to the narrow channel below [5-12].

From the pool on the Delegates Patio the water passes through a narrow and shallow channel/cascade that hugs the walk and terminates at the annex, initially known simply as Building IV [5-13; 5-14]. Although one of the garden's simplest features, the waterway might be its most clever and lucid facet. Rather than following common practice by setting the leading edges of the water terraces perpendicular to their sides, Noguchi cranked them at alternating angles, thereby diverting the flow this way and that to enhance the sense of journey as the water falls within the channel's elongated rectangle. A row of cherry trees planted parallel to the length of the channel reinforces in vegetal material the linear descent of the water. This simple row of trees is also one of the garden's most consequential uses of plants, as it defines the path, graces the garden with bright-pinkish blooms in spring, and brightens the atmosphere with orange-yellow leaves in autumn.

As part of its support for the project the Japanese government provided funding to purchase river stones in Japan and, as mentioned above, sponsored a small team of gardeners from Kyoto to set the stones and assist in the selection and installation of the plantings. Stones had been a major garden element from its inception; considering the garden's sponsorship, their incorporation was inevitable. In April 1957 Noguchi spent several weeks in Japan searching for the right stones, aided by the prominent landscape designer Mirei Shigemori, whom he met on the island of Shikoku for the first time [5-15]. Together, they "fished" for the celebrated blue rocks found most desirable, in Noguchi's view, because "they [are] very bright blue, almost too beautiful, and not at all subdued like those used in a tea ceremony garden. But I didn't need anything subdued in my Paris garden so they would be just fine."[15] After a scouting for a week and a half, Shigemori and Noguchi had found and secured about eighty stones. They then traveled to Kyoto, where Shigemori had arranged for their participation in a tea ceremony at Kômyô-in—he had designed a garden for the temple before the war—while also visiting his other gardens at Tôfuku-ji [5-16].[16]

Following this sojourn in the Old Capital they returned to Shikoku, to the city of Tokushima, where a mockup of the proposed arrangement of the stones had been constructed to test how the stones would be installed in Paris. Finding the design overcrowded Noguchi reduced the number of stones, which were then crated and shipped to the port of Marseille, and from there to the construction site in Paris. Construction progressed slowly: untrained for such work, the Algerian and Spanish workers hired to build the garden took three weeks to move one stone.[17] Money was getting tight. The arrival of skilled gardeners from Kyoto must have been very warmly welcomed.

Unfortunately, the first gardening team, which Shigemori had recommended to Noguchi, decided to return home a month earlier than planned; a second team, also selected on Shigemori's recommendations, replaced them. This team was led by Tôemon Sanô, scion of a sixteen-generation Kyoto gardening family whom Noguchi had met in 1955 when the Kyoto prefectural government had asked Sanô to assist the artist, presumably in gaining access to gardens in Kyoto.[18] With extensive experience garnered almost from birth, Sanô was a master of traditional garden making. On his visits to Japan Noguchi had visited many gardens and had also been coached on the aesthetic ideas that shaped them by artist Saburo Hasegawa, with whom he had traveled in the early 1950s.[19] Despite his direct experience of the gardens, Noguchi was not really knowledgeable about their creation, the botanical and aesthetic factors governing plant selection, or the realities of garden maintenance. His view, quite understandably, was that of an artist making a garden intended as a work of art. Consequently, the relationship between Noguchi and Sanô was respectful but at times strained, with frequent differences of opinion that on occasion led to heated disagreements. On the other hand Noguchi was fifty years old, while Sanô was only thirty; this gave Noguchi an edge, bolstered by the basic fact that it was his garden for which Sanô was only a consultant. Sanô recalled that once at work Noguchi displayed absolute concentration, paying no attention to anything beyond the task at hand.[20]

In sharing his UNESCO experience with Noguchi biographer Dore Ashton, Sanô noted that Noguchi always wanted every element of his work to be visible, evident, while the Japanese tradition embraced partial or complete occlusion, followed by subsequent revelation, to produce a stronger design and greater intrigue. "The Japanese spirit," Sanô believed, was not to show

your hand. Hide it and make it stronger." Noguchi, he felt, "always wanted to make everything prominent."[21] In the Japanese tradition, the garden's elements were a means to an end: beauty, serenity, and an appreciation of nature. To Noguchi, in contrast, the plants and stones possessed their own intrinsic interest; some stones could even be regarded as artworks in themselves.

At the center of the great biomorphic plateau in the middle of the garden, Noguchi installed a stone lantern, virtually on axis with the bridge of a single stone over which one enters. Noguchi conceived the piece—which confronts the visitor upon entry—as at once a rock, a lantern, and a sculptural form [5-17]. Such a positioning of a garden element was anathema to traditional Japanese practice, and curiously contrary to how Noguchi himself would approach the shaping of his later works in basalt. Noguchi wanted no part of his stones and sculptures to be concealed in any way, even if only by plants.

Despite their relatively small number, the "Japanese" elements of the garden, such as the stones, became the most problematic aspects of the construction process. Noguchi and the Japanese gardeners rarely worked in accord: while the latter sought a beautiful garden rooted in tradition, Noguchi sought a modern sculpture in the form of a garden, or a modern garden in the form of a sculpture. He neither understood nor desired the practices and forms that for centuries had guided the creation of gardens in Japan. As a result, there were many back-and-forths between the two protagonists, as well as considerable frustration. For his part, however, Sanô seems to have maintained his respect for Noguchi despite the differences in their philosophies and approaches. "Once we had agreed upon the procedure and begun working," Sanô reflected, "all of a sudden, Isamu's eyes glowed and he became full of spirit."[22] Despite their differing viewpoints on garden philosophy and design, the two men evidently maintained a friendship and an appreciation for one another's knowledge and contribution. The two shared an apartment while working in Paris; each morning Sanô prepared a breakfast they took amicably and thereafter traveled together by Metro to the construction site.[23] Noguchi stayed in Paris for as long as his other obligations would allow, troubleshooting glitches in the construction and deflecting the desires of the gardeners that diverged from his own.

5-15 *[above]*
Noguchi and Shigemori on Shikoku "fishing" for stones for the UNESCO garden.
[© The Noguchi Museum/ARS]

5-16 *[below]*
Mirei Shigemori.
Komyô-in, Tôfuku-ji.
Kyoto, Japan, 1939; 1960s.
The garden, which uses unconventionally large stones, as seen from the adjacent pavilion.

5-17
UNESCO garden.
Paris, 1958.
Entrance to the lower garden with stone lantern on axis.

As the garden's construction progressed, problems continued to hamper its completion: the trees had been planted too late in the year to support their immediate growth, the installation of the stonework for paving and the walls of the plateau was behind schedule, and a cement mixer used to construct the annex remained on-site. These and other factors delayed the completion of the lower garden. The source stone to be installed on the Delegates Patio still lacked its inscription.[24] In spite of these issues, by mid-September the garden's construction was substantially complete; as a memo stated: "to all intents and purposes except for some finishing touches and additional plantations which had to be deferred until the autumn."[25] UNESCO House, that is the main building, was ultimately inaugurated on 3 November 1958, coinciding with the tenth session of its General Assembly.[26] The garden and its contoured surfaces, still partially unfinished, were ready for the building's opening; its trees and shrubs were freshly planted and remained small in stature. Finally, in late 1958, the realization of the garden had been substantially achieved, although its inauguration was postponed for some months, until May 1959.

Seen from above at the time of its opening, the garden appeared as sculptured terrain set within a rectangular frame, not unlike *Contoured Playground* and certain of Noguchi's early reliefs. As sculpture, the UNESCO garden is best viewed from above during the winter months, when the deciduous trees are bare and more of the ground plane is visible, or in the autumn, when some sparse tints of autumn color excite the molded ground plane [see 5-1].

>> A *SOMEWHAT* JAPANESE GARDEN

In their literature UNESCO refers to Noguchi's creation as *Le Jardin japonais*, the Japanese garden. The name presumably derives from the Japanese government's sponsorship of the project as well as certain of the garden's elements—the blue stones, for example—rather than reflecting Noguchi's own artistic intentions. In terms of concept and general aspect there is little of Japanese origin in this garden, although in certain materials and forms a whiff of the island nation is evident. The walls of the central plateau for example, are surfaced with small granite blocks in a manner reminiscent of the wall construction of Japanese castles [5-18]. Historically, however, the walls of fortifications were carefully configured as catenary curves to efficiently repel the overturning forces of the earth behind them and to achieve increased integrity. At each corner, larger stones were angled to enhance the strength of the wall's construction. At UNESCO, in contrast, the wall profiles are set at a more vertical angle and the size of the facing element is more or less consistent throughout. In shape and material the Japanese castle may have provided a distant inspiration for the walls in Paris, but while sculpturally attractive, Noguchi's application provided only limited structural efficacy. In all, the stonework is more effective aesthetically than functionally.

Other garden elements display vague references to Japanese techniques—references, yes; deferences, no. Unsurprisingly, a sculptural sensibility prevails. For example, in the lower garden Noguchi continued the pebbled surface of the ground plane beneath the water as the lining of the pond bed, using this continuity of materials to link two areas of the garden [5-19; see also 5-11]. One possible source for this detail might have been the *ariso* (also written *aliso*) shore of the pond at the Sentô Gosho, an imperial retirement villa in central Kyoto that employs a similar use of small stones [5-20]. The biomorphic shape of the UNESCO pond itself continues the vocabulary of the central platform, although reversing the balance of solid and void, and solid and liquid. Continuities, repetitions, and cross-references grant coherence to the composition although the materials differ.

So just how Japanese is the UNESCO *Jardin japonais*? To my mind, not very much, except in a most superficial way.[27] The seating on the upper terrace is completely of the West, perhaps colored by a distant hint of Brancusi. Yes, the various clusters of natural stones, many of them untraditionally upright, and the planting on the terrace render an association with Japan unavoidable—but mainly Japanese landscapes of the modern period. Perhaps only in gardens by Noguchi's friend Mirei Shigemori do we find a related, if not precisely comparable, use of rocks.[28] Shigemori challenged tradition—and in the process tried the patience of Japanese-garden aficionados—by turning stones on end rather than burying them in the earth as was the norm. At gardens such as at Kômyô-in, a sub-temple of Tôfuku-ji in Kyoto, the plethora of vertical stones that peppers the gravel field of Shigemori's 1971 garden appears erratic and excessive [see 5-15]. There remains in Shigemori's designs a greater incorporation of stones than in Noguchi's gardens, where stones serve primarily as natural sculpture.

Considering Noguchi's love of things archaic, he probably would have more greatly appreciated Shigemori's freely composed groupings of massive stones in his 1975 garden at the Matsuô Taisha shrine in Kyoto, where references to the setting of stones in ancient *iwakura* inspired the composition [5-21]. In contrast, Noguchi tended to use individual stones as singular sculptural elements and positioned them in his own manner, whether as spatial markers or as sculptures. Despite Sanô's best efforts, the planting at UNESCO bears little resemblance to how shrubs and trees are used in gardens in Japan, except perhaps in their species and original shaping.

In my estimation, the use of vegetation is the weakest aspect of the UNESCO design, as it neither reinforces nor subverts the presence of the garden's hard forms and surfaces. At the time of inauguration, the trees in the garden stood as only small saplings, and the great plateau at its center dominated the composition. Its identity as a true abstract relief upon which one could walk was obvious [see 5-1]. The trees and shrubs, which over the decades have lacked the care of a Japanese gardener, have reached sizable dimensions; their placement has always appeared haphazard, having been determined with little regard for their patterns of growth or their later effect on the garden's composition. As noted earlier, the row of cherry trees that parallels the path to the annex is the notable exception, a symbiotic relationship between the trees and the water channel adjacent to them.

All in all, is this a Japanese garden just because it was designed by a Japanese American and built with the aid of a Japanese team? The simple answer is "no." "It is true," Noguchi admitted, "that I have paid a more obvious homage to the Japanese garden in the lower area. This follows the nature of the commission, and because of the very generous gift of all the stones from Japan."[29] But in all fairness it should be noted that Noguchi never attempted to create a truly Japanese garden. He was a sculptor and not a gardener, and more American than Japanese. He was perhaps inspired by Japanese tradition, accepting the incorporation of stones and stonework identified with Japan, but in reality he sought only to create a modern garden to accompany a modern building. The challenge, as he saw it, was, "[to] learn but still to control, not to be overwhelmed by so strong a

5-18 *[left above]*
White Heron Castle.
Himeji, seventeenth century.
Although the castle's stone walls may have provided the inspiration for those supporting the central plateau of the UNESCO garden, their address of structural demands is more efficient and thus structurally more appropriate.

5-19 *[left center]*
UNESCO garden.
Paris, 1958.
Stones set in the water continue the path begun on land.

5-20 *[left below]*
Sentô Gosho Imperial Villa.
Kyoto, ca. 1630.
The *ariso* stone shoreline.

5-21 *[above]*
Mirei Shigemori.
Matsuô Taisha shrine,
Kyoto, Japan, 1975.
A garden featuring ancient rock arrangements known as *iwakura*.

tradition."[30] "It was my first great lesson in the sculpture of space through making a *somewhat* Japanese garden," he later commented.[31] In his final assessment he would downplay the role of influence: "It would be almost more correct to say that the truly Japanese part is that which is least obviously so."[32]

A "somewhat Japanese" garden. Without question, certain features directly invoke the landscape traditions of Japan: the water basin with its bamboo spout on the upper terrace; the reuse of a millstone as a paving element; the slightly arching bridge that forms the entrance to the lower garden; the use of natural stones; certain species of plants such as cherry trees and dwarf bamboo; the basic coloration of planting, stone and concrete; and even some compositional strategies. But I would suggest that in the scheme of things these are relatively minor, and that the garden is far more modern and Western in both its conception and realization [5-22].

>> RECEPTION

The critical reaction to the UNESCO garden at the time of its inauguration was largely positive; most of the negative invectives were hurled against the building, whose exposed concrete was taken by some as an affront to Parisian heritage. For several European writers, the garden was too nationalistically Japanese; for the Japanese it was too Western; for certain UNESCO representatives it was too modern. Architectural critics seeking a more humanistic aspect to the New Brutalist architecture held up the garden as a mirror to the forms of UNESCO House, and in the comparison the garden emerged the victor. On the one hand architectural historian Bruno Zevi, editor of the Italian journal *L'Architettura*, believed that "[UNESCO's] beautiful Japanese garden is superimposed on the site in the same way that the paintings in the interior spaces are superimposed on the walls."[33] While Zevi's displeasure with the art program probably stemmed from his predilection for the natural materials with which Frank Lloyd Wright built his "organic" architecture—and thus his distaste for the standardization and sculptured concrete surfaces of Le Corbusier—this does not invalidate his observation.

Noguchi's future collaborator, architect Gordon Bunshaft, summarized his reaction in two words: "It stinks." After meeting Noguchi on-site, however, he expressed a rather different opinion of the sculptor's work in his diary: "Looks like a fine garden."[34] In general, critics judged the artworks as valuable additions to the UNESCO complex by adding color and pattern to the otherwise gray and plain surfaces of concrete. While the architecture critic Reyner Banham decried the architecture and its lack of relation to the Place Fontenoy, he appreciated Pablo Picasso's mural on the theme of the fall of Icarus. He lavished most of his praise, however, on the Noguchi terrace and garden, which he described as a "significant contribution" to the total UNESCO environment. While perhaps placing too much emphasis on his mistaken reading of the work as a Zen garden, Banham was most positive about the Delegates Patio: "dotted with stone objects, some geometrically fine hewn, others in a state of highly sophisticated nature, the abstract artefacts of the Thirties informed with a meaning that no Hepworth or Nicholson ever gave them." The lower garden, as he deemed not unfairly, was overcrowded with elements, although it "strikes a note freshness that is not to be found elsewhere."[35]

Lewis Mumford condemned the new headquarters on both social and aesthetic grounds, encapsulating the dilemma of modernist spatial planning by using UNESCO House as his whipping boy. "This scheme conforms neither to the old block pattern of Paris nor establishes a better order based on free-standing buildings," he declaimed. Faring little better in his eyes was the art program, which he summarily dismissed as comprising "scattered objects of art, which are disposed almost at random about the open spaces."[36] Amid this modernist desert, filled with architectural clichés and so lacking in humanity, the Noguchi garden occupied a difficult position. Mumford accepted the sculptor's heroic task but sadly concluded that "for all its romantic ingenuity, there is no getting away from the looming glass façade of the Secretariat." The result: a "garden [that] seems like a curio snatched by a tourist on his travels, not an integral part of this complex of UNESCO buildings."[37] Showing grudging respect but ultimately condemnatory, Mumford concluded: "Even if this garden were not too heavily charged with ancient, narrowly national idiosyncrasies to represent an emerging new universal order in both art and life, it would have been nullified by its hostile surroundings."[38]

>>REFLECTION

In May 1988, on what would be his last visit to the UNESCO site, Noguchi supervised renovations, which included the restoration of both the hard surfaces and the planting of new vegetation. The team of three gardeners from Japan—with Sanô again as their head—were once more sponsored by the Japanese government and completed the necessary work. The *Jardin japonais* is now over sixty years old; the vegetation has reached adulthood and has acquired considerable height and volume. The lack of continuous pruning and meticulous care characteristic of the Japanese gardener has allowed the greenery unbridled growth, which has resulted in vegetation that is today unsympathetic and out of scale with Noguchi's original intentions. While a major renovation took place in 2002, maintaining truly sympathetic vegetal forms requires frequent pruning and shaping. One cannot expect the desired results by pruning adult vegetation left on its own for many years. On the other hand, it must be admitted that the *Jardin japonais* is today a far more pleasant place in which to sit or walk than it was years ago, when it offered only a sculptural relief of hard surfaces. On a visit to the garden some years later, even Noguchi derived some pleasure from its condition, untroubled by the lack of proper maintenance: "[N]othing is being done, and the garden had overgrown with weeds, jabbering away and having a wonderful time. The trees have grown to the max, and the garden is all its own with nobody taking care of it. I've never seen it look so beautiful. . . . I cannot imagine a landscape or a sculpture that is mute."[39]

The progression of the planting and the consequent increase in personal pleasure, however, have come at the expense of sculptural identity. The Delegates Patio remains much as it was, and still offers a fitting point of entry to the garden below; the descent along the walkway from the source stone, particularly in spring or autumn, offers one of the Noguchi landscape's most pleasurable moments. The garden is heavily used by staff as an escape from the hubbub of activities inside the building and quite frequently as a place to smoke. The ban on tobacco within the building has given additional life to the *Jardin japonais*, countering the restrictions on public visits to the site in a post-9/11 and Covid era. Unlike in earlier days, when you were permitted to be on your own and enjoy the garden at your leisure, access today is possible only on a ticketed guided tour. This is a sad state of affairs, although understandable given the state of society, disease, and the world.

The UNESCO garden represents a pivotal point in Noguchi's development as a maker of gardens. Here, for the first time, he realized ideas for making gardens formulated almost two decades before. The project evinced his ability to create an outdoor work of relatively large dimensions, working with others as a team to bring it to fruition, only after personally securing the necessary funding for its construction. While I do not believe the lower garden at UNESCO is Noguchi's greatest work, as an overall ensemble, it was one of his most successful landscapes in its exploration of form, and in demonstrating how a garden can be sculpture and vice versa. "Nothing could have been more opportune or rewarding in showing me the way I must go," he reflected,

> *toward a deeper knowledge through experience of what makes a garden, above all the relation between sculpture and space which I conceived as a possible solution to the dilemma of sculpture, as it suggested a fresh approach to sculpture as an organic component of the environment.*[40]

The UNESCO project also firmly established Noguchi's credentials as the maker of gardens conceived and regarded as art. His meeting architect Gordon Bunshaft had already led to one commission; in the years to come there would be others.

5-22
UNESCO garden.
Paris, 1958.
The garden seen from the top-floor cafeteria in Summer 2022.

> 6.

Gardens within Bounds

Few Noguchi landscapes transformed open land with expansive horizons; to the contrary, most of his gardens were enclosed by walls. In historical gardens such as the Middle Eastern *bagh*, the Italian *giardino segreto*, and the *karesansui* gardens at Japanese temples, walls directed the focus inward. Noguchi visited many of these gardens on his travels in India, China, and Japan during the 1930s and 1950s, discovering the beauty of their forms and spaces and gleaning their lessons firsthand. Of these, the gardens of Japan were the most influential, not only for their appreciation and setting of stones, but also for their restraint and the way in which the elements cohered as a whole constrained by walls. Although the analogy may be strained, we might propose that, like the edges of a two-dimensional painting, the boundaries of the walled site establish both the dimensions of the garden and a direction for its design. The majority of Noguchi's bounded gardens are centripetal and inwardly focused, yet his most moving works psychologically transcend the physical limits established by the walls around them. His mediums and forms vary; some include vegetation, others restrict materials to only one. The number and types of materials were never the issue. "I am not concerned here with a monument or embellishment but with gardens," he wrote, "by which I mean that self-contained sculpturing of space with whatever medium, be it trees, water rock, wire, or broken-down automobiles."[1]

>> INTERIOR GARDENS

If given the latitude to metaphorically regard an interior space as a landscape, we could include the Faculty Retreat at the Keio University campus in southern Tokyo as a Noguchi garden [6-1]. Founded in 1858 by Yukuchi Fukuzawa (1835–1901) with a focus on Western studies, Keio is among Japan's premier educational institutions, today comprising almost a dozen faculties.[2] Around 1950, to meet its growing needs and replace facilities lost during the war, Keio commissioned Yoshirô Taniguchi (1904–1979) to design a new classroom building that would also include a faculty lounge. Noguchi's father, the poet Yonejirô (Yone) Noguchi, who had died only recently, had taught on the Keio campus for forty years, and the room would be dedicated to his memory. Noguchi *fils* had maintained sporadic contact with his father and was familiar with his writings, as Yone had been the first Japanese poet

6-0
1 Chase Plaza.
New York, 1964.
Water and stone.

6-1
Shin-Banraisha.
(Yoshirô Taniguchi, architect).
Keio University, Tokyo, Japan, 1951.
The left column serves
as the flue for the fireplace.
[Chuji Hirayama, © The Noguchi Museum/ARS]

to write principally in English. Yone had traveled widely; well versed in other arts, he had even authored a small book for the Japanese Tourist Library on the woodblock prints of Hiroshige and their relationship to Japanese landscapes.[3] "Art is something like love or flowers or the moon," he wrote in 1935, "the mission of which is, with an intangible but real power, to develop our sense of living to something higher and nobler."[4]

His son, in all probability, shared this sentiment. As the new Faculty Retreat would be dedicated to Yone's memory, Taniguchi invited Isamu to collaborate on its design. The project became a vehicle for restoring ties; Noguchi confessed that after being invited to design the memorial room he "became preoccupied with [it] as [his] own act of reconciliation to [his] father and to the people."[5] The space would be known as the Shin-Banraisha, the New Banraisha, a replacement for the original lounge destroyed in the war.[6]

The room was planned on two levels using three surface materials, a triad that parallels the three zones of the rural folk house [6-2]. Stones of irregular shapes pave the entry and the primary circulation areas; the raised wooden platform doubles as seating and supports circulation; the tatami zone accommodates repose and conversation in a more traditional manner. Complementing the stone floor and the wooden platforms are furniture also of Noguchi's design, likely the result of a collaboration with his friend, interior designer Isamu Kenmochi [see 6-6].

Flanked by two stout columns of concrete, a circular firepit about fifteen feet in diameter is the dominent element of the room. Only one of these columns is structural, however; the second cleverly conceals its identity as the flue for the firepit. Resembling the petals of a flower, the radiating stones that surround the fire have been spaced to facilitate airflow. Perhaps its flames were intended to evoke the sanctity of the memorial to Yone Noguchi [6-3, 6-4]. Spanning the pillars, a wedge-shaped mantle of copper collects the smoke that mysteriously disappears within it. The curving edge of the wooden platform and the wall of scratch-patterned terracotta tiles behind it define a zone for reading. On the stone floor facing the garden a long table, bracketed by benches with backrests elliptical in section, melds with the total composition of the room [6-5, 6-6].

To Noguchi, room and garden were a single entity. Through the glass doors the space flowed, its continuity ensured by using the same

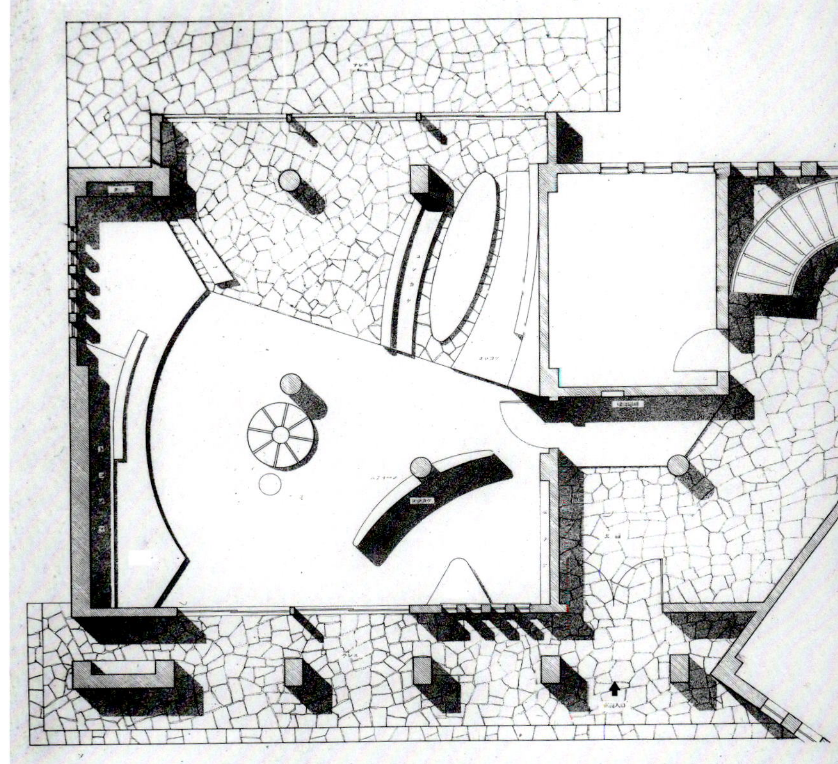

6-2
Shin-Banraisha.
Floor plan showing the three levels surfaced with stone, wood, and tatami.
[*Shin Kenchiku*]

6-3
Shin-Banraisha, remade.
(Kengo Kuma, architect, 2015),
Keio University, Tokyo.

6-4 *[above left]*
Shin-Banraisha, remade.
Keio University, Tokyo, Japan, 2015.
Hearth detail.

6-5 *[above right]*
Shin-Banraisha, remade.
Original table and chairs.
Collaboration with Isamu Kenmochi.

6-6 *[above]*
Shin-Banraisha, remade.
Original table and bench (detail). Collaboration with Isamu Kenmochi.

6-7 *[right]*
Shin-Banraisha,
Garden with sculpture *Mu*, above center.
[© The Noguchi Museum/ARS]

stone to pave the exterior patio [6-7]. The soft greenery of the garden supplied the antidote to the hard surfaces within the room and created the setting for the freestanding sculpture *Mu*, its title referring to the Zen concept of void or nothingness. A sizable and somewhat chunky piece, it was carved in Stony Creek granite after a full-size plaster study first displayed at Noguchi's 1950 exhibition at the Mitsukoshi department store in Tokyo. By positioning the sculpture to the west, Noguchi hoped that the twisted horns of its "broken circle" would collect the rays of the sun as it sets, "making of it an *ishidoro* [stone lantern] of celestial illumination."[7]

As a totality the Shin-Banraisha—room and garden—can be read as a hybrid of internal and external objects that, despite their differences in shape, material, and finish, cohere as a single entity. Like the dance sets for Martha Graham, each element retains its distinct identity, with unity deriving from the relationships among them and their confinement within walls.

Despite massive protests from the international art community the Shin-Banraisha was demolished in 2003 to provide land for Keio's new law school. Its furnishings were spared, however, and reassembled on the roof of the new building in a reconstructed version weakly reminiscent of the original space. While we must be thankful that the furnishings of the original room survived, the new space designed by Kengo Kuma, although respectful, lacks any feeling of authenticity. Neither does the concrete terrace perforated with circular planting holes by landscape architect Michel Desvigne suggest much of the original garden setting for *Mu*. As a result, the Shin-Bairaisha today has been reduced to the status of a period room, curiously displaced on a rooftop five floors above the ground to which it was originally so strongly united.

>> COLLABORATION

The commission for a courtyard for the Lever House in New York City, would be Noguchi's first collaboration with architect Gordon Bunshaft (1909–1990), senior designer and partner in the New York office of Skidmore, Owings & Merrill (SOM). Their projects together would span a decade. Born to immigrant parents in Buffalo, New York, Bunshaft had studied architecture at the Massachusetts Institute of Technology and quickly rose within the ranks of one of the United States' fastest growing corporate practices.

Since the end of the earlier Beaux-Arts era the place of art in architecture had withered precipitously. As modernism took hold in the United States and internationally the importance of the frieze, sculpture, and mural as integral elements of architecture atrophied, and had largely disappeared. To a degree unusual among architects at that time Bunshaft had developed an appreciation for modern and tribal arts, and eagerly sought a place for art within his buildings.

Noguchi and Bunshaft met through Hans Knoll, who with his wife, interior designer Florence, had founded the high modernist furniture company that bears their name. While excited by the prospect of a major sculptural commission, Noguchi was wary of the working relationship, as he found most architects to be "egotistical" and "wanting to hog the whole thing." He saw working with architects as "a test of my competence to contribute something in spite of the so-called collaboration, which is so one-sided."[8] While always forceful in advancing his ideas, he understood the nature of commissions and who ultimately holds the decision-making power. By accepting commissions where sculpture and building maintained autonomous identities, Noguchi buffered potential confrontations. "I myself have tried to get around this difficulty [collaboration with architects]," he admitted, "by seeking commissions which are separate but in counterpoint to the architecture, with an equivalent scale and using the creation of space as an extension of sculpture."[9] In reviewing a project as outlined by the architect, Noguchi would either accept it outright, modify its scope, or simply reject it. Architects rarely enjoy ceding control of their determination of form and space; artists, for their part, may consider themselves the sole masters of their domain. As early as 1946 Noguchi declared that if someone needs to be in control, "I say it is the sculptor who orders and animates space, gives it meaning."[10]

For his part, Bunshaft thought "collaboration" was the wrong term for these interactions of artist and architects, as so "few artists know much about architecture."[11] He regarded Noguchi as "one of the two or three greatest sculptors in the United States. I know a lot of people think he's commercial. . . . The thing about Noguchi, he's one of the few artists in the world who understands architectural space. Very few design to scale, to a space enclosed by a building."[12] In the Bunshaft-Noguchi collaborations the two men would first jointly agree on an approach, after which the sculptor would conceive the work and present it to the architect and client for review. "We didn't talk about what [the sculpture] should be, but had he [Noguchi] come up with something lousy I would have told him so."[13] That said, Bunshaft seems to have established the parameters for the sculptures, but then gave Noguchi relatively free reign by which to respond.

Although their collaborations produced interesting results, neither Noguchi nor Bunshaft found the actual process of working together very comfortable. Yet each expressed an appreciation, even an admiration for the other. Noguchi considered Bunshaft among the few architects who understood the place of sculpture in architecture; Bunshaft admired the sculptor's understanding of architecture, going so far as to say that Noguchi thought like an architect. Despite the frequent feather ruffling, an affinity of some sort developed through their collaborations that extended over a decade. As he recalled years later in *The Sculptor's World*, this was a relationship that Noguchi openly appreciated:

> *The architect with whom I have worked most is Gordon Bunshaft of Skidmore, Owings & Merrill. It is due to his interest that projects were initiated, his persistence that saw them realized, his determination that squeezed out whatever was in me. Indeed I am beholden to him for every collaborative architectural commission I have been able to execute in the United States.*[14]

Over time their professional relationship became a friendship. In October 1960 Noguchi guided the Bunshafts during their visit to Kyoto, introducing them to a number of great landscapes like the tiny courtyard at Daisen-in and the splendid moss garden at Saihô-ji.[15] Unfortunately Bunshaft, without further comment, jotted down only the names of the gardens in his travel diary, and he seemed more impressed by the tea ceremony they attended at the "House of Sen," in a 400-year-old teahouse, than any of the gardens.

6-8
Red Cube, 1968.
New York.

>> *RED CUBE*

The negotiations that shaped Noguchi's *Red Cube* (1968), commissioned for Bunshaft's Marine Midland Bank in Lower Manhattan, are indicative of the manner of their collaboration. Perhaps reflecting Bunshaft's suggestion of a megalith following the architect's recent visit to Stonehenge, Noguchi first proposed a composition using several rocks. Its estimated price tag of $90,000 caused the client to balk, and the proposal ended there. Bunshaft also began to question the use of natural forms in an urban setting, proposing "some bright abstract metal forms" as a better option. Noguchi responded with studies using bent sheet metal. Reviewing the model together they agreed that the space for the irregular arrangement of the cubic elements Noguchi envisioned would be insufficient. One element of the model proposed a cube balanced on its corner, rehearsing a marble form in the Beinecke courtyard at Yale University discussed below. In its final form, Noguchi's *Red Cube* bonds sculpture to architecture through its dissonance with the black façade of the bank building [6-8]. A hole through the cube invigorates the purity of the geometry and lures passersby with its lens-less spyglass through which to view the black steel façade.[16]

>> LEVER HOUSE

The first collaboration between the sculptor and the architect was for Lever House (1951), a new high-rise to be built in Midtown Manhattan. The client, Charles Luckman, was trained as an architect, but fate had other plans for the ambitious young man. With intelligence, guile, and an almost manic work ethic, Luckman had worked his way up from newsboy to president of Lever Brothers, the American subsidiary of the Dutch conglomerate Unilever. Studies determined that distributing Lever's staff and executives over several cities was inefficient, and despite the significant cost, Luckman proposed centralizing all operations in a single building in New York City. Luckman reserved for himself the task of selecting the architect and determining the size and concept for the building. "After all," he bragged, "I was an architect."[17] Given that Luckman wrote his memoirs long after the fact, we must allow for considerable exaggeration and self-aggrandizement.[18]

For his architect Luckman selected Skidmore, Owings & Merrill, with Bunshaft as the partner in charge of design. New York zoning codes allowed an increased number of stories for a tower that occupied less than 25 percent of its site. The central, open space at street level acquired through zoning allowances would feature a garden with a pool, "not unlike the atrium of classic Roman houses." Contrary to the norm for most urban towers, there would be no shops on the ground floor, and the lobby at the base of the tower was the only enclosed space.[19] Luckman calculated that the free access across the site would create a positive corporate image and garner millions of dollars of free advertising—and he was right [6-9]. Bunshaft and his staff delivered an elegant slab sheathed in a blue-green glass curtain wall that soon became an icon of midcentury American modernism.

During the design process Bunshaft proposed a sculpture/garden to enliven the courtyard and soften the transition to the walls of the adjacent property to the west. "We hoped to have sculpture integrated with the total design, including landscape," said Bunshaft, "and Noguchi was the only sculptor that I knew of in the world who had the requisite knowledge of architecture, of plant material and space design."[20] Noguchi accepted the commission and began to work. Over a period of almost three years he produced two schemes that occupied much of the building's street-level open space. "My concept," said Noguchi, "was to eliminate the bed of green in the central marble planting box which had already been determined and to cover it with marble from which would rise sculptures with small risings and apertures in the marble for planting. The rest of the ground floor was related to this with mound shapes and stone and soft seating areas."[21]

Creating a template for many of his landscapes to follow, Noguchi's design composed sculpture, greenery, and water elements on a stone plinth, opposing hard with soft, solid with liquid, and vertical with horizontal [6-10]. While one of the two columnar sculptures recalls Brancusi's *Endless Column* (1918)—and prefigures Noguchi's own *Endless Coupling* (1988)—here the shaft is freely treated and enhanced by organic forms clinging to its surfaces. The cylindrical pillar of its shorter sibling supports a sculptural object that recalls the soft contours of the prewar *Miss Expanding Universe*.

Within what appears to be a pool of irregular ovular shape were paired horizontal and vertical elements probably destined as fountains, with the taller form possibly its source and conspicuously similar to Brancusi's horizontally oriented *Fish* (1930); from the second element water fell as a continuous curtain. Noguchi probably felt that vertical forms were needed to counter the flatness of the ground plane and to lead the visitor's eyes upward upon entry into the courtyard. The taller element would also provide a subject of interest for those having a drink or a meal in the employee cafeteria on the second floor. The green areas, as in many of Noguchi's early garden works, appear gratuitous and do little to enhance the space or the sculpture. Noguchi was unclear as to why the scheme was not accepted but suspected it stemmed from union interference. As he was then in Tokyo at work on the *Reader's Digest* garden he had to manage the Lever House project from afar and accept its rejection.

The second scheme retained the initial layout and elements, but like a chess master, Noguchi now shifted the pieces upon the field of play [6-11]. The original two verticals have become three pieces that share the idiom of the first proposal's shorter element, now placed within the pool. Given their relative heights, it is difficult to avoid reading them as an abstract family group, with the "father" retaining the horned form reminiscent of the nearly coeval *Mu*; the stacked forms of the "mother" cite Japanese *haniwa* burial figures or Noguchi's *haniwa*-like ceramic pieces, especially *The Queen* (1931). The short form looks to be its parents' child. A tree and four grassed/vegetal areas converse with the sculptures across the court. In terms of spatial definition, their effect is unconvincing.

For whatever reasons, Noguchi's second proposal was also rejected, or died a lingering and unhappy death. He believed that when the building construction costs overran the established budget, the funding for the sculpture fell victim.[22] In place of the Noguchi sculptures, SOM's in-house landscape architect Joanna Diman designed a simple, rectangular plot planted with low vegetation; the space was left devoid of sculpture. While the Lever project went unrealized, Noguchi did not discard his ideas or the monumental works he had proposed. In 1958 he realized two sculptures, now in the Sheldon Museum of Art in Lincoln, Nebraska [6-12], that together comprise a single work, *Song of the Bird*. The shorter figure was carved from white marble. The taller column, whose stacked forms and curious growths upon its shaft exude a distant echo of Brancusi's *La Negresse blonde* (1926), was executed in gray granite.

>> CONNECTICUT GENERAL LIFE INSURANCE

Despite the unhappy ending to the Lever story, it appears that Bunshaft judged Noguchi's proposal a success, as he returned to Noguchi for several additional landscape in the years to follow. Noguchi's next opportunity

6-9
Skidmore, Owings & Merrill.
Lever House.
New York, 1953.

6-10
Courtyard.
Lever House, New York, 1952.
First Proposal. Model.
[Charles Uht, © The Noguchi Museum/ARS]

6-11
Courtyard.
Lever House.
Second proposal. Model.
[Charles Uht, © The Noguchi Museum/ARS]

arrived with the commission for the light courts in the new headquarters of Connecticut General Life Insurance (1957) in Bloomfield, Connecticut. For decades, nearby Hartford had been the home of several major insurance companies, and in the postwar period their number was increasing. To implement new ideas concerning organization and management, the corporation was moving to the suburbs, where land, light, greenery, and parking would be abundant; where the offices and staff could be consolidated; and where its architecture could speak of progress and modern business practices. To design their new headquarters, they turned to SOM and Gordon Bunshaft. The original building was of three stories, its ground floor primarily glazed to provide visual permeability and ease the meeting of the structure with the ground.[23] To minimize the need for artificial light in the offices, the block was perforated by four glass-walled courtyards. Noguchi would design gardens for three of the four original courts [6-13].[24]

Compared with *Play Mountain* or the more recent Lever House proposals, Noguchi's courtyard designs are rather restrained—possibly at Bunshaft's request, possibly from Noguchi's belief that simplicity was required. All three courtyards remained relatively flat, with their horizontality broken only by a Japanese maple in one and shrubs in another [6-14, 6-15]. A shallow pool of irregular profile played against panels of gravel and grass as the court's sole occupants. The stepping stones that crossed the pool echoed Noguchi's use of stones at UNESCO House in Paris, designed around the same time. The most formally complex and visually interesting of the courtyards featured a panel of ground cover in a modernized version of the double-gourd motif found in historical Japanese gardens and a lone tree that shades one lobe of the panel in counterpoint to a circle of low, flowering shrubs. Using smaller and delicate species like Japanese maple allowed the passage of light into the offices while tinting the courts with color, seasonal change, and perhaps also offering a rare instant of movement. These were light courts rather than employee oases and were entered only for maintenance. On the ground floor the spaces were glimpsed in passing; from above, they served primarily as sources of light and visual relief.

In contrast to the internal courts, the Employee Terrace provided respite from the building's sealed environment and was open to all. Raised above the adjacent greensward, the terrace was read by some as a "moat between technology and nature."[25] Using rectangles of stone paving

6-12
Song of the Bird, 1958.
[Sheldon Museum of Art]

6-13 *[above left]*
Courtyards.
Connecticut General Life Insurance, Bloomfield, Connecticut, 1957.
Model.
[Charles Uht, © The Noguchi Museum/ARS]

6-14 *[above right]*
Courtyard.
Connecticut General Life Insurance.
The central biomorphic form recalls the traditional double-gourd motif used in Japan.
[Ezra Stoller / ESTO]

6-15 *[below left]*
Courtyard.
Connecticut General Life Insurance.
A minimal vocabulary of gravel and water, dotted with panels of floral color.

6-16 *[below right]*
Employee Terrace.
Connecticut General Life Insurance.
Photographed in the 1990s.

and gravel, and with only limited ground cover, the color scheme was predominantly black and white [6-16]. Unlike the internally focused courts, here the thrust was outward, toward the softly contoured landscape designed by Joanna Dimon. The terrace's rectangular panels were planned with sufficient dimensions to support tables and chairs for use by individuals as well as groups.

From the main office block, two smaller volumes protruded: on the entrance side, the executive offices; facing the landscape on the opposite side, the employee cafeteria.[26] With glass walls on three sides to maximize light and view, and raised several feet above the landscape, the cafeteria hovered above the reflecting pool that optically doubled its presence on three sides. As the cafeteria would be visible from the offices on the floors above, the black-and-white gravel on its roof was configured in a diamond pattern for visual interest [6-17]. While no record shows this to be Noguchi's work, he may have had a say in its design.

In addition to the courtyards and the terrace, Noguchi was commissioned to create a sculpture identifiable as a work of art. "At that time," recounted Bunshaft, "Noguchi was monkeying around with a quarry in Connecticut and was very excited about doing work cut right in the quarry; he was fascinated with the idea of doing handwork."[27] The issue was scale, or more accurately, size. Size denotes a work's actual dimensions; scale, how large it seems. To ensure that the proposed size was correct for its location, Bunshaft had plywood mockups constructed at heights of twelve, fourteen, and sixteen feet. These tests successfully determined the preferred height but revealed that the terrace was not the ideal location for the sculpture, whether because of its height, mass, or craggy surfaces. The sculpture Noguchi created, *Family*, consists of nine roughly hewn stone blocks, whose number and relative heights evoke the nuclear family of father, mother, and child [6-18]. Looking beyond their coarse demeanor, one can detect vestiges of sculptures first proposed for Lever House several years earlier. Bunshaft credits "the owner" with the suggestion that *Family* be installed on a hill across the meadow; consensus determined that this was the correct location for the sculpture.[28] "So we got a truck," explained Bunshaft, "and rushed them out . . . Very scientific."[29]

For his part, Noguchi accepted the verdict, at least as reported in retrospect. "I do not deny that the result seems to have justified

6-17 *[above left]*
Employee Terrace.
Connecticut General
Life Insurance.
Bloomfield, Connecticut, 1957.
Patterning in black and white.
[Ezra Stoller / ESTO]

6-18 *[below left]*
Family, 1957.
Connecticut General
Life Insurance.

the dispute," he confessed, "which teaches me not to be tied to preconceptions, to be open to change and chance to the end."[30] To confirm the work's proper siting, the company solicited the opinion of Christopher Tunnard, then a member of Yale University's planning faculty; author of *Gardens in the Modern Landscape* (1938), the ur-manifesto on modern landscape architecture; and arguably the field's most prominent theorist.[31] Tunnard confirmed the prior decision made by the parties involved. Although the management of the buildings had changed and parts of the site redeveloped, as of 2022 *Family* remained in its original location.

>> BEINECKE LIBRARY COURTYARD

Around 1960 Bunshaft solicited Noguchi's involvement on two important projects: the courtyards for the Beinecke Rare Book and Manuscript Library at Yale University in New Haven, Connecticut; and 1 Chase Plaza, to accompany the new headquarters for Chase Manhattan Bank in New York City.[32] Although both courts occupied sites below ground level, Noguchi's response to their respective conditions would differ significantly.

Bunshaft's design for the Beinecke library is essentially a transparent box within a translucent box, supported by a structural concrete frame infilled with panels of white alabaster [6-19]. The inner box of glass—a *sanctum sanctorum*—houses the stacks for the rare books. Surrounding the lower-level courtyard are the reading room, library offices and support services; their rooftops align with the surface of the Hewitt Quadrangle plaza fronting Woolsey Hall and the Schwartzman Center. Thus "sunken" in relation to the plaza and the surrounding buildings, the court would be viewed by most visitors from above; only library staff, readers, and researchers were able to view the court from eye level [6-20]. On the lower level, walls of floor-to-ceiling tinted glass provide a strangely sympathetic backdrop to Noguchi's white marble forms. Viewed head on rather than from above, two of the geometric sculptures—the torus and the cube—rest lightly on the ground; their fugitive reflections in the dark glass panels double their presence, while shifting with vantage point and intensity of sunlight.

There would be no vegetation in the courtyard, a proscription decided early on.[33] Preceding the geometric objects that today populate the courtyard, Noguchi first proposed one softly modeled circular mound

6-19
Skidmore, Owings, & Merrill (Gordon Bunshaft).
Beinecke Rare Book and Manuscript Library.
Yale University, New Haven, Connecticut, 1963.

6-20
Courtyard.
Beinecke Rare Bcok and
Manuscript Library.
Yale University, New Haven,
Connecticut, 1963.
As seen from the plaza above.

balanced by a corresponding circular depression. This simple play of positive and negative embodied at large scale Auguste Rodin's belief that sculpture was essentially "the art of the bump and the hole" [6-21].[34] While not directly evident in the final design of the court, Noguchi cited memories of the Indian astronomical observatories in Delhi and Jaipur as inspiration, in addition to those garnered working in the marble quarries of Italy [6-22].[35] A second, mounded scheme rehearsed the shapes found in one courtyard of the Connecticut General offices.

While up to that point Noguchi had never supported his garden designs with either mythical references or more pragmatic explanations —the *Monument to the Plough* being the main exception—for the Beinecke he announced the symbolic program that would guide his work. As the project progressed, a cluster of three geometric objects supplanted the naturalism of the ground forms of the first scheme. Like the courtyard paving beneath them, white marble would be the material for the ring, the cube, and the pyramid. Noguchi composed these elements from the belief that in groups, objects "accumulate energy between them—they call to each other."[36] The objects and ground of the Beinecke court became literally mono-lithic, with geometry and stone replacing nature and vegetation.

The courtyard, like the building, would be constructed by the George A. Fuller Company—perhaps no surprise, given that one of the Beinecke brothers was president of the firm; their personal investment in the project ensured an excellent product.[37] The Vermont Marble Company would fabricate the elements of the courtyard to Noguchi's design and specifications. The architects, contractor, and sculptor established a working method whereby Noguchi would prepare—in addition to drawings—a half-size model of "The Sun" and a one-third-size model of "The Cube." From these, "the marble sub-contractor ... under the supervision of Mr. Noguchi, would cut, carve, and finish the sculptures," and would be "responsible for their delivery and setting."[38] Presumably, drawings would suffice for constructing the pyramid and fabricating the paving.

As Noguchi described it, the new approach produced "a dramatic landscape, one that is purely imaginary; it is nowhere, yet somehow familiar. Its size is fictive, of infinite space or cloistered containment [6-23]."[39] Every element became a symbol as well as a form, with each

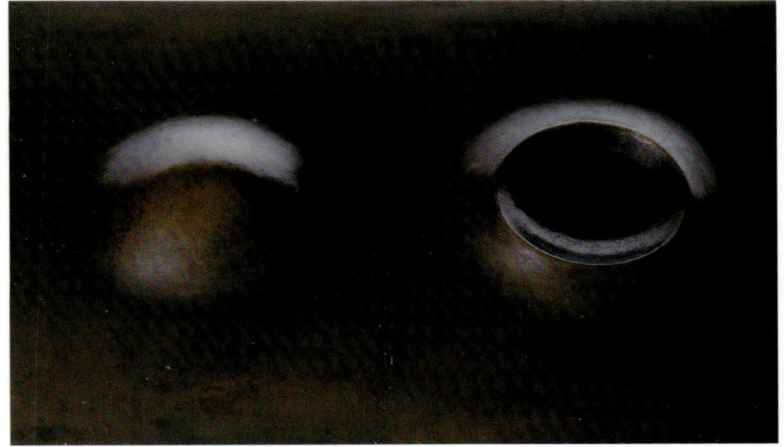

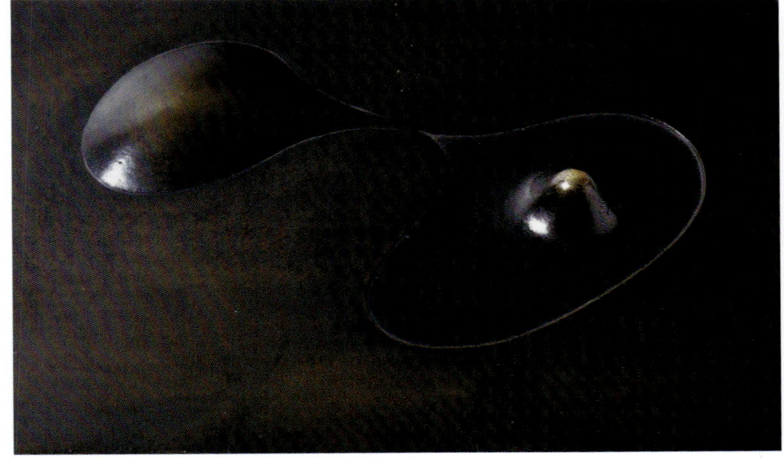

6-21 *[right above]*
Courtyard.
Beinecke Library.
Early studies, 1960.
A play of opposites.
[Kevin Noble, © The Noguchi Museum/ARS]

6-22 *[right below]*
Jantar Mantar observatories.
Jaipur, India, 1734.
[Wikicommons]

6-23
Courtyard.
Beinecke Rare Book Library.
Yale University, New Haven,
Connecticut, 1963.
The principal elements
seen from the lower floor.

6-24
Courtyard.
Beinecke Rare Book Library.
Chips and deformations along the edges enrich the form of the torus, intended by Noguchi to symbolize energy.

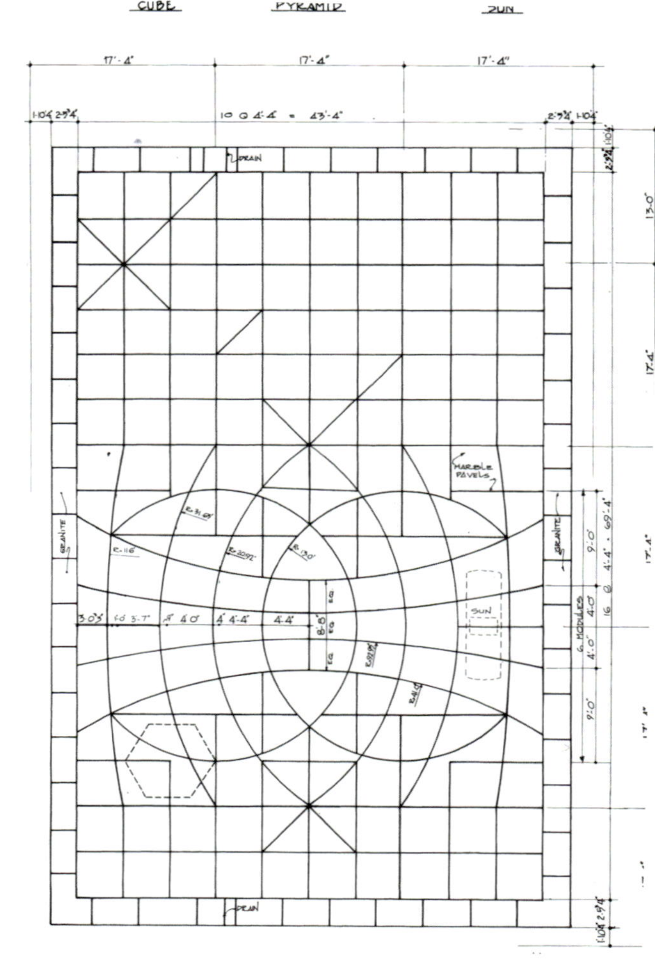

6-25 *[above]*
Courtyard.
Beinecke Rare Book Library.
Yale University, New Haven,
Connecticut, 1963.
The Pyramid symbolizes
stability; the Cube, chance.

6-26 *[above right]*
Courtyard.
Beinecke Rare Book Library,
Plan with paving pattern.
[© The Noguchi Museum/ARS]

assigned a set of meanings. The torus, or ring, symbolized energy, with the sun as its reference.[40] Unlike a disk, the torus frames a void, defining space while occupying it. Noguchi rarely left any form or surface in its pure state, however. In studying the sculpture he called "The Sun," he sought a form "that was harmonious and also disharmonious. If you have complete harmony, nothing happens, whereas if you have an element of disharmony, energy enters as a disequilibrating factor. Things start to happen."[41] The sun was a potent symbol: a "coiled magnet, the circle of ever accelerating force."[42] Noguchi claimed that "the hole is an abyss, the mirror, or the question mark."[43] The ten-foot-high ring varies in thickness; bites and chips taken from both its outer and inner edges add to the intricacies of its form [6-24]. Whether this torus is ultimately read, as Noguchi suggested, as a sun or an energy source may be questioned, but not its role and importance in the Beinecke ensemble [6-25].

Unlike the triangular *Monument to the Plough* or the nose of *Sculpture to Be Seen from Mars*, the base of this pyramid is square. To Noguchi, the pyramid symbolized the earth, the "man-made pile of carbon blocks by which [man] has learned to simulate nature's presence."[44] Similar to the *Red Cube* that followed several years later, the marble cube at the Beinecke stands on one point as an embodiment of chance, "like the rolling of dice."[45] Its uneasy balance confronts gravity and natural forces; its precariousness complements the stability of the ring, and especially the pyramid.

Although normally underappreciated, the scoring in the Beinecke's marble floor plays a crucial role in structuring the composition, especially those lines radiating from the torus and the cube. Noguchi likened these joints between the paving units to the line of the rope in his early dance set for *Frontier*: "The lines on the marble ground give a kind of perspective. It opens up. I have often used the ground artificially—that is to say, I think of the ground not just as ground but as a kind of geometry of ground."[46] To some, these lines in the Beinecke court floor suggest waves or lines of force that radiate outward from origins in the court's primary forms, terminating only at the walls that enclose the space.

The beauty of the Beinecke garden benefits considerably from its restriction to a single material [6-26; 6-27]. As maquettes all Noguchi landscapes appear continuous and monolithic, their small size permitting an understanding through even a single view. In contrast, a landscape comprises varied materials, some living, some mineral. Only very rarely is the coherence characterizing the relief or maquette achieved in an actual landscape. The pattern of linework at the Beinecke is so carefully plotted and immaculately crafted that the composition is transformed into a habitable maquette. Therefore, although many consider the Beinecke court to possess only three constituents, in fact there are four: the torus, the pyramid, the cube, *and* the ground plane. The relationships among them are precise, resulting in a formal checkmate: no further movement or change can be made without causing the garden's destruction.

I seriously doubt that anyone has ever or will ever decode Noguchi's intended symbolism by looking at the sculptures, even when viewed from above, when the regulating lines in the paving gain increased presence.[47] The untitled courtyard will not be appreciated for its symbolism, but rather as a beautiful and seamless composition of geometric forms of marble set before them. Designers must always distinguish their intentions and aspirations from what they can realistically expect visitors to sense and discern. In this case, symbolism aided, and perhaps even propelled, Noguchi's conception of the work, just as his scenario also instigated the design of the courts at the IBM offices in Armonk, New York, described below.

>> 1 CHASE PLAZA

The sunken court at 1 Chase Plaza in New York City was created nearly contemporaneously with the Beinecke library garden, although in terms of form the two designs could hardly be more different [6-28]. Noguchi's participation was again solicited by Gordon Bunshaft. Wrapped in a highly refined aluminum curtain wall, the somewhat staid tower for the new Chase offices contained nearly two million square feet of floor space distributed over sixty floors. Among the services accommodated in the building would be the bank's public banking hall, by necessity set below plaza level. Given the building's constricted footprint allowed a taller building, the resulting open space would provide an appreciated breath of air for the congested streets of the city's Financial District. A lower-level courtyard, circular in plan—perhaps in response to a Noguchi suggestion—brings light into the banking hall enclosed within floor-to-ceiling glass walls [6-29].

6-27 *[opposite below]*
Courtyard.
Beinecke Rare Book Library
Lines in the paving radiating from the principal elements enfold them as a composition.

In starting work on the garden Noguchi faced the problematic site, or, as architecture critic Paul Goldberger judged it, "awkward surroundings" adjacent to a tall building that rose from a "stark plaza."[48] Noguchi's original charge included a sculpture for the upper plaza and the design of the lower court. For the that site he produced several studies, each of them a gateway executed in rough materials, possibly stone; at least two of the studies suggest the forms of the later Dodge Fountain in Detroit, although in this version they appear as if a relic of Neolithic times [6-30]. For unexplained reasons these proposals were rejected, and in the end Jean Dubuffet's monumental black-and-white *Group of Four Trees* was commissioned and installed on the plaza in 1969 [6-31]. Approbation for the sculpture was not universal, and at the presentation of the maquette, the critic David L. Shirey described the resin-and-epoxy work as "a weird cross-pollination of mammoth Alice-in-Wonderland mushrooms and a jig saw puzzle for giants."[49] For his part, Dubuffet believed the sculpture of the trees "belong[ed] to the world of spiritual creation . . . [Trees] embodied in a form suggesting trees . . . [but] operations and structures belonging to a strictly mental realm."[50] While one might have wished for a second Noguchi contribution to the Chase environment, the scale and black-and-white tones of the Dubuffet sculpture feel appropriate, with their willy-nilly forms providing an agreeable contrast to the rigidly orthogonal architecture.

Below the plaza Noguchi produced one of his most remarkable and unified spatial sculptures, a garden he described as "my version of Ryoan-ji."[51] As unworked stones were the principal sculptural objects, the reference seems apropos. In Noguchi's view, the stones in the dry Ryôan-ji garden felt that they,

> *were not just placed there,* [but] *that they grow out of the earth (the major portion buried), their weight is connected with the earth—and yet perhaps for this very reason they seem to float like the peaks of mountains. Here is an immaculate universe swept clean* [see 1-3].[52]

While he may have drawn inspiration from the temple's celebrated stone garden, there is little at Chase that in any way resembles its putative prototype. For one thing, the Chase garden is viewed more often from the plaza above than from eye level within the banking hall below [6-32]. Ryôan-ji is permeated by a still and contemplative air, whereas the circular Chase court is active, dynamic, and devoid of visual rest. Clients circumambulate the glass walls of the court to enter the banking hall; hundreds, possibly thousands, of passersby traverse the plaza every day. Unlike the gravel surface of the celebrated stone garden in Kyoto, the ground plane of the fountain court is fully paved and contoured as an undulating landscape of low hills and shallow depressions enlivened by bubbling sprays. Not least, and most dramatically, these are not rocks solidly grounded, but in heretical opposition to traditional practice some have been lifted above the granite ground. When conditions are at their best the rocks seem to hover or float in the air. "Some [rocks] will seem to soar, others remain close to the earth"; the total effect will be that of a "moonscape."[53] Noguchi explains,

> *In viewing this garden one has the sense of being transported into a vast void, into another dimension of reality—time ceases, and one is lost in reverie, gazing at the rocks that rise, ever in the same but different spot, out of the white mist of gravel.*[54]

During the course of design Noguchi considered adding plants and trees, and at one point the architects proposed the addition of carp or goldfish to swim in its pools. All of these were dismissed as unnecessary and requiring too much care.[55]

This is in no way a true garden design in the Japanese tradition, as any forms or materials suggesting some historical antecedent have been filtered through a mesh of Western modernity. Even in their number, the rocks conflict with the traditional Japanese preference for odd numbers. The fifteen stones at Ryôan-ji are arranged in groups of three, five, and seven; in New York, eight large stones prevail.

In search of stones Noguchi returned to Japan in September 1960 and spent two months there aided by Tôemon Sanô, with whom he had worked on the UNESCO garden, and who would serve as Noguchi's purchasing agent for the Chase project. Even before the bank granted him permission to do so, Noguchi had begun his search for appropriate stones: first along the Kamogawa river in Kyoto, then in Uji south of the city, and finally in Ujigawa near Ôtsu.[56] His success was limited. Chase took so long to approve his design that by the time their consent was finally received on 9 October 1961, the one rock Noguchi prized most highly had already been sold.[57] Presumably

6-28
Sunken Garden.
1 Chase Plaza, New York, 1964.
The court-garden viewed from above; the banking hall is located on the lower floor.
[Arthur Lavine, © The Noguchi Museum/ARS]

6-29
Sunken Garden.
1 Chase Plaza.
Contrasts of rises and depressions, and seasonally, wet and dry.

with Sanô's aid, he was able to track down the wayward stone and manage to convince its owner to sell it to him for installation in New York.[58] Without question, the stones are the most prominent elements of the composition but, as at the Beinecke, the ground is of no less significance.[59] By using small granite setts Noguchi evoked the raked-gravel patterns of the historical dry garden and the seas rendered in Chinese painting.[60] The patterns of the paving stones and their joints unify the composition with a network of lines that function as if the structure of a board game [6-33].

The presence of water, the third element of the garden, is only seasonal, yet it is the critical ingredient for conjuring the impression that rocks can rise in the air. Groups of jets gush vertically from below some rocks and from two of the rocks themselves. The water then collects in the depressions, gives dimension to the ground, and distinguishes durable from volatile. In winter the garden is left dry to avoid damage from freezing to the stones and piping.[61] At that time, when the garden is drained of the drama that the water creates, the sculptural aspects of the stones and the ground plane read more strongly. Thus, in its own way, the Chase courtyard reflects the passing of the seasons although without the use of vegetation as its gauge.

Despite the sizable gulf that separates inspiration from final form, Noguchi's reference to Ryôan-ji, along with the traditional Japanese regard for stone, cannot be dismissed out of hand. Compiled by Tachibana Toshitsuna in the mid- to late-eleventh century, the *Sakuteiki* is regarded as one of the world's earliest garden manuals and provides a considerable number of directives for the selection and placement of stones. "Compare the various qualities of the stones," Toshitsuna instructs his reader, "and, keeping the overall garden plan in mind, pull the stones into place one by one."[62] At first the garden at Chase seems to have closely followed this precept. However, the *Sakuteiki* also tells us that "stones must be set powerfully, which means that the 'roots' of the stone must be set deeply."[63] Turning this dictum on its head, Noguchi made no effort to deeply root the rocks in Manhattan's soil. Quite the opposite, in fact. While perhaps not as great in dimension, or as psychologically disturbing as the great boulder afloat in René Magritte's *The Castle of the Pyrenees* (1959), the stones hovering above the water at Chase provoke a similar sense of delicious unease [6-34].

6-30 *[above left]*
Study for a plaza sculpture.
1 Chase Plaza, New York,
ca. 1960.
[Kevin Noble, © The Noguchi Museum / ARS]

6-31 *[below left]*
Jean Dubuffet.
Group of Four Trees, 1972.
1 Chase Plaza, New York.

6-32
Sunken Garden.
1 Chase Plaza, New York, 1964.
A landscape animated by water,
seen from the banking hall.

6-33
Sunken Garden.
1 Chase Plaza, New York, 1964.
A terrain of small granite setts modeled as knolls and lakes in miniature.

6-34
René Magritte.
Castle of the Pyrenees, 1959.
[Wikicommons]

And what of their freely arranged composition, set on a calligraphic bed drawn with mortar and expansion joints? The *Sakuteiki* might have been describing the Chase garden when it states that stones might also be placed as if "those of a rolling meadow [that] are like a pack of dogs at rest, wild pigs running chaotically, or calves frolicking with their mothers."[64] That is to say, although lacking an apparent order, an order governs the Chase garden nonetheless. Noguchi wrote that in the Japanese garden, if done well,

> *One feels that the rocks were not just placed there, that they grew out of the earth (the major portion buried), their weight is connected with the earth—and yet perhaps for this reason they seem to float like the peaks of mountains.*[65]

Within the sunken courtyard of 1 Chase Plaza, however, he applied this principle only metaphorically—and literally made the peaks of mountains float—or at least appear to do so.

>> PAIRED COURTYARDS

The project for the courtyards at the IBM offices in Armonk, New York, again designed by Gordon Bunshaft, broadened Noguchi's consideration of spatial design. For whatever reason, IBM chose to contract with the architects and not with Noguchi directly, while firmly establishing the budget at $100,000—perhaps having heard rumors about the artist's tendency to enlarge the scope and cost of his commissions. Early correspondence suggests Noguchi's creation of a piece identifiable as sculpture, prefiguring a similar client interest at *California Scenario* a decade later.[66]

Rather than the single spaces available in New Haven and New York, the Armonk site offered a pair of courts separated by three floors of corridors that connected the long sides of the building [6-35]. From these glazed "bridges" both courts could be viewed almost simultaneously, which may have contributed to Noguchi's use of time as his theme: "One part of the garden would represent the past, a composition of blasted rock. The other half would be of today, with carvings of the significant symbols of science, inscribed as in Egypt, for future generations to read."[67] In terms of effect, one court was "to provide rest for the soul" for the employees, while the other would "provide 'stimulus for the brain.'"[68]

The past, to Noguchi, had been green. Half the court was planted with lawn, with six large rocks installed either erect or prone. A peninsula of grass extended from one wall and penetrated the sheet of white gravel upon which additional stones were installed; a pine grove on the edge of the lawn greeted pines planted on the lawn. Set at a slight angle to the buildings, the walkway of dark-gray stone that traverses the lawn once again recalls the *hanamichi* entrance path of the traditiona Japanese Noh and Kabuki theaters. Thus, from the choice of their materials and disposition we may deduce that the past was natural, and filled with grasses, trees, and stones that ranged in size from pebbles to boulders [6-36].

If the past was natural, the present and the future were driven by science and mathematics as conveyed through geometry. In its design the present more closely resembles the marble forms of the Beinecke court, while the past called to mind the flat courtyard landscapes at Connecticut General [6-37]. Two shallow domes, one upright, one inverted, expressed the achievements and contributions of science to contemporary life. Incised in the smooth granite surface of the black dome were inscriptions drawn from chemistry, computer circuitry, stellar constellations, and physics, including Albert Einstein's celebrated $E=mc^2$. The inverted dome was treated as a red saucer whose pool could remain still or be activated by jets [6-38]. Complementing the dome and saucer were a stone-faced pyramid and a freestanding sculpture of intertwined bronze tubes intended to evoke the interlocking helix of DNA, "the code of life" [6-39].[69] For privacy, three trees along one wall screened the offices behind them; others were planted with no apparent order. The sculptural presence of these trees is strongest in winter, when their nude branches play off well against the geometry of the sculptural elements and the walls of the building.

By the time Noguchi designed the Armonk courtyards, his approach and repertoire for working in bounded spaces had been established. Once again, the composition appears as an assembly of sculptural and natural elements rather than one that began as a fully integrated whole—unlike the courtyards at Yale, Chase, or even Connecticut General. This was due in part to the loose gravel that precluded the use of joint lines to unite the features within the space. In some ways, then, the paired courts at IBM Armonk return to Noguchi's earlier landscape designs and are less satisfy-

6-35 *[above]*
Mankind's Past Courtyard.
IBM offices, Armonk, New York, 1962.
Glass bridge in the rear of the photo provides views into both gardens.

6-36 *[left]*
Mankind's Past Courtyard.
IBM offices, Armonk.
Two large stones establish a relationship between the two differently surfaced zones of the courtyard.

6-37 *[opposite above]*
Mankind's Future Courtyard
IBM offices, Armonk.
The gravel surface coheres the sparce planting and geometric elements of the composition.

6-38 *[far left]*
Mankind's Future Courtyard.
IBM offices, Armonk.
The stone-faced pyramid with shallow dome beyond.

6-39 *[left]*
Mankind's Future Courtyard.
IBM offices, Armonk.
Freestanding sculpture of patinated tubular forms, intended to express the complexity of DNA.

ing than Chase, Beinecke, or *California Scenario*, which followed decades later. In an honest act of self-judgment, Noguchi agreed that the work was less than perfect. There were too many elements, he concluded, and would have preferred the courts to be free of the trees.

Given the care that all living materials demand, the IBM maintenance staff may have shared his opinion. And yet one wonders whether the grass and other vegetation contribute a needed vehicle for marking time in an otherwise unchanging composition. That thought could also apply to Chase or Beinecke, of course, but in those works the composition had reached a state of perfection that did not require change to maintain interest. When questioned about what in particular he would revise, Noguchi replied: "I would take out the trees first, then get rid of the bronze sculpture and put it on a truncated pyramid in front of the building. It would look nice there" [see 6-39].[70] Despite any misgivings Noguchi might have had, the trees and the sculpture remain in place.

>> THE WESTERN WALL

With the termination of the British Mandate and the founding of the State of Israel in 1948, Jerusalem was divided into eastern and western sectors. The Western, or Wailing, Wall (*ha-kortel* in Hebrew, *al-buraq* in Arabic), the sole surviving fragment of Herod's Temple and the most sacred of all Jewish sites, had lain within the Muslim eastern zone.[71] Israel's dominance in the so-called Six-Day War two decades later resulted in the reunification of Jerusalem and facilitated access to sacred sites within the sector. At that time only a sliver of space merely thirty feet wide separated the Western Wall from the houses of the Muslim residential neighborhood that bordered it.

In June 1967, even before hostilities had ceased, the Israeli authorities called for the demolition of the buildings of the Mughrabee quarter to increase space for those in prayer at the Wall. No design for the site had as yet been determined, however, not to mention compensation for residents displaced by the process.[72] In addition to accommodating the predicted influx of observants, the newly won space would create an urban plaza that reflected the sanctity of the site. After some debate, at times contentious, the area was placed under the authority of the Department of Holy Places, a unit of the Ministry of Religious Affairs, rather than the National Park Authority, as the city's urban planners had wished.[73] Apparently impressed with Noguchi's design for the sculpture garden at the Israel Museum constructed several years earlier, in 1970 the agency offered the artist the commission to design the space now bounded on one side by the Western Wall. For an agnostic and a foreigner this was both a compliment and an honor, especially given the contentiousness that hampered the design process and the development of the site.

Noguchi evidently worked on his design for the Western Wall in the office of landscape architect Shlomo Aronson (1936–2018). Aronson had received his degree in landscape architecture from the University of California, Berkeley, and had worked for several years thereafter in the San Francisco office of landscape architect Lawrence Halprin. In his early adulthood Halprin had lived on an Israeli kibbutz for several years, during which time he had become familiar with the land and its people, and his ties to the country ran deep. Halprin would also become a member of the Jerusalem Committee, formed in 1969 by Mayor Teddy Kollek to advise on the planning and urban design of the unified city.[74] Noguchi and Louis I. Kahn—with whom the sculptor had collaborated on the ill-fated design of the playground for Riverside Drive Park in New York—were also members of the committee.[75]

Noguchi proposed a plaza with two distinct levels joined by a sculpted terrain of stone. Above ground the plaza would reflect and address contemporary conditions and needs, its paved surface serving simultaneously as the roof of a lower level excavated to the stratum of Herodian times. These excavations would also increase the height of the exposed wall by some thirty feet and add to its physical presence and grandeur. The edge of the plaza would be pulled back from the wall along a biomorphic curve to retrieve its original height [6-40]. No vegetation or constructed objects interrupted the flow of paving stones that gently undulated across the contoured surface of the plaza, inflected by the shallow rises derived from the shallow domes that roofed the spaces of the lower level. From above these appear as circular patterns, although on the ground the continuity of the stone surface would efface the identity of any geometric figure. A staircase treated almost as a bridge brought the secular and the religious from the plaza through a gateway to the Temple Mount, which

6-40 *[left]*
Proposal for the Western Wall.
Jerusalem, 1973.
[Model, Israel Pavilion,
Venice Biennale 2018]

6-41 *[below left]*
Office of Shlomo Aronson.
Western Wall.
Section.
["Research for the Design for the
Area of the Western Wall"]

6-42 *[below right]*
Cenotaph.
Peace Park, Hiroshima, ca. 1951.
The wall of names continues
through the lower and upper
levels of the memorial.
[© The Noguchi Museum/ARS]

stood about forty-five feet above it. A far broader and more monumental staircase in the southeast corner of the site linked the plaza with the newly excavated base of the Western Wall.

Joining the plaza and Herodian levels was a black stone wall, or stele, two stories high with battered ends and rounded edges that rose from the understory through the surface of the plaza [6-41]. Noguchi used the wall to define a more intimate zone within the confines of the greater plaza to increase privacy for those at prayer. In its shape and general tone the wall echoed the black basalt wall in the nearby Israel Museum sculpture garden, and, more distantly, the two-story vault Noguchi had proposed in the early 1950s as the central feature of the subterranean cenotaph for the Peace Park in Hiroshima [6-42]. Walls of black stone are easily misread and open to unintended interpretations, and this proved to be the case in Jerusalem.[76] To Noguchi the wall symbolized the ability of the Jewish people to survive the worst of situations over the course of centuries.[77] But to architect Moshe Safdie, who would develop his own designs for the plaza and the neighborhood over the following decade, the black wall was an affront. "[Noguchi] spoke of worship and I thought of his pagan altar. I felt my blood boiling. I wanted to scream out . . . You do not understand the fundamentals of Judaism."[78] For their part, neither Noguchi nor Kahn thought much of Safdie's proposals.

The scheme was documented in "Research for the Design for the Area of the Western Wall," a report Aronson and architect Arthur Kutcher— also a Berkeley grad and alumnus of the Halprin office—prepared for the Ministry of Religion in 1973.[79] In several aerial perspectives Kutcher and Aronson proposed an arrangement of stepped terraces that would support the descent to the level of the Herodian temple—unlike Noguchi's distinctly two-floor solution, which in the report was presented by an aerial view of a study model and a section/elevation presumably drawn by someone in the Aronson office. Neither proposal was accepted, much less adopted and realized. Nonetheless, Safdie continued his studies, rethinking and modifying them in response to the continued criticism. Given that Noguchi's involvement may have been little more than that of a consultant, and that the preliminary model and section/elevation drawing are the only records of his efforts, his engagement was probably short-lived.[80]

>> *TENGOKU*

For *Tengoku*, a permanent transformation of the lobby of the Sôgetsu School of floral arrangement in Tokyo, Noguchi crafted an interior world of water still and flowing, using rough and polished granite as its principal material. The founder of the school, Sôfu Teshigahara (1900–1979), had been a close friend of Noguchi's since the artist's stay in Japan in the early 1950s, and they shared a sensibility that interrogated both modernity and tradition. Teshigahara had founded the school in 1927 based on precepts that differed markedly from other approaches to flower arrangement such as Ikenobu, whose roots extended as far back as the eighth century, and whose practices had become more codified over the centuries. Sôgetsu represented a confrontation with, if not complete rebellion against, convention, accepting a broader range of materials, scales, and acceptable manners of composition. At its most extreme, Teshigahara's own floral art, often gestural in its use of forms and materials, suggests parallels with the paintings of the Abstract Expressionists in the United States and the Art Informel group in France.

Teshigahara admired Noguchi's ideas and art and had purchased several of his ceramic pieces produced during the artist's stay with Rosanjin Kitaôji in 1951. For Japanese artists working in the immediate postwar period, Noguchi suggested a path beyond tradition, although he himself looked as much to Japan's past as to the Western present. That their respect was mutual is confirmed by Noguchi's having invited Teshigahara to create a grand work of *ikebana* for the shallow pool beneath the main stairs of the *Reader's Digest* building to welcome the three hundred prominent guests who attended the building's inauguration in May 1951.[81]

In 1957, with the school's resources having become sufficient, Teshigahara commissioned architect Kenzô Tange—working with Masamitsu Nagashima and Koichiro Okamura—to design a Brutalist building of three floors, constructed of concrete and partially faced with cobalt-blue tiles. Set back from the street, its plaza was enlivened by sculpture and seating by Teshigahara and other artists. Less than two decades later, however, more extensive premises were needed. Commissioning Tange a second time, Sôgetsu now planned an eleven-story office tower on prime real estate in Akasaka, in which the school would occupy only several floors. Its rather anonymous façade confounds the realization that the building is the home of the most radical school of flower arrangement in Japan. A second-floor café and meeting room overlook the two-story lobby; due to the ceiling height required by a lower-level theater, the floor of the lobby would need to be sloped or terraced.

Construction was well underway when graphic designer Yûsaku Kamekura suggested to Teshigahara that Tange's proposed lobby design was not quite right, and that they should invite Noguchi to create a work for the space.[82] Teshigahara agreed and essentially granted Noguchi carte blanche. That Noguchi and Tange had collaborated on the Hiroshima Peace Park in the early 1950s and were amiable acquaintances no doubt helped soften any blow to the architect's pride. When informed of Teshigahara's decision to commission Noguchi to create a work for the lobby space, Tange is said to have replied, "Is that so? I understand," and the matter was settled. To assist Noguchi in his work, Tange assigned the recently hired Jun'ichi Kawamura and generously offered the use of his own office as base.[83]

Noguchi's solution to the problem of the theater below was to treat the floor as a "steep hill," terraced rather than sloped. The various levels would serve "as one enormous and integrated setting for Ikebana," almost as a gigantic reinterpretation of the traditional *tokonoma* of the temple, teahouse, and residence in which flower arrangements are commonly displayed [6-43].[84] Teshigahara accepted the idea, perhaps stemming from his belief that flower arrangement demanded greater aspirations if it were to endure: "Ikebana has to be divorced from the toko no ma. There is no future for ikebana as an accessary to the toko no ma."[85] If the floral master sought a space in which ikebana prevailed, the space of *Tengoku* provided him with the platform. Noguchi's terraces would integrate numerous surfaces and receptacles for flowers rather than disturb their beauty through "the egoism and eccentricity of sculpture." For Noguchi, "the totality became ... a sculpture and not merely sculptures in space."[86] In all, *Tengoku*—"heaven" in Japanese—joined three levels and the ground floor with ranks of stairs and the fall of water that flows from its summit.

Noguchi's design required minor modifications to the building design, principally the position of the skylight that diminished the gloom that would otherwise have resulted. The terraces and the ground floor, and indeed all the subsidiary elements, were shaped from Inada granite, an off-white stone with a remarkably consistent salt-and-pepper texture, from Miyagi Prefecture.[87] From its light tone and texture, Noguchi believed the stone would sparkle, brighten the space, and give it life. At the limits of the terraces that accommodate circulation, display and viewing the rough edges of the slabs lend a sculptural presence to otherwise ordinary construction. Boulders at the end of each terrace replace railings, although just how this was accepted by the Tokyo city building department is not known—presumably only after long negotiations.

Holes were drilled in the slabs to support floral displays, their voids recalling a certain Noguchi clay sculpture with hollows for water once in Teshigahara's possession [6-44; 6-45]. In this play of rough and smooth, geometric and irregular, and solid and void, Noguchi shared his patron's adage: "Be sure to make definite points of emphasis and avoid redundancy in the arrangement."[88] The stairs, which also lack handrails, are generous in width but staggered to connect level to level without drawing undue attention. Benches integrated into the edge of each level invite visitors to linger, contemplate, or rest.

If the staircases support physical movement from terrace to terrace, it is water that joins the levels aesthetically. "Incorporating water into the ikebana," Teshigahara believed, "is part of the Sogetsu style. Water not only nourishes the flowers," like Noguchi's water path, "it also creates an important visual link."[89] The source for *Tengoku* is found in a cylindrical *tsukubai* (water basin) from which water softly overflows [6-46]. From there a small rivulet trickles into a coiled stone basin, reappears in another *tsukubai* on the level below, and terminates at ground level in two shallow pools set askew to one another. Like the visual presence of water that softens the hardness of the stone, the sound of water adds to the calm with which *Tengoku* is infused. In December 1977 the work was inaugurated to general acclaim.[90]

Dore Ashton has suggested an intriguing historical parallel if not direct source for *Tengoku*, in Swedish art historian Osvald Sirén's *History of Early Chinese Art*. Sirén describes the Altar of Heaven in Beijing in this way: "most of the space is planted with trees but there are also a number of buildings for ceremonial purpose ... The circular 'altar' is arranged in three terraces ... all the terraces are covered by white marble and enclosed in sculptured balustrades."[91] Noguchi had visited Beijing for six months in

6-43
Tengoku.
Sôgetsu Kaikan, Tokyo, 1977.
Seen from the entry.

6-44 *[below]*
Tengoku.
The downward flow of the water integrates the levels of the work.

6-45 *[opposite above]*
Three-legged Vase, 1952.
Once owned by Sofû Teshigahara.
[Sogetsu Foundation, © The Noguchi Museum/ARS]

6-46 *[opposite below]*
Tengoku.
From its source water flows through rills and runnels, collects in shallow pools, and falls to the level below.

1930 and studied calligraphy with Qi Baishi. Could his conception of the heaven of *Tengoku* derive from a buried memory of the city's Altar of Heaven, as its title suggests?

Regarded critically, *Tengoku* falls short of perfection, a judgment that can be applied to several Noguchi landscapes where he spent insufficient time on-site to control every aspect of the installation. Taken individually, the shaped slabs along the terrace edges and the water sources are quite handsome, whereas the vertical granite panels that edge each level are more commonplace. The ground level entry feels compressed and crowded, and the reception desk perhaps a bit too massive. Teshigahara's son Hiroshi, the noted filmmaker—and then head of the school—offered an honest appraisal of how *Tengoku* had fared in the two decades since its opening: "Despite Isamu's instructions, during the ensuing 20 years and more this space has hosted numerous flower exhibitions, though the number that I consider to have been successes is small. From this I have learned the valuable lesson that in order to stand up to the severity of such a space, the work on display has to have a robustness of its own."[92]

These shortcomings, like those in most of Noguchi's landscapes, are easily forgiven. Once beyond ground level, visitor focus falls not on the project's deficiencies but on the jagged slabs along the terrace edges, the delicate descent of water, and the enlivening quadrangles of light cast by the skylights upon the floor and walls. The window at the intersection of the walls on the top level opens to the greenery beyond, a most welcome and powerful psychological release. Returning the view inward, the staged terrain appears as an internal garden of hard materials and water. *Tengoku* may not have reached the level of heaven, but it certainly achieved a level far above purgatory.

>> DOMON KEN MUSEUM OF PHOTOGRAPHY

The courtyard for the museum in Sakata City built to honor the memory and work of photographer Ken Domon (1909–1990) followed in the wake of three of Noguchi's most successful gardens. The building was designed by architect Yoshio Taniguchi, the son of Yoshirô Taniguchi, with whom Noguchi had collaborated on the design of the Shin-Banraisha at Keio University decades before. Responding to my question as to whether the building had resulted from a direct commission or a competition, Taniguchi replied that it had come about "by a misunderstanding."[93] In his sunset years Domon, a major figure in postwar Japanese photography, offered his works and archives to his hometown if the city would build a museum to house the collection. To this gracious offer, the municipality readily agreed. When asked if he had a particular architect in mind, he apparently responded, "Taniguchi."

The building committee traveled to Tokyo and arranged a meeting with Taniguchi, but partway through their meeting it became obvious to the architect that Domon had actually suggested his father, the late Yoshirô Taniguchi. Taniguchi *fils* brought this delicate matter to the attention of the committee, who, after some deliberation—and no doubt consternation—decided that since Yoshio was Yoshirô's son, it would be quite suitable to offer him the commission. In response, the younger Taniguchi designed a sensitive, handsomely composed, and finely detailed building sited on what had been a rice paddy on the northwest edge of the city. The architect conceived the museum as "almost half buried in the ground—a static space that never changes—and half floating on water, changeable [6-47]."[94] Building construction was completed in 1983.

Although in plan the museum fills the figure of a square, the experience of its architecture is more attenuated and complex than the shape would suggest. To structure the sequence of internal spaces, Taniguchi routed circulation around a courtyard, using a series of right-angled turns analogous to movement across a *yatsuhachi*, the eight-part zigzag bridge common to Edo-period stroll gardens. To Noguchi the building recalled "ancient juxtapositions of nature and architecture" [6-48].[95] The pond, easily secured from the high-water table in the marsh beneath the rice paddy, furthers the parallels.

Tending to be skeptical of architect and developer solicitations, Noguchi first demurred when Taniguchi approached him about designing the museum's courtyard. The architect had brought a model of the scheme, however, and Noguchi soon began to reconsider, telling the architect that changes to the building would be needed. Taniguchi agreed. The design that resulted is restrained and masterful, graced with sufficient variety and change to create continued visual interest.

Noguchi's garden comprises a set of shallow terraces that step downward from gallery level to the surface of the pond; upon these stands an erect basalt stone sculpture titled *Mr. Domon*. Over their rough stone terraces flows a continuous sheet of water that appears to empty into the pond—in fact, a small dam collects the spillage, which is then filtered and recycled [6-49]. The confrontation of the two materials reflects the opposition of variation and stasis. As Noguchi saw it: "Stone in nature is the thing which undergoes the least change, and water the most change—because of this contrast they belong together" [6-51].[96] A wall spanning high over the court as it joins the pond frames the view and suggests a gateway not unlike the *torii* of Shinto shrines.

The beauty of the courtyard lies in its motion and affect; though appearing endlessly repetitive, it constantly mutates and is never the same. Variations in wet and dry surfaces result from irregularities in the rough surfaces of the stone and deviations in evaporation rates caused by fluctuations in temperature. Despite its simplicity of idea—or because of it—the effect is hypnotic. In contrast to the animation provided by the subtle current, *Mr. Domon* stands noble and unchanging, a sculpture Noguchi regarded as "a silent witness, a gnomon, a sentinel, a point from which the viewer can seize all the connections of mountain, sky, and water."[97] The lesson learned from the courtyard is that seeming austerity can produce artworks and perceptions of considerable complexity. In all, the courtyard represents Noguchi at his most mature and sophisticated, exploiting the properties inherent to stone—whether left rough or worked—to produce an unpretentious work of intricacy and richness.

As a group Noguchi's bounded gardens, as he called them, share some characteristics and qualities while differing in others. Most have been conceived as elements composed within a frame; the feeling is inwardly focused. Exceptions to this generalization exist, for example, at the Domon Ken Museum of Photography, where the flow of water across the terrace leads the eye outward to the surrounding landscape through the "missing" wall. The bounded gardens at 1 Chase Plaza and the Beinecke Rare Book and Manuscript Library at Yale University also achieve their beauty by being complete and unified works. They are aided to considerable extent by their visually activated ground planes whose scored lines unify their features and forge a bond difficult to achieve in courts with grounds of grass or gravel. Chase and Beinecke rank among Noguchi's best works,

6-47
Yoshiô Taniguchi.
Domon Ken Museum
of Photography.
Sakata, Japan, 1983.
Viewed from across the pond.

6-48
Yatsuhashi bridge.
Korakuen, Okayama,
late seventeenth century.

not only for their harmony but above all for their presence as sculptures in themselves rather than as sculptures on display. As an interior work *Tengoku* warrants a different categorization, like the earlier Shin-Banraisha faculty room at Keio University. Yet in its terracing, watercourses, sculptured platforms, and exterior stone sculpture, with little jump of faith and imagination it, too, could be regarded as a garden. Or so Noguchi would like us to believe. Whether to be entered or only viewed, all these works employ sculptural objects to modulate spaces within their boundary walls and render the space as sculpture. That said, perhaps they are really not gardens as we normally consider them, but "rather, compositions in topological space," as Noguchi once told Dore Ashton.[98]

6-49 *[opposite]*
Water Garden.
Domon Ken Museum
of Photography.
Sakata, 1983.
Noguchi's intervention included the stone surfaces of the court; the flow of water; and the erect stone sculpture, *Mr. Domon*.

6-50 *[left]*
Water Garden.
Domon Ken Museum
of Photography.
The vertical form of *Mr. Domon* plays against the descending terraces over which water flows toward the pond.

6-51 *[above]*
Water Garden
Domon Ken Museum
of Photography.
View from the water garden to the pond.

> 7.

Sculptures for Sculpture: Jerusalem; Houston

Any outdoor space for art—whether court or garden—faces far more variables than the white cube long the norm for modern gallery design.[1] Outdoors, change occurs hourly, daily, annually, and over time.[2] The first three of these trajectories are somewhat cyclical, the fourth is linear. Fluctuations in the intensity, direction, and quality of light follow the diurnal cycle of day and night. Seasons affect the advance or retreat of vegetation that may subtly or radically influence the point of display. Over the years other dimensions also enter the mix: the growth of the vegetation, the aging of the sculpture, perhaps even the increase or decline in the number of viewers. Designing a sculpture garden can be a complex task.

>> JERUSALEM

In creating the sculpture garden for the Israel Museum in Jerusalem, Noguchi faced his greatest topographic challenge, a challenge that resulted in his most consequential reshaping of terrain [7-1]. The project also tested his patience and resolve when dealing with its patron, Billy Rose, who battled the artist over virtually every form and surface. Recalling the process years later, Shula Eisner of the American Friends of the Israel Museum noted the discord that troubled the project's realization, disputes that "often turned into full-fledged battles." Antagonism came from both sides: "Each morning Noguchi resigned, each afternoon Billy Rose fired him."[3] This was hardly a marriage made in heaven, but somehow both parties stuck with it until the garden's opening on 11 May 1965. Rose died of pneumonia the following year, but Noguchi continued to consult on the maintenance and modifications to the garden over the ensuing decade as the number of museum buildings increased. While the favorable display of sculpture was the ultimate goal, mastery of the hillside topography was the immediate and primary objective. Models provided the principal vehicle for studying and communicating the design, supported by drawings, photographs, and on-site discussions as construction progressed.

The UNESCO garden, completed several years prior to the Israel Museum commission, inserted a habitable relief into a flat urban site. In stark contrast, Noguchi's first task in Jerusalem was to create quietly undulating land on which to display sculpture and leisurely promenade, and from which to gaze across the Valley of the Cross. To reshape the rocky hill-

7-0
Billy Rose Art Garden.
Israel Museum, Jerusalem, 1965.
Walls and courtyards create
settings condusive for the display
of smaller sculpture.

7-1
Billy Rose Art Garden.
Israel Museum, Jerusalem, 1965.
Selected walls of the courtyard
are faced with the same stone
as the walls of the museum.

side into suitable terrain required significant earth movement. To address these issues Noguchi relied on both his artistic abilities and his intuitive understanding of engineering.

>> *FOUNDING A MUSEUM FOR ISRAEL*

The founding of the Israel Museum followed the country's achievement of independence from the British Mandate in 1948 and the successful waging of war with the surrounding Arab nations immediately thereafter. The museum, to be filled with Judaic antiquities as well as contemporary art, was envisioned as a repository and showcase presenting the past and the present as a foundation for the future. It was conceived as early as 1953 as an amalgamation of the Bezalel Museum and a new art museum, for which a collection would be needed.

Two sites were proposed: the first on the campus of Hebrew University; the second, and ultimately the site selected, stood on the Neva Sha'anan, the Hill of Tranquility, at a remove from the core of the old city. The site was spectacular in terms of views, but its steep slopes, rocky substrate, and meager topsoil were far from ideal. An early proposal by artist Leopold Krakauer suggested what might be the look of a new national museum, although in the end an architectural competition was held, and won by Alfred Mansfeld (1912–2004) and Dora Gad (1912–2003).[4] Born in St. Petersburg, Russia, Mansfeld emigrated to Berlin with his family while still a child. He began his studies at the Berlin Institute of Technology but in 1933, amid the rise of National Socialism, he moved to Paris, where he completed his architectural training at the École Spéciale d'Architecture two years later. That same year he emigrated to Palestine. Dora Gad was also born in Russia but studied architecture at the Technical University in Vienna. Like Mansfeld, she emigrated to Israel shortly after completing her studies in 1936. Unlike Mansfeld, Gad focused her design practice on interiors. In 1959 they won the competition for the new museum and collaboratively produced a concept that featured the integration of landscape, architecture, and interior design.

The existence of the Israel Museum largely depended on funding and artworks donated by the American Jewish community. As a result, there was some ambiguity as to who exactly was to be Noguchi's client. Was it the America-Israel Cultural Foundation (AICF) or Billy Rose, the garden's sponsor? Perhaps any official designation would hardly have mattered, as the arrogant Rose was someone who always got his way—or at least, always wanted to. Keep in mind that during the time of the garden's making, between 1960 and 1965, fax, email, and the internet did not yet exist; even commercial jet travel on the Boeing 707 had begun only around the start of the project. Meetings with clients, site inspections, and construction supervision were difficult to arrange, and many things—both good and bad—could transpire between visits to the construction site, which were spaced several months apart, often when Noguchi was en route to or from Japan.

>> *BILLY AND ISAMU*

Billy Rose (1899–1966) was a Jewish-American theatrical producer known for the musical and burlesque productions from which he had amassed the sizable wealth that supported his art collecting. When a house fire in 1956 destroyed most of his paintings and drawings, Rose shifted his interests to sculpture. Despite the sometimes-questionable tastes represented by his theatrical extravaganzas, he had developed an interest in nineteenth- and twentieth-century sculpture and had acquired a substantial number of significant works that he intended to donate to the Israel Museum, then under design. How he came to select Noguchi is not known. It may have come about through New York's art/theatrical circles or possibly through the artist's collaborations with Martha Graham. Just *why* he would select an artist to design a garden is open to question, since artists are notorious for being difficult to work with.

No evidence suggests that Rose knew of the UNESCO garden at the time he offered Noguchi the commission, but he no doubt learned of it thereafter; perhaps he had encountered the proposals for Noguchi's conceptual playgrounds. Noguchi initially declined Rose's request to design the garden but Rose repeated his offer, seemingly moved by the fact that Noguchi "had voluntarily incarcerated [him]self with the other Japanese Americans from the West Coast in the War Relocation Camps."[5] Noguchi was intrigued by the comment and later explained that "those who object to segregation often feel that Israel was itself a protest and a haven against it."[6] He ultimately accepted the commission, embarking on the design with an optimism that would dissipate during the course of the garden's design and construction. As Hayden Herrara explains, "In Billy Rose Noguchi met his match in ambition, egotism, and willfulness. Short and plump but with a wonderful, animated face, Rose was passionate, ebullient, and quick-witted." Though their interactions were often confrontational, "they respected each other's intelligence and strength" and somehow managed to persevere in their goal to create a remarkable work.[7] In January 1960 they traveled to Jerusalem together to meet the museum representatives and the architect, and so that Noguchi could make a careful survey of the hillside that would be the site.[8] Although Rose was the donor and person to whom Noguchi was responsible, the commission actually came about through the Israel-American Museum Foundation or the Israel Cultural Foundation. Leading players included Elaine G. Rosenfeld, museum project coordinator; Yonatan Beham, director of the Israeli Tourism Office and member of the museum committee; and Teddy Kollek, mayor of Jerusalem. These groups were responsible for raising money to construct the museum, while Rose was committed to funding the garden.

In June 1960 Noguchi was presented with a brief specifying the character of a garden, planned to comprise roughly five acres: "When completed [it] will, insofar as feasible, achieve the feeling and effect of a parklike oasis in an arid land."[9] The physical comfort of museum visitors was a concern, as was the requirement that "the sculptures effectively will be given due regard." The brief further specified that Noguchi's contribution would be divided into a "creative period" and a "supervisory period."[10] The breakdown of phases and payments followed, with an agreement that first-class air travel would be provided the artist. The brief, essentially a letter contract, established a maximum figure of $25,000 for Noguchi's fee. As in many of his projects, the fee would become a point of contention after Noguchi surpassed the directives of the contract and thereafter sought remuneration for his additional work. Lastly, it was stipulated that Noguchi would "submit all design information to the Architect [Alfred Mansfeld] in clear, concise and comprehensive form and context so that the Architect can incorporate your design information in his final architectural plans or blueprints." The creation—and approval—of the work would "rest with the sculptor," the buildings and site planning with the architect. The architect was allowed a final say on "aesthetic and practical considerations," even those that might be at variance to those of the artist.[11] In actuality, Noguchi's relationship and collaboration with Mansfeld were smooth; his problems usually resided with Billy Rose. A proposed time frame concluded the document.

As revealed in his notes written while reading the prospectus, Noguchi maintained some level of uncertainty as to the conditions it stipulated. He questioned the fee for supervision, the amount of the per diem, and the number of trips necessary to ensure the proper execution of his design. He questioned the upset figure—wisely, as it turns out—and would accept that amount only if no additional work would be required. He also questioned what was meant by "comfortable," especially considering the rugged conditions of the site's surfaces and contours, and his goal "to make something new which may not fit preconceived notions [of a park]." He questioned the very idea of "comfort and physical well being," asserting that "beauty should not be limited by such matters." Not that he was against providing comfort, of course, only that it would not be his primary concern. Most of all, he wondered, "If my setting does not turn out to be more important than the sculpture, why hire me?"[12] Why, indeed.

Given that he had not yet seen the site nor met the various parties involved, Noguchi's reactions were all based on anticipation of what might happen, in all likelihood informed by lessons learned from prior landscape projects. Recall that Noguchi's playground designs were self-instigated, with their program and concept determined solely by the artist. The UNESCO garden did have a client and a program, but specifics were few and only implicitly stated, leaving Noguchi enormous latitude for self-expression. But designing a garden whose purpose was to maximize the aesthetic effect of works by other artists was a task of far greater complexity, both physically and morally. Despite his hesitancy or misgivings, there was the lure of Israel. Something about Israel drew him to the project, and in comments written at the time of the garden's inauguration he expressed a feeling of connection with the country, its people, and its land.

I have not located any documents that discuss the evolution of Noguchi's ideas and their presentation and ultimate acceptance by Rose and the museum committee. It appears that when first presented they were favorably received by all parties. In 1960, at the start of the commission, Israel as an independent state was hardly more than a decade old, and threats to its existence persisted along its border. The museum site lay within the range of hostile artillery fire, and therefore building the museum was not an enterprise without risks, although those risks were shared by the other major government institutions that faced the museum across the valley.

Commissioning an artist to provide the setting for the work of other artists was also risky business, inherently an act of faith as well as one of questionable sanity. How could the garden's design enhance the presence of sculpture? To what degree would the garden's forms confront or even overwhelm the individual pieces? How could Noguchi reconcile his sculpture garden as a work of art, as a personal expression, with the objective of providing a suitably benign or enhancing setting for experiencing the sculptures on view? The garden design would need to balance the functional requirements for display and walking with a significant work of terrestrial sculpture: a task neither easy nor enviable.

>> *ARCHITECTURE*

Massive amounts of financial support for the museum's founding had been raised beyond Israel's borders.[13] Donations of art and artifacts came from abroad as well as from Israeli artists and findings from the new nation's archaeological sites. Willem Sandberg, former director of the Stedelijk Museum in Amsterdam, would serve as the museum's founding director. Versed in modern and contemporary art, he was well equipped to develop a collection of international significance to be housed in a building modern and functional, yet respectful of its physical context and cultural matrix.

Mansfeld's design for the building employed the modular structuralism that pervaded architectural design in the late 1950s and early 1960s. The latter was premised on the belief that architecture, like life-forms, should be flexible and adaptable to needs that change over time [7-2]. Similar to trees or fields or flowers, buildings should appear complete at each stage of their lives, from construction through years of use and occupation, and even in decline. The incremental addition of the three *shoin* pavilions of the seventeenth-century Katsura Imperial Villa in Kyoto exemplify this idea. A reformalization of this concept adapted to contemporary urban conditions emerged in 1960 with the launch of the Metabolist group at the World Design Conference in Tokyo. In their work, architects Arata Isozaki, Kiyonori Kikutake, Kisho Kurokawa, and Fumihiko Maki employed repetitive units amalgamated into buildings whose structure and services were distinguished from the living units they supported.[14]

Although the work of the Metabolists was widely published, whether Mansfeld and Gad knew of their projects is not known. Their use of

7-2
Alfred Mansfeld and Dora Gad.
Israel Museum, Jerusalem, 1965.
Noguchi's curved walls were cut into the contours of the architectural site model.
[Courtesy Alfred Mansfeld]

7-3
Frederick Kiesler and Armand Bartos.
Shrine of the Book.
Israel Museum, Jerusalem, 1965.

staged modular pavilions for the museum suggests an affinity with international architectural currents, however. By the time of the museum competition, Aldo van Eyck's orphanage in Amsterdam, completed in 1960, had also received broad coverage in the architectural press. Units square in plan, each roofed with a vault, were set individually or conjoined into larger spaces, with circulation used to join the modules. The composition of these modules was informal, suggesting incremental growth and addition, with their arrangement addressing functional and environmental factors; some units defined exterior courtyards while other, larger spaces accommodated group activities. The entirety was carefully scaled to the measure of the child. In their competition site plan, Mansfeld and Gad determined the locations of any future pavilions that could be constructed individually or as a group. To a significant degree if not precisely, further additions have followed this original directive.

Also occupying the site was the Shrine of the Book, an independent pavilion designed by Frederick Kiesler and Armand Bartos to house the Dead Sea Scrolls [7-3]. Quite unlike the cubic volumes of the museum, the Shrine was circular in plan and capped by a roof with a curving profile that one journalist described as resembling a giant Hershey's chocolate kiss. An additional challenge Noguchi faced was to configure the sculpture garden as a fitting transition to the Shrine as well as the main museum buildings.[15] The garden would stand in relation to, and yet oppose, the geometries of both buildings, an antidote as well as antagonist to the architecture.

>> *THE ART GARDEN*

From its inception, the Noguchi landscape was referred to as a garden, as he preferred, although the qualifier before it varied. To some people in Israel "sculpture garden" suggested the display of works considered "graven images," which for the Orthodox community was seen as a violation of the Second Commandment. Rather than on biblical grounds, Mansfeld interpreted their rancor as artificial "'indignation' built up for political reasons."[16] Rose brushed off the protests, noting that "gentlemen of political persuasion like nothing better than to hide behind a chapter of the Bible, let alone one of the commandments."[17] Over time the protest subsided, and the project proceeded. The official title of the project became the Billy Rose Art Garden, a name that fulfilled the dual purpose of thwarting arguments against the figurative works in the collection—although the majority of them were abstract—as well as suggesting that the garden should itself be considered a work of art.

Noguchi stated on more than one occasion that he regarded "the whole hill as a sort of new Acropolis," to which he wished to "raise a song of praise."[18] The medium would be the earth itself. Noguchi's first task was to create surfaces sufficiently level to facilitate walking and the display of sculpture. To do so he proposed five massive walls of local stone to retain the soil as a dam retains water [7-4]. "My walls are not the demarcation of property," he explained. "They rise from the earth and return to it, permitting the flow of topography around them."[19] From within the garden, the walls appear as concave curves that bulge toward the greater landscape. Rather than in sketches,

> *Working together and alone, I devised a model showing five curved retaining walls some thirty feet high and over one hundred feet long . . . By curving them both in plan and elevation, and by placing them at different levels, I hope to create an undulating and walkable landscape, something memorable born out of the adversity of the terrain* [7-5].[20]

When I visited Al Mansfeld in his office in Haifa in 1993, he pointed out that structurally the walls curved in the wrong direction, that they should have been oriented toward the hillside for maximum resistance against the overturning forces exerted by the earth. It was the mass and the number of the large stones, reinforced by concrete foundations if needed, that rendered the walls structurally sound.[21] The stones were laid without mortar, so provisions for drainage were not needed. At its center each wall rose to roughly two feet above the surface of the terrace to preclude the need for railings, and diminished to only six inches at each of its ends.[22] Arriving at the correct contour of the walls proved to be a difficult task, exacerbated by changes in road elevation and the floor levels of the museum. Coordinating these levels itself proved a challenge. Mansfeld did his best to solve these problems, although his solutions did not always meet with Noguchi's approval.[23] The artist maintained reservations regarding the profile of the walls and the quality of their stonework; nevertheless, Billy Rose was delighted by the photos of the walls sent to him. To the contractor Rose wrote: "The retaining walls you have built, judging by the photographs, look as if

7-4 *[opposite above]*
Isamu Noguchi working on architectural model of the Israel Museum, ca. 1962.
[Courtesy Alfred Mansfeld]

they were carved out of the Bible with Moses himself collecting and setting the stones" [7-6].[24] High praise indeed, especially when describing a site in the Holy Land.

Accommodating people and sculpture on-site demanded substantial earth movement, originally estimated at some thirty thousand cubic meters of soil. Fortunately, that total was almost halved by using soil and materials excavated for the foundations of the museum buildings. The freer forms of the terraces also served as formal foils for the orthogonal modules of the museum's architecture. As the bases for sculpture displayed on these sculpted terraces, Noguchi positioned several square or rectangular slabs and a platform of sufficient area to display several small sculptures to their best advantage [7-7].

Rose, and perhaps Sandberg and other parties as well, expressed some concern that the smaller works might be lost in the sea of space on the open terraces. After extensive discussions, Noguchi acquiesced and created a zone defined by curved and straight walls that define a series of more intimate spaces in which to display works more closely matching the size of the human body. This area also supported the transition from the architectural zone of the museum to the open spatial flow of the landscape. After the opening of the garden Noguchi admitted that this addition to the original brief was a correct decision. "That it has turned out well may prove that Billy Rose was right or that I am an architect. I wonder? It may at least prove," he continued, "that the way it blends into the hill proves me a better sculptor than most architects."[25]

Due to the undulating surface of the garden as designed, using asphalt or concrete as paving proved impractical. A mix of gravel was determined as the best option, although the material ultimately turned out to be problematic [7-8]. For one thing, its white color was too brilliant and caused considerable glare. In addition, its instability was uncomfortable to walk on and even contributed to several accidents. After several trials, however, a reasonable balance of gravel and stabilizers was attained.

By 1962 construction was well underway when issues arose concerning the size and placement of the stones in the retaining walls and the elevations of several display surfaces. The nature of Noguchi's design made it difficult to specify precise heights in the drawings. What drawings

7-5
Billy Rose Art Garden.
The arcs of the retaining walls, built of stone found on site, seen from downhill.

7-6 *[right]*
Billy Rose Art Garden.
Israel Museum, Jerusalem, 1965.
The curve of the stone retaining wall seen obliquely.

7-7 *[below left]*
Billy Rose Art Garden.
Rectangular sculpture terraces adjacent to the museum.

7-8 *[below right]*
Billy Rose Art Garden.
Paved and gravel surfaces; sculpture terraces with the museum buildings behind.
[Steven Koch, 2022]

were provided by the artist, and their exact types, is not known; presumably many of the details and grades were determined in situ. Noguchi spent several days in Jerusalem in August 1966 inspecting the walls, the grading, and the quality of the stonework. Three of the walls were finished or projected to be completed within a few weeks. Still unresolved was the land at the meeting point between the sculpture garden and the Shrine of the Book.[26]

Noguchi was sensitive to the disturbance of those parts of the hillside caused by grading and construction, and called for their restoration to as great a degree as feasible. While his garden would hardly qualify as the "parklike" setting specified in the original brief, he used trees and shrubs to soften the starkness of the walls and the paved surfaces. Evidently, vegetation never appeared on any of the models, yet greenery remained an aspect of the artist's design, to be planted only after the garden's major features had been constructed. A November 1962 memo called for planting 100 pines and 100 olives, although just where they would be planted was not noted.[27] In time their total number was reduced to 160, although of what species is also unknown.[28] Supplying a sufficient volume of soil for the trees required pits to be dug into the stony hillside, thereafter filled with fertile topsoil. Vegetation was never a primary motivating factor in Noguchi's landscapes, even for the creation of spaces. Indeed, at UNESCO the trees and shrubs appear almost as an afterthought, installed seemingly without any clear intention. Their role in Jerusalem was again subsidiary.

Horticulturalist Abraham Karavan had been recommended to Noguchi as a consultant and was ultimately responsible for selecting and installing the plants.[29] While well regarded, Karavan was slow to act, which frustrated Noguchi's efforts to keep the project moving and completed to his satisfaction. Not one to leave the technical side of things to others, Noguchi took an active role in the placement of irrigation piping, the positioning of sprinkler heads, electrical services and outlets, and lighting for nighttime visits. A drawing submitted in March 1963 specified those areas to be "returned to nature," an action that would require additional rocks and topsoil.[30] He then turned his attention to the fountain atop the mound and the watercourse that issued from it.[31]

Noguchi returned to Jerusalem in February 1963 and found that most of the work met with his approval. He instructed the contractor to begin construction of the large mound near the entrance and the basalt pyramid, among the few geometric forms in the garden. A final curved wall remained to be positioned and its precise shape determined.[32] Yonatan Beham, director of the Israeli Tourism Office and a member of the museum committee, wrote to Rose acknowledging Noguchi's presence and that "he is working very hard, very satisfied with the progress accomplished so far and quite sure that the garden will be the showpiece of the hill." He closed by saying that "all Israel is waiting to see what can be done with a barren hilltop."[33] They would have to wait.

During the last weeks in July a bellicose meeting took place on-site, with all the garden project's dramatis personae participating in the almost theatrical production. At Mansfeld's request, Noguchi had arrived the day before and, although generally satisfied with the progress of the work, agreed with the architect that the quality of construction of certain walls was unacceptable. Noguchi was forced to admit, however, that any of his dissatisfaction with the profile of the central mound was his own fault, as the contractor had accurately executed the design as drawn. "Finally, it came to a showdown about the rough area," those transitional zones at the periphery of the garden. "At this point," wrote Beham in a letter describing the meeting, "Noguchi stood up like a man and said that this was the way he wanted it. If Billy didn't like it, he, Noguchi was willing to resign." And that was not the end of his outburst: "With tears in his eyes and in quite a huff he walked away."[34] End Act I. Act II began with Rose's soliloquy declaiming that "he wouldn't have gotten his fat *** out of a comfortable chair on East 93rd Street if all he was expected to do was to build a rock garden for Jerusalem which is full of rocks anyway." No, the problem was that Noguchi was basically "anti sculpture, (except for Noguchi's sculptures)," while he, Rose, was "trying very hard to create a beautiful garden in which no sculptures would interfere with the harmony." In addition, it was evident that the second phase of construction had not been completed, as Rose had been led to believe.

Beham responded, "at the top of [his] voice"—thus initiating Act III—"that he [Rose] was all wet," that the specified work had been completed, and that the funding had not been exhausted because some money had been held for contingencies. By the end of the meeting, he wrote with no apparent irony, "everybody, and I mean everybody, was completely fed up."[35] The following day it was the contractor, Hillel Fefferman's, turn onstage, thus opening Act IV. "Meanwhile, out at the ranch," Beham reported with a touch of American humor, "Hillel had told Noguchi in no uncertain terms that he was a weakling, a cheat, and a liar because everything had been completed during his last visit and only after he had countermanded some of his instructions, were things changed again." To prove his point, the contractor took Rose and Noguchi to the last completed retaining wall "and convinced both that they were all wet and finally proved that Billy owed him $19,000 and not $9,000." The plot continued to thicken. "Billy will never admit that he is wrong," continued Beham. "He did not this time either but became Sweetness and Charm Inc." Apparently, it was ultimately the contractor who emerged the victor, while Noguchi and Rose agreed to disagree about how the garden should be completed. Noguchi aspired to the ideal of a true sculptural work derived from the harsh environmental conditions on the site, whereas Rose sought a "manicured park which might be right for the backyard on East 93rd Street but not for Jerusalem."[36] In a true theatrical denouement all parties shared a dinner the following night—although there was no agreement on how to proceed or when.

Several weeks later Noguchi sent Fefferman a new drawing for the mound, with no hint of any residual animosity from their heated encounter in Jerusalem. "With caution and ingenuity and thought and taste on the part of those who actually lay the rocks," the sculptor wrote, "as well as on the part of he who supervises it—it should succeed."[37] And it did. But the overall question of how to continue was left unresolved. It seems obvious that Noguchi did not want to deal with Rose if there was any possible way he could avoid it. He had spoken with Elaine Rosenfeld, who wrote to Beham that Noguchi wanted clarification on just for whom he was working: Was it the museum or Billy Rose? "Isamu," wrote Rosenfeld, "also indicated that if he works for the Museum, and if Billy is out of the project altogether, he will charge one half of his usual cost; but if Billy reimburses the Museum, he must charge the regular rate."[38] In addition, one last trip would probably suffice to resolve all the details—as it turned out it was not, as Noguchi returned to Jerusalem again in early December, using the opportunity to supervise the grading of another area of the garden.

No doubt aware of lingering hurt or doubts on the part of his patron, after visiting Rose in New York in March, Teddy Kollek sent him a placating letter. He expressed his appreciation for the impresario's continued support for the garden and stressed that although he may not say it often enough, Rose should be "aware of the limitless measure of [his] unspoken though deeply felt gratitude." In the following paragraph he added: "Billy, you have been wonderful, utterly selfless and dedicated," a sentiment that Noguchi and Fefferman may not have shared. Still, it poured some oil on those troubled waters and may have had a positive effect.[39] Despite any remaining animosity, work on the garden continued, and in April Noguchi was once again in Jerusalem. After his visit he issued a memo listing the tasks still awaiting completion, which included two areas requiring additional topsoil, missing water and electrical services, and curbs along the edges of the asphalt paved areas. He specified that "at least 12 Olive trees and about 10 Cedars" should be planted, understanding that planting the trees would require some excavation, perhaps even blasting. Other problems involved the motor, the water-circulation test and electricity for the fountain, and the ever-present need to stabilize the gravel; the latter could possibly be achieved by having gravel "rolled into place and stabilized with stone dust prior to final gravel finish."[40] Letters from the AICF discussed the loan of Rose's works—prior to eventual donation—and proposed the opening day for the museum and the garden.

In mid-May a memo from Noguchi—no recipient is indicated but perhaps Hillel Fefferman—revised the list of the remaining work. It included the pruning of the olive trees to ensure their survival. Like the gravel surfaces, the topsoil required stabilization to prevent its being washed away by the first rains; carefully placing rocks in "key places" might solve this problem. Noguchi called for planting ground cover, noting that "the advice of a man such as Mr. Karavan in Tel Aviv would be most useful." The issue of the gravel, however, continually nagged at all the parties, and in the memo Noguchi suggested that limestone powder might be an effective stabilizing agent; but in order to be effective, the top layer of gravel should be scraped and reinstalled thereafter. Drainage pipes might prevent unwanted erosion.[41] Lists such as this one reveal the depth of the sculptor's involvement with the technical aspects of the undertaking, an understanding that should functional issues be left unresolved, the aesthetic concept would be undermined, or worse.

Noguchi returned to the construction site in June and found that although "we now have the appearance of a garden ... much of the work *is unsound* and must be done over." Nevertheless, he believed that Fefferman should be paid for his work up to that point. He closed by saying, perhaps with a sigh: "Ah well, live and learn—I couldn't retire from the battle—I'm glad it's over for me. To try not to think of it any longer but to give you all fair warning of what to expect."[42] Of course, he could not help but think about it and had tendered a request for an additional $10,000 above his upset fee. Nor had Fefferman been paid for additional work beyond that listed in the contract. Discussions continued for months. A letter to Teddy Kollek from the AICF, possibly from Elaine Rosenfeld (the second page with a signature is missing), admits that "I for myself tend to lean towards the artist and not towards the rude and rich donor, although I have been informed that Noguchi is not the easiest to deal with when it comes to money."[43] Was that because he always expanded his scope of operations, whether it was approved or not, and then wanted payment for the additional work?

Although the museum and garden had opened in spring 1965, Abraham Karavan continued his deliberations on plant selection throughout the summer, postponing any final decision until the temperatures had cooled sufficiently to allow planting—which would be in September.[44] The trees already planted had not done well; of the seventy olives that had been planted nine had already died, while "20 more have not taken root properly."[45] However, with proper care the majority of them could still be saved, and every effort was being made to ensure their survival.[46] In August Noguchi conceived some broad ideas regarding transitions and effects, and offered detailed thoughts on possible solutions for the gravel areas, which remained problematic. He stressed that on a natural hillside, large stones reduce erosion and provide a foothold for the plants that subsequently take root. Meeting this functional demand should be an effective means of merging the garden with the greater landscape.[47]

Karavan's deliberations over the planting dragged on. Once again, Rose bristled and wrote that if the projected vegetation could not be installed by spring 1966, "then at least have a good quality grass to cover all the earth spots."[48] Although Daniel Gelmond, museum administrator, supported the choice of Karavan as their consultant, he too was troubled by the slow pace at which the landscape architect was working. In Gelmond's view, he had designed some beautiful gardens in Tel Aviv, "but ... he is very slow and I personally do not like it. I also think he is angry at me because of my constant phoning and frequent requests for a result of his planning. Apparently, he does not like when somebody 'keeps on his back.'"[49]

The survival of plants, the proper handling of stone and vegetation in the transition areas, and safety continued to test the Noguchi design. Several visitors had already tripped on the gravel surfaces; one had even broken her leg stepping down from one of the display platforms.[50] Single-step situations are often prohibited by many building codes, as distinguishing one edge from another can be difficult; these accidents proved the validity of that proscription. Noguchi's suggestion that discreet signs warning visitors to enter at their own risk was hardly a viable or empathetic solution.[51] Beham had a different proposal—to install railings—and cautioned Noguchi that "we must very seriously consider the possibility of substituting a more suitable surface for the gravel which is bad for ladies' heels and everybody's eyes because the glare is really overwhelming."[52] Of course, to Noguchi this proposal was not acceptable.

>> *FORM*

In designing the Billy Rose Art Garden, Noguchi faced more complex and very different challenges from those he had faced in Paris, New York, and New Haven. This was not a constricted urban site but rugged hilltop terrain ruled by severe topographic and environmental factors such as slope, substrate, aridity, and inhospitable soil. The solution lay in reforming the slope as a set of interlinked terraces, some cut into the terrain, others formed by backfilling the massive walls of stone with new soil. The terraces were not completely level but slightly inclined, so that visitors would most often view a sculpture against the sky [7-9]. This was an insightful and prescient solution, as in the decades that have followed the original construction the land around the museum has been highly built up, creating a backdrop that could most kindly be described as "distracting." The tops of the walls were sloping, reaching a high point at their middle and tapering down nearly to ground level at their ends. Seen from above, the gravel ground plane prevails; from below, the walls appear as powerful sculptures in themselves. In the early years, the dearth of sizable vegetation and major sculptures made the terraces feel overscaled, no doubt contributing to Rose's initial dissatisfaction with the design. Although this impression has diminished in the succeeding decades, in several areas the garden still appears to isolate the artworks rather than joining them in any sort of dialogue. Of course, this is a curatorial issue as much as, if not more than, one of landscape design.

The composition of terraces and walls adjacent to the buildings represents Noguchi at his most skillful, both in his selection of shapes and in construction. A battered wall of dark basalt—foreign to the local Jerusalem limestone—effects the transition between architecture and garden [7-10]. The "rooms" defined by paired concrete arcs, or walls triangular in elevation, secure a continuity and spatial flow offering continued variation. In his specifications, Noguchi required that the stone facing on the triangular walls match the material of the building façades and be set horizontally on one wall and vertically on the other—a dialogue with variations, subtle but effective. In places the paving changes from the gravel on the terraces—retained by concrete curbs—to irregular stone flags configured as a circle. A semicircle cut from the top of one wall softens the distinction between architecture and sky [7-11]. As Noguchi envisioned it, there would be "within the garden a sufficient area of fixed geometry—of base, vertical, and horizontal—where the more conventional Euclidean sculptures might be better placed," along with areas employing "Non-Euclidean" geometry and asymmetry.[53]

Near the summit of the rocky hillock at the museum entrance is a fountain Noguchi titled *The Source*, comprising a single stone, roughly carved but still reading as sculpture [7-12, 7-13]. From it issues a stream of water that wets the stone face of the mound as an irregular sheet, finally disappearing below and recycled thereafter [7-14]. Arriving at both the form and the technology of this modest fountain to meet Noguchi's standards was no easy matter, and in several letters the troubles are enumerated. At least for a period, the fountain flowed in appreciation of the water needed in this dry land, symbolizing the triumph of making the desert flower.

>> *EPILOGUE*

Billy Rose died in 1966. In June 1967 war broke out following the Arab states' attack on Israel; although lasting only six days, the hostilities had serious consequences. Among those killed was Beham's son.[54] The garden was still incomplete and the problems with the gravel surfaces of the terraces remained unresolved. Additional trees, shrubs, and ground covers were planted; landscape architect Lawrence Halprin became a consultant to the museum. In 1968 Noguchi requested, "When the season is suitable I shall appreciate if a large quantity of desert plants may be planted among the stones."[55] At that time Noguchi regarded the garden as only a partial success and the experience of making it bittersweet. Shortly before the museum's opening he wrote that while he had been able to realize many of his original ideas, he had been forced to compromise and make changes that were not to his satisfaction [7-15].[56] While this is a common sentiment among designers, it is less so for artists, whose shortcomings are more easily dismissed. Up until his death in 1988 Noguchi continued to visit Jerusalem and tended to any issues that had arisen, for example, when an expansion to the garden had been projected to accommodate more works. Clearly, he remained fully invested in the project and maintained an affinity for the young nation and the challenges it faced.

My visit to the garden took place in 1993, and I have not been able to return during the course of the book's writing. Since its inception the museum itself has grown fivefold, with the number of sculptures in the garden keeping pace through donation and purchase. James Turrell's *Space That Sees* was installed under one of the terraces in 1992, a clever solution albeit an unfortunate one in terms of the Noguchi design. A recent video features the current museum director, Ido Bruno, among olives and pines now mature, with the ground covers and low shrubs playing counterpoint to the gravel terraces.[57] Despite the urban development around the site, the garden today appears to be far more hospitable to the visitor but, like the UNESCO garden, less evident as a work of sculpture [7-16]. One wonders whether it is possible to achieve both aspirations to equal measure.

Happily, it seems that the recent renovation and additions to the museum by Jamie Carpenter Associates have had little or no effect on the garden. In all, the Billy Rose Art Garden remains the most challenging

7-9 *[above left]*
Billy Rose Art Garden.
Israel Museum, Jerusalem, 1965.
The sculpted terraces with mature, if limited, vegetation.
[Steven Koch, 2022]

7-10 *[above right]*
Billy Rose Art Garden.
The curving black basalt wall at the entrance to the garden echoes the form of the stone walls retaining the terraces.
[Steven Koch, 2022]

7-11 *[below left]*
Billy Rose Art Garden.
The zone for small-scale sculpture intermixes rectangular, triangular, and curved walls, some faced with the same stone as the museum.

7-12 *[below right]*
Billy Rose Art Garden. Today vegetation defines the paths to a sculpture terrace, under which James Turrell's *Space That Sees* (1992) has been installed.
[Steven Koch, 2022]

landscape Noguchi created during his lifetime and was only partially successful in both functional and aesthetic terms. Nonetheless, it perhaps best embodies Noguchi's ideas and approach to landscape and culture, in this case the landscape and culture of a land with which he felt a strong bond. "Jerusalem is an emotion shared by all of us," he claimed. "It gains new meanings and it is my hope that the Garden and the Museum, of which it is a part, will come to be a very integral part of this new image—an acropolis of our times."[58]

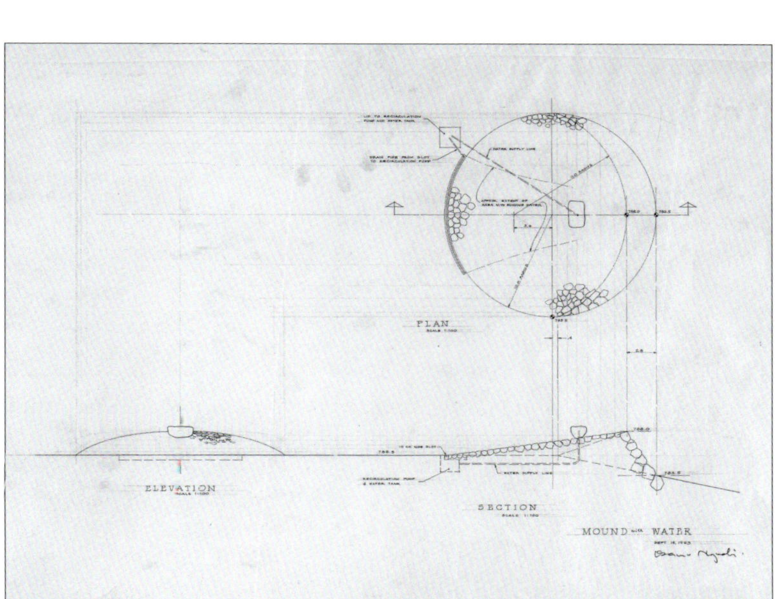

7-13 *[opposite]*
Billy Rose Art Garden.
Israel Museum, Jerusalem, 1965.
The knoll and fountain,
called *The Source*.
[Steven Koch, 2022]

7-14 *[left above]*
Billy Rose Art Garden.
The Source.

7-15 *[left below]*
Billy Rose Art Garden.
Plan and section through the
circular knoll at the entrance
with the fountain at its summit.
[© The Noguchi Museum/ARS]

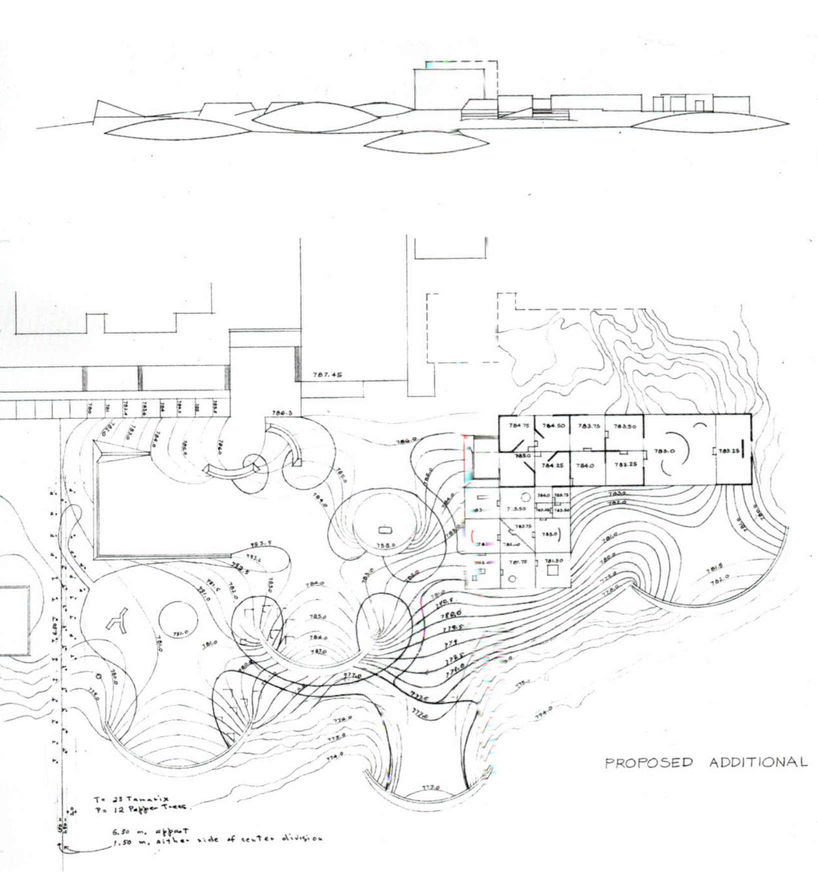

7-16
Billy Rose Art Garden.
Israel Museum, Jerusalem.
Site plan and elevation, 1968,
showing proposed additions.
After the opening of the garden,
Noguchi continued to suggest
improvements.
[© The Noguchi Museum/ARS]

>> HOUSTON

Like many of the stories surrounding Noguchi landscapes, the history of the Cullen Sculpture Garden is both fraught and prolonged.[59] Alice Pratt Brown a museum benefactor, had visited the Billy Rose Art Garden in Jerusalem in 1970 and not long after suggested that Noguchi might be the ideal designer for the sculpture garden long envisioned for the Museum of Fine Arts, Houston.[60] The commission followed in 1976. Noguchi's first presentation was made late that year, but his initial ideas were vetoed. Having arrived in Houston on his first visit after a heavy rainfall, he found the site a giant puddle. "As people had no means of escape from the flood, I immediately thought of an elevated area."[61] This would be the first of a series of his proposals to be rejected.

In the years since the museum's founding in 1924 there had been several proposals for the outdoor display of sculpture on the triangle of land to the south of the original building by William Ward Watkin. Garden designs by Thomas Church, Ruth London, and Mies van der Rohe had all attempted to mitigate the effects of passing traffic while addressing the original entrance to the museum.[62] By the late 1960s, however, the museum had acquired land one block to the north, once the site of a church and a six-story apartment house demolished some years earlier.[63] The two major arteries that bordered the site—Bissonet Street to the south and Montrose Boulevard to the west—rendered crossing from the museum a challenge.

Noguchi made little attempt to structure the garden in accordance with the north façade of the museum or the other buildings around the garden; the garden would employ its own formal language rather than acknowledge or emulate any of its neighbor's [7-17]. In some ways this strategy represented a lost opportunity to develop a garden space that would enfold the surrounding buildings. Nothing in the brief for the garden called for that relationship; in fact, there was every indication that the museum wanted "a Noguchi" and not a plaza as might be conceived by an urban designer or a landscape architect. Noguchi's intention was simply to provide places for displaying sculptures to their individual advantage and to conceive the entirety as a spatial sculpture. When faced with requests for changes later in the course of design, Noguchi emphatically responded that he was an artist and not an architect, and that he would consider modifications only if they did not undermine the integrity of the work.[64] The pieces to be viewed and their exact disposition were not his responsibility; these would be determined by the curatorial staff. In that sense, the program was vague.

From his first proposal Noguchi conceived the garden as an interior world not unlike those of most major Western gardens or the gardens of Buddhist Japan [7-18].[65] Varied in height as it circumscribed the site, a concrete wall buffered the domain of art from the mundane worlds of residence and commerce beyond. Inside the precinct were zones paved and zones grassed, balanced in nearly equal proportions. The freestanding concrete walls that subdivided the whole diverted movement without directing any specific itinerary. This was to be a conglomerate landscape that fused individual spaces into a whole: a composition that moved from the part to the whole rather than vice versa.

After the presentation of the first design, reservations lingered in the minds of the trustees, and in a November 1976 letter to Noguchi the museum's director, William Agee, requested a revised scheme. A response written the following January suggests that Noguchi had been unprepared for criticism and gave little hint that he understood or accepted the objections raised by the various parties. "Needless to say," he wrote to Alice Pratt Brown,

> *I am distressed by this as I had worked hard to solve a difficult problem. To clarify what I sought to do may I give you the following as the assumptions under which I worked: 1. To show sculpture and be practical for active use. 2. To make an environment both ennobling and distinct, that is parklike and not a private spot. 3. To be strongly visible to effectively contain and complement the Museum"*[66]

In terms of earth shaping, the first scheme was far more dramatic and ambitious than in the realized design.[67] Noguchi mounded an arc, "raising it as an embankment"; entry was positioned deep in the curve, using a double ramp to change levels.[68] In sum, the garden's earth forms suggested a minor acropolis with a corresponding flat area at its base, the two levels connected by ramps—a design bold, sculptural, and dynamic. In the balance of the letter, he remained defensive and showed little interest in revising the proposal. But he modified the scheme nonetheless.

That same day he wrote to Agee, arguing that "cozy nooks of bamboo without sufficient barriers would be meaningless and an architectural barrier would simply remove the garden from its surroundings."

7-17
Ludwig Mies van der Rohe.
Cullinan and Brown Pavilions,
Museum of Fine Arts,
Houston, Texas, 1974.
North façade.

7-18 *[below]*
Cullen Sculpture Garden.
Museum of Fine Arts, Houston, 1985.
Study model.
[MFA, Houston]

7-19 *[opposite]*
Cullen Sculpture Garden.
Earth mounds and variation in height reduce the impact of the perimeter walls.

Using earth forms, he believed, was the correct approach: "For a moment I thought of making a giant earth sculpture (with shade too for that matter). Then you would not need to fear vandalism or have to buy sculptures ever."[69] Agee replied in February 1977 with news that the museum had "acquired a new parcel of land which presents several additional alternatives," and he requested the artist's forbearance.[70] A grant from the Cullen Foundation in May 1978 injected new life into the project, providing funds both for the acquisition of land and for constructing the sculpture garden.[71] Agee contacted Noguchi in September confident that the project would reach fruition.[72] "I'm delighted to know my plan with further study may now be realized," Noguchi responded.[73] The following February the director reported to the museum's executive committee his pleasure, as well as that of the Cullen family, with the revised scheme.[74] That pleasure was not shared by all Houstonians, however, and the display of the model of the revised design provoked a number of critical responses.

Although reconfigured to address the negative reactions and opposition to the first scheme, Noguchi's 1979 design proposal drew carping responses from neighbors, local architects, those accustomed to the site as a vacant lot, and even some of its sponsors. Their collective gripe was that the wall bounding the site, to range in height from eight to fourteen feet, cast the sculpture garden as a private preserve for the elite. The point was well taken.[75] Additional complaints were submitted both to the museum and the local newspaper. But despite this "storm of controversy," calmer heads prevailed. Members of the design team had pointed out that walls were necessary buffers against the noise and visual distraction of the passing cars; the question concerned their form and height. "A study of the model shows that outside the walls, Noguchi has devised grassed berms set against the walls that would reduce the amount of exposed concrete while creating an additional sound barrier."[76] There were other suggestions from the community, however, primarily related to access.

Other factors ruled against the immediate realization of the garden—some of them economic, as the projected costs had risen dramatically from the original $400,000 budgeted sum—and the project languished.[77] It was not until about three years later, with the appointment of Peter Marzio as museum director, that work on the design and construction drawings

proceeded anew. Noguchi's new proposal largely maintained the original interior configuration in the model presented by Shoji Sadao on 4 April 1983, but the design of the wall enclosing the garden had been substantially softened.[78] Because the height of the boundary wall had been lowered, the art, the grassed areas, the trees and shrubs—now open to view—would generate a feeling of a public amenity rather a restricted enclave [7-19]. This modification to the prior scheme mitigated criticism against the design; construction began, progressed well, with the garden opening in April 1986.

In some respects the Cullen Sculpture Garden design is less assertively a Noguchi artwork than a sympathetic setting for sculpture in relief and in the round—quite understandable, as Noguchi himself had said that he wanted "the garden to be beautiful with or without sculptures."[79] Warmed by the pink grout that fills the wide joints between the units, the Carnelian granite paving plays well against the carefully poured and finished concrete walls [7-20]. While the perimeter of the garden is emphatically defined, the ordering of the various internal zones and display surfaces is less apparent. Only in the grassed mounds contained by the angled walls does sculpted topography produce any minor drama [7-21]. Like the Billy Rose Art Garden, concrete walls define distinct spaces that enrich the readings of the place, but in some ways diminish any evident sense of unity. Thus, the design is less concerned with being immediately legible and more with being an assembly of charged spaces apprehended through time.[80]

At the time of its opening the garden still had its critics. Susan Chatwick, fine arts editor at the *Houston Post*, thought the garden "has the appearance of a compromise, a jumble of mismatched elements, a place in which many of the museum's sculptures seem awkward and out of place, overwhelmed by the design of the garden itself."[81] The trees were small—primarily native species including pine, magnolia, crape myrtle, and mimosa—and did little at that time to either shade the space or alleviate the impact of the concrete and granite surfaces.[82] She cited Houston's often hot and humid climate, and the intense heat and glare reflected from the walls. But hedging her bets, she left an opening for the improvement that the passage of years might bestow: "Time, of course, is on the side of the garden for, over the years, the newly planted trees will grow and, it is hoped, lush vegetation will replace the uninspiring grass that now covers the berms inside and outside the walls."[83]

While one may not agree completely with Chatwick's initial assessment, on this point she was correct. Noguchi himself expressed his own reservations about the garden in the book accompanying the opening of the Isamu Noguchi Garden Museum in 1987: "After eight years of changes and reduced in scale, the garden is now illusionistic and will be a difficult site for sculpture, but it does wonders for the Mies museum, the contemporary museum, and the whole area."[84] As the trees have matured and the collection enriched by additions, and as the curatorial staff has become attuned to the spaces and the siting of sculpture within them, the Cullen Sculpture Garden, like the UNESCO garden, is today a more welcoming place both to its visitors and to its art [7-22, 7-23]. At the time of its opening Noguchi spoke of the garden as a "a very quiet conversation between walls and spaces, people and sculptures," and that relationship endures as a restrained but animated discourse.[85] As at UNESCO, the increased prominence of the vegetation has dampened the apparent sculptural aspects of the Noguchi design and diminished its identity as itself a work of art.[86] That is not necessarily a bad thing. It suggests that Noguchi's sculpture for sculpture has succeeded, and that an artist—like a landscape architect or an architect—may capably subdue his or her ego to create settings conducive to the appreciation of the work of others while instructive and pleasurable as art in themselves.

7-20 *[left]*
Cullen Sculpture Garden.
Museum of Fine Arts, Houston, Texas, 1985.
Entrance.

7-21 *[below]*
Cullen Sculpture Garden.
Mature vegetation helps define the various "rooms" and provides much-needed shade.

7-22 *[above]*
Cullen Sculpture Garden.
The play of walls, trees, shapes, and space.

7-23 *[right]*
Cullen Sculpture Garden.
Planting softens the presence of the concrete perimeter wall.

> 8.

Water: Furor and Stillness

Despite periodic excursions into the use of materials such as metal, wood, or bronze, stone remained a constant in Noguchi's art in his later decades. Stone served as the anchor for many of Noguchi landscapes, but his interest in natural processes—and more philosophically in the flow of life—fueled his use of water. In describing his courtyard for the Domon Ken Photography Museum in Sakata for example, Noguchi noted how in its design he joined the timelessness of stone with the ephemerality of water in a play of oppositions [see 6-51, 6-52, 6-53].[1] Still or moving, in puddles or streams, small basins or large ponds, water gives life to the sculpture, the room, and the garden [8-1]. Stone is fixed, inert, of a definite form with time embedded. Water, in contrast, is impermanent, in flux. Stone is solid, water liquid. Stone possesses a shape, while water responds to gravity and the form of its container. Unlike stone, water exists in three states; two of these, liquid and solid, are found in gardens—and if we include steam and clouds, possibly all three. Stone and water both occupied places in Noguchi's palette, individually or used in tandem: water complemented the armature provided by the earth—and in some gardens, by the stones. Paired with the seasonal change reflected by plant form and color, water granted life to otherwise static landscapes.

>> WATER IN JAPAN

Water in streams, cascades—and in larger gardens, ponds—was an element common in several types of historical Japanese gardens, the notable exception being the *karesansui* dry garden. The eleventh-century *Sakuteiki* declared that "Earth is lord, water servant. If earth permits it, water will flow."[2] That is to say, the shape of the water in both movement and repose derives from the shape of its vessel. Water dwells in the small hollow of the *tsukubai* or in a pond measured in acres, like those at the Shugaku-in imperial villa in Kyoto [8-2, 8-3].

Historically, geomancy influenced the location and nature of water in the garden, requiring that it should enter from the northeast and flow toward the southwest. In the great stroll gardens, particularly those of the imperial family, the pond was used physically for boating and aesthetically as a mirror to double the presence of vegetation and capture the sky on its surface. In a brook water carried verses floated in paper boats to be inter-

8-0
Horace E. Dodge Fountain. Detroit, 1976.
The downward fury of masses of water
[Wikicommons]

8-1 *[above left]*
The Well (Variations on a Tsukubai),
1982.
[Marc Treib, © The Noguchi Museum/ARS].

8-2 *[below left]*
Tsukubai.
Koto-in, Daitoku-ji.
Kyoto, early seventeenth century.

8-3 *[above]*
Emperor Gomizuno-o, gardeners, and workers.
Shugaku-in Imperial Villa, Kyoto, 1660s.
A giant dam retains seepage and rainfall to create a lake for active boating and the passive capture of reflections.

8-4 *[opposite above]*
Mirei Shigemori.
Tofuku-ji Hôjo. Kyoto, 1939.
Raked gravel.

8-5 *[opposite center]*
Von Sternberg pool.
Northridge, California, 1935.
Maquette.
[Kevin Noble, © The Noguchi Museum/ARS]

8-6 *[opposite below]*
The Chassis.
Ford Pavilion, World's Fair, New York, 1939.
[© The Noguchi Museum/ARS]

cepted downstream by a guest who contributed the next stanza to the evolving poem. In dry gardens water appeared only by analogy or symbol, for example, represented by raked gravel or by the composition of the stones [8-4]. Noguchi's attitude toward water, like his use of other materials, accepted Japanese traditions at times, but most often skewed them. At an extreme he turned tradition on its head. Following historical practices he shaped water as streams and pools; unlike tradition, he created fountains in which water pulsed, rose, and fell—at times as a mass, at times as a mist.

>> WATER IN POOLS AND SHEETS

Perhaps Noguchi's earliest aquatic work was his commission for a swimming pool for Richard Neutra's 1935 house for Hollywood film director Josef von Sternberg. The relatively flat and unremarkable site in the San Fernando Valley, California, offered Neutra virtually no geographic features with which to design and in response he turned the house inward. Just where on the site Noguchi's swimming pool was to be located is not known. Biomorphic curves set off by a straight line folded the water within the pool [8-5]. A sloping band surrounded the entirety, rising until it reached a height sufficient for use as a seat. The pool was never built, but its maquette was later cast in bronze to be regarded as a sculpture.

Among Noguchi's several projects for the 1939 World's Fair in New York was *The Chassis*, a fountain for the Ford Pavilion [8-6]. The design, based on the Ford V-8 engine, was held aloft by a column graced by spiral flutes and a diagonal shaft that emerged from the hemispherical forms at its base. Here water rather than gasoline fueled the engine, its sprays radiating from jets distributed around the paired central forms. The sculpture rose from a circular basin surrounded by beds of flowers and upright evergreen Italian cypresses, the totality encircled by the curving ramp that brought visitors to the entrance of Ford's popular "Road of Tomorrow" exhibition. Just who designed the setting is not known, but it is doubtful that it was Noguchi. The fountain with its garden were intended to provide a rest stop for those visitors weary or overwhelmed by all the fair had to offer. Looking back Noguchi had little to say about this work other than its "only virtue" was "to teach me the use of magnesite (MgO Cl_2)."[3]

>> WATER IN STREAMS & SHEETS

As discussed in chapter 3, Noguchi was briefly interned at the relocation camp for "those of Japanese ancestry" at Poston, an arid desert site on a Native American reservation in Arizona. Water was a prime concern for both reservation and camp, and had been diverted from the Colorado River using irrigation canals whose insufficient yield was augmented by wells dug on site. Noguchi created a plan to redirect the flow from the channels into a series of shaped basins, and to intermittently widen the ditches to become swimming pools [see 3-11, 3-13]. The project was stillborn, and the benefits of enhanced water sources never materialized.

Noguchi also used the canal and the pool to complement the earth mounds at the *Reader's Digest* garden in Tokyo (1952). These were augmented by a fountain within a twenty-foot-high cage of iron, said to have been inspired by the city's Edo Period fire towers. Water from the fountain first spouted upward, but thereafter fell into a rectangular basin that transformed into a sinuous channel that meandered through the flat lawn [see 3-28]. The garden wisely collected the water from the air conditioning system and used it to feed the water features adjacent to, or that passed beneath, parts of the building.

At the headquarters for Connecticut General Life Insurance Corporation (1957) water remained in a passive state, as shallow pools within the courts, and as the reflecting pool surrounding the Employee Cafeteria [8-7]. The fluidity of water complemented the solidity of gravel and moss within the light courts, an immobile pool in the tradition of the water parterres of seventeenth-century French gardens. In the courtyards water received a biomorphic contour free of the regularity of the circle or rectangle.

In the UNESCO garden (1958) water traced a complex trajectory. On the Delegates Patio water issued from a large vertical stone standing erect in a shallow pool, then passed through a composition of rectangular steppingstones before spilling into the narrow channel that paralleled the inclined path leading to the Annex on the site's eastern edge. Rather then allowing the water to descend freely as a cascade, or tumble in regular stages, Noguchi angled the leading edge of each level so that water would first fall toward one edge of the channel and then to the other [see 5-15]. The result was a flow that injected considerable vigor and presence to the water's descent. At the path's midpoint the stream widened into a semicircular pool whose missing half, executed in low plants, completed the circle. From this point the profile of the water became more naturalistic, descending as a twisting stream that emptied into the biomorphically shaped pool on the garden's lowest level. Here the treatment became more traditionally Japanese, although the shapes of the stepping stones that traverse the pond are more modern than historical. The use of water at UNESCO represents Noguchi's most complete exploration of its possible effects—that is to say, water flowing, plunging, gushing, or still and reflective. Only twenty-five years later, as source and stream in *California Scenario*, did the uses of water rival the variety and sophistication of its appearance in the UNESCO landscape.

The principal task facing Noguchi in the design of the sculpture garden for the Israel Museum in Jerusalem was to recontour the hillside into terrain suitable for visitor movement and the display of sculpture. The garden's story, told in the preceding chapter, shows how Noguchi addressed that challenge with seven massive arcs of local stone. Jerusalem receives twenty-three inches of precipitation annually, almost all of which falls between November and March. The remainder of the year the land is dry. In response Noguchi conceived the garden as a dry landscape with one notable exception: a rock from which flows a nominal stream. Like the stone at the UNESCO garden, *The Source* was left in an almost naturalistic state, with water issuing from its upper surface, then dividing into a sheet that glazes the rocky slope beneath it. Rather than collecting in any visible receptacle at base of the slope, the water mysteriously disappears into the earth beneath the rocks. The idea of fountain has been distilled to its essence: an oasis in miniature, flowing gently on the Hill of Tranquility.
At the Domon Ken Museum of Photography, in contrast, a sheet of water emerges from a source unknown and mysterious, slowly flows over the stepped terraces, and empties—or so it appears—into the adjacent pond. Its somewhat erratic and hypnotic tide conjoins architecture and water despite differences in their kinetic and material properties [8-8].

In the fountains cited above water takes form as a source or a sheet, most often assuming an irregular profile. In reality, the fountain at the New York World's Fair was more an identifiable sculpture set within

8-7 *[opposite above]*
Courtyard.
Connecticut General
Life Insurance, Bloomfield,
Connecticut, 1957.
Still water as reflecting pool.

8-8 *[opposite center]*
Water Garden.
Domon Ken Museum of
Photography, Sakata, 1985.
A sheet of water in constant
motion, water flows over the
stone surfaces.

a pool than a fountain. The water in Paris and Jerusalem, more significantly wedded water and rock. In that same category falls the fountain in the court of the IBM headquarters in Armonk, where five jets unite as an aqueous vault at the center of the red enameled saucer which contains it [8-9]. Although in these gardens water added a dimension to an otherwise dry landscape, their impact was minor. In other Noguchi projects, however, water figured more consequentially as an energizing counterpoint or as the garden's principal subject.

In the sunken courtyard for 1 Chase Plaza in New York City (1963), Noguchi used water dynamically and illusionistically to "float" stones above the paved surfaces. In clement seasons water carpets the undulating white-granite ground, pooling in some areas, left only as a thin coat in others [8-10]. In places stone surfaces rise through the water and assume the guise of softly contoured islands that support boulders imported from Japan. Spurting jets from beneath the stones exert a force seemingly sufficient to elevate them above the ground—an effect seriously dissipated in winter when the pool is drained. In the warmer months, water and stone share equal roles in making the sculpture. Seen from the plaza above, the masterful composition of stones and the undulations of granite surfaces below dominate the view. Seen from from the lower banking level, however, water governs the rocks, visually suspending them in carefully composed groupings. It is little surprise that Noguchi referred to this work as his Ryôan-ji, although here in New York the water of river or sea, only suggested by the raked gravel in dry gardens, is real—at least at certain times of year..

The source of the central stream at *California Scenario* (1982) commands the garden—a roughly thirty-foot-high, sandstone-faced wedge called Water Source, down whose slope the waters first plunge. From its base the stream commences its meandering course that varies in width as it winds through the plaza, finally terminating in the low pyramid intended to symbolize water use in California [8-11]. In contrast to the quiet of this slowly flowing stream, the sound and sparkle of the Energy Fountain dazzle by day and by night [8-12].

The uniting of source and stream in a pool recurred in several Noguchi landscapes: first in the *Reader's Digest* garden, then at UNESCO garden and in the lobby of the Sôgetsu ikebana school, and ultimately

8-9 *[left]*
Mankind's Future Courtyard.
IBM offices, Armonk,
New York, 1962.
Fountains in a shallow saucer.

8-10 *[above]*
Sunken Garden.
1 Chase Plaza, New York, 1963.
Water in animated and animating volume.

8-11 *[center]*
California Scenario.
Costa Mesa, California, 1982.
Meandering stream.

8-12 *[below]*
California Scenario.
Tumbling water of Energy Fountain.

in Moerenuma Park. All these works shared a progression of flow that adapted the movement of water in nature. In the Sôgetsu lobby, water furtively emanates from a stone cylinder with rounded base on its uppermost level and then hugs the sides of the stone before passing through a narrow trough excised from the granite floor, then falling to the next lower level [see 6-46, 6-48]. From that point the stream continues ever downward from terrace to terrace to terminate in a pair of shallow pools at ground level. While serving primarily to animate and unify the installations on its four levels, the water also broadcasts an ambient murmur that muffles human voices and other sounds within the lobby. In the Moerenuma Park a sculptured stone once again feeds a winding stream that extends beyond the paved surface of the Aquatic Plaza between Mt. Moere and Play Mountain. [see 11-10, 11-15]. Water joins disparate surfaces, here more distinguished by their materials than their elevations. Regarded critically the Moerenuma stream suffers to some degree from its limited dimensions, which appear underscaled in relation to the park's massive earthworks.

>> FOUNTAINS

>> *NEW ORLEANS*

Almost all the water features described above possess an identifiable source, whether of metal or stone, whether left more natural or highly worked. Regardless, they are their garden's primary feature. Noguchi also designed a series of fountains that stood boldly as independent works of sculpture, especially evident when missing the water that gave them life. Although today left dry, water originally issued from the top of the fluted, horizontally set crescent atop *The Mississippi*, a fountain sculpture in New Orleans [8-13].[4] While its overall form reprises two sculptures originally proposed for the garden at Lever House in New York, here the reference cites its setting in the Crescent City. With or without this particular allusion, the sculpture of Minnesota granite referenced the mighty river that passes through New Orleans before debouching in the Gulf of Mexico. The John Hancock Insurance building, on whose plinth the fountain was installed, occupies one side of Lee Circle, whose prominence was historically augmented by the 1884 statue of Robert E. Lee by Alexander Doyle that until 2017 stood atop a column in the circle's

center.[5] Gordon Bunshaft of SOM was the lead architect for the building, a seven-story block with open interiors, whose elegant frame of concrete both supports the building and shields its glass walls from the intense southern sun. The plinth, with parking below, was designed to compensate for the differences in level from one end of the site to the other. Noguchi recalled that a tree was originally proposed for the plaza, but structural deliberations judged that idea to be impractical; in its place, a fountain was proposed. The fountain's basic form is a T, with water falling from the crescent-shaped bar at its crest; *The Mississippi*, its title, refers to both its use as a source and its location.[6] The fountain was positioned for view by anyone mounting the stairs to the plinth level to enter the building. Building construction was completed in 1961; *The Mississippi* followed a year later.

Within its form the fountain comprises two elements: a stone lintel half-moon in shape with upturned ends; and its columnar support, whose fluting echoes the treatment of the column that formerly bore the statue of Lee that stood across the Circle. All sides of this element have been smoothed and polished, except its curving outer edge which was left coarse.[7] From both sides of the summit, water flowed as a curtain, hugging the sides of the pillar as it descended. No pool at its base collected the water, which mysteriously disappeared into a circle recessed in the surface of the plaza. The fountain exudes a monumental air, which some have claimed favors form over water, an impression perhaps derived from the height and solidity of the fountain, or from the archaic aura produced by the simple act of placing a lintel upon a post. Like the statue of Lee, water is today missing, but *The Mississippi* retains its dignity and presence, even without the liquid that once graced its surfaces life [8-14].

In several water features presented to this point, the volume and flow of water was relatively subdued, with their power and presence derived from understatement and refinement rather than volume and bombast. Their antheses are found in the fountains from which masses of water rose and fell in Osaka, Detroit, and Sapporo.

>> *OSAKA; CHICAGO*

In preparation for Expo '70 in Osaka, architect Kenzô Tange invited Noguchi to design nine fountains to be installed in the expansive water parterres as

8-13
The Mississippi.
New Orleans, 1962.
[Ezra Stoller / ESTO]

8-14
The Mississippi.
The lintel, dry.

part of the Festival Plaza fronting the colossal space frame of his design and the monumental *Tower of the Sun* by Tarō Okamoto (1911–1996). While the fountains exploited the latest technology to maximize the wonder and memorable effects of water, it was the artist's intention that, "the object-nature of the fountain must not be strong enough to overshadow the water-nature itself —which must be emphasized."[8] More significantly, Noguchi challenged traditional fountain forms that spewed water only upward. Instead, directions and effects were increased by shooting water downward and sideways as well as upward, water left stationary, and water that twisted and rotated as it left the nozzle. "My fountains," he asserted, "jetted down one hundred feet, rotated, sprayed, and swirled water, disappeared and reappeared as mist."[9] In developing the necessary technology for his water sculptures, "the fountain manufacturers responded enthusiastically."[10] How many of the proposed number of fountains were actually produced has been difficult to ascertain. In photos only three or four works are illustrated, each of them painted steel, and configured either as a narrow cylinder, two cubes, a half dome, or intersecting disks.[11] Whatever their number, these supports and sources generated a true aquatic spectacle: a cylindrical column transformed into a pillar of spray; water shooting from the bottom of cubes as if the tail of a comet; a half dome of water that transmuted water into space; and a liquid three-quarter sphere that emerged from a group of disks, with its rotation propelled by the horizontal jets installed on their edges [8-15, 8-16]. That Noguchi was successful in his quest for creating a sculpture of and for water was confirmed by the sculptural presence of almost all the fountains when dry. Water made the sculpture; the structure provided their only source.

As part of the celebration of the American Bicentennial, Noguchi designed a less assertive fountain and basin of Minnesota rainbow granite for an addition to the Art Institute of Chicago designed by architect Walter Netsch. The fountain's composition paired a pylon some forty feet high with a forty-foot-long horizontal cylinder split into halves; between the halves a sheet of water fell downward [8-17]. Horizontal flutes etched deeply into the surface of the pylon disturbed the flow of the water down its surface, aerating and rousing the water as it descended into a pool at its base. The opposition of a tall and slender waterfall with a sheet of water, was a theme Noguchi had previously explored in the 1961 sculpture *Study for a Waterfall.*

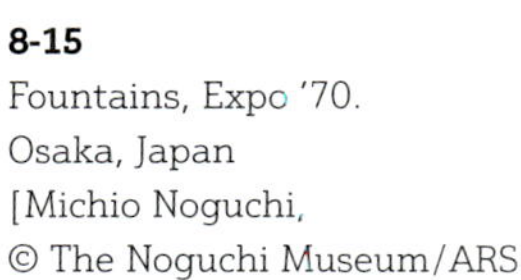

8-15
Fountains, Expo '70.
Osaka, Japan
[Michio Noguchi,
© The Noguchi Museum/ARS]

8-16
Fountains, Expo '70.
Water as propulsion
as well as emission
[Michio Noguchi,
© The Noguchi Museum/ARS]

Perhaps a sculpture with similar properties would have better served as a Bicentennial commemoration; banished to the less trafficked side of the museum, the fountain was dry on my two visits several years apart, although its operation may only be seasonal, as at 1 Chase Plaza.

>> HORACE E. DODGE FOUNTAIN

Shortly after the stunning success of the Osaka Expo fountains, Noguchi was invited to design a monumental waterwork at the head of Woodward Avenue in Detroit, funded by a two-million-dollar donation from philanthropist Anna Thomson Dodge in memory of her husband, Horace E. Dodge [8-18].[12] Stemming from various socioeconomic factors that included reduced industrial production, job losses, and population shifts to the suburbs, the city had been suffering economic decay for over a decade. As in so many American cities, by the 1960s Detroit's downtown witnessed a population decline that yielded a neglected infrastructure. In the 1970s, however, due in part to the infusion of sizable amounts of capital for mixed-use developments such as the city's Renaissance Center, the movement for a revivified urban heart had gained momentum.

The Horace E. Dodge Fountain, as it would be named, was intended as the central feature of a major redevelopment project. Sited on a former parking lot in downtown Detroit, the original program for Hart Plaza ranged from "a skating rink and amphitheater to a covered performance area, gallery, restaurant, and twenty-six kiosks."[13] Noguchi once again swelled the scope of his commission, envisioning a monumental fountain to embrace the entire setting, a plaza to include an additional sculpture, sculpted seating, and an event space. As he described it, the site would provide "an opening to the sky and to the Detroit River. A horizon for people."[14] Somewhat surprisingly, he received complete support for this expanded regime from the executive architects Smith Hinchman & Grylls, especially architect Robert Hastings, who chaired the Dodge Fountain Committee and who had solicited Noguchi's participation in September 1972.[15]

>> *INITIAL DESIGN*

In his design for the new fountain Noguchi greatly increased the volume and impact of water used to "float" the rocks in the Chase plaza. Located on the

8-17
Bicentennial Fountain.
Art Institute of Chicago, 1976.
[Oliver Andrews, © The Noguchi Museum/ARS]

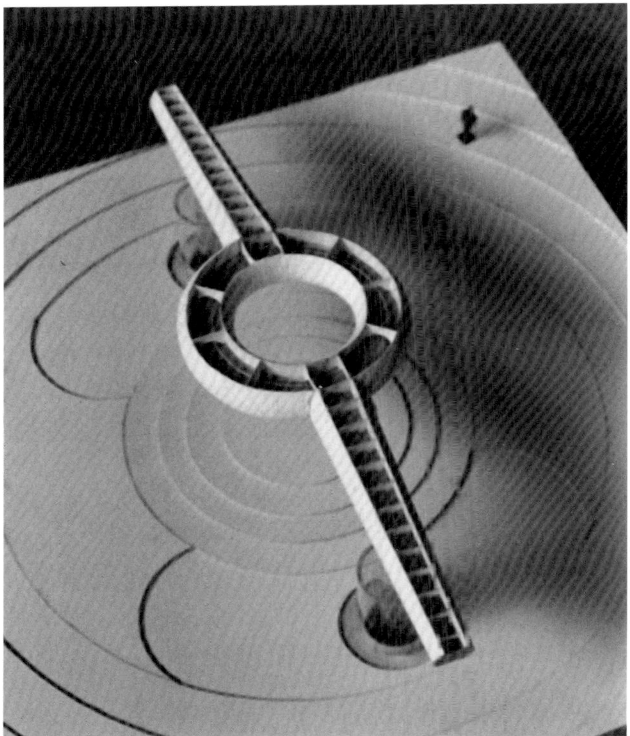

shore of the Detroit River, Hart Plaza was less confined and of far greater dimensions than the bounded and sunken garden in New York. No number of rocks, even large rocks, could effect the spatial definition and visual interest demanded by a site of this scale. Eschewing the use of stone, Noguchi proposed a ring of stainless-steel tubes supported by two hefty legs of the same material. The resulting volume of water far surpassed that of any other Noguchi fountain until that time—and by an exponential degree. In the manner common to most fountains, water would shoot upward—but it would also shoot downward in a complex cycle of aquatic choreography controlled by computer. The design intention pushed the limits of the available technology, which at that time unfortunately fell short of what was needed to realize the artist's vision.

Noguchi's first proposal differed substantially from the fountain as constructed. A monumental, if hollow, metal beam spanned two granite piers and supported a ring from which dense volumes of water shot downward, countered by an opposing field of upward-thrusting jets [8-19]. Together, they fashioned a grand entry arch of water under which only the eye was allowed to pass. To the Fountain Committee, he sold the design as an "engine for water," plainly associating the aquatic spectacle with the automobile motor so integrally a part of Detroit's history: "the dream that has produced the automobile, the airplane, and now the rocket. The machine now a poem."[16] The area surrounding the fountain had been assigned to parking, which Noguchi considered unsuitable for such an artwork; in response, he sought to magnify his field of intervention to include the entire project area. Somewhat miraculously, his proposal was accepted, and he began to work closely with the architects on the design of the plaza as well as the fountain and the sculptures.

The Dodge Fountain thus became only one element, albeit its focal point, in a landscape that ultimately included an amphitheater, a 120-foot-high aluminum-clad twisting pylon, a stepped pyramid to be used for seating, a restaurant, a riverfront promenade, and shops [8-20]. Noguchi explained the revised 1973 scheme as follows: "The plaza, viewed as a whole, will present a series of pyramidal shapes: that of the fountain, that of the stepped pyramid of the theater, the blue exhaust stack of the road and the greater pyramid of the festival amphitheater as it rises to the plaza plane"

8-18
Isamu Noguchi at the Dodge Fountain, Detroit, 1975.
[City of Detroit, © The Noguchi Museum/ARS]

8-19
Dodge Fountain.
First proposal.
[© The Noguchi Museum/ARS]

[8-21, 8-22]. The pylon, which was to be Noguchi's gift to the city, was carefully positioned in the plaza's northeast corner to serve as a visual beacon terminating Woodward Avenue while announcing the plaza as a civic space. Furthering his description Noguchi then played his trump card, no doubt devised to win the heart of the Middle American: "I like to think that the effect will be American, unlike anything elsewhere." He assured the populace that it would not be a monument but a "people's park."[17]

Because the unstable clay soil and existing seawall were incapable of supporting the truckloads of earth necessary to raise the grade to the desired elevation, the plaza would be constructed on a deck supported by a field of some 500 piles and columns. The lower story would be assigned to stalls used during the city's various fairs, including its annual and highly popular Ethnic Festival. The main plaza was surfaced with a red Carnelian granite, the same material later used in the sculpture garden for the Museum of Fine Arts, Houston.

The scale of this design task was far beyond any that Noguchi had previously undertaken as well as beyond his technical expertise. The architects at Smith Hinchman & Grylls would address the technical issues and produce the construction documents, coordinate with Noguchi's colleague Shoji Sadao (1927–2019) and the engineers, and manage the project and its realization—and they remained dedicated to executing the design as Noguchi envisioned it. If the architects are to receive such credit, enormous recognition must also be given to Sadao, who developed Noguchi's design ideas, directed the work with consultants, and produced the necessary drawings and documents. Much of the work on these landscapes took place while Noguchi was traveling or residing in Japan, and considerable responsibility thus fell to Sadao to make decisions and carry them through—with the artist's review and consent, of course.

>> *THE CONTRIBUTIONS OF SHOJI SADAO*

Born in Los Angeles in 1927, Sadao received his architecture degree from Cornell University in 1954. He had met Buckminster Fuller in 1952, when Fuller had taught at the university as a visiting professor. Shortly after graduation Sadao began working for Fuller in his office in Raleigh, North Carolina, on projects that ranged from the Dymaxion map to the geodesic dome that

8-20
Isamu Noguchi with Smith, Hinchman & Grylls. Hart Plaza, Detroit, 1976. [Balthazar Korab, © The Noguchi Museum/ARS]

8-21
Hart Plaza. Pylon.

8-22
Hart Plaza. Seating steps with fountain beyond.

housed the US Pavilion at Expo '67 in Montreal. As Fuller's partner he would become responsible for developing, resolving, and managing all the office projects—that is, bringing them into reality from a state of theory and proposition. Sadao later played a similar role for Noguchi, whom he had met through Fuller, Noguchi's longtime friend, in 1956.[18]

Sadao described the differing characters of his two partners in this way: "[Fuller's] discourse was marked by rationalism and science, [Noguchi] explored the world of dreams and nuanced areas of human emotion."[19] In his relationship with Noguchi one could comfortably substitute "Sadao" for "Fuller" in this description. As the scope and intricacy of Noguchi's landscape commissions increased over time, Sadao assumed greater responsibility, especially as the artist spent more and more time away from his New York studio.

As we have seen, Noguchi had difficulty accepting the economics of his garden projects—or at least the rationale behind those economics—and had other difficulties working within the constraints of time and budget. When Sadao raised the issue, Noguchi would usually respond by claiming, "I'm only trying to make the project better! Why are you causing all these problems. I'm trying to improve it!"—arguing that it wasn't for himself that he was taking on this additional work but for the client and the potential visitors.[20] Rarely satisfied with any existing scheme, he was unable to accept the design at any stage as final, nor keep to his assigned task—or the architect's task, for that matter. "He would change the façade," noted Sadao, "he would change the orientation of the building, he'd push it in the back to create a larger plaza, and so he designed the total environment, not just a piece of sculpture to sit there."[21] Collaboration with Noguchi, Sadao recalled, could be difficult. "He could be mercurial, obstinate, moody or charming as the situation suited him."[22] But despite these problems —and there were many concerning the design of the Dodge Fountain—their close relationship continued until the artist's death and even endured beyond, as Sadao continued working on the park in Sapporo through its completion and for many years served as executive director of the Isamu Noguchi Foundation.

>> *THE FOUNTAIN RECONSIDERED*

Noguchi's initial proposal for the fountain met with severe criticism and was rejected. Skeptics saw the project as an ungainly white elephant. Despite its fronting a sports arena and a future convention center, and sited adjacent to the Ford Auditorium, they questioned why people would be attracted to the space other than during scheduled events. The riverfront location made the space vulnerable to wind, rain, and especially snow in the winter. Noguchi's metallic doughnut hardly suited the image of a monumental fountain in the minds of Detroit's citizens, lacking as it did all traditional iconography.

After due consideration, the essentially post-and-lintel scheme bothered Noguchi as well, and he began to revise its form. In the new design a central torus, clad in stainless steel, would be supported by two inclined metal legs, joined in a composition marked by a far greater sense of unity. Despite its own beauty and identity as sculpture, the metallic structure was not the real essence of the work. Water makes a fountain, and water—at 45,000 gallons an hour—would be ejected from some 300 jets controlled by a software program. Given these enormous volumes, water danced upward to the sky and thrust earthward as dense, fluctuating showers: a truly modern fountain of stainless steel and water [8-23]. Gone were the river gods, the seahorses, and the allegorical deities that had once dominated classical fountain design, for example, as found in the monumental fountain by Cass Gilbert on nearby Belle Isle [8-24].[23] "Today electronically programmed fountains have done a complete about face," asserted a hyperbolic press release for the Renaissance Center. "Today water is the star; decoration is minimal or non-existent."[24] Even the traditional basin at the base of the fountain was eliminated in favor of a continuous pavement that allowed the use of the complete space when fountain was dry.[25]

All well and good—if the water had performed correctly and the drains remained unclogged. But from its opening day on 24 July 1976 the fountain never functioned properly, confirming the dire predictions of its pessimistic critics. The grandeur of the artist's vision seemed to have surpassed contemporary technological capabilities. Even prior to its official inauguration, the fountain had been slated for renovation, a victim of apathy and vandalism. Costs grew, as did criticism of the project. Irritation plagued the designers, the builders, and the public alike. "What a mess," exclaimed a 1979 *Detroit Free Press* editorial. "If the Dodge Fountain were Detroit's only place to get

8-23
Dodge Fountain.
Detroit, 1976.
In splendor.
[Wikicommons]

a drink, the population would have perished of thirst years ago."[26] Maintenance had not been factored into the expenditures, and to keep such a finely tuned engine running smoothly, maintenance was mandatory. Achieving the symphony of water effects—downward, upward, and outward sprays—required faultless execution and upkeep, neither of which had been in great supply.

Fortunately, Noguchi and the fountain had a strong ally in City Engineer Louis Klei, who took on the fountain's proper operation as a personal crusade and did not rest until everything was working smoothly. The process took years, and Klei spent much of his free time trying to make all the parts function satisfactorily; he was described as obsessed. "I call him Bela Lugosi," said Carl Miles, a construction inspector who worked with Klei. "You see him in the control room at night turning knobs and punching buttons on the computer panel, and he looks just like the Phantom of the Opera. He wants to see it dance." It had to work, Klei argued, or there was no sculpture. He had adopted Noguchi's own litany that regarded the fountain as a water and light show. The water and lights are the sculpture. The actual structure is secondary, it is simply a means to carry the water and lights. The sculpture itself is constantly changing.[27] True, but only if the water design performed correctly, which it often did not. As one would-be wit phrased it: "How do you squeeze some pizzazz out of a lemon that looks like a doughnut?"[28] Only with yet another renovation in 1988, after fountain technology had sufficiently advanced, were the hydraulics reliable.[29] To quell anxiety over the spartan quality of the plaza, Noguchi stressed in writing that "we have reserved at least a third of the area to grass or trees."

Despite the less than perfect results of the downtown-renewal efforts, the Dodge Fountain saga had a happy ending. Although without question a sculptural object set on the surface of the plaza, this is indeed a mighty fountain; if it is an engine for water, it is definitely a V-8 or a high-performance diesel.[30] Supported by its inclined legs, the ring spews water downward as a dense cylinder countered by upward-surging jets thrust into numerous configurations. "The fountain rises 18 feet in the air," Noguchi wrote, "hovering in a cloud of water, incandescent at night."[31] Computer controlled, the thirty-one variants offer a play of liquid in constant movement.

Photos record the public's fascination with the dancing waters that draw everyone to them, especially children. As a social design, it has unquestionably triumphed. As one writer described it:

> *Emerging out of classical symmetry toward a controlled asymmetry and the river beyond, the mood is that of the primeval land we inhabit within America. The vista is defined by primary forms which themselves invite participation as places of relaxation: to sit, listen to the sounds of the river, the sounds of voices, or even music and theater at times. There are in effect four such communally enjoyable configurations."*[32]

As a form, it is a stunning sculpture of water supported by a metal armature. For Noguchi, "This work [was] a synthesis of unity and plurality, of balance and imbalance, of fusion and fission, of stability and change, of all imaginable pairs of opposites."[33] As a technological accomplishment, however, systemic flaws have continued to mar its performance and appreciation; the vision behind it may have pushed the limit of hydraulic equipment a bit too far, a bit too fast, and a bit too soon. As a sculpture, however, the Horace E. Dodge Fountain is arguably the most handsome of later twentieth-century fountains, a credit to its design and construction teams and the city to which it was given. More recently, however, the integrity of the plaza has been seriously compromised. A gaggle of flagpoles has been installed as well as a memorial to a labor movement, the form of which is unsympathetic to the plaza design. And it seems that the magnificent display of what water can do, or can be made to do, is only seasonal at best.

>> MILDRED AND CLAUDE PEPPER FOUNTAIN

Set on the shore of Biscayne Bay, Bayfront Park in Miami had long served as the site for the Miami Public Library at its southern end [8-25]. In the course of redesigning the twenty-eight-acre landscape, Noguchi convinced the city to remove the vacated building to increase green space for recreation; thereafter, the area became the site for the memorial to the astronauts who perished in the 1986 Challenger explosion [8-26]. The design and execution of the project extended from 1980 into 1996 and included an amphitheater, a major fountain, abundant green space, and the memorial itself. It also welcomed another iteration of the sculpture *Slide Mantra*—this version executed in white marble.[33]

From the time of its initial planning in the early 1900s, Bayfront Park benefitted from the rapid growth and hardiness of tropical

8-24 *[opposite above]*
Cass Gilbert.
James Scott Memorial Fountain.
Belle Isle, Detroit, 1925.

plantings. Miami architect and landscape designer Lester Pancoast consulted on the selection of plants to support the artist's design. The large, circular Pepper Fountain is a welcome feature although, as with the overall site plan, the rationale behind its form and location is not apparent [8-27]. From Noguchi's detailed scenario, however, it becomes obvious that despite any shortcomings in its design, he had considered the water sequence in detail:

> 1. *Entire basin is filled and still.*
> 2. *Outer rim flows centrifugally. Its effect controlled by water pressure. This is almost continuous.*
> 3. *Upward jets are introduced with turbulence like sea waves and increasing waterflow over rim.*
> 4. *Central drain is opened causing upward jets to rise gradually to full height as desired.*
> 5. *When the central drain is closed, jets decrease in height to sea waves as basin fills with water from jets.*
> 6. *The inward spiral may be maintained by controlling upward jets. Thus there would be two factors for control.*
> 7. *The drain at the base of fountain is an integral part of the fountain operation. Normally there is no water visible in the red sandstone catch basin, which is only filled occasionally.*
> 8. *The fog jets on the exterior rim of the fountain must be synchronized with the rest of the water display.*
> 9. *The fog is lighted as is the centrifugal spray by eighteen lights within the drain.*[34]

Unfortunately, due to budget constraints the program was realized only in a far more subdued form.[35]

Clad with gray granite today stained to rust color by the iron in the Miami water, the fountain sits as an independent feature in the landscape and does little to engage the adjacent parts of the park. It is an element one skirts on the way to somewhere else rather than a central feature to linger and enjoy. Bayfront Park will not be a landscape for which Noguchi is remembered, perhaps because of its size; perhaps due to the complex collaboration that involved so many other parties; perhaps due to the lengthy period demanded for its planning, design, and construction that continued for years after Noguchi's passing.

8-25
Pepper Fountain. Bayfront Park, Miami. Satellite view. The Challenger Memorial is at the lower left. [Google Earth]

>> SEA FOUNTAIN

Similar in idea and configuration to the Mildred and Claude Pepper Fountain, Sea Fountain at Moerenuma Park more successfully produces an engaging, memorable experience. Like the other features of Moerenuma Park on the northern Japanese island of Hokkaido, Sea Fountain was inaugurated in 2005, seventeen years after the artist's death. A dense band of red larch trees embraces the great fountain at its center to mark it as a significant feature. One enters the circular space without quite knowing what to expect, as few clues about the fountain's program are apparent between cycles or as perceived from beyond the ring of visually impermeable trees. Unlike the Dodge Fountain, which rises from its plaza, the Sapporo fountain is contained within a shallow bowl set slightly below ground level. But similar to the Dodge Fountain, the drama lies not so much in the form of the support structure as in the dramatic oscillations of water forms that characterize the fountain's periodic displays [8-28, 8-29]. In quiet times the water remains a low stack of spurting liquid but at the moment of peak performance, a single jet rises far above the treetops. At night, changes in lighting add to the effect.

>> QUIET WATER

The water in the Noguchi landscapes we have seen enlivens and amplifies, with volumes of water that vary from trickle to flood. In contrast to the energy and clamor of the grand fountains are a series of fountains of greater restraint that suggest a more inward path. In the seven fountains for Japan's Supreme Court, Noguchi most closely approached a sense of the sublime that pervaded the reductive dry gardens of the Muromachi period (1336–1573) [8-30]. Absent is the furor of the Dodge and Moerenuma fountains. In its place is a series of small fountains harbored in the courtyards of a Brutalist building designed by Shin'ichi Okada (1918–2014). Inaugurated in 1974, the Supreme Court is a tough, concrete fortress of monumental scale on a site facing the Imperial Palace. Within the building's innermost spaces—inaccessible to nearly all but the justices and staff—are a series of fountains Noguchi claimed had been inspired by the *chôbachi* of the traditional garden: a small basin within a rock that, like the *tsukubai*, provides water for washing hands and rinsing the mouth.

8-26 *[above]*
Challenger Memorial.
Bayfront Park, Miami, 1989.
Seen from an adjacent hotel.

8-27 *[left]*.
Pepper Fountain.
Bayfront Park, Miami,1989.
Iron in the water has stained the original gray granite setts that cover the fountain.

8-28
Sea Fountain.
Moerenuma Park,
Sapporo, Japan, 2005.
Low cycle.

8-29
Sea Fountain.
High cycle.

Each of the seven Supreme Court fountains is octagonal in plan, its water softly trickling from the underside of the lid at its summit. The fountains, aligned along a visual axis that connects the internal courtyards, mitigate—at least to some minor degree—the severity of the architecture. To Dore Ashton, "The sobriety of this black and white garden certainly suggests Noguchi's idea of the stern principles of justice dispensed within the building."[36] Perhaps. Or perhaps these fountains, pared down to their essence, responded to the bleakness of the architecture or the realization that today's judicial processes continue a tradition with roots extending back centuries, despite the country's postwar constitution.

Furthering the quest for depth through reduction were a series of *tsukubai*, or washbasins, long a requisite element of the Japanese temple garden [8-31]. *Waterstone* (1986), on permanent display in the Metropolitan Museum of Art's Japanese galleries represents the Noguchi fountain at its most transcendent [8-32].[37] Here, in the smallest of sizes, in the quietest of ways, Noguchi showcased and unified the inherent properties of the sculpture's two constituents: stone and water. Stone establishes the base, water provides the life. As the animating factor, water invisibly issues from the top of the stone and continuously overflows its small basin. Lightly coating the sides of the stone as it descends, it mysteriously disappears into the bed of gravel that supports the fountain. In its form, and in the experience it stimulates, the fountain offers an answer while provoking questions as well. Why is the pool carved from its summit shaped as a circle whose pure geometry softly contrasts with the still-rough sides of the stone? From where does the water come and where is it received? Its glacial seepage marks the flow of time, and yet the sculpture appears to be removed from that passage. In its austerity, in its reduction to its basic elements, *Waterstone* achieves the quality of *yûgen*, that Japanese aesthetic category marked by profundity and the ineffable, both of which are to be found in this very small work in which Noguchi nonetheless approached the unbounded dimensions of the sublime [see chapter 10].[38] Water, quiet water, provided the path.

8-30
Fountains for the Supreme Court. Tokyo, 1974. Austere elegance.

8-31
Tsukubai,
1962.
Marc Treib, © The
Noguchi Museum/ARS]

8-32
Waterstone,
1986.
[Metropolitan Museum
of Art]

> 9.

California Scenario, Costa Mesa

In conception and execution *California Scenario* fully merits its rank as Noguchi's most perfect landscape, a landscape in which California's varied ecotones have been abstracted, distilled, and recast as sculpture [9-1]. It is at once a place, a space, a sculpture, and a garden, where the visual sense obtains the greatest reward. Physical accommodation is admittedly minimal, with seating primarily set on the periphery of the site. While the sculptural experience derives largely from movement through the space, the garden is also appreciated by those looking down upon it from the floors of the adjacent office towers [9-2].

>> VISITS

On my first visit many years ago, having been schooled in architecture and design, and at the time knowing little about Isamu Noguchi and his work, I found *California Scenario* lacking. It was near midday in Costa Mesa, and the temperature was high. Heat radiated from the white walls of the parking garage with little shade to provide relief. While the forms, the materials, and the quality of light were provocative, my overall impression was not positive. Without question its forms held some interest, but I wondered why the garden seemed so inhospitable. The thin stream of water flowing through the sandstone paving provided no physical relief, although I did appreciate the detailing of its edges. I wondered why anyone would want to enter this space and concluded that it had been designed mainly to be seen from above, from the comfort of air-conditioned offices. I left unimpressed.

That impression changed radically on a second visit about a year later. It was afternoon, just after a rainstorm, probably in spring, when some rain still falls in California. The majority of the garden had been thrown into shade by the low-lying sun. Gradually, from beneath the cloud layer, light began to beam intensely into the space, creating deep shadows that dramatically transformed the garden into sculpture [9-3]. In contrast to the arid torture of my first visit, this was gripping visual theater. Perhaps there was something here after all. That night I returned; my altered opinion was confirmed. Life and shape within the space appeared as high drama. At night, visitors appeared as moving silhouettes cast upon the walls of the garage, especially those of the valet parking attendants as they ran to retrieve the restaurant clients' cars. After seeing one of Noguchi's early proposals

9-0
California Scenario.
Costa Mesa, California, 1982.
Water Use and stream
at night.

9-1
California Scenario.
Costa Mesa, California, 1982.
Garden by day,
theater by night.

9-2
California Scenario.
Seen from the roof of
the parking garage.

9-3
California Scenario.
Costa Mesa, California, 1982.
In afternoon light.

for the garden, Henry T. Segerstrom (1923–2015), the project's client—or, better termed, patron—told Noguchi that the space would be a garden by day but a theater by night.[1] Mr. Segerstrom got it exactly right.

>> CHRONICLE

A century and a half ago, the land in the part of Costa Mesa today occupied by a major shopping mall, office towers, restaurants, shops, and parking was agricultural. The Swedish immigrant Segerström family settled in Orange County's Santa Ana in 1898 and purchased some forty acres of land; by the late 1940s their holdings had grown fiftyfold. During its first fifty years on the land, the family worked two of the largest dairy farms in the state; additional crops included alfalfa and lima beans.[2] By the 1940s, into the 1950s, and even today, they were the nation's largest producer of the legume. Lima beans had originated in lands around Lima, Peru, and benefitted from cool coastal climates, seasonal moisture, and periods of high heat.[3] The region extending from Santa Barbara to San Diego shares similar environmental conditions and is ideal for the bean's propagation.[4] The harvests were plentiful; the family prospered and continued to acquire more land. Seriously affected by estate taxes, however, the family sought investment opportunities beyond agriculture. Nevertheless, as late as 1948, 100 percent of the Segerstrom holdings remained in farmland.

In time, Harold T. Segerstrom Jr. and his cousin Henry Thomas Segerstrom saw other and greater financial potential by developing the land. In 1967 they built South Coast Plaza, which through periodic expansions today ranks among the largest shopping malls in the United States. In time, there followed a series of office towers set in a sea of greenery and parking garages, not unlike the future city proposed by Le Corbusier early in the twentieth century. Sites near the mall and offices serve cultural as well as mercantile purposes and today host the Segerstrom Center for the Arts (formerly the Orange County Performing Arts Center), and the adjacent Renée and Henry Segerstrom Concert Hall, the Samueli Theater, the Lawrence and Kristina Dodge Education Center, and most recently, the Orange County Museum of Art.

With Prudential Insurance, the C. J. Segerstrom firm planned to construct two office towers adjacent to the San Diego Freeway, just off Bristol Street and across from South Coast Plaza. Town Center Two, each a 15-story tower, would be served by a parking structure of five floors. Together, the garage and the offices would define a space of some 70,000 square feet (approximately 1.6 acres) ultimately to become *California Scenario*. With their earlier project for the nearby Westin South Coast Plaza hotel, the Segerstroms had included a small park as part of the development. As it had been well regarded by guests, Segerstrom thought that a similar park would be a positive complement to the new complex and had begun working with landscape architect Ken Kammeyer and architects A. C. Martin and Associates, who had proposed a terraced green space that was more a park than a plaza.[5]

The idea for commissioning Noguchi to design another "park" was Henry Segerstrom's. A dramatic photo of the Dodge Fountain on the April 1978 cover of *Smithsonian* magazine had caught his attention—his first exposure to Noguchi's work. Reading the article Segerstrom learned that Noguchi also designed landscapes, and almost immediately he reconsidered the nature of the park and terminated further work on the initial project. In its place Segerstrom wanted Noguchi to design something: perhaps a plaza, a park, or a sculpture. He then hired art consultant Tamara B. Thomas (1940–2004) to broker the commission and establish a relationship with the sculptor.[6] Thomas, in turn, wrote to Noguchi in September 1979, conveying Segerstrom's interest in the sculptor's involvement and expressing his fervent wish that Noguchi accept the commission. Noguchi was apparently noncommittal but agreed to meet with Thomas and Segerstrom sometime before 13 November.[7]

Noguchi was ailing with a cold and apparently gave Segerstrom a correspondingly cold reception, telling him flatly that he didn't work for developers.[8] When Segerstrom mentioned that two of the boundaries of the site were defined by a parking garage, Noguchi grumbled that people should drive less and walk more as they did in New York—apparently overlooking problems of transportation in the urban sprawl so characteristic of Southern California.[9] Rather than a sculpture for a commercial property in Costa Mesa, Noguchi suggested that Segerstrom sponsor a piece for Stanford University, his alma mater.[10] Segerstrom had no interest in sponsoring a project in Palo Alto, however; he wanted Noguchi to create something for his familial homeland in Costa Mesa.

The existing documents confirm that Segerstrom was not a person to give up easily, and in a series of handwritten letters he expressed his deep appreciation for the sculptor's work and his belief that the garden could be a landmark project for both patron and artist. A visit to the Costa Mesa site was proposed for some time in the coming months, but on 3 December 1979, before the date of the visit had been set, Segerstrom again wrote to Noguchi explaining how "deeply meaningful" his visit with the sculptor had been and that he had been inspired by his philosophy and art. "There has long been a dream in my mind and heart, that I would be responsible for bringing your art and creation to South Coast Plaza." He added that to him "the sensitivity and expression of your sculpture is without peer," and that with it he experienced "an almost emotional bond."[11] As in several other commissions, Noguchi initially said "no," but after some period of time he returned with a proposal; that is to say, despite his immediate refusal, his mind kept mulling over the possibilities until his creativity got the better of him. Was it the flattery to his ego that changed his mind, or was it the excitement that accompanies a new commission so rich in potential, bolstered by a sizable budget?

After the visit to the site and further conversations with Segerstrom and his architectural and landscape teams, the artist relented and accepted the commission. His January 1980 letter to Thomas matter-of-factly outlined the issues of logistics, fees, and the method of payment for a piece of his own making—in addition to a plaza of his design. The December meeting was probably the first time that the subject of a distinct sculpture had been raised. In reconsidering the scope of the project, Segerstrom realized that he had secured Noguchi's services as a designer but would not have a sculpture specifically identified as "a Noguchi."[12] Installed on the site almost a year before overall construction was completed, the sculpture was eventually titled *Spirit of the Lima Bean*—referring, of course, to the Segerstrom family's principal crop, whose annual yield arguably remains the world's largest.[13]

When Segerstrom, Thomas, and Noguchi met in December 1980, the artist convinced them that a "bare plaza" was better than a green park. Noguchi questioned Segerstrom's "courage and who has the greater imagination or at least the courage to do the ultimate within our limits."[14] That Segerstrom possessed the "courage" is attested by the fact that immediately after their meeting he had halted all further work on the earlier park design.

Serving as broker, Tamara Thomas outlined the conditions of the contract in a letter of 26 March 1980. Noguchi would "undertake this design work" for a fee of $110,000, payable in four installments beginning with the signing of the agreement and ending with the completion of construction. The construction drawings would be the responsibility of landscape architects Kammeyer, Lynch, and Partners, Inc. (later Kammeyer and Partners) of Irvine, who would also supervise construction. Kammeyer had launched his practice in 1966 and had met Henry Segerstrom when working as a landscape contractor. Segerstrom had given Kammeyer field ruffage left after harvest as organic enrichment for the soils in his landscapes.[15] For prior building projects, Segerstrom had commissioned other landscape architects, including Peter Walker, but had selected Kammeyer because he was local and had previously collaborated with the architects A. C. Martin and Associates. As neither Segerstrom nor Kammeyer had ever undertaken a project with so many unknowns, they agreed that rather than a fixed fee the landscape architect would bill for his time and materials. Liability in terms of safety and building codes would be the responsibility of the landscape architects.

Segerstrom approved the letter-contract the following day. Although never specifically stipulated, the budget probably hovered around $1.2 million, which would mean that Noguchi was receiving a commission based on about ten percent of the construction costs. Segerstrom was concerned that his partners at Prudential Insurance might not support a garden as involved and costly as the one Noguchi would no doubt propose, and so there was never a line item for the garden's design and construction apart from the general building costs. In effect, he buried the cost to secure a great artwork never tagged with a precise price.[16]

>> *SPIRIT OF THE LIMA BEAN*

On a more personal level, as noted above, Segerstrom sought a sculpture that would "not only be an expression of Noguchi's mind but also of his hand," perhaps for the lobbies of the towers or sited at some focal point near the garden's entrance.[17] Thomas prepared a separate agreement for *Origin Stone*, as the sculpture was first called, in July 1980.[18] Segerstrom admitted to Noguchi that, "it has troubled me for many years that we will soon no longer be able to grow beans on our native soil." Therefore, the sculpture would be "our most precious connection with the source."[19] To occupy the space of an 8.5-foot cube, the sculpture would be fabricated at Noguchi's studio in Mure, Japan, shipped to California, and assembled on-site. *Sculpture of Origin*, its second title, would itself be succeeded by *Spirit of the Lima Bean* [9-4]. Noguchi's technical support for the garden would come from Fuller and Sadao, with Shoji Sadao taking primary responsibility. This was the first time the firm was mentioned in relation to the project; their responsibilities would include all the elements of the plaza in addition to *Origin Stone*. Although it was not specified what percentage would be directed toward the whole and what toward the sculpture, the total fee had escalated, in fact more than doubled, to a quarter of a million dollars—exclusive of sales tax, should any be involved. Through Thomas, Noguchi cautioned Segerstrom that although *Origin Stone* might bear certain similarities to a fountain sculpture for Miami then under study, it should be regarded as a unique work of art.

The massive stones for the sculpture were shaped and preassembled at Noguchi's studio in Japan, shipped to Los Angeles arriving around the end of February 1981. The elements were then joined using stainless steel dowels to ensure structural integrity, especially against seismic disturbance. Well before the completion of *California Scenario*, on 10 March, *Spirit of the Lima Bean* was christened before an invited crowd of some 200 "art museum directors and board members, media representatives and business men who will be resident in the office building." A lithograph commemorated the event and was given to each guest.[20] The acclaim by those in attendance was unanimous.

>> DESIGN AND PROCESS

While the contractual relations and the creative aspects of the project have considerable interest, they need to be seen in relation to the difficult site conditions that governed the shaping of the topography and infrastructure. The rich farmland so beneficial to raising lima beans presented structural problems for both buildings and garden. Among those troubling conditions was the spongy nature of the loamy soil, which proved insufficient to support the sandstone slabs proposed for the paving. In response, the existing surface of the land was taken down several feet below the ultimate floor level of the building lobbies. After the loam had been removed, the site was

9-4
Spirit of the Lima Bean,
1981.
California Scenario.
Viewed from inside the garden.

backfilled with about a foot of sand as the bed for the paving stones set level with the floors of the towers.

It appears that as early as June 1980 Noguchi already had a concrete, although preliminary, proposal for the work. Kammeyer recalls that biweekly meetings were held in the contractor's trailer, and that everyone attending—except Noguchi—wore a coat and tie. Although Segerstrom gave no specific date in his reminiscences of the project, he recalled that Noguchi arrived with a small sheet of cardboard, perhaps about twenty inches square, with maquettes of each of the garden's major features (Kammeyer believes the sculptures were modeled with Play-Doh bought at the Tokyo airport).[21]

The landscape architect was dismayed at the unprofessional nature of Noguchi's presentation, but in time he became excited and completely engaged in the project, and ultimately considered it the most interesting of his career.[22] Noguchi requested that Segerstrom alone first review the proposal, which the latter found "brilliant."[23] "I was so convinced of the purity of what he had created," said Segerstrom, "that I told him I thought it was absolutely perfect . . . He had a singular ability to translate the scope of the universe the size of the State of California into symbolics that could be places on a small-scale area. There was no redesign" [9-5]. Had the sculptor considered a name for the project? Noguchi had described his idea for the garden as a scenario, as in a film; perhaps *California Scenario* might be suitable. It stuck. Segerstrom expressed his "shear exhilaration for the design," and to the Noguchi team he forwarded the architects' site plan and sections that included the floors of the parking garages.[24] These would help determine more precisely the overall planning of the site as well as the relationship among the levels of buildings and garden. The architects also offered a plan for what they envisioned would be circulation through the site, the most critical feature being a ground-level door at the intersection of the wings of the garage, subsequently positioned adjacent to the future Desert Land.

One amusing aspect of the *California Scenario* story relates to the procuring of the large stones, preferably from a Californian source, to be used as sculptural objects throughout the garden. In their search for boulders of suitable size, form, and character, Noguchi and Ken Kammeyer scouted the desert areas east of Costa Mesa, including a ranch

9-5 *[above]*
California Scenario.
Study model, 1980.
[Kevin Noble, © The Noguchi Museum/ARS]

9-6 *[below]*
California Scenario.
Desert rocks.

owned by the contractor C. L. Peck. Noguchi found the rocks too soft. The search continued, and in their odyssey they included a visit to Joshua Tree National Monument in the Coachella Valley near Twenty-Nine Palms. At Joshua Tree, Noguchi found rocks much to his liking and wondered whether he might acquire them for installation in the plaza. After preliminary discussions with the National Park Service, Kammeyer wrote Noguchi explaining that Joshua Tree was a protected national monument and that only under very strict and certain conditions could any materials, mineral or vegetal, be removed from its jurisdiction. The specifications for any removals, Kammeyer informed the sculptor, were threefold: the materials had to be required for scientific or educational purposes; they could not be found in any other location; and if their removal were finally approved—the chances of which were very slight—the source of the materials at Joshua Tree had to be credited.[25]

On 1 August 1980 Noguchi wrote Joshua Tree Superintendent Rick Anderson and explained why he wanted these five particular rocks: the plaza's design would be "very bare," and "the stones will be used in the Japanese manner as focal elements." The purpose, he assured Anderson, was "to ennoble the stones, and in that sense I believe it will be significantly educational in furthering appreciation of the original beauty of California." He then offered his artistic credentials and requested Anderson's "kind intervention."[26] In a measured yet gracious reply, Anderson wrote of his appreciation for such a public space but that it was "completely against . . . policy to remove any object from areas administered by the National Park Service." He noted, however, that there was land surrounding the park with similar geographic characteristics and geological compositions—perhaps Mr. Noguchi could find stones on those lands.[27]

Kammeyer continued the quest for stones after Noguchi's return to Japan, and on a ranch in the Yucca Valley found what he considered excellent candidates, flagged them, and arranged for their purchase. C. L. Peck photographed the rocks and sent them to Noguchi for his approval. But then the rancher died, and the ranch—and the rocks with it—were put into probate. Alas, given the tight construction schedule any delay was unacceptable. Happily, Kammeyer found similar stones on an adjacent ranch; Peck again photographed them, and Noguchi's approval was secured. Moving rocks of these weights and proportions was no simple matter, and it required building a road several miles long just to haul the rocks off the ranch. Some issues at a weigh station troubled their passage, as did another concerning bridge clearance, but ultimately the rocks arrived and were installed on-site under Noguchi's supervision [9-6].[28]

The sandstone for the plaza's extensive paved surfaces remained to be selected. Although materials from California and Mexico were deemed acceptable, stone from Arizona was thought to be the best option. A chartered flight to the quarry allowed the group to review the material firsthand. By September 1980 samples of the cut stone provided by the supplier had been accepted. In writing to Noguchi in Mure, Segerstrom displayed remarkable acumen, distinguishing the precise differences among the various possible cuts of stone and their resulting aesthetic properties. He ranked at the top those merely quarried and thus more natural, although the width of the joints between the stones would be larger and more irregular than those between stones with straight cuts. "My own reaction leans toward the random pattern," he wrote, "which I feel gives a much more natural look to the surface—a contrast which should emphasize your precise design of the walkway areas."[29] As this was the look apparent in the final form of the paving, Noguchi must have shared the values of his patron.

The following month a meeting of those involved with the project took place on-site, its minutes recording the issues raised by the contractor and the actions to be taken and by whom. Shoji Sadao represented Noguchi's interests in the meeting. The question of the paving cut remained undecided, and specifications governing the sprinklers and plant materials were still lacking. Kammeyer would address these. The minutes of the meeting attest to the significant role Sadao played in the development and construction of *California Scenario*, by questioning conditions such as the intersection between the stone paving and the walls of the garage and the office towers, and details regarding the features Desert Land and Water Source. Given the weight of *Spirit of the Lima Bean*, predicted to be some 67,000 pounds, foundations would be needed, which would be calculated by the architects.[30]

Many of the items discussed in the meeting were still unresolved when the group met the following month, this time with two representatives of the architect in attendance. Among the issues were how the joints between the stones should be treated and the subsurface preparations needed to best address the problematic soil.[31] The 7 November meeting, which included the masonry contractor George Gusky, focused on the paving and determined that the stones should be set in a bed of mortar rather than sand, with the variation between the stones allowed to vary between 1" and 2.5".

Light sand blasting would remove any mortar overage; a penetrating sealant was recommended for protection against staining (an issue with sandstone) but avoiding any gloss that was unappealing to Noguchi. Gusky noted that "very few stone jobs have been done on the West Coast in the last 10 years" and that there were only a handful of individuals capable of executing the work at the high level that was required. He recommended that one small crew do the work to produce the best results. In the end, nearly five months were required for installing the sandstone by three crews of about seven or eight men.[32] The trial paving—with sandstone from Arizona, south of Flagstaff—was installed around Water Source, testing stone approximately two inches in thickness. By general agreement these were judged too thin, and together Noguchi and Kammeyer ordered the work halted; the final material thickness was increased to almost six inches. While Noguchi provided the directives, verbally and in letters, most of the work was executed based on concept sketches without the particulars of construction drawings.

The following week, Kammeyer proposed the selection of plant species for Desert Land and noted that he had already contacted nurseries in Riverside and Palm Springs about their availability. His letter included photographs of the cacti from which Noguchi and Sadao could select. These included aloes, agave, cereus, opuntia, and echinocactus of various varieties—a substantial menu. He also provided specifics regarding horticultural practices, noting that a special soil mix and good drainage would be required, and recommended transplanting in late spring, as the summer heat would stimulate root growth thereafter.[33] The rocks, drawn from desert sources in the Yucca Valley, were soon due on-site. By the following February the selection of species had been finalized and Kammeyer had staked out their locations within Desert Land. The final selections were Palo verde, Trichocereus, aloe, *Agave americana*, Beavertail cactus, Golden Barrel cactus, Red Barrel cactus, and ocotillo, all arranged for their sculptural properties. The construction of Desert Land, described in detail later in this chapter, ensured both the survival of the plants and the contour of the shallow dome.[34] Other trees were chosen based on the tint of their blossoms or the color of their bark.[35]

The delivery date for the granite from the Cold Spring Granite Company in Minnesota— presumably the material to be used for the Water Use pyramid, curved benches, water fountains, and cigarette urns —had been set for some time in July. Clearly, the pace of construction had slowed in prior months, as in June Segerstrom was expressing his anxiousness to the artist. More happily, construction was apparently now progressing at a speedier pace, with most of the cactus and trees already planted.[36]

A nagging issue concerned the wall surfaces of the parking structure. Before Noguchi entered the scene, the architects had specified a split-face concrete block, brown in color, to create a more attractive surface. Noguchi was not looking for surface texture, but walls smooth and neutral. To achieve the desired look, the concrete blocks were rotated to have their textured surface turned inward. The outer faces of the walls were initially only painted white, but the lines of the joints between the blocks remained too evident, causing that option to be rejected. The final solution applied a skim coat of stucco over the entire walls to transform the individual units into a monolithic backdrop for the garden's elements. Painted white, the walls also provided a reflective surface for night lighting.

As construction neared conclusion, Segerstrom began envisioning a major event to celebrate the opening of the garden.[37] Rather than inaugurating *California Scenario alone*, the event would also honor Noguchi himself. Writing to Hisashi Yamada, executive director of the Urasenke school of tea, Segerstrom inquired whether it might be possible to schedule a ceremony as part of the festivities.[38] The program assigned the first day to events associated with the Japanese American Cultural and Community Center, including a tea ceremony. The following day the Los Angeles Museum of Contemporary Art would present an audiovisual presentation introducing the design of its new building by Japanese architect Arata Isozaki. On the third day, the Orange County Performing Arts Center would host traditional Japanese music and dance as well as a performance of Indonesian gamelan.

Segerstrom also wrote to Noguchi to confirm his interest and participation in the events. In his view, "'California Scenario' will symbolize a unity in our art community never before realized."[39]

Detached from the celebration planning, Noguchi was reconsidering his fee, and in April wrote his patron to review the work already done and their previous financial arrangement, and suggested that the fee—which at that point would have totaled $350,000—was somehow insufficient. He told Segerstrom that he had signed the contract because he wanted to realize the project; it would be his most significant garden, and a tribute to the state in which he was born. "I did not want to jeopardize its realization," claimed, adding:

> *and I must say, I did not expect such terms, which I deemed patently unfair, to be either adhered to or upheld by law considering that all my subsequent costs for preparation and supervision of construction were loaded onto the initial over all design to which I had already given my full contribution.*[40]

It is unclear to which particular costs Noguchi referred, as travel expenses and other incidentals were paid outside the contract. But as we have seen in other projects such as those in Paris and Detroit, he often swelled the scope of the project far beyond the one originally agreed upon. "If you had not asked me to be concerned with these I suppose I would have had to retroactively include them myself as part of the design . . . What is the role or process of art if not continuous development and refinement from vague beginnings to the clarity of its final exposition?" He continued, "Nothing may be known in advance, nor can contracts be defined ahead in legal terms without getting in return the kind of response that is seen everywhere in architecture, design, or the arts which are minion to the commercial world."[41] It is true that given the extent to which Noguchi engaged in his designs—in this case down to the benches, water fountains, and cigarette receptacles—he would have been quite displeased should a stock item be installed in place of one of his own making. On the other hand, designers and even artists work under economic and time constraints, presumably to terms agreed upon in advance that would not constrain their creativity.

In essence, Noguchi was asking Segerstrom for carte blanche and his support regarding changes to the program, materials, or time frame, in pursuit of his art. While to some his point might appear valid, it was a lot to ask of a client who had already done everything in his power to ensure that the design would be carried out to the level of detail and excellence Noguchi desired. Segerstrom could have played hardball by simply referring to the contract and demanding that Noguchi stick to it. After all, almost all the major decisions had been made, and the inaugural "Noguchi Celebration" was scheduled for the following month. Although I have not found any document indicating the final resolution of the matter, I suspect that Segerstrom and Noguchi negotiated a fee to some degree of mutual satisfaction.

It is important to note that throughout the entire process Segerstrom was more than kind to Noguchi, held the design in the highest regard, and had supported its realization to the level at which the sculptor aspired, whether in the selection of materials, craft, care for detail, or the revisions to work already completed. As expressed in Segerstrom's letters, on the one hand, his successful negotiations with the sculptor can be attributed to the prior experience of a businessman accustomed to dealing with difficult colleagues and clients, who used this experience to diplomatically avoid conflict with an artist known at times to behave like a maverick. On the other hand, one also senses in Segerstrom's letters a genuine warmth and respect for the artist, as well as his wholehearted support for realizing the design precisely as Noguchi conceived it. If there were problems along the way, he found the best way to solve them. Even when forced to address many of those problems himself, usually due to time limitations, he always wrote Noguchi immediately, seeking his approval for his decision and offering to modify it if Noguchi so chose. There is never a mention of his partner, Prudential Insurance, or what they thought of the project or its costs. For the most part, Segerstrom had buried the high cost of the plaza within the total costs of the buildings so that its actual cost will never be known.[42]

Even in letters essentially regarding some factual matter, Segerstrom always included effusive praise for the design and his complete support for its realization. From Segerstrom's side there seems to be no question of the cordiality and depth of their friendship, one hopes that deep down Noguchi respected Segerstrom as well, and that he saw their relationship as more than a mere business arrangement. Supported by a talented team of landscape architect, architects, and lighting and fountain consultants, their partnership produced a garden, which, as noted at the start of this chapter, I regard as Noguchi's masterwork.

California Scenario opened, as initially proposed, with a three-day celebration starting on 11 May 1982, enacted according to the original program described above. No doubt the Segerstroms and the cultural and arts communities of Costa Mesa were more than thrilled, perhaps more so than the creator of the project, whose mind was already on other works in other places. Records show that Noguchi was pleased with the final form of the garden and its reception. He noted that people were "stunned," and that Costa Mesa had pulled off something that Los Angeles had been unable to do by creating a work of that inventiveness, scale, and quality.[43] In his own retelling of the course of the *California Scenario*, Segerstrom noted that the opening was a major regional event whose program spanned three days —and that Noguchi left after only two of them.

>> ELEMENTS AND COMPOSITION

California Scenario represents through abstraction five landscape types that characterize the Golden State—Water Source; Water Use; Desert Land; Forest Walk; Land Use—in addition to Energy Fountain and the somewhat independent *Spirit of the Lima Bean*. Like the title of a painting or a poem, these should be considered as abstractions rather than replicas, as a portrait is to a sitter, or an Impressionist painting to a scene: interpretations rather than reproductions. Forest Walk, horseshoe in plan, rises as a slope toward the office buildings behind it [9-7]. Its central area was originally planted with wildflowers—today replaced with grass—and ringed by a path and plantings of California redwoods (*Sequoia sempervirens*) that have grown to impressive proportions.

To use plants in a synthetic ecosystem far from their native environment often causes problems: the semi-arid landscape of Southern California hardly provides the same rain, streams, and snow of the High Sierras, but irrigation and periodic replacement have maintained this zone in excellent form, and it offers a welcome respite from the air-conditioned office spaces within the towers. All gardens modify natural processes to some degree as they bring into close contact species hailing from locations far from their usual neighbors. In this regard *California Scenario* has posed some challenges to the maintenance staff. Set at the opposite end of the plaza is Land Use, a mound shaped in plan as a bar with rounded ends, whose sloping sides were planted with honeysuckle [9-8]. Along its ridge extends a bar of granite beside which Noguchi proposed running fluorescent lights in a shallow trough.[44] Originally, mist—perhaps to evoke the thick Tule fogs that periodically obscure visibility in California's Central Valley—was to emanate from the bar and hover above the mound, but early on this idea was scrapped over concerns about maintenance and liability.

Other than the redwoods and eucalyptus, Water Source is the tallest element in the garden, standing proudly against the north wall of the garage [9-9]. Viewed from the side, it is a pure triangle faced with the same sandstone as the paving but given a geometric cut and a smoother finish. The origins of the form probably stem from Noguchi's travels in India, with an itinerary that included the astronomical observatories commissioned for Delhi and Jaipur by Sawai Jai Singh II in the eighteenth century—including one structure that might rank as the world's largest sundial [9-10].[45] In Costa Mesa, however, the giant wedge stands as an abstraction of the slopes of the Sierras and the rivers and streams produced by the springtime snowmelt. Inside its hypotenuse, a bed of stones modulates and aerates the downhill tumble in a spray of white and blue, much in the manner of the *chadar* in Indian Moghul gardens [9-11].[46] Noguchi's saw the observatories as:

> *mystic sculptures that define space... You might call them useless architecture or useful sculpture. They imply a use—much sculpture does that. Whether or not they were intended so, Jai Singh's works have turned out to be an expression of wanting to be one with the universe.*[47]

His translation of these forms—which he had already used in the walls of his sculpture garden in Jerusalem and to which he would return in Houston—grants a new function to this "useless architecture": the form remains, but now serves a new purpose.

The stream emanating from Water Source winds its way through the sandstone surfaces and terminates beneath the low, polished granite pyramid that symbolizes Water Use [9-12; 9-13]. To Segerstrom the opposed wedges suggested the erosion and deposition of soil from sources in the mountains to the flatlands of the valleys.[48]

Unlike the wedge and the pyramid, Desert Land is based on the circle [9-14]. Here, cactus, agave, and other desert species are employed according to the modernist ideal: an ecological assemblage whose plants are particularly striking in low sunlight or at night, when silhouetted against the white walls of the garage [9-15].

Energy Fountain stands in a leafy setting between the office towers, framed by pink-flowering trees like the Brazilian silk floss (*Ceiba speciosa*) and crape myrtle (*Lagerstroeumia indica*) [9-16]. The shape of the fountain possibly derives from early space-capsule designs, with a conical form sheathed in granite setts originally capped by a cylindrical stainless-steel tube. Water pulses from the top of the tube and hugs its sides until it engages the top rank of granite setts, at which point it tumbles, bubbly and frothy, over the uneven surface of the cone. Early difficulties with overspray were solved by adjusting the height of the lip atop the tube and by the installation of an anemometer, which shuts off the water when the wind blows too strongly. Dramatically illuminated at night, the fountain provides a welcoming feature for those who enter the garden from the west and those in search of a cooling overspray [9-17]. The last player in this theater of water, leaf, and stone is *Spirit of the Lima Bean*, a stack of massive stones that anchors one corner of the garden.

Whether consciously intended by Noguchi or not, the plan can be read as a series of correspondences in opposing pairs: like Energy Fountain across the plaza, Water Source also refers to water; both Desert Land and Forest Walk feature vegetation rather than stone; and Land Use and Water Use not only reflect the appropriation of California's natural resources, but also anchor the composition at the west and east, respectively. Relations evident in plan can only suggest those actually perceived in three dimensions, so here the game becomes trickier. There is little question that the fifteen-story office buildings and the five-level parking garage define the garden within which Noguchi worked that parallels, if in a more open way, the sunken courtyards in New York and New Haven. Almost all Noguchi's gardens and courts follow the same pattern of composing distinct features within the confines of a space usually not of his making.[49] We might characterize this pattern as a constellation—an appropriate word because it suggests a coherent figure, even if imagined by the observer; a cohesive relationship among the various elements; and a whole that surpasses the sum of its parts. Indeed, most Noguchi gardens could be grasped and summarized by this one word.

9-7
California Scenario.
Costa Mesa, California, 1982.
Beyond the stream, Forest Walk is bounded by a stand of mature redwoods

9-8
California Scenario.
Land Use.

9-9 *[left]*
Astronomical observatory.
Jaipur, India, eighteenth century.
[Isamu Noguchi, © The Noguchi Museum/ARS]

9-10 *[above]*
California Scenario.
1982.
Water Source at twilight.

9-11
California Scenario.
After tumbling down Water Source, the narrow stream weaves eastward through the paving toward Water Use.

>> DETAILED DESIGN AND CONSTRUCTION

The beauty and impact of *California Scenario* derive as much from its details and construction ingenuity as from its guiding myth and formal invention. Much of the credit goes to Shoji Sadao and Ken Kammeyer, who brought Noguchi's ideas into reality [9-18]. Sadao was responsible for the preparation of many of the construction drawings, executed in cooperation with the architects. For his part, Kammeyer invented and developed various critical solutions that elevated the quality of usually mundane details to the level of artwork. Noguchi himself, of course, was responsible for many of the details, among them those concerning the grouting between the stones used for the paving.

> *About the joints of the sandstone paving. Of a natural gray to darker cement without added color, a fine sand should be used with an additive, to allow for smooth troweling without cracking, with the finish 1/8-inch below the edges of the sandstones. This must be maintained without too much concern for keeping a uniform level. In other words, the level of the cement at the groove edges should conform to the level and character of the stones, whatever the rises and depressions.*

He further directed that special attention be paid along the edges of the stream, where "the vertical mortar should be recessed fairly deep, 1-inch or more at the corner where this meets the surface[,] not a sharp square as I saw, but rounded: the troweling of the joints should carefully follow the irregularities of the stone going deeper into the crevices at water's edge."[50]

It is easy to consider this concern for the detail of the mortar joints as something just short of maniacal until one considers the role the joints play in the garden and their number [see 9-24]. Noguchi also instructed Kammeyer that on the facing of the Water Use pyramid a noticeable joint between the stones would compensate for irregularities in their surfaces. In the end, it should come as no surprise that Noguchi devoted so much attention to the installation and details of the stonework; after all, stone was his principal medium.

Noguchi had learned from the Japanese garden that the stones were its "bones" and that all other elements were secondary. In this tradition the primary stones are usually positioned first, set deeply to appear

9-12
California Scenario.
The stream varies in width and intensity as it meanders.

9-13
California Scenaric.
Water Use.
Miraculously, the heat of the stone facing in the sunlight does not deter children's play.

9-14
California Scenario.
Desert Land.

9-15 *[opposite]*
California Scenario.
Mound of earth separating the garden zones, planted with crape myrtle and other species.

as if they had always been a part of the land. Secondary stones and plants adhere to this initial structure. To some degree this process also governed the construction of *California Scenario*, with the desert boulders initially installed using cranes and a trained crew while supervised by Noguchi. In Japan a stone has live sides that possess more than visual attraction. In directing the setting of the stones Noguchi looked to find each stone's "best" side and considered its relation to the other stones, and to the sculptural objects and vegetation to come.[51] Turning the boulder, dropping it a bit, raising this edge—all were necessary adjustments to ensure that the rock would function aesthetically as an integral element of the garden's composition.

The sandstone throughout the project is unusually thick for public spaces; the thickness increases where its edges are visible. Along the rims of the stream the paving on each side cantilevers over the water and conceals the carefully placed jets installed to boost the perceived vigor of the stream.[52] These were installed when it was found that after its exuberant fall along the inclined surface of Water Source, the velocity of the stream quickly dissipated and continued with hardly a ripple as it approached the inclined pyramid of Water Use [9-18]. Throughout the entire garden, all the drains have been concealed beneath the edges of cantilevered sandstone paving blocks. While this may appear as a minor detail, masking the drains prevents visual disruptions to the continuity of the pavement.[53] Needless to say, the irrigation needed to support the planted areas is apparent only when in use.

All the furnishing required by public use—such as benches, water fountains, ashtrays, and lights—were Noguchi's design [9-19]. Although Noguchi had once joked to Kammeyer that the latter had a "trash mind," the landscape architect understood how poorly designed features could undermine the design integrity of the garden. Noguchi agreed and told him there should be no trash, no smoking in "his garden." Reality said otherwise, and the receptacles for both trash and smokes were installed adjacent to the benches on the periphery of the central area. These functional elements were all executed in granite and represent a collaboration among Noguchi, Kammeyer, and Sadao. Apparently, when Noguchi first showed his design for the benches to Segerstrom, the patron jokingly questioned how he was going to bend the granite into the curves shown in his drawing. The solution was not to bend the granite, Noguchi replied, but to create the semblance

9-16
California Scenario.
Energy Fountain with the redwoods of Forest Walk behind.

9-17
California Scenario.
Energy Fountain at night.

of a curve by assembling the bench in segments. Like the supporting actors in a movie, these furnishings do not attract the visitor's attention but stand quietly aside, ready for use when needed. More significantly, their design does not detract from the unity of the space.

Perhaps the most adroit resolution of a challenging task involved the construction of Desert Land. Early on Noguchi had established its design as a shallow dome, circular in plan, and graded to increase its visual presence. After Kammeyer provided a menu of desert plants from which to choose Noguchi made his selection and determined the position of each plant within the circle. The main task was to determine the best method for shaping and constructing the contour of the dome to resist rain, wind, and the curiosity of visitors and children.

The solution devised was ingenious. First, the required volume of soil was dumped into the bounds of the circle after the necessary services and irrigation piping had been installed.[54] A plywood template, whose lower edge was cut to the desired profile of the dome, was attached to a sturdy pipe inserted in the circle's center. The template was then rotated around the pipe several times to screed the earth into the desired contour. Steel-reinforcing mesh was then carefully positioned over the soil, and covered with concrete to create a dome of the perfect slope. Following Noguchi's design, holes had been cut into the steel mesh in appropriate positions, and the cacti, agave, and other species planted. Upon review, Noguchi requested that the positions of some plants be shifted and additional holes cut into the covering shell. In this manner, the final composition was achieved. A carpet of brown pebbles approximating the color of sand was then set in a bed of matte epoxy resin to fix the stones in place. Segerstrom wrote Noguchi telling that he was impressed by Kammeyer's method, and that "all of us are very pleased with the final finish on the Desert Land. The epoxy is phenomenal. The large rocks are so firmly attached they cannot be displaced even by kicking. The color is excellent and the texture and look of the 'sand' is remarkably desert-like."[55] Although today one sees some scattered pebbles lying beside the circle—some of them no doubt added at a later date and not adhered to the slab—in large measure the resolution of the design and the construction method have both functioned without incident.

9-18
California Scenario.
Boulders and stream,
with Land Use beyond.

>> NIGHTTIME

Segerstrom was prescient in understanding that the garden would become a theater by night, with the experience after sunset even more dramatic and impressive than during the day [9-20]. For the garden to be occupied at night, building codes required a minimum number of lumens, the measure of visible light relative to a certain measure of time. That is to say, the illumination of the garden had to be sufficient to ensure the safety of its nighttime visitors. Noguchi would accept no light standards within the garden; the architects wanted no light fixtures attached to "their" buildings.[56] Apparently in an act of self-contradiction and prompted by his dissatisfaction with the lights installed under the stones along the edge of the stream, Noguchi proposed short bollards as light standards. This solution proved untenable, however, and was dismissed as a potential disruption to the harmony of the design. In the solution that ultimately won out, the white walls of the parking garages reflect the light cast upon them by lamps set within short granite posts.

Noguchi's second requirement was that the wash of light upon the walls be consistent throughout their lengths, as it was by day. Lighting specialist Paul Marantz consulted on the lighting design but offered no solution generally accepted. In the end it was Noguchi himself who suggested the successful path by which to proceed. Or almost successful. Apparently, the light reflected from the walls fell slightly below the required measure.[57] To increase that number a giant light fixture—originally a group of four 1,000-watt arc lamps—was installed on the roof of the west tower. Mounted on tracks, it rolled out to the edge of the rooftop each evening and increased the light level by an amount sufficient to meet the demands of the code [9-21]. With a diameter of roughly two feet and covered by paired blue and purple filters, the impression was that of a soft blue moonlight with a slightly romantic air.[58] The effect was subtle, of course, and I suspect it was only very rarely that any visitor noticed either the source of the augmented light or its benefits. Every visitor, however, would notice the animated shadows cast by anyone or anything passing between the lamps on the ground and the wall surfaces of the garage. Like an Indonesian shadow play, or a simple hand shadow, visitors—especially children—delight in seeing their forms writ large upon the walls, zooming larger and smaller depending on their proximity to the light source. The effect is indeed theatrical.

9-15
California Scenario.
Bench, table, and ash tray.

9-20 *[opposite]*
California Scenario.
Water Use with Desert Land and Water Source at night.

Lights mounted beneath the stones that protrude over the banks of the stream and beneath the sides of the Land Use pyramid complement the wash of light reflected from the garage walls. Perhaps the the most exciting effect is found at the Energy Fountain, where the uplights in the pool at its base enhance the dazzle of the water plunging down the slopes of its granite cone. Noguchi specified that the metal surfaces of the fountain be given a "swirl finish" similar to that on the Dodge Fountain in Detroit.[59] Not only does this conceal blemishes or irregularities in the finish of the stainless steel, but it also enhances the play of light on its surface.

>> RECEPTION

From the time of its completion, most of the response to *California Scenario* was laudatory—especially from the art world. Over time, the garden received design awards from the American Society of Landscape Architects, and Henry Segerstrom himself received their award for his continued patronage of the arts. Sharing my own initial reaction to the garden, architect Jay Todisco, whose firm later designed the adjacent Copa de Oro restaurant, felt that the courtyard "seemed to alienate the people who would really use it, by not having more seating. It's a viewing, not a people-oriented space." On the more practical side, executive secretary Susan Fuller, who worked in one of the towers, thought that "it's really cute from up there. But the one thing I don't like is that my new spike heels get caught in the unevenness of the pavement," and felt that she "was going to fall and break [her] neck."[60]

Although the public was a bit hesitant about the garden's success, there is little question that both patron and artist were quite pleased with the results of their collaboration. Henry Segerstrom had brought into existence a work unique to California, if not the world; its conception, resolution, and realization produced Noguchi's most outstanding garden, perhaps his only landscape where every aspect of its design had been executed as he wished. There were no agencies to decry its design, no stringent code requirements to compromise its form, no governmental bodies to interfere when an administration changed. Segerstrom had stated at the outset that he sought an "aesthetic dictator" for the project, and he had found a great one in Isamu Noguchi. Of the series of artworks Segerstrom had commissioned, this was by far his most significant.

In reminiscences appearing in the *Los Angeles Times*, Segerstrom recounted how he first noticed Noguchi's work, visited him in New York, and coaxed him to accept the commission. Although Noguchi had never previously worked with a developer—he often said he didn't trust them—Segerstrom persevered, writing Noguchi a longhand note telling of his admiration for the sculptor and his belief that it was important for Noguchi to have a work in the region of his birth. Perhaps Noguchi had been interested from the start but played hard to get to secure the best terms. When Segerstrom "told him a figure that [he] thought was less than the actual budget cost but still a significant budget," Noguchi responded: "That's not enough." Segerstrom assured him that he would do what was necessary.[61] In the end Segerstrom provided an opportunity unmatched by any public agency, giving the sculptor virtually free rein and rarely questioning the many changes that accompanied the development and realization of the design.

In a letter written to support the nomination of Henry Segerstrom for the American Institute of Architects' award for the promotion of "the understanding, appreciation, and advancement of Art and Architecture," Noguchi recalled the origins and the course of the project with a warmth expressed in no previous document. In the letter he noted how his proposal was for "something entirely different: For a cubic volume of clear California air, not earth." He then described the meaning of each of the features: "the revealed beauty of the garage walls. A sculpture of great proportion to give weight and meaning . . . Waterflow directs us from one awareness to another, from 'Water Source' to 'Water use.'"[62] Redwood trees become sculpture; a fountain symbolizes energy. Land Use represents "a passage of life and a testament to those who made America." He makes certain to note that "Henry went along with all this and more: Needling me to figure out how to bend stone into circular seating and wood benches made integral to the landscape. He accepted that every element was integral to the integrity of the work as a whole." And in closing, as if to dispel any doubt, Noguchi wrote that "the rare individual who abetted all this with warm personal involvement was Henry Segerstrom, and I am grateful."[63]

>> AFTERMATH

Like the natural environment itself, every aspect of the built environment changes over time. In the forty-odd years since its creation, *California Scenario* has experienced changes to its fabric, some of them for the better, some not. While constructed elements such as Water Source and Water Use have retained almost all their original character, the trees planted throughout the site have matured to impressive dimensions, especially the eucalyptus (*Eucalyptus citriodora*) and redwoods (*Sequoia sempervirens*). Sandstone spalls, water jets clog, mortar joints crack and crumble—all require periodic maintenance. In 2001 Prudential Insurance expressed their wish to sell their stake in the development, and for certain reasons C. J. Segerstrom opted not to buy out their interest.[64]

The sale to CommonWealth Partners caused an existential crisis for those to whom the garden had become a precious resource. How would *California Scenario* fare under new ownership? Would the new owners treat the landscape with the respect accorded an artwork or would they destroy parts or all of it for new construction or other use? Various art and cultural parties lobbied the municipality to attach its approval for the sale to the contingency that *California Scenario* be conserved in the form in which Noguchi had conceived and constructed it. Segerstrom did not want to sell but for some reason found it was the best—or only—way to proceed. Apparently, the new owners did not intend to change the garden in any way; the question was to what level of maintenance they would commit, for how long, and whether the adjacent parking garage should be considered a part of the work. Fortunately, with the calling of the question by Costa Mesa Mayor Libby Cowan at a meeting on 23 May 2001, the story was granted a happy ending: CommonWealth Partners received the approval to make the minor modifications to the property they planned while agreeing to maintain the garden in its original form for fifty years.[65]

California Scenario is regarded as an amenity and an attraction for tenants, a portion of whose rents support the cost of upkeep based on the square footage of their rental. Visiting in August 2004, I toured the site with Karen Graham, who then headed its management.[66] I learned that although any tenant can host an event in the garden, its use requires prior approval. Of course, cultural and community events also take place there, as do weddings. However, no events that would disturb normal business activities are permitted, and therefore most of these are held at night or on the weekends.

Some changes have been fortuitous.[67] Under the searing sunlight of a Costa Mesa summer maintaining mountain meadow flowers was untenable, and that area of the Forest Walk was long ago replanted with grass, with a substantial annual savings. The original irrigation for the Desert Land cacti did not function as desired and over time was replaced by hand watering; some cacti have been replaced, but with the original species. In contrast, the honeysuckle planted on the side of the Land Use mound has thrived and requires periodic thinning. With fertilizing and pruning, these are all normal issues involved with the maintenance of any garden.

The moon lamps mounted on the roof of the west tower were changed to more energy-efficient LEDs. Energy Fountain is now controlled by a variable speed drive that adjusts the rate of flow based on wind conditions or the need for water conservation. The wood seats of benches have been renewed, as have the filtration system and light fixtures in the stream; new directional and identification signage today proudly identifies the "Noguchi Garden" and explains its elements. Less auspicious has been the repointing of the joints between the sandstone paving blocks, which have been rendered flush with the surface of the stone, lacking the subtle reveal on either side of the joint that lent the stones an air of elegance. Perhaps this was required by universal access requirements that came into force after the opening of the garden; perhaps it came about due to lack of awareness of the subtlety of the original technique. *California Scenario* stands today much in its original state, other than the welcome growth of its trees The water is flowing; the lights are working; the visitors are coming.

Admittedly, the visits upon which certain of these observations are based occurred some years ago, and I have been unable to determine whether the property has been sold again to new owners in the interim. On a more recent visit at the end of 2019, however, the conditions of the sculpture and the plants were happily similar to those I had encountered a decade before.

>> REFLECTION

Like most of Noguchi's landscapes, *California Scenario* is perhaps more for the mind than the body. True, its beauty and complexity derive and benefit from movement through the space to relate the garden's principal features to one another and experience the sculpture as a whole. In that sense, the garden does engage the body. Yet it must be admitted that the comfort offered the visitor is meager. Yes, there are benches for seating, two of them agreeably shaded by trees, and another at the crest of Forest Walk. But throughout much of the site there is little shade and little seating to offer respite from the sun and heat in the warmer months—or protection from the rain. Standing within the space in summer can be brutal, with the intense light reflected from the walls of the garage exacerbating its presence.

Landscape architects are educated to consider the human presence as well as the natural environment, and their investigations of form are usually tempered or even guided by their potential service and user response. The artist, should he or she so choose, can mute the impact of this aspect of their work—the reason I was so troubled by *California Scenario* on my initial visit. In time I came around, however, realizing that comfort is only one aspect by which to valorize experience. Should it always be the most important one? Can a landscape not challenge its visitors, assuming that entry to the place is voluntary and not forced upon them?

In the 1990s I again visited *California Scenario* to see if any major changes had been made in the several years since my prior visit and to take some new photos. When I arrived, I was shocked to find a caterer setting up for an event, perhaps a wedding [9-22]. Tents had been erected to shelter guests from rain and sun, beneath which were some Astroturf carpets to cover the sandstone and presumably soften the hardness of the paving. I assumed that chairs would be brought in later. I found it awful and was somewhat sickened by it. As the caterers went about their work and I tried to take photos without including them, I began to reconsider. "Well, maybe this isn't such a bad idea. When physical comfort is required in a landscape conceived as an artwork, let the caterers bring it in. And more importantly, when the event is over, let them take it away." Why can't physical amenity be transitory while the value of the work endures?

9-21
California Scenario.
Original lights on roof of office tower, today replaced by LED.

As a place for the eye, there is little argument that *California Scenario* is stunning. The play of forms, the babbling of water falling and streaming, the shifts in materials, the flowering of plants in spring —all become elements of temporal flow as well as visual delight. This interest and delight apply equally to views of the garden from the offices in the towers, as well as from the ground. Some of my more socially minded colleagues are troubled by *California Scenario*, which they term "inhuman." *California Scenario* is not a work of landscape architecture as normally practiced; it is a work of art. If you build it, they will come—but perhaps for different reasons.

Interestingly, even curiously, changes in California smoking laws have increased the use of the garden—in direct contradiction to Noguchi's wish that smoking be prohibited. Municipal codes today forbid smoking inside buildings and within twenty or so feet of a window or door. Like those seeking privacy beyond the earshot of their coworkers when making cell-phone calls, smokers have retreated ever more deeply into the garden in their lust for that delicious cigarette: thus adding to the garden a new use and a new user group with a different type of appreciation for this exceptional sculpture.

9-22
California Scenario. The importation of caterer tents, tables, and chairs.

> 10.

Noguchi and Japanese Aesthetics

In reviews of Noguchi's exhibitions over the years, American critics have often referred to the artist's Japanese heritage and its influence—both broadly in regard to his approach to sculpture and more specifically as it pertains to his selection and handling of materials. During his residence in Japan in the early 1950s, in contrast, Japanese artists regarded him as an American artist and a representative of Western modernism. These divergent readings of Noguchi and his work recall the alternative interpretations of the shoreline city of Despina, among the fanciful stories told by Marco Polo in conversation with Genghis Kahn, as related by Italo Calvino in *Invisible Cities*.[1] To those approaching Despina from the surrounding desert, Calvino offers, the city's form suggests that of a ship at sea, whereas those approaching the city from the water see Despina as if a camel, the ship of the desert. As with art, perceptions of the city vary with personal experience, location, and intention, and are only very rarely neutral or objective.

While in the West it is easy to interpret Noguchi's art and gardens through a lens of "Japan-ness," we need recall that his earliest studies, guided by Onorio Ruotolo at the Da Vinci Art School, introduced him to traditional Western genres, at which he soon became adept.[2] A six-month apprenticeship in the Paris atelier of Constantin Brancusi in 1927 prompted his embrace of modernism—Western modernism—and furthered his quest for simplicity and concern for revealing the essence of each form and material. Despite this conversion to more modernist thinking, it was his commissions for figurative works that supported him through the 1930s. This series of portrait heads varied in material and manner, including an almost classic realism, expressionism, and minimalism, although not in any particular order. To my mind, Noguchi remained a Western modernist touched and enriched by his knowledge of Japanese aesthetic philosophy and the approaches it fosters. But in what way, and to what degree?

>> INFLUENCE

Influence is a notoriously tricky subject to tackle with any convincing degree of accuracy. Unless the artist or writer happens to admit to the specific inspiration, its presence may reside more in the eyes of the viewer than in the mind of the artist or the work itself. I once suggested that there are four degrees of influence, traceable along a gradient: replication, citation, adap-

10-0
Bring to Life (detail), 1979.
[Marc Treib, © The Noguchi Museum/ARS]

tation, and abstraction. Each corresponds to the extent to which the original source is apparent in the conception or realization of the new work.[3] Replication is the easiest to identify because it produces a demonstrable match with its source; citation rehearses the precedent to a lesser degree and may adopt it only in part. Adaptation often involves the appropriation of thought more than the resulting form; abstraction furthers the distance between a work and its referent, and may result in a total lack of resemblance between the two. Assigning a work to any of those categories is troubling at best.

For well over a century critics and historians have traced Japanese influence in painting, printmaking, and, of course, garden design; the influence of Japanese woodblock prints on nineteenth-century European painting and printmaking being among the strongest and best known. Here one must distinguish between a substantive application of influence and a superficial borrowing and replication. Vincent van Gogh's repainting of Utagawa Hiroshige's *Bridge in the Rain* (1837) is more an homage than an example of influence, as the reference is overt and little has been changed beyond the medium of the work, its size, and the artist's manner. An arrangement of rocks on a gravel bed, perhaps garnished by a miniature *torii* or pagoda, or graced by a Japanese maple (*Acer palmatum*) usually suffices to be read as "Japanese garden." But such landscapes are only iconographic constructs rather than landscapes that grasp and utilize the essence of Japanese garden making. Where would a garden such as this fall on the scale of influence? Probably nowhere—or replication at best, if very loosely translated. The elements of a garden are much like words in language; while each carries semantic content even when regarded independently, meaning ultimately derives from its association with other words in sentences and paragraphs. So too with the elements of a designed landscape: a true garden is more than a collection of features.

Introducing boulders into a garden may reflect Japanese inspiration, but it could also derive more pragmatically from the incorporation of materials found on-site that are too difficult or costly to remove. A material is only a material, like a word is only a word, and how and where it is used—and with what intention—are the consequential factors. Taliesin West (1941+), Frank Lloyd Wright's home, school, and atelier near Scottsdale, Arizona, skillfully integrated the rocks found on-site within its walls and throughout

10-1
Frank Lloyd Wright.
Taliesin West.
Paradise Valley, Arizona, 1941+.
Boulder as sculptural subject.

its grounds [10-1]. Standing independently as sculptural objects, the rocks may indeed express Wright's lifelong interest in things Japanese, which may have prompted his display of natural elements for their sculptural properties. Wright also devised a completely new way by which to integrate local stones into the walls of his buildings. As only his apprentices' unskilled labor was available for building construction, skilled masonry was precluded. In its place, native field stones were piled within the wooden formwork that shaped the walls; once they were in position, concrete was poured over the rocks to fill the form. The result was a composite of concrete and stone—a new material, which Wright termed "desert stone." Did this constitute Japanese influence, or was it pragmatism and just savvy invention?

If it may ultimately prove impossible to establish influence with great precision, one can nonetheless attempt to identify ideas or sensibilities that suggest a Japanese presence in Noguchi's aesthetics and handling of materials. These may have begun with his first stay in Japan as a child; exposure to the writings of his father, Yonejirô Noguchi, may have deepened his knowledge, as did his residence in the compound of Kitaôji Rosanjin (1883–1959) in the early 1950s. Restaurateur and aesthete of the highest order, Rosanjin initally turned to clay to craft exquisite plates and wares for use in his restaurant. He provided the newly wed Noguchi and his wife, the actress Yoshiko Yamamoto, with a place to live in his compound in Kamakura, and in their conversations and exchanges the sculptor no doubt acquired further insights into Japanese arts and thought. During Noguchi's travels through Japan in 1950, the painter and author Saburo Hasegawa (1906–1957) augmented the American sculptor's growing knowledge of things Japanese as they visited key sites that included gardens in Kyoto.

It is said in the *Tao Te Ching* (Book of Tao) that "learning is forgetting," that until what has been acquired consciously has been transferred to the subconscious—or preconscious, if you prefer—you have not really learned and understood.[4] Gaining skills in the martial arts is but one obvious example of this process: to be truly effective one must act without thinking. Similar to the swordsman, until an artist has fully absorbed any or all of these concepts, influence would probably manifest in his or her work without nuance—like adding a miniature pagoda to your front yard and calling it a Japanese garden.[5]

Donald Richie quotes the architectural historian Teiji Itoh on the complexities of trying to explain Japanese thinking in Western terms: "The dilemma we [Japanese] face is that our grasp is intuitive and perceptual rather than rational and logical."[6] I have found this to be the case when asking Japanese friends in architecture and the arts to explain certain aesthetic concepts to me. Each has offered his or her own version of what, for example, *shibui* might mean, but these have tended to be individual interpretations difficult to combine into one shared definition. I claim no deep understanding or knowledge of these ideas, of course, but perhaps even a skewed and imperfect interpretation by a Western historian may be of some use when associated with the sculpture and gardens produced by Isamu Noguchi.

Of the rich palette of Japanese aesthetic concepts reflected in its philosophies, I have selected only five: *ma* and *kûkan*, the concern with space and void, which lies at the root of Japanese architecture and which Noguchi once proclaimed to be the essence of his sculpture; *shin-gyô-sô*, the intermixture of formal, semiformal, and informal orders; *sabi* and *wabi*, the sense of ephemerality and the passage of time, often signaled by patina and other products of aging; three categories of beauty, *jimi*, *hade*, and *shibui*; and *yûgen*, an ineffable aspect of a work perhaps related to the Western concept of the sublime. We could also add simplicity, suggestion, and irregularity as much appreciated aesthetic qualities, but these five should suffice in the context of this book.

>> SPACE/VOID

The composite characters 空間 are read as *kûkan* and usually translated together simply as "space"; the first character suggests the notion of void. The composition of the second character, with *ma* (space-time) and *aida* (interval) among its alternate readings, incorporates both space and time: 門 for *gate*, 日 for *sun*, which also signifies *day*. Thus, *ma* integrates aspects of both place and time and parallels the post-Einstein concept of space-time that figured so largely in Western modernist architectural thought in the first half of the twentieth century.[7] There is little doubt that Noguchi would have been exposed to the term, as what might be described as rooms by Western visitors to Japan are labeled as different *ma* in Japanese. Noguchi's associations with the artist Saburo Hasegawa and the architects Yoshirô

Taniguchi and Kenzô Tange must also have contributed to his knowledge of this concept.

As early as the 1930s Noguchi had declared that space lies at the root of sculpture, although the monolithic basalt works executed in his later years might appear to favor solidity over space. In the display of his works, however, it is clear that he carefully considered the space in which each sculpture would be displayed. Although the object/sculptures in the courtyards at the Beinecke Library and 1 Chase Plaza each possess its own merit, they also affect the reading of the space itself and the relationships among its elements. Frank Lloyd Wright often quoted Lao Tzu in his belief that the reality of the vessel lies not in the container but in the space contained. This idea is obvious in Noguchi sculptures such as *The Void* (1969) or the floor-piece *This Earth, This Passage* [see 2-16]. These works rely as much on the space or interval between the elements as the elements regarded in and of themselves. The aesthetic presence of a large work like *Portal* (1976) in Cleveland derives in large degree not only from its scale but also from the space defined by its steel frame, with the readings of both the frame and the space it defines changing as one walks around the sculpture [10-2, 10-3].

>> MIXED FORMALITIES

The tripartite classification *shin-gyô-sô*—whose terms loosely translate as "formal," "semiformal," and "informal"—originated in calligraphy, where the terms described modes of writing. Over time, the categories and their application were adopted and became a mainstay of many arts including flower arrangement and garden making [10-4]. The formal mode, *shin*, is dignified and clear, used in Japan as we might employ Roman letters for inscriptions on governmental buildings or on official documents. Its ideograph also implies "true" or "truth." The informal embraces cursive forms, flowing and continuous; the character used to write *sô* represents grass. *Gyô* occupies the terrain between the formal and the informal. Looser in its definition, *gyô* is largely dependent on context for its definition and affect. Its character suggests movement.

The interplay of these formalities has informed Japanese arts since the Edo period (1603–1867), although each mode has received

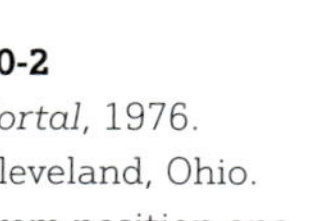

10-2
Portal, 1976.
Cleveland, Ohio.
From position one.

10-3
Portal, 1976.
From position two.

appreciation even when used individually. The potential benefit of this thinking, however, lies less with the individual merits of the three modes than in their combination and embedding within one another. The overall plan of a major temple complex such as Daitoku-ji in Kyoto, for example, may be read as semiformal, but the plan includes a central axial core and semiformal groupings of sub-temples. Semiformal in themselves, the entry courts of the sub-temples may intermix formal, semiformal, and informal features in their use of stone or the treatment of vegetation [10-5]. In addition, within the essentially *sô* inner garden appear elements with any or all of the three orders. At Shôden-ji, formally clipped azaleas replace stones as the principal subjects; at Ginkaku-ji, mounds of sand—one raised, flat, and sprawling; the other a truncated cone—play against the informality of the vegetation and the formality of the temple architecture [10-6; see also 2-11].

The stepping stones and pathways at the seventeenth-century Katsura villa outside Kyoto superbly represent stones of the three orders used alone and in combination [10-7; 10-8]. A single formal pathway may contain all three formalities or perhaps only one, demonstrating that in fact rather than just three combinations, there are at least nine: *shin-shin*, *gyô-shin*, *sô-shin*, and so on. It is important to note that these are concepts, not rules. As Sôfu Teshigahara—founder of the Sôgetsu school of ikebana—taught: "True ikebana is not isolated from times or our lives," and "The spirit of ikebana applies to all periods while the style of works may change over time."[8] Modern sculpture and landscape design are the products of an era, and as such should reflect that era.

At this point, I will leave the discussion of historical applications and turn to Noguchi's work and how it might be read using these orders. Many basalt pieces on display at the Isamu Noguchi Garden Museum in Long Island City play surfaces left natural against those that have been substantially worked, smoothed, or given a more geometric aspect. In other works, for example *To Bring to Life* (1979), the semiformal aspect prevails as a basically cylindrical form with a rough surface marked by patches of smooth black stone. When applying these ideas to gardens we find that Noguchi frequently used the formal figure of the circle. It appears as both dome and dish at the IBM headquarters in Armonk, New York; it governs the configuration of the central mound at the Israel Museum sculpture garden;

10-4
Ikebana flower arrangement,
Ikenobu School.
Takashima Department Store,
Kyoto, November 2015.

10-5
Sub-temple, Daitoku-ji.
Kyoto, seventeenth century(?).
Entry court.

10-6
Kobori Enshû.
Shôden-ji.
Kyoto, seventeenth century.
View through the *shoji*, over the clipped hedges, to Mount Hiei in the distance.

10-7
Katsura Imperial Villa.
Kyoto, seventeenth century.
Shin path composed of *shin*,
gyô, and *sô* stones.

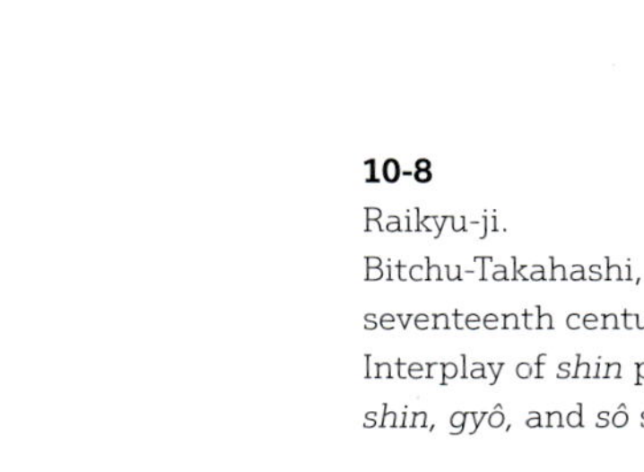

10-8
Raikyu-ji.
Bitchu-Takahashi,
seventeenth century.
Interplay of *shin* planting with
shin, gyô, and *sô* stones, .

it is the footprint of Desert Land and Energy Fountain at *California Scenario*; the slide hill for the Riverside Park playground and the plan of Mount Moere in Sapporo. Noguchi frequently used the circle as a foil for orthogonal geometries, but also as a statement of order opposed to the natural, the *sô*. Did these formal preferences derive from Japanese aesthetic dicta? Possibly. Did he apply these ideas to his work consciously? Probably not. Developed over time, Noguchi's personal aesthetic appreciated these plays of embedded opposites; he employed them to avoid Western dualism in favor of nuanced, softer differences lying between the two extremes.

>> BEAUTY

Japanese culture and Japanese language contain more than a single idea or word for what might be translated in English simply as "beauty." Needless to say, the definition of beauty itself varies across time, as it does across cultures. Of the group of words in the Japanese language that denote beauty, three in particular suggest the range of classes or types. *Jimi* connotes a harmonious beauty, possibly represented by an unglazed earthen bowl that is admired for its simplicity of form and homogeneity of material; an oatmeal-colored kimono paired with a chocolate-brown *obi*; or a green bamboo grove with brown leaves collected at its feet [10-9]. Beauty in this understanding derives from coherence, from a lack of disruption. It issues from a sense of the whole; no single component demands attention.[9] *Hade*, brilliance, stands in almost diametrical opposition. If *jimi* suggests the mellow tone of a cello, *hade* is the sharp blare of the trumpet. *Jimi* recedes, *hade* advances. In Japan *hade* suggests an aesthetic imported from the Asian mainland, one mixing brilliant golds with vermilion or white, possibly featuring elaborate carvings and architectural forms made up of distinct pieces. The elaborately ornamented Tôshôgû shrines at Nikkô could stand as the prime embodiments of *hade* in Japanese architecture [10-10].

Though in some ways dependent on personal values, *shibui* is commonly regarded as the highest form of beauty as well as the most difficult to achieve.[10] The word in its common usage translates as "astringent," like the reactive puckering of the lips when tasting an unripe persimmon. *Shibui* often plays the dissonant tone against the harmonic, as in the introduction to Mozart's Symphony No. 39 just before the introduction

10-9
Kôraku-en.
Okayama, seventeenth century.
Bamboo grove.

10-10
Tôshôgû Shrine.
Nikkô, early seventeenth century.

10-11
Daichi-ji.
Shiga Prefecture, 2012.
Matcha and sweets: *shibui*.

of the first principal melody. *Shibui* may develop from the unintended drop of glaze on the surface of a plate acquired in the kiln; a scarlet cloth set beneath a moss-green, gray-glazed plate; or it may be found in the blue-and-white checkerboard screens set against the muted grasses and natural wood of the Shokin-tei tea pavilion at Katsura [10-11; 10-12]. *Shibui* thus derives from the interplay of harmony and dissonance, and therefore rejects the complete accord that characterizes *jimi* [see 10-16].

The Beinecke Courtyard could be read as *jimi*, as it uses only a single material; conversely, one could interpret the play of the geometry of its major forms against chips and bites taken from its edges as aspiring to *shibui*. The late basalt works oppose areas of worked and finished stone against those left natural, using ideas from *shin-gyô-so* to pit consonance against dissonance. *Waterstone* and its related fountains counter the smooth top surface and circular pool to the rough sides of the stone [see 8-32]. It needs to be stressed, however, that none of these aesthetic ideas exists in isolation and that all readings are contingent.

>> POVERTY, VENERABILITY, PROFUNDITY

Although independent concepts, *wabi* and *sabi* are often paired as related qualities. *Wabi* suggests a restraint resulting from a reduction of means, whether by self-imposed restriction or imposed by others. "It is concerned with manner, with process, with direction."[11] The setting and utensils for the tea ceremony (*cha-no-yu*) reflect this preference for simplicity and "refined poverty," at times elevating the qualities of rural existence to the level of high art [10-14]. The direct translation of *cha-no-yu* is simply "hot water for tea"—and Sen no Rikyu, a tea master who shaped the ceremony at the end of the sixteenth century, claimed that what we call the tea ceremony in English is simply the act of boiling water, making tea, and drinking it.[12] The teahouse or tearoom is usually small, its architecture simple and restrained, and constructed using a frame of unpainted wooden posts and beams infilled with earth-plastered walls and roofed with reed or straw.

Kakuzô Okakura referred to the realm of tea as the "abode of asymmetry," in which imperfection was favored over perfection.[13] Ceramic ware used in the ceremony tended to be rough and expressive; the products of fortuitous accidents occurring during firing at low temperatures were

10-12
Shokin-tei, Katsura Imperial Villa.
Kyoto, seventeenth century.

praised for their idiosyncrasies and confounding of expectations. Containers for flower arrangements within the alcove (*tokonoma*) that greeted the guests upon entry might even be left as unpainted bamboo. At the very least, the resulting aesthetic was *jimi* although *shibui* was the aspiration.

The complement to *wabi* is *sabi*, a sense of venerability giving rise to tranquility and peace.[14] *Wabi* may result from intention, but *sabi* usually requires the passage of time. In time, glazes crackle and pottery chips; wood twists, darkens, and rots; mud plaster erodes and exposes its straw binder; stone surfaces acquire robes of moss [10-13, 10-14, 10-15]. Through these phenomena we understand that we exist in but one small moment of a grand continuum. The realization that time is not static but continually flowing stimulates contemplation and deepens our relationship to the proximate and greater environments—and causes us to reflect on our place and time within it.

The greatest artistic aspiration was to attain *yûgen*, a word variously defined and broadly interpreted, suggesting "a sense of mystery, depth, elegance, calm profundity, mixed with a feeling of mutability."[15] *Yûgen* was an idea advanced by the early Noh dramaturge Zeami (Kanze Motokiyo, 1363–1443), who described it as an attribute of true beauty and gentleness, an interior quality as well as an exterior form. In explaining the term, Zeami compared the Noh author to the landscape gardener by noting their shared need for grasping essences. "The gardener sees and understands the river and recreates its spirit in the garden, though he does not replicate its form." In writing a Noh play its author puts forth the "garden within his soul."[16] In writing his *Kadensho*, a secret teaching manual—a reference to Zeami's own *Kadensho, The Transmission of the Flower of Acting Style*—Sôfu Teshigahara, who founded the Sôgetsu school, believed that one must seek the essence, stating, "Concentration in art means looking far beyond the mask of things." Like the components of any great work of art, "Flowers become concentrated in ikebana."[17] Noguchi once told Teshigahara that "if you set a pine, it should not look like a pine," but admitted that "it is very difficult to make it not look like a pine."[18] The best of Noguchi's works captured the essence of the stone or the site conditions, a quality not easily realized.

Since interpretation and meaning ultimately reside with the individual, it is more difficult to achieve in the landscape than in sculpture.

10-13
Oku-no-in, Koyasan.
Jizô deity figures.

In the garden the factors affecting perception and thought are so much more complex and multidimensional, compounded by variations in location, the availability of plant species, weather conditions, and light. In the gallery and the museum these conditions can be controlled and stilled, but exterior works, whether sculpture or gardens, possess no such luxury.

Nominations for Noguchi sculptures that have achieved this level of profundity will vary with the individual. Of the landscapes, I would again cite 1 Chase Plaza and the Beinecke courtyard but also add *California Scenario*, each reaching this higher aesthetic level if in differing ways. In New York, the selection and elevation of the rocks, the play of water, and the undulating ground plane with its inscribed lines cohere as a landscape that fuses as an engaging whole. As the seasons change the plaza shifts from wet to dry and suggests an accord with its environment and the passage of time. *California Scenario* is in some ways more static and timeless with its recollections of desert, mountain, and valley remaining essentially constant throughout the year. The flow of the water from its source in the wedge and the aquatic animation provided by Energy Fountain rupture that static state by playing liquid against solid, and movement against stillness.

As he worked, did Noguchi deliberately draw on these concepts from Japanese aesthetics, for example, the interplay of formalities or the pursuit of venerability?

I would think not, at least not consciously. But I would venture that they resided—at least to some degree—within a personal aesthetic developed over his decades of practice, experience in Japan, and that he too sought profundity, whether he thought to call it *yûgen* or not.

10-14
Tsukubai.
Koto-in, Daitoku-ji.
Kyoto, early seventeenth century.
Moss = Time

10-15
Rinnon-ji.
Nikko, seventeenth century.
Moss on rock, rock in pool;
autumn leaves.

> 11.

Sculpture(d) Park: Sapporo

At the time of Moerenuma Park's origin as a garbage dump in the late 1970s, there was good reason for selecting a site on the northeast edge of Sapporo, the prefectural capital of Hokkaido, away from the housing, schools, and shopping in the city's core [11-1].[1] But in the 1980s Mayor Nobuo Katsura had begun to entertain greater visions for the landfill after it had reached its projected capacity and closed to further deposits. Katsura saw the years of waste deposited on-site transformed into a public park of a rather heroic scale. A park of that aspiration, size, and quality did eventually materialize, although its realization would require more than two decades.

In January 1988, in the last year of Noguchi's life, a delegation from Sapporo that included Hiroyuki Hattori, a prominent local computer entrepreneur, and Jun'ichi Kawamura, an architect based in Tokyo, met with the artist in his New York studio. Their intention was to commission a sculpture. Noguchi declined their offer, telling the committee he was not interested in creating a work for the northern city, whether in a sculpture park or on some other site within Sapporo.[2] As in the past he again held a larger vision, and in time that request for a single sculpture burgeoned into a commission for a garden in the form of a park of colossal dimensions.[3]

On Noguchi's initial visit to the city in late March, Hitoshi Yamamoto, director of Moerenuma Parks, offered Noguchi three sites for his consideration. The first was in a sculpture garden south of the city center; the second, on the proposed site for a future university of the arts. Noguchi had already expressed his lack of interest in creating a discrete sculptural object, wherever it might be installed. He was also offered a third option, however: the possibility to somehow reform the city's landfill in Higashi Ward, already slated to become a public park.[4] There was no question in Noguchi's mind as to which alternative was the most attractive, and his acceptance was immediate. "When we reached the [Moerenuma] site, the marshland surrounded by winding river," architect Kawamura recalled, "[Noguchi] joyfully stepped into the remaining snow, saying 'This land needs form. This is my job.'"[5] Agreeing to Noguchi's conditions, the city commissioned him to convert the wasteland not only into a major park but, even better, into a work of art.

The on-site operations of deposit and reformation had been underway for nearly a decade before the city turned to Noguchi, and

11-0
Moerenuma Park.
Sapporo, Japan, 2005.
Aqua Plaza with Mount Moere beyond.

11-1
Moerenuma Park.
Sapporo, Japan, 2005.
Play Mountain, modified from the original 1933 design, with Aqua Plaza in the foregroundand Tetra Mound and the band shell in the distance.

certain aspects of the original pastoral vision for the park had already been realized. A horseshoe-shaped waterway had transformed the site into a peninsula; a new bridge had been built, although several more were needed [11-2]. These engineering tasks, rather than any elevated vision for a design, had governed ground operations from the start of the construction. On the northeastern end of the site thousands of cherry trees had been planted, a forest that Noguchi would retain despite its lack of a distinctive design profile. In his future plan, Cherry Forest would become the vegetal matrix from which areas for play and other activities would be extracted. In addition, the wooded areas effectively marked the limits of the park along the banks of the canal, and, perhaps more importantly, buffer the site from the development projected to grow around it in the future.

Noguchi proceeded swiftly—of necessity, given the volume of his prior commitments—and in fewer than three months he produced his first design. In May, at a meeting on-site in Sapporo, he presented a small model to the politicians supporting the project and the consulting architects [11-3]. In all Noguchi would have only ten months to bring the design to a definitive stage, as he died in December of that year.[6] All design modifications and developments followed one after another in rapid succession.

The brief for the landscape was both simple and complex. It was simple in its asking Noguchi to provide facilities for outdoor performance, and active recreation such as baseball diamonds, a running track, and other sports. More unusually, the program included the request for a mountain. Always concerned with play and the well-being of children, Noguchi dedicated the park to them. "I like to think of playgrounds as a primer of shapes and functions," Noguchi had written in his 1968 autobiography, and that the "simple, mysterious, and evocative [are] thus educational."[7]

In accordance with his vision of the park as a sculpture of vast dimensions, he retrieved elements and forms from prior sculptures and landscapes but enlarged them to gargantuan scale. In some ways this approach is highly problematic, certainly at a conceptual level, and such a design risks descending to the level of pastiche. Nevertheless, that is how the landscape was designed and realized, how the park is perceived, and how it works incredibly well on those terms. Without question, Moerenuma Beach—a shallow pond with a sandy shore—has been an outstanding success offering Sapporo's landlocked kids a shoreline that nature herself did not provide [11-4]. Like many of the park's principal features, the irregular shore of the sandy beach is itself defined by a purely geometric figure, in this case a circle.

In his first scheme Noguchi accepted the site work already completed, primarily the considerable engineering efforts to drain the marshland, grade the tons of waste deposited over the years, dredge the belt of waterway surrounding the site, and plant thousands of trees. In his design for Moerenuma Park, Noguchi revisited ideas and forms from garden and playground designs long left unrealized and reassembled them to create a new composite. In response to the dimensions of the site, the key elements would be enormous. As noted above, the program had required a design for a mountain, presumably to introduce a vertical element into the terrain, and to provide an overview for the park and slopes for winter sledding. It took little prompting for Noguchi to construct new topographies from the heaps of nonflammable garbage deposited over decades, capping the forms with clean landfill from excavations then underway for the city's new metro system. The forms shaped from these deposits included the conical Fuji-like Moere Mountain; an open-air amphitheater configured as a vast, inclined, rectangular plane; and—finally, half a century after its original design—a realization of *Play Mountain*. Initially proposed for an urban site in 1933, the design had remained solely as a maquette until its execution in Sapporo [see 3-9]. These major topographic units became the superstructure for the overall landscape, bolstered by subsidiary elements such as playgrounds, sports fields, and what in time became a pyramid of glass and steel [11-5, 11-6]. Perhaps unconsciously, Noguchi was working in the manner of the Japanese gardener, albeit at a far greater scale, first setting the key "stones" to establish the garden's structure and direct the placement of the lesser garden elements thereafter. Smaller stones and plants—here, features such as Sea Fountain, Cherry Forest, and the play areas—were then conceived and positioned in relation to the primary earthworks.

This first scheme employed an organizational strategy common to many of Noguchi's landscapes. While Play Mountain modified a form retrieved from the original 1933 proposal, the circle once again appeared and reappeared as the fundamental shape of several park elements; their

11-2
Moerenuma Park.
Sapporo, Japan, 2005.
Aerial view from southeast.
taken at the year of opening.
[Courtesy Architect 5]

11-3 *[above left]*
Moerenuma Park.
Study model.
[Courtesy Architect 5]

11-4 *[above right]*
Moerenuma Park.
Moere Beach.
[Courtesy Architect 5]

11-5, 11-6 *[below left, right]*
Moerenuma Park.
Glass Pyramid houses offices and exhibitions, hosts events, and offers an observation deck to visitors.

11-7
Moerenuma Park.
Sapporo, Japan, 2005.
The risers facing Play Mountain used stone brought from Mure.

relationship to one another reflected a carefully conceived composition more evident in plan and model than as perceived through experience on-site [11-7; also 11-3]. The base of Moere Mountain, the enclave including Sea Fountain, and the boundary of Moere Beach were all planned on the circle. Partial circles, in turn, shaped the berms that anchor the west ends of the baseball fields and the running track. While the circles were composed within an orthogonal field, the triangular forms of Tetra Mound and Aqua Plaza, and the amphitheater's great rectangular wedge confront the prevalent order and complete the composition of geometric shapes [see 11-8].

Like the play of formal elements in Japanese aesthetics, these slightly dissonant notes articulate an otherwise purely harmonious composition [see chapter 10]. Viewed as a two-dimensional compression of the park's primary features, the plan suggests associations with Suprematist paintings by Kazimir Malevich or improvisations by Wassily Kandinsky. Of course, it is far easier to discern such geometric play in a drawn plan grasped by the eye in a single take than it is at the huge scale of the park itself. As experienced, the relationship among the key elements must be appraised as volumes in space rather than as flat shapes in a drawing. On-site, the relationship among the forms is sensed rather than read.

11-8
Moerenuma Park.
Sapporo, Japan, 2005.
Amphitheater seen from below.

>> DESIGN

In Noguchi's first schemes the primary features were proximate and in places conjoined. As a whole, the shaping of the land appears more integrated in the early designs than in those that followed, with Moere Mountain and the amphitheater merged into a single mass, although the two were distinguished by the low saddle extending between them. Circular in plan, like the baseball field on an adjacent site, they conceptually "answered" the circular Sea Fountain and the playground voids extracted from Cherry Forest at the opposite end of the park. While the steps on the front face of Play Mountain embody an accurate realization of the original design proposed in 1933, the rear of the mound was distended into a more gently graded slope to allow visitors to reach the summit by means of an inclined walk rather than by climbing the steep stairs on the face of the hill. The contours of the steps are retained by stone slabs used as risers selected by Noguchi's longtime friend and colleague Masatoshi Izumi and brought to Sapporo from Mure [see 11-5]. In addition to its identity as a sculpture, as seating, as a belvedere, and as a physical challenge, Play Mountain helps protect the park against winds coming from the northeast.

In early studies, circulation through the park relied on a set of curving paths and roads to link the principal forms, counterposing the straight line to the curve, and paved surfaces to those planted with grass and trees. Being clustered as a unified group, the central features were somewhat removed from the perimeter of the site, positioned much like the central plateau of the UNESCO garden. At this stage of design, Noguchi appears to have been more focused on determining the plans and profiles of the landforms rather than the spaces generated by and between them. For unexplained reasons—perhaps modified in response to questions concerning construction over an extended period of time or simply for clarity as an aesthetic statement—in his revised scheme Noguchi separated the elements of the first composition and more clearly defined major features like Play Mountain and Mount Moere as autonomous forms. Although this separation reduced the sense of the park as a single sculpture, the independent landforms could better accommodate the activities programmed for them. In its final rendition—as in so many other Noguchi landscapes—the ground and its structures became a gathering of related elements, as opposed to a completely geometrically ordered scheme or a loose composition characteristic of some types of assemblage.

In the years following Noguchi's death, and as design and construction progressed, the paths as initially proposed began to resemble axes, although none of them extended uninterrupted from one side of the park to the other. The roads also straightened during design development but they neither directed views aesthetically, nor pedestrian circulation pragmatically.[8] Without question, the paths support the east-west, and to a lesser degree the north-south, movement across the site. But only in places do they truly link the various nodes of the design and rarely serve any aesthetic function. Of course, functional requirements, like the need for emergency-vehicle access, also affected the park's planning. As landscape architecture, circulation may be the weakest aspect of the park design as executed; or, kindlier put, the paths accept their supporting role in relation to the leads played by the earth forms. In terms of accommodating walking and bicycle riding, the paths function well; it is in terms of enfolding the experience of movement with the encounters of Noguchi's compositions that they offer relatively little. One feels that the paths are not quite where you would want them, nor do they engage the mountains and the constructed earthen features in a manner that would intensify the visitor's experience.

>> REALIZATION

Isamu Noguchi died on 30 December 1988 at the age of eighty-four, leaving the Sapporo authorities and its design team in a quandary as to how to proceed with the construction of Moerenuma Park. Some sketches, plans, and two or three stages of design-development drawings and models produced with his Japanese collaborators recorded their efforts and would have to serve as guides in realizing the park's design and construction. Were these sufficiently complete to the degree that the park's design could still be credited to Noguchi? The three schemes Noguchi had produced at lightning speed over a very short period record the major changes to the forms and associations among the park's components in each version. In his usual working method, the sculptor designed landscapes using sketches and models to explore ideas at a conceptual level. These were adjusted and modified on-site—often substantially—utilizing his design studies, and even construction documents, only as a record of the intentions and to serve as a guide for construction [11-9]. Or it fell to his partner Shoji Sadao to solve any functional problems that might trouble the fulfillment of Noguchi's aesthetic proposals. In addition, Sadao was usually responsible for producing the construction documents as well as troubleshooting any difficulties that arose during construction.[9]

But now the master was gone; he would make no additional visits to the site nor propose further modifications and adjustments during construction. Despite the need for the extensive design and construction documentation required to build a park with forms of such immense scale, Noguchi had produced its design in fewer than nine months and had left few records to direct construction. Thus, to architects Jun'ichi Kawamura and Takahiro Terasawa of Architect 5, Shoji Sadao of the Isamu Noguchi Foundation, Kôji Saitô of Kitaba Landscape in Sapporo, and others working in the various Sapporo city departments fell the task of scaling up the small-scale models and sketches, and from them bringing the park to fruition.[10] The process of Moerenuma's design development and construction would span almost eighteen years. In July 1998, ten years after Noguchi produced his design, the park announced its "soft" opening, although construction was only 60 percent complete. The official inauguration followed seven years later, in summer 2005.

Noguchi was notorious for producing limited project documentation in advance of construction, relying on extensive interventions and adjustments on-site—at least where time and the clients allowed. In Sapporo, however, as there were no other alternatives, Noguchi's models and handful of sketches with specified elevations and dimensions became the basis for the park's design development and realization. Consulting with Sadao, year after year Architect 5 and the Sapporo Parks Department continued their efforts to execute the project in accordance with Noguchi's original concept. As the years passed the garbage deposits were capped, the waterways cleaned and their banks given definite contours, and more of the projected 10,000 cherry trees were planted on the park's eastern tip. Clean fill was brought to the site, piled, and graded into the topographies represented in Noguchi's model for Play Mountain, Moere Mountain, the amphitheater, and the berms that shelter the sports fields.

In addition to these earthworks, the architects and their consultants developed the once-schematic form into the handsomely detailed Glass Pyramid that serves as the park's service, administrative, and exhibition center. In all their efforts the design team attempted to remain faithful to the original concepts, diverging from them only when the exigencies of site work or building codes determined otherwise. These were relatively minor, however, with no radical departures from the ideas and forms that Noguchi had articulated in his studies. Nor, fortunately, were there any cataclysmic surprises caused by soil conditions or accompanying the process of filling and grading. It was just a matter of time, patience, and economics. Time was prescribed; patience and funding were demanded.

>> EVALUATION

Then there is the question of scale. Nature tells us that the size and structure of any organism are related. A bird has bones thin and lightweight because

11-9
Noguchi at work on the courtyards for the IBM offices in Armonk, New York, early 1960s.
[Dan Butnik, © The Noguchi Museum/ARS]

it is relatively small and must leave the ground and fly. An elephant is terrestrial, large, and heavy, and its stocky skeleton must address those constraints. You cannot simply scale up the bone structure or organs of a bird to support or nourish an elephant; the entire organism must be rethought in order to function at the enlarged scale.

In designing Moerenuma Park, Noguchi willfully mined forms and designs from his past, and in some ways the entire park could be read as a collection of motifs produced or proposed for prior landscapes. Late in life Marcel Duchamp produced small-scale replicas of his works and collected them inside a suitcase. The series *Boîte-en-valise* (1936–41) allowed Duchamp to replicate his past achievements at a size that would allow them to be coherent, portable, and easily viewed as a life's work. In contrast, at Moerenuma, Noguchi retrieved—but enlarged—prior designs or finally executed sculptural ideas that had long lain fallow. As we know, Play Mountain at Moerenuma Park rehearsed a giant play sculpture of that same name from years earlier but it also drew upon certain features of Noguchi's *Monument to the Plough* from that same time. In the figure of a three-sided pyramid—in structuring one of its sides as a giant flight of granite steps, and in its use of differing plantings on each of its faces—Noguchi selected and applied ideas selected from a single, now-lost drawing of the proposal, a photograph of which constitutes its sole surviving evidence. More than half a century after their original conception these early landscapes, somewhat surprisingly, finally attained their status as landscapes and as art.

Like moths to a flame, visitors are drawn to the summits of Moere Mountain, Play Mountain, as well as the viewing terrace of Glass Pyramid, within which are located a gallery, a performance space, a viewing platform, a café, and administrative offices. Is there a basic human instinct that, like climbing Mount Everest, lures visitors to the tops of these hills? This enticement—and the reward for the ascent—is among the park's unquestionable triumphs, confirming Moerenuma as one of the very few landscapes that, similar to the great Pre-Columbian complexes of Mesoamerica, dramatically encourage upward movement. On Mount Moere one can literally get high from the delicious thrill derived from reaching the apex and surveying all that lies before you. Compound this mild euphoria with the novelty of assessing the sculptural elements of the park in terms of new relatioships: for example, the play between Play Mountain and the circular belt of larch that surrounds Sea Fountain, whose jet reaches heights far above the treetops. From the air or hilltop, Noguchi's forms and strategy become more legible including, as has been noted, his reliance on the circle in the planning of Larch Forest, the footprint of Moere Mountain, and the collection of play areas. Given their scale and distinct geometries—the pyramid and the cone—it is no surprise that these landforms dominate the Moerenuma landscape. And in the relationships among Play Mountain, Mount Moere, and the raked slope of the amphitheater, the design's aesthetic moments are at their highest [11-10].

The design is not without its shortcomings, however. Through the triangular Aqua Plaza at the foot of Moere Mountain, a watercourse flows from a stone fountain whose profile seems lifted directly from *California Scenario*. But as one minor element in a vast space, the stream and fountain feel small in relation to the colossal scale of the hills at whose bases they lie. Tetra Mound creates the opposite impression: a gigantic sculpture that marks the park's northern entrance but lacks any second dimension or greater detail that might induce visitors to view the enormous form more closely [10-11, 11-12]. Constructed of tubular stainless steel finished with the same brushed swirls as the Dodge Fountain in Detroit, the giant tripod suggests no purpose beyond marking the northern entrance to the park. Tetra Mound is the park's most purely sculptural moment, whose existence can be argued in no other terms, as its interaction with the other earthworks is minimal. Sculpture can be its own justification of course, and in any event, the bulky tubular structure of Tetra Mound does frame views of other of the park's forms, especially Play Mountain nearby [11-13].

If filling, piling, and grading of earth were the initial operations at Moerenuma, it is water that vivifies the stable landforms. The canal and its banks provide additional recreational opportunities to accommodate boaters and picnickers, respectively. The constructed Moere Beach attracts hundreds of people in warm weather, and it is especially appealing to children, who flood the sandy shores that surround its pool. Noguchi would be pleased. It is unfortunate that the use of the pond is seasonal, and that it is drained and covered during the winter months—unfortunate, but hardly avoidable in a location whose subfreezing winter temperatures support the mounting of the annual winter festival of snow sculptures.

11-10
Moerenuma Park.
View from Play Mountain
to Mount Moere beyond.

Sea Fountain continues Noguchi's series of animated waters and most closely resembles, in program if not in actual form, the Dodge Fountain—as well as its later reincarnation in Bayfront Park in Miami half a world away. Set within a ring of densely planted larch trees the fountain is programmed to cycle through various states: initially nearly dry, as a low, tingling heap of water, and then, after several other iterations, culminating in a geyser some eighty feet high [see 8-28, 8-29]. Its forty-minute cycle draws people from all parts of the park to watch the performance, oohing and aahing at the spectacle, and indiscriminately taking hundreds of photos, most of which are selfies. Alas, the dense plantings that ring the space and comfortably buffer the fountain from the winds also isolate the fountain from the park's other features, thus preventing any synergy among them. That is not unusual in a Noguchi landscape, however, and in many ways the composition of elements at Moerenuma recalls similar gatherings of forms found at much smaller scale in projects such as the Beinecke Library and *California Scenario*. Or perhaps Noguchi was consciously appropriating the Japanese-garden concept of hide-and-reveal to increase the presence of the fountains and their cycles.

The standards for the design of the fields and courts for baseball, tennis, and track dictate standard solutions, and they cannot be faulted. They provide the needed settings and they work efficiently. The numerous spaces assigned to play have been created as voids within Cherry Forest, which carpets the northeastern end of the park. The play equipment in these spaces revisits the forms of many works the sculptor designed in the 1970s, only a fraction of which had been realized in his lifetime. As he himself had reclaimed playground equipment from the early Ala Moana Park in Hawai'i, the swings and the spiral slides from the 1976 *Playscapes* in Atlanta reappear in Hokkaido [11-14]; other pieces, such as the wavelike Play Sculpture, refer more directly to Noguchi sculptures such as the 1977 *Sky Gate* in Honolulu [11-15; 11-16]. Here, the gently undulating surfaces encourage straddling and climbing on the part of their young users. In one zone, the play landscape is constructed in concrete and looks credibly Noguchian, recalling smaller elements from his 1960s collaboration with architect Louis Kahn for Riverside Drive playground in New York; in fact, it is the work of Architect 5 and their consultants [11-17]. Most of the play structures are

11-11
Moerenuma Park.
Tetra Mound seen from behind the band shell.

brilliantly colored in oranges, yellows, and seafoam green set off by contrasting surfaces of chocolate brown and black [11-18]. They are handsome sculptural settings in and of themselves, and there is little doubt that children encounter, negotiate, and invent among them as they would among an abstract set of blocks.

In a world in which standardized play equipment of red, blue, and yellow fiberglass cubes has become the kudzu of playground design, the formal invention and spatial dispersal found in the Moerenuma playgrounds is a most welcome antagonist. Their distribution within spaces defined by the forest of cherry trees stimulates the children's discovery of the other locations —which, in turn, may stimulate their exploration of further sections of the park. This is a collection of Noguchi's playground forms, all abstract, first proposed or used in other projects but filtered through the sensibility of Architect 5. As a totality the playgrounds constitute a small empire of highly shaped and colorful sculptures fabricated with hard materials—a far cry from the mess, dispersal, and discovery so characteristic of the adventure playgrounds of the 1960s with their celebration of society's detritus and emphasis on combination rather than encounter and use alone [see chapter 4]. But that was then and this is now, and the liability that burdens municipalities everywhere around the world has vastly increased, even in the far less litigious Japan.

>> REFLECTION

Moerenuma Park is well maintained despite its size and distance from the eyes of the city government seated downtown; it is a popular destination despite the severe weather characteristic of Hokkaido. In 2005, the time of my first visit, the larch and cherry plantings—still quite young—were growing well; the grass planted on the contours only slightly less so. Now, some eighteen years later, the trees have reached sizable proportions and the forests have matured. The slopes of the earth forms show no sign of major deterioration, which is a credit to the Parks Department's maintenance staff. Given an annual precipitation of forty-four inches, coupled with periods of heavy snowfall—not to mention the very size of the park—upkeep is no doubt a challenge. As in all landscapes public and private, maintenance remains the key to sustaining the qualification of the park as artwork.

11-12 *[above]*
Moerenuma Park.
Tetra Mound with Play Mountain behind.

11-13 *[below]*
Moerenuma Park.
Band shell with Tetra Mound in the distance.

11-14 *[above left]*
Moerenuma Park.
The spiral slide, also drawn from Playscapes, rehearses a form used in one of the Osaka Expo '70 fountains.

11-15 *[center left]*
Moerenuma Park.
The undulating play sculpture shares an affinity with *Sky Gate* in Honolulu.

11-16 *[above right]*
Sky Gate,
1977.
Honolulu, Hawai'i.

11-17
Moerenuma Park.
Architect 5 designed the stepped play form, drawing on Noguchi's designs for the United Nations and Riverside Drive playgrounds proposed for New York.

Moerenuma is a large park of 467 acres, about half the surface area of Central Park in New York City. But central it is not, located as it is on the northeastern edge of Sapporo. Frederick Law Olmsted regarded Central Park as a work of art from which nothing could be removed, changed, or added; his model was nature and his aesthetic primarily naturalistic. While sharing the belief that a park can be a work of art, Noguchi thought differently regarding an approach to nature. "It is not wise to mimic nature within nature," he told Hitoshi Yamamoto, Moerenuma Park's director on his first visit to the site.[11] Even in the mid-nineteenth century, New York and the Central Park site were hardly nature; neither was a twentieth-century garbage dump and landfill. While Moerenuma Park offers little of the variety and subtlety of the richly variegated Central Park, as well as far less tree cover, it is an impressive place of another type and order: a park that in its scale and abstraction simultaneously acknowledges its location in Sapporo, the open landscape of Hokkaido and the ambitions of its sponsors and designers.

Is Moerenuma Park really a landscape designed by Isamu Noguchi? Hard to say, although all the city's publicity for the park credits Noguchi as its creator. Creator, without question; designer, only perhaps. Does Moerenuma Park today represent what Noguchi himself would have designed had he lived through the almost two decades required to bring the project to completion? Probably not, at least not in the details and less so in the adjustment of forms. Given that nearly eighteen years had elapsed between the year of his design and the year of its inauguration, it is safe to assume that the sculptor himself would have developed as an artist, and thus on subsequent visits would have modified the design accordingly. However, it is also doubtful that he would have lived to witness the park's 2005 opening date. And so, the design of Moerenuma Park in many ways must be regarded as a collaborative project: although based on an original concept and design by Noguchi, its realization derived from the efforts and contributions of a design team comprising Jun'ichi Kawamura and other members of Architect 5, Shoji Sadao, and many individuals in the municipal government of Sapporo. That in itself is no mean feat, of course, and despite any shortcomings in form and feeling one must be grateful for this sculptural park's realization. No doubt, the residents of Sapporo share my sentiment.

11-18
Moerenuma Park.
The play equipment throughout the park is vividly colored, although without the clichéd use of the primary hues.

> 12.

Mure, and Reflection

>> MURE

From the 1960s on Isamu Noguchi returned to Japan more frequently, spending half the year there, often three months in the spring, three in the fall. Knowing the artist's considerable success reviving the lantern-making industry with his Akari light sculptures, in 1958 the governor of Kagawa Prefecture on the island of Shikoku invited him to explore artistic possibilities using the local gray Ajishi granite [12-1]. Noguchi was already familiar with the island and its granite, having sought stones there for the UNESCO garden with the aid of landscape designer Mirei Shigemori and having returned some years later in search of rocks for his sunken garden at 1 Chase Plaza.

Nothing of substance came of that initial invitation and visit but his meeting with the Izumi family at that time proved to be significant, leading as it did to the sculptor's being granted ground in their stoneyard in Mure, a small stone-working community near Takamatsu, the prefectural capital. Here, Noguchi would profit not only from the land graciously offered to him upon which to live and work, sources of material, and the use of specialized equipment, but even more consequentially from the experience and considerable knowledge of the people working there—above all Masatoshi Izumi (1938–2021).

Born into a lineage of stoneworking artisans, Izumi started carving in 1953, and with the years of apprenticeship and experience that followed he had become an expert craftsman with an understanding of the aesthetics as well as the physical properties of stone.[1] Noguchi once told his young assistant that he had three things working in his favor: he hadn't gone to art school; he didn't speak English; and, like Noguchi himself, he loved stone. Over the years of their association Izumi evolved from a skilled craftsperson to a significant artist in his own right, with numerous gallery exhibitions and public works installed in Japan and abroad. Noguchi came to rely on Izumi for stoneworking expertise, just as he relied on Shoji Sadao for his architectural knowledge and construction-management skills. For decades Izumi would serve as Noguchi's assistant, fabricator and resident expert on the stone used in the sculptures. In addition, he and his crew produced elements of Noguchi's landscapes, their association beginning with carving *Black Sun* (1969) and ending with the risers for the steps of *Play Mountain* at Moerenuma Park, supplied by Izumi long after the master's death.[2]

12-0
Sculptures as legacy.
Mure, Japan.

At times in their relationship Izumi was puzzled by Noguchi's comments; for example, when Noguchi once told his collaborator—almost in the manner of a Zen koan—that he wanted to make "heavy stones look light, hard stones soft, and immobile stones look like they were in motion." This paradoxical request squares with his comment to *ikebana* master Sôfu Teshigahara that if one wanted to set a pine into a garden, it should not look like a pine.[3] It is the act of transformation that renders an object or situation art, but only with transformation derived from the true nature of the tree. Or the stone.

The Izumi family's ownership of the stoneworks and quarry in Mure extended back over 150 years; Masatoshi Izumi had assumed its directorship when his father retired.[4] In 1966 Noguchi requested Izumi's assistance in carving a major stone sculpture for the Seattle Art Museum, *Black Sun*, installed in front of the museum in 1969 [12-2]. The Izumi family generously granted Noguchi a piece of land on which to work, and, in time, a piece of land on which to build a house and live. In sequence, he relocated several historic structures to the site, first an eighteenth-century house (to be named Isamu-ya) from Eihme Prefecture that he believed to be the former residence of a samurai, although it was more likely that of a merchant. Later came a storehouse (*kura*) that would serve as his indoor studio, and finally a larger storehouse used to stockpile sculptures underway or completed, but still being reconsidered prior to shipment [12-3]. The studio buildings were restored, left with dirt floors, and furnished only modestly. The house was remodeled to suit the artist's hybrid lifestyle and completed by the small, simple garden that occupies a narrow slice of land to the rear of the structure [12-4, 12-5; 12-6]. To provide sufficient level ground for the house and garden required cutting into the hillside and constructing a stone wall to retain the slope. Other than a stand of bamboo, there are virtually no plants within the garden [12-7]. For years the sculpture *Ground Wind #1* (1968) has occupied the space, the simplicity of its long bar enhanced by a gradual twist that subtly catalyzes a more complex reading of its form. Complexity within simplicity.

Noguchi worked on his sculptures both outdoors in the yard and, when required, within the shelter of the old storage buildings transferred to the studio area. To distinguish his terrain from the other oper-

12-1
Akari ceiling light sculptures *E* and 31N (1954), on display at The Hepworth Museum, Wakefield, England, 2017.

12-2
Black Sun, 1969.
Seattle Art Museum.

12-3
Storehouse converted to use as studio. Mure, Japan.

12-4 *[above left]*
Isamu-ya (Noguchi house).
Mure, Japan.
Entrance.

12-5 *[above right]*
Isamu-ya.
Entry vestibule.

12-7 *[below left]*
Isamu-ya Garden.
Minimal space featuring
Ground Wind #1, 1968.

12-6 *[below right]*
Storehouse (*kura*).
Converted to storage
and display space.

12-8 *[left]*
Noguchi Studio.
A curving stone wall encloses the work and display areas.

12-9 *[right]*
Noguchi Studio.
Sculpture finished or nearly finished, displayed for review.

ations of the Izumi stoneyard around it, to define his personal work area, and to demarcate a space within which to appraise the sculptures placed there, Noguchi built a roughly four-foot-high dry stone wall shaped as a grand, if segmented, arc [12-8]. In actuality less an arc than a parenthesis, the wall gathers within it almost 15,000 square feet of sandy ground and joins the work area with the storehouse/studio. In this zone he installed sculptures in process or possibly regarded as complete. Here, they would be studied, in some cases for years, under changes in light and differences in weather. Some 150 of these pieces occupied the yard at the time of Noguchi's death; nearly all remain in place [12-9].

Virtually all the sculptures created in Mure are of stone, although many if not most did not use material locally quarried. Rather ironically, after only a relatively short period of time Noguchi began to import blocks of granite, marble, and other stone from Africa, Sweden, and diverse countries—all types foreign to Japan. When selecting materials abroad, Izumi explained, "We went directly to the place and selected them from the quarry." The pair's association had become so close and so enduring that, although "there were hundreds to choose from . . . I could tell which stones Mr. Noguchi would choose simply when he stood next to them, because he and a particular stone would look so good together."[5] For the sculptor the color of the stone was a major factor, its working properties were another. Like most artists, Noguchi chose his material to suit his idea, although at times selecting the material came first; the idea for working it followed later on. As he also worked with materials ranging from paper to sheet metal to wood, so too did he explore and exploit the properties of a particular stone, even if it required the material's importation to Japan.

>> NOGUCHI'S LANDSCAPE

The Izumi stoneyard, Noguchi's house, and working and display areas, all occupy land on basically the same level. Behind the house, however, the land rises quickly, revealing that much of the working terrain has resulted from excavation and regrading. To the rear and the left of the entrance to the Isamu-ya runs a set of narrow rough stone steps that mount the slope and lead to an open space with sculptured landforms whose elevation offers views over a Shikoku landscape of forested mountains, and, in places, glimpses of the sea [12-10; 12-11]. This is a landscape shaped by the sculptor and his team, first by terracing the land to provide suitable surfaces for work, walking, or display, and then by shaping the adjacent hillside as if a giant terrestrial sculpture. Into the grass-covered slopes, stone slabs, circular or square in shape, have been inserted, possibly intended as bases for the future display of sculpture.[6] Today, only the stone bases themselves occupy the otherwise uninterrupted slopes.

Complementing the earth forms are three major sculptures. Upon reaching the top of the stairs, directly before one's eyes is a massive stone shaped by natural forces; its twisted surfaces and and deep concavities bring to mind the stones harvested from Lake Tai, the stones so prized by Chinese scholars and garden makers in eras past [12-12]. The two sculptures that accompany this large stone are more obviously of Noguchi's mind and hand. The first, to the right of the stairs, is a simple platform paved with linear stone planks of mixed finish—some smoother, some rougher, some intact, some with holes cut through them [12-13]. Its constituents may formerly have served as structural posts, but here they have been installed horizontally rather than vertically and set adjacent to one another rather than as vertical lines spaced at appropriate intervals. The quality and overall effect of this platform suggest the rough stone terraces in the courtyard of the Domon Ken Museum of Photography and, far more distantly, minimalist floor sculptures by Carl Andre.

The third sculpture is a large work with a form that, considering its location, is more than a bit puzzling [12-14]. Extending more than some thirty feet in length, the piece comprises three parts. A cairn of stones—not dissimilar to *Spirit of the Lima Bean* at *California Scenario* or his major sculpture *Time and Space* (1991) at the Takamatsu airport—anchors its far end. From these stacked rocks extends a long gray granite plank that could be used as a seat or read in relation to the linear stones that form the platform sculpture nearby. At its end closest to the platform and the stairs *Sky Mirror*'s plane of steel rises obliquely from the granite—the sole obvious use of metal in the entire site. The sculptor's intention and the meaning of the sculpture are unclear, and to some visitors the composition of the piece and the materials used in its fabrication may appear discordant. All the sculptures fit comfortably within the contours of the land, however, as if each had been conceived and sited in relation to the other and contrived for their mutual support.

12-10
Stairs to upper level, above Isamu-ya (Noguchi house).

12-11
Reaching the upper level, eyes fall on the stone.

12-12
Eroded stone as sculpture. Or had it been shaped, at least in part?

12.3 *[above]*
Platform composed of reused stone planks.

12.4 *[right]*
Sky Mirror, 1990, installed on a low stone wall.

>> AFTER LIFE

In preparing for his afterlife Noguchi designed an urn of sorts to hold his ashes.[7] While the final forms of the two works are quite different—one sculpted and reassembled, the other left in halves—the urn at Mure and *Momo Taro* (1978) at the Storm King Art Center in New York share their use of stone left partially in its natural state, but divided during their creation [12-15]. On an expedition to secure stones for sculpture on the island of Shodoshima in the Inland Sea, Izumi spotted a huge stone that he thought might be suitable for a new sculpture. As it was "too big to handle," Noguchi remembered, "it was broken in two to get it to [the] studio." As the piece evolved, when the void was cut in one half, "everyone said: 'Oh, that's Momo Taro.'"[8] Momotarô is a character drawn from Japanese folklore. Reportedly born from a giant peach, he grappled with troublesome demons among his many heroic acts. Today he is associated with the region around Okayama and Kurashiki across the Inland Sea from Mure: thus, the association of the a hero born of a peach with a sculpture derived from a single stone and reconfigured as a composition of solid and void.

After Noguchi's passing in 1988 Masatoshi Izumi became responsible for the fabrication of the artist's memorial stone to his directives. Once the granite boulder had been selected, chisel cuts were made halfway around its middle [12-16]. These cuts were left evident, reprising a similar aesthetic that had informed Noguchi's making of several works, among them *Integrity of Ideology* (1981). The stone was then pried apart, the two halves divided. A vessel for the ashes was chiseled out of the stone in its middle, into which the ashes were deposited. The two halves of the boulder were rejoined thereafter. Although the chisel cuts on the stone remain visible, the natural seam of the fracture is so minimal that after the two sections of the stone had been reunited, few clues remained to reveal that the boulder had ever been sundered. The stone—both rent and restored by human effort —stands at rest on the hillside overlooking Mure; one trusts that Noguchi's spirit, too, rests within it—at least six months of the year [12-17].

Today, the Noguchi compound at Mure, like its sibling in Long Island City, New York, is a museum and open to the public. And here remain a substantial number of works either left unfinished or recently completed at the time of Noguchi's death, placed in the yard surrounding the

12-15 *[above]*
Momo Taro, 1978.
Storm King Art Center,
New Windsor, New York.

12-16 *[below]*
Noguchi cenotaph.
The marks of the
chisel remain.

buildings for the artist's prolonged examination and evaluation [12-19]. As an agglomeration, the buildings and grounds at the Isamu Noguchi Garden Museum in Mure present an indicative presentation of the sculptor's world, a world that thoroughly enfolded Japan and the West, the archaic and the modern, the organic and mineral, the inchoate and the complete.

The landscape, like the gardens Noguchi created, is a place "where the human heart can come into direct, pure contact with the world of plants and flowers . . . a space in which art itself is so artless as to be totally unapparent."[9] Within St. Paul's Cathedral in faraway London, an inscription circling the interior of the church's magnificent dome instructs visitors that if you seek his monument—that is, the monument for Christopher Wren, the building's architect—look around you. While the sculptor's ashes may be interred within the giant granite stone that is his cenotaph, his true monument is all that surrounds it.

>> REFLECTION

The phrase "Life is a journey" has been repeated so freely and frequently that for most of us, especially those of us who live in California, it has become a tired and annoying cliché. Yet for Isamu Noguchi the phrase remains apt, not only spiritually but also literally, in reference to the inordinate number of miles he logged during travels throughout the United States, Europe, and Asia—and his quarterly commutes between his studios in Long Island City in New York and Mure in Japan. Authors writing about the artist have frequently commented on, or even stressed, his ethnic and spiritual position that spanned two worlds and two cultures—Japan and America—and the contribution that each made to his formation and production as an artist.

However much we may wish to stress or dismiss the influence of these cultures and voyages, it seems only logical that both played a significant role in shaping Noguchi's ideas, sensibility, approach, working methods, and choices of materials. He continued to travel until the end of his life, like the seventeenth-century Japanese poet Bashô, who shared his peripatetic nature. Bashô writes: "There are a great number of ancients, too, who died on the road. I myself have been tempted for a long time by the cloud-moving wind—filled with a strong desire to wander."[10] A more contemporary parallel to Noguchi is the celebrated composer Toru Takemitsu, who was also drawn to travel. "A journey's significance," Takemitsu wrote, "lies not in its destination in the sense of traveling from one place to some other designated one, but in the process of extending one's will into the realm of the uncontrollable."[11] For Noguchi, however, the issue seems to have been less about ceding control and more about escaping the everyday in search of fresh situations and sensations.

Almost every artist transitions through "periods" during which he or she works in series, exploring a certain idea or ideas, material or materials, executing variants developed from the same basic concept or using the same material.[12] Yet like children of the same parents, each work reveals differences as well as genetic similarities. The same qualification applies to Noguchi and his art, for example, his early sculptures influenced by Constantin Brancusi or the impressive series of portrait heads—with variations even within each series—and the late works in basalt. That said, there have been few artists working in the twentieth century who have exhibited an equally restless shift from one style or medium to another. In Noguchi's case, drastic diversity distinguishes the paper-thin Akari light sculptures from his furniture or interiors—and, most of all, from the landscapes. Noguchi himself referred to these landscapes as gardens—including naming the repository of his own oeuvre as a "garden museum"; of course, we could do the same.

A garden, for Noguchi, was a respite from the exigencies and pressures of everyday life, a place of escape and solace—and potentially a site of contemplation and reflection as well. In scale, however, these works occasionally possessed dimensions far beyond those we normally associate with gardens, whether because they were too small or, as in the case of the Moerenuma Park, too large. But should we think less in a Western manner and more in a Japanese way, the limited scale of some of the courtyards and perhaps even some of the sculptures could nonetheless rightly be termed gardens. Many of the traditional *tsuboniwa*, for instance, are far smaller than any landscape of Noguchi's design. *Tsubo* is a historical Japanese unit of areal measurement roughly equivalent to thirty-six square feet, or the area comprising two tatami mats; *niwa* translates as "garden." For centuries minuscule gardens have provided relief from the tight confines of the house and the densely populated city beyond, and have brought light, increased space,

12-17
Noguchi cenotaph in the landscape. Mure, Japan.

release, and perhaps also some greenery or a *tsukubai* with the sound of softly flowing water. In theory, with the correct mindset a garden can be perceived to be of any dimension, small or large. This was probably Noguchi's own view of the garden; for him, it was intent and intensity rather than magnitude that was consequential. It was the idea more than the form, a sensibility beyond the space, much as a poem transcends its assembly of words.

Should we look at Noguchi's landscapes as landscape architecture or design, as noted in the individual chapters, some projects may come up short. *California Scenario* in full sunlight during warm weather can be a challenge to the body, compounded by its lack of places for sitting comfortably. To some degree this is also true of the Billy Rose Art Garden in Jerusalem. Other landscapes, like the Beinecke and Chase, can only be viewed from above or below but never entered, much less touched. In contrast to this removal, one welcomes the physical engagement offered by *California Scenario*, the UNESCO garden, or Moerenuma Park—the lone work planned to accommodate team sports and other organized active recreation. For several of the other Noguchi gardens, the landscape resides in the mind more than in the body—unless one regards the mind and body as one. In that sense these are spiritual works, most obvious perhaps in the program for IBM's Armonk offices, where Noguchi attempted to express the human past and the future through form and vegetation—no mean feat.

Landscape architects have acknowledged, and sometimes appreciated, the formal inventiveness and use of materials in Noguchi's landscapes while to some degree disparaging their performance in the manner expected of landscape architecture: that is, applying the trio of social, physical, and environmental criteria. In terms of performance this assessment is valid. But we need to keep in mind that Noguchi made no attempt to create landscapes that operated in the manner common to landscape architecture. Instead, he sought to create an artwork, a spatial sculpture of human scale, at times to be entered physically, at other times to be entered only visually. To evaluate the production of fruit or the percolation of water is usually a far easier task than measuring the effect of a landscape on one's well-being or thought. Gauging the effect of a garden at the psychological and spiritual levels is a still more difficult task.

In a conversation between sculptor Richard Serra and architect Peter Eisenman, Serra gave a one-word response to the moderator's question as to what distinguished their two disciplines: "plumbing." Sculpture answers to no functional demands. We could extend that distinction to artists' gardens by dismissing the normal functional demands—although, as it happens, Noguchi certainly did address the issue of plumbing in his monumental fountains. In several interviews Noguchi stressed that he worked as an artist. "I am not a Landscape Architect," he once stated emphatically. "It is a separate profession. You must understand codes, you must be able to cope with varying states of hypocrisy and once more, you are essentially a machine bound to respect business hours." No, he was a sculptor, with that mindset as well as the required skills. "My work is a creative act, not a professional discipline bound to degrees and building codes."[13] He typically left to Shoji Sadao the task of dealing with building codes and the "varying states of hypocrisy," although he certainly was forced on several occasions to personally address his share of the latter.

We can fault Noguchi's gardens for their shortcomings but we cannot dismiss their validity or success as works of art based on functional criteria alone. Conceived and regarded as artworks, they should be granted a free pass on function. But why should they?

> *Now I am a sculptor and I've worked with gardens and attempted the design of playgrounds, all with the idea of being able to have an area that I could control and work as a sculptor. Some people say, "Aren't you being an architect, too?" I don't think so, because I am little concerned about the mechanics of shelter and so forth, which is a very important part of architecture and which I am quite willing to leave to architects; I don't want to get involved in these difficult problems.*[14]

The big question remains as to why and by what criteria we should or can regard a garden, a plaza, or a park as an artwork rather than as design, as landscape architecture. For that matter, how do we even define art? Nicolas Bourriaud proposes, "Artistic activity is a game, whose forms, patterns, and functions develop and evolve according to periods and social contexts; it is not an immutable essence."[15] If we accept that assumption, surely in our time we can regard landscapes—or at least *some* landscapes—as art. Personally, I feel that while the best of the Noguchi landscapes achieve the status of art, others fall short. That is a value judgment, I admit, rooted in my belief that art is a quality rather than a category of object, the quality that touches you in a particular way—you, personally and individually. Naturally, this stance may be dismissed by some as invalid or at best problematic. However, I support my belief using the analogy of language and speech as proffered by the Swiss linguist Ferdinand de Saussure in the early years of the twentieth century.[16]

Saussure saw language (*langue*) as the overarching structure of grammar and vocabulary that governed communication among individuals. Granted this apparatus, we can understand new and unique sentences we have never heard or read before; we are able to comprehend because we know the language. Speech (*parole*), in turn, is our ability to create new and personal utterances, invented variations that rely upon the greater sphere of language. Objects, ideas, and writings operate within the language of art, but whether we regard them as art is ultimately personal. It is not a question of whether the object is functional or conceived free of function, as is most sculpture. That value is independent of the medium. Of course, one can take issue with this stance, and many have, such as those supporting the ideas of John Dewey and the pragmatists.[17] I just do not share their values.

To return to Noguchi. Appraising his landscapes using this value system I find that Chase, Beinecke, and *California Scenario* achieved a level higher than the others, although in some ways I probably would have to add the Jerusalem sculpture garden and UNESCO to that list. A gigantic—and posthumous—work like Moerenuma Park occupies a class of its own. Having been realized by other parties, it must be judged on other terms.

So where does that leave us? As presented in the opening chapter, Noguchi provides us, especially designers, with lessons both syntactic and semantic. But in the end, perhaps neither represents the ultimate value of his contributions. Perhaps one should leave the last word to Isamu Noguchi himself. In his guide to the Isamu Noguchi Garden Museum, he concludes with a simple measure that we could also apply to his gardens: "Call it sculpture when it moves you so."[18] Or call it a garden—or just call it art.

>> NOTES

>> CHAPTER 1

1 Author's conversation with Kirk Varnedoe, then Chief Curator of Painting and Sculpture, Museum of Modern Art, New York, in Chatham, New York, October 1991.

2 Nikolaus Pevsner, *An Outline of European Architecture* (Harmondsworth: Pelican, 1943), p. 15.

3 Several philosophers have ruminated on that possibility. See Mara Miller, *The Garden as Art* (Albany: State University of New York Press, 1994); Stephanie Ross, *What Gardens Mean* (Chicago: University of Chicago Press, 1998); and David E. Cooper, *A Philosophy of Gardens* (Oxford: Oxford University Press, 2006).

4 Hayden Herrera, *Listening to Stone: The Art and Life of Isamu Noguchi* (New York: Farrar, Straus and Giroux, 2015), p. 360.

5 For the dangers lurking in the private/public ownership of "public" spaces, see Kristine F. Miller, *Designs on the Public* (Minneapolis: University of Minnesota Press, 2007).

6 Isamu Noguchi, quoted in M. M., "Exhibitions," *International Sculpture* 95 (March 1931): p. 80; cited in Nancy Grove, *Isamu Noguchi Portrait Sculpture* (Washington, DC: Smithsonian Institution Press for the National Portrait Gallery, 1989), p. 10.

7 Marc Treib, "Must Landscape Mean? Approaches to Significance in Recent Landscape Architecture," *Landscape Journal* (Spring 1995): pp. 46–62, reprinted in Marc Treib, ed., *Meaning in Landscape Architecture & Gardens* (Oxon: Routledge, 2011), pp. 82–165.

8 Isamu Noguchi, *A Sculptor's World* (New York: Harper & Row, 1968), p. 28, quoting from Dorothy C. Miller, ed., *Fourteen Americans* (New York: Museum of Modern Art, 1946).

9 Isamu Noguchi, "New Stone Gardens," *Art in America* (June 1964): p. 64.

10 The catalogue raisonné on the Isamu Noguchi Museum website testifies to this fact; noguchi.org/CR/Index.

11 Ana Maria Torres, *Isamu Noguchi: A Study of Space* (New York: Monacelli, 2000).

12 Herrera, *Listening to Stone*; Dore Ashton, *Noguchi: East and West* (New York: Alfred A. Knopf, 1992); and Masayo Duus, *The Life of Isamu Noguchi: Journey without Borders*, trans. Peter Duus (Princeton NJ: Princeton University Press, 2007).

13 See Treib, *Meaning in Landscape Architecture & Gardens*.

>> CHAPTER 2

1 In this, Noguchi seems to have shared the opinion of Ray Kroc, the man who built the McDonald's fast-food empire, who once asserted that "nothing recedes like success." Ray Kroc, *Grinding It Out: The Making of McDonald's* (Chicago: H. Regnery, 1977).

2 Complete biographies, well told, are found in Ashton, *East and West*; Duus, *Journey without Borders*; and Herrera, *Listening to Stone*. On Noguchi's mother, see Edward Marx, *Leonie Gilmour: When East Weds West* ([Santa Barbara, CA]: Botchan, 2013); on his father, Edward Marx, *Yone Noguchi: The Stream of Fate*, vol. 1, *The Western Sea* (Santa Barbara, CA: Botchan, 2019).

3 Noguchi, *A Sculptor's World*, p. 12.

4 Duus, *Journey without Borders*, p. 89.

5 Isamu Noguchi, "Noguchi on Brancusi" (1976), in *Isamu Noguchi: Essays and Conversations*, ed. Diane Apostolos-Cappadona and Bruce Altshuler (New York: Harry N. Abrams, 1994), p. 111.

6 There were seven marble interpretations of the theme of the bird in flight, from which issued nine bronze casts; metmuseum.org/art/collection/search/486757.

7 Eric Shanes, *Constantin Brancusi* (New York: Abbeville, 1989), p. 106.

8 Like Brancusi, Henry Moore believed that simplicity as an end in itself tends toward emptiness and monotony, but that simplicity in carving—interpreted as the lack of surface trimmings—"reveals the contrast in section, axis, direction, and bulk between different shapes and so intensified the three-dimensional power in a work." Both Brancusi and his short-term assistant no doubt shared Moore's attitude toward form and carving. Henry Moore, "On Carving" (1932), reprinted in *Henry Moore: Writings and Conversations*, ed. Alan Wilkinson (Berkeley: University of California Press, 2002), p. 188.

9 On the portrait heads, see Nancy Grove, *Isamu Noguchi: Portrait Sculpture* (Washington, DC: Smithsonian Institution Press for the National Portrait Gallery, 1989).

10 Grove, *Noguchi: Portrait Sculpture*.

11 Noguchi, *Sculptor's World*, p. 27.

12 Because of the fragility of the stone used in such thin sheets, certain pieces originally executed in Georgia marble, such as *Avatar*, were later cast in bronze.

13 Noguchi, *Sculptor's World*, p. 28.

14 Reprinted in *Noguchi, Sculptor's World*, p. 28.

15 Isamu Noguchi, *The Isamu Noguchi Garden Museum* (New York: Harry N. Abrams, 1987), p. 126.

16 Isamu Noguchi, quoted in Sam Hunter, "Isamu Noguchi," in *Isamu Noguchi: 75th Birthday Exhibition* (New York: André Emmerich Gallery / Pace Gallery, 1980).

17 The piece is alternatively known as *The Seed* and *Red Earth*.

18 "An Interview with Isamu Noguchi by Katherine Kuh" (1962), reprinted in Apostolos-Cappadona and Altshuler, eds., *Isamu Noguchi: Essays and Conversations*, p. 131.

19 noguchi.org/artworks/collection/view/practice-rocks-in-placement/, accessed 9 October 2021.

20 Ashton, *East and West*, p. 163.

21 This technique derived from Noguchi's "kneading clay for firing ceramics in 1931 in Kyoto." noguchi.org/artworks/collection/view/this-earth-this-passage/, accessed 12 December 2020.

22 The play of hill and valley, mound and depression, reappears in Noguchi's early studies for the Beinecke courtyard.

23 "Thinking of the floor, I made Floor Frame. I made many other pieces in relation to the floor space at that time, but this seemed to best define the essentiality of floor, not as sculpture alone but as part of the concept of floor." Noguchi, *Garden Museum*, p. 124. *Floor Frame* is roughly contemporary with Noguchi's gardens at the Beinecke Rare Book and Manuscript Library at Yale University and the Chase Manhattan Bank in New York, in both of which the floor plane figures prominently.

24 The floor plane would play a major role in the two gardens cited in the previous note.

25 He is also credited with the garden at the nearby temple of Tenryû-ji.

26 Musô Soseki, "Poem on Dry Mountain," in *Sun at Midnight: Musô Soseki, Poems and Sermons*, trans. W. S. Merwin and Sôiku Shigematsu (San Francisco: North Point Press, 1980), p. 32.

27 Noguchi, *Garden Museum*, p. 88.

28 poetryfoundation.org/poetrymagazine/poems/14575/anecdote-of-the-jar, accessed 20 July 2019.

29 Ashton, *East and West*, p. 16–17.

30 "He [Noguchi] loved to watch dance performances. Years later Noguchi recalled how much he had learned from Ito as well as from Ito's younger brother Yuji, a set and costume designer." Herrera, *Listening to Stone*, p. 72.

31 Herrera, *Listening to Stone*, p. 217.

32 Herrera, *Listening to Stone*, p. 217.

33 Robert Tracy, *Spaces of the Mind: Isamu Noguchi's Dance Designs* (New York: Limelight, 2000), p. 19.

34 David Sylvester, *Looking at Giacometti* (London: Chatto & Windus, 1994), pp. 102–03.

35 Hunter, "Isamu Noguchi."

36 Martin Friedman, *Noguchi's Imaginary Landscapes* (Minneapolis: Walker Art Center, 1978), p. 27.

37 Friedman, *Noguchi's Imaginary Landscapes*, p. 29.

38 Choreography by Martha Graham, music by Louis Horst, 1935. Graham herself danced the part.

39 Noguchi, *Sculptor's World*, p. 222.

40 Ashton, *East and West*, p. 54.

41 Tracy, *Spaces of the Mind*, p. 24.

42 Noguchi, *Sculptor's World*, p. 23.

43 *Embattled Garden* showed "the apple on a grand scale. The platform is colored like an apple skin. Quivering branches spring from it, like worms, between which the dance proceeds. A tree to one side forms the remainder of the set." Noguchi, *Garden Museum*, p. 210.

44 Tracy, *Spaces of the Mind*, p. 207.

45 See Gladys Fabre and Doris Wintgens Hütte, eds., *Van Doesburg and the International Avant-Garde: Constructing a New World* (London: Tate Modern, 2010); and Theo van Doesburg, *Principles of Neo-Plastic Art*, trans. (1925; London: Lund Humphries, 1966).

46 H. Allen Brooks, "Frank Lloyd Wright and the Destruction of the Box," *Journal of the Society of Architectural Historians* (March 1979): pp. 7–14.

47 Friedman, *Imaginary Landscapes*, p. 29.

48 Ashton, *East and West*, p. 16.

49 Noguchi, *Garden Museum*, p. 11.

50 Nicolas Bourriaud, *Relational Aesthetics*, trans. Simon Pleasance and Fronza Woods (Dijon: Les Presses du Réel, 2002), p. 13.

>>CHAPTER 3

1 Isamu Noguchi, "The Sculptor and the Architect," *Studio International*, 1968, reprinted in Apostolos-Cappadona and Altshuler, eds. *Isamu Noguchi: Essays and Conversations*, p. 50.

2 That the documentation of these works in drawings, photographs, and maquettes was displayed and sold undermines this assertion.

3 Isamu Noguchi, legend on drawing, Isamu Noguchi Archive (hereafter INA). In reviewing Noguchi's exhibition at the Marie Harriman Gallery in New York, the critic Henry McBride noted that Noguchi's preferred location would have been at "the geographical center of the United States." Noguchi, *Sculptor's World*, p. 22. The text on the drawing does not indicate a location, however.

4 Thomson reshaped the music into an orchestral suite in 1942.

5 Wright's forebears had been farmers, and as a youth he had spent summers on the farm of his uncle Richard Lloyd-Jones; throughout his life he professed an attachment to the land and its folk. And it was there, in Spring Green, that he established his home and studio, Taliesin. Frank Lloyd Wright, *An Autobiography* (New York: Duell, Sloane & Pearce, 1943), pp. 6–9. "On the only existing drawing of the chapel, Wright wrote a description of his design as a 'Memorial to the tiller of the ground,' making the earth a feature of the monument or vice versa." Frank Lloyd Wright's Chapel for Cooksville." cooksville-news.blogspot.com/2012/12/frank-lloyd-wrights-chapel-for.html, accessed 19 March 2021.

6 Grant Wood, "A Definition of Regionalism," 17 November 1937, Grant Wood Archives, Davenport Museum of Art, Iowa, quoted in Brady M. Roberts, "The European Roots of Regionalism: Grant Wood's Stylistic Synthesis," in *Grant Wood: An American Master Revealed* (Davenport, IA: Davenport Museum of Art; Rohnert Park, CA: Pomegranate Artbooks, 1995), p. 34.

7 Noguchi, *Sculptor's World*, p. 21. Just how an earthen monument in the middle of the country would be a part of daily living is left unexplained, although one can say that commemoration is a value shared commonly, if not always at a specific site.

8 Quoted in Amy Lyford, *Isamu Noguchi's Modernism: Negotiating Race, Labor, and Nation, 1930–1950* (Berkeley: University of California Press, 2013), p. 13.

9 Lyford, *Isamu Noguchi's Modernism*, p. 13.

10 "My model indicated the wish to belong to America, to its vast horizons of earth." Noguchi, *Sculptor's World*, p. 22.

11 "John Deere was born in Vermont in 1804. In 1825 he started his career as a blacksmith. He moved west in the 1830s when times got tough. Many problems prevented the making of the steel plows. Steel was hard to find. In the beginning steel had to come from Great Britain. Ten years after the first plow was made, Deere's company was making 1000 plows a year." iwest.k12.il.us/schools/thawville/projects/1800/index–017.htm, accessed 3 April 2017.

12 "In recent years, farmers are moving away from disk-ing and plowing and exploiting non-till options that use the residue of the prior crop as fertilizer." Rae Tyson, "As New Ground Is Broken, Plow Is Dying Out," *USA Today*, 23 May 1994.

13 The pyramid appeared throughout history in tombs or memorials. For his final place of rest, in 1854 Prince Herrmann von Pückler-Muskau constructed a sizable earthen pyramid in the middle of an artificial lake on his estate in Branitz, near Cottbus, Brandenburg, Germany. Michael Jakob, *Faux Mountains* (Novato, CA: ORO, 2022), pp. 81–82.

14 Noguchi's description given on the drawing.

15 Amy Lyford also suggests that the sides were too steep to have been plowed by a tractor and that anyone farming the monument would have had to resort to a horse-drawn plow. *Noguchi's Modernism*, p. 34.

16 Noguchi hoped that his patron/mentor, Dr. Edward Rumley—who was himself involved with the production of tractors—would persuade John Deere or some other tractor manufacturer to build the project "in the middle of the West Prairie" or "somewhere in Oklahoma." Herrera, *Listening to Stone*, p. 135.

17 Herrera, *Listening to Stone*, p. 136.

18 "Architects Would Come to Him . . . and He Would Redesign the Architecture. Interview with Shoji Sadao," *Casa Brutus* (special issue, "A Century of Isamu Noguchi") (2005): p. 82.

19 Isamu Noguchi, "I Become a Nisei," draft, 5 October 1942, unpublished typescript for *Reader's Digest*, October 1942, INA. Although solicited by the magazine, the text was only recently published for the first time.

20 "Nisei Writers and Artists Mobilization for Democracy," memorandum, 1942, INA.

21 Isamu Noguchi, memo, ca. 1942, INA.

22 Poston was then called Parker because its land would be irrigated by the Parker Dam. John Collier, Commissioner of Indian Affairs, negotiated Noguchi's entry into the camp. Herrara, *Listening to Stone*, p. 178.

23 The Bureau of Indian Affairs considered this an expeditious means by which to develop the infrastructure of the reservation at no cost. The Native Americans themselves were against the use of this land for what they regarded as unjust purposes. The Army overruled them. Thomas J. Fujita, encyclopedia.densho.org/Poston_%28Colorado_River%29/, accessed 28 March 2017.

24 janm.org/projects/clasc/poston.htm, accessed 23 March 2017.

25 Isamu Noguchi to Mr. Fryer, 28 July 1942, INA.

26 Isamu Noguchi, "Projected Creation and Recreation Center for Poston," 1942, INA.

27 Noguchi, "I Become a Nisei."

28 Fujita, encyclopedia.densho.org/Poston_%28Colorado_River%29/.

29 After the war, Webb (1899–1974) became a major developer in the Phoenix area, the Sun City retirement community being his best-known project. He no doubt used the efficiency techniques developed and tested at Poston and other military undertakings to rationalize the construction of his housing developments.

30 Paul Bailey, *City in the Sun: The Japanese Concentration Camp at Poston, Arizona* (Los Angeles: Westernlore, 1971), p. 100.

31 "Report on Cemetery and Mortuary Project," 9 June 1941, Evacuee Case File: Isamu Noguchi, War Relocation Authority Records, RG-210, National Archives, Washington, DC; cited in Lyford, *Noguchi's Modernism*, p. 118. These materials were presented to the relevant government agencies in Washington.

32 Kinoshita turned to Hollywood after the war and had a long and successful career as an art director and set designer, with a specialization in science-fiction films. He was the creator of the celebrated Robby the Robot, which appeared in the 1956 production of *Forbidden Planet*.

33 According to one source, 221 internees died in the camp, while there were 6,623 births. javadc.org/poston.htm, accessed 11 May 2021.

34 The initials GE penciled on the top of Cairns's copy of the letter are those of Garrett Eckbo, indicating that he had read the memo and had reviewed Noguchi's plan(s).

35 Bailey, *City in the Sun*, p. 111.

36 Herrera, *Listening to Stone*, p. 180.

37 Isamu Noguchi to Man Ray, 7 May 1942, INA.

38 Lyford proposes an additional reference: the USS Arizona, sunk in the attack on Pearl Harbor. Amy Lyford, "Noguchi, Sculptural Abstraction, and the Politics of Japanese American Internment," *Art Bulletin* (March 2003): p. 144.

39 Hunter, "Isamu Noguchi," n.p.

40 These reliefs contributed to the shaping of the ceiling for the American Stove Company in St. Louis (1948), which is essentially treated as a reflection of a landscape that might have existed below it. Illumination is accommodated within the flat voids cut from the ceiling plane, rather than modeled like the Lunars. These voids were revealed when the dropped ceiling that covered Noguchi's work was recently removed.

41 "We were at war then, you know. The earth was being bombarded and torn up by bombing, just like Vietnam. In this piece I conceived of the earth as tortured by these bombardments." Isamu Noguchi, quoted in Martin Friedman, ed., *Isamu Noguchi: The Sculpture of Spaces* (New York: Whitney Museum of American Art, 1980), p. 43.

42 Herrera, *Listening to Stone*, p. 178.

43 Photographs show that the piece was also displayed vertically as a relief, however.

44 Noguchi, *Sculptor's World*, p. 250.

45 Friedman, *Sculpture of Spaces*, p. 43.

46 The venture was the brainchild of Luther Ely Smith, a leading St. Louis citizen and booster, who contributed a substantial sum toward the instigation and design of the memorial. Smith believed the memorial should be "transcending in spiritual and aesthetic values," which would attract people of all nations. "Luther Ely Smith: Founder of a Memorial," *Museum Gazette* (March 2001): n.p.

47 The demolition of the district did not receive universal praise. "A lot of people felt that it was the heart of St. Louis and it was being ripped out." Luther Ely Smith's granddaughter, quoted in "Luther Ely Smith," n.p.

48 In terms of architectural style, the jury was evenhandedly constituted, however, balancing modernist Californians Richard Neutra and William Wurster—who chaired the jury—with the more traditional Fiske Kimball and the St. Louis architect Louis LaBeaume.

49 Sharon Brown, "Jefferson National Expansion Memorial: The 1947–48 Competition," *Gateway Heritage: Quarterly Journal of the Missouri Historical Society* (Winter 1980): pp. 40–48.

50 Construction of the arch would be completed only in 1967, with its inauguration the following year.

51 Noguchi, "Sculptor and the Architect," p. 53.

52 Antonin Raymond to Isamu Noguchi, 22 November 1950, INA. In a letter to Macalester College (the ultimate recipient of the metal sculpture/fountain), 18 February 1987, INA, Noguchi writes: "[Raymond] proposed that I do a garden covering the large space around the building which must have been at least an acre. To do this, he had saved $1,500 by substituting gravel for cement on the parking area. Considering the airfare back to Japan this hardly left anything for my time. However, I was eager to continue my study of the Japanese garden

which I had started the year before with a memorial to my father at Keio University."

53 Antonin Raymond, *An Autobiography* (Rutland, VT: Charles E. Tuttle, 1973), p. 219.

54 Paul Cummings, "Oral History Interview with Isamu Noguchi," 7 November–26 December 1973. Typescript, Archives of American Art, Smithsonian Institution, Washington, DC.

55 Kurt Helfrich and William Whitaker, eds., *Crafting a Modern World: The Architecture and Design of Antonin and Noémi Raymond* (New York: Princeton Architectural Press, 2006), p. 275. See also Herrera, *Listening to Stone*, pp. 278–79.

56 "The costs were covered by the cement saved by doing a garden instead of a parking lot." Noguchi, *Sculptor's World*, p. 163.

57 Noguchi claimed that he was applying the mixing of orders, in Japanese known as *shin-gyô-sô*. See chapter 10.

58 Noguchi to Macalester College, 18 February 1987.

59 Noguchi never executed the *kokeshi* at full-size for the *Reader's Digest* project; they were produced at a later date but have been lost. The artist's longtime assistant, Masatoshi Izumi, created new versions, which are in the collection of the Museum of Modern Art in Kamakura. The untitled steel fountain sculpture today resides at Macalester College in St. Paul, Minnesota, the gift of DeWitt and Lila Acheson Wallace.

60 Noguchi, *Sculptor's World*, p. 131.

61 Herrera, *Listening to Stone*, p. 283.

>> CHAPTER 4

1 Joe L. Frost observed that in the 1950s and 1960s, "Although the motives were worthy, play sculptures were frequently more appealing to adults than to children." Joe L. Frost, "Play Environments for Young Children in the USA: 1800–1990," *Children's Environments Quarterly* (Winter 1989): p. 21.

2 M. Paul Friedberg and Ellen Perry Berkeley, *Play and Interplay: A Manifesto for New Design in Urban Recreational Environment* (New York: Macmillan, 1970), p. 35.

3 Amy Ogata, *Designing the Creative Child: Playthings and Places in Midcentury America* (Minneapolis: University of Minnesota Press, 2013).

4 Aldo van Eyck "On the Design of Play Equipment and the Arrangement of Playgrounds" (1962), in Francis Strauven, ed., *Aldo van Eyck, Collected Writings* (Amsterdam: SUN, 2008).

5 Norman Brosterman, *Inventing Kindergarten* (New York: Harry N. Abrams, 1997). I thank Susan Herrington for bringing this book to my attention. On the influence of Froebel in his education, see Wright, *An Autobiography*, pp. 33–34.

6 Although Brosterman provides several provocative illustrations of children's exercises that bear formal similarities with works by name-brand artists, I cannot wholeheartedly support his conclusion. Brosterman, *Inventing Kindergarten*, p. 106.

7 Noguchi, *Sculptor's World*, p. 12.

8 Ashton, *East and West*, p. 52.

9 Ashton, *East and West*, p. 52.

10 Noguchi, *Garden Museum*, p. 144.

11 When a version of *Play Mountain* was finally realized at Moerenuma Park in Sapporo in 2005—some seventeen years after Noguchi's death—stone served this purpose [see 11-7].

12 See Robert Caro, *The Power Broker: Robert Moses and the Fall of New York* (New York: Alfred A. Knopf, 1974).

13 Noguchi, *Sculptor's World*, p. 22.

14 Herrera, *Listening to Stone*, p. 141.

15 Noguchi, *Sculptor's World*, p. 22.

16 Herrera, *Listening to Stone*, p. 176.

17 Herrera, *Listening to Stone*, p. 25.

18 In *Towards a New Architecture*, Le Corbusier designates the plan as the generator of architecture: "Without a plan, you have lack of order, and wilfulness. The Plan holds in itself the essence of sensation." Le Corbusier, *Towards a New Architecture*, trans. Frederick Etchells (1927; New York: Dover, 1986), p. 45.

19 See Marc Treib, "On Plans," *Utblick Landskap* 4 (1998), reprinted in Marc Treib, ed., *Representing Landscape Architecture* (London: Taylor & Francis, 2008).

20 While this is far from the most desirable way to create architecture, it was probably the most common method until recently, when, with the aid of the computer, architects could freely design from the outside in—an approach anathema to modernist thinking.

21 John Gordon, *Isamu Noguchi* (New York: Whitney Museum of Art / Frederick Praeger, 1968), p. 13. Beekman Place runs north–south from 48th to 51st Streets, and other than FDR Drive, is the last street before the East River. The northern limit of the United Nations precinct is 48th Street. The established landscape architect Gilmore Clark, who was designing the United Nations grounds, would also consult on the relationship of the playground to the greater landscape. Untitled timeline, typescript, INA.

22 Julian Whittlesey studied architecture and civil engineering at Yale University and in 1935, after working for New Deal agencies such as the Settlement Administration, cofounded Mayer & Whittlesey; in time the office was restructured as Whittlesey Conklin + Rossant. The design work of his firms spanned apartment houses, housing, and institutional projects, as well as the planning of new towns such as Kitimat, British Columbia, and Reston, Virginia. en.wikipedia.org/wiki/Julian_Whittlesey, accessed 1 April 2021.

23 Thomas Hess, "Playgrounds," *ArtNews* (April 1952).

24 The work is today in the Peggy Guggenheim Collection in Venice, Italy.

25 "Playground for the United Nations," *Interiors* (April 1952).

26 Hess referred to Moses as "the Cheops of toll bridges." Hess, "Playgrounds."

27 Shaina D. Larrivee, "Playscapes: Isamu Noguchi's Designs for Play," *Public Art Dialogue* (March 2011): pp. 53–80, reprinted in *Isamu Noguchi: Parques / Playscapes*, ed. Ariela Ramírez Moyao and Mara Garbuno (Mexico City: Museo Tamayo, 2016), p. 64.

28 "Playground for the United Nations."

29 Reuben M. Rainey and J. C. Miller, *Public Gardens: The Suburban Parks of Robert Royston* (San Francisco: William Stout, 2006).

30 Although known as an adventure playground, it embodies nothing of the ideas for adventurous play as they appeared in Europe.

31 While admitting that her research has tended to be qualitative and that greater risk appears to be taken by male preschool children, Ellen Sandseter has proposed that "risky play" is both attractive and necessary for children's development. Ellen Beate Hansen Sandseter, "Characteristics of Risky Play," *Journal of Adventure Education and Outdoor Learning* no. [illegible] (2009), pp. 3–21. I thank Susan Herrington for bringing Sandseter's research to my attention. See also Shirley Wyver et al., "Ten Ways to Restrict Children's Freedom to Play: The Problem of Surplus Safety," *Contemporary Issues in Early Childhood* no. 3 (2010), researchgate.net/publication/236986877_Ten_Ways_to_Restrict_Children's-Freedom_to_Play_The_Problem_of_Surplus_Safety.

32 Lady Allen of Harwood (Marjory Allen), *Planning for Play* (London: Thames & Hudson, 1968).

33 Susan Herrington, *Cornelia Hahn Oberlander: Making the Modern Landscape* (Charlottesville: University of Virginia, 2013), p. 106.

34 Herrington, *Cornelia Hahn Oberlander*, p. 108.

35 "Out of the Sandbox," *Newsweek*, 17 February 1964.

36 Levy died in 1960.

37 Barry Gottehrer and Tim Hutchens, "Court Battle and Confusion Over Playground," *New York Herald Tribune*, 27 February 1965, reprinted in *Play Mountain: Isamu Noguchi + Louis Kahn*, ed. Shizuko Watari (Tokyo: Watari-um, 1996), p. 61.

38 Gottehrer and Hutchens, "Court Battle and Confusion Over Playground."

39 Gottehrer and Huchens, "Court Battle and Confusion Over Playground."

40 Considering the eclecticism of Johnson's architecture in the 1960s, imagining a work stemming from their collaboration is a fascinating exercise.

41 Isamu Noguchi to Louis I. Kahn, 27 August 1961, quoted in Watari, ed., *Play Mountain*, p. 47.

42 Richard Saul Wurman, ed., *What Will Be Has Always Been: The Words of Louis I. Kahn* (New York: Access Press, 1986), p. 31.

43 Noguchi, *Sculptor's World*, p. 177–78

44 Noguchi, *Sculptor's World*, p. 177.

45 The original three-block area was reduced to one. *New York Times*, 4 February 1963; cited in Watari, ed., *Play Mountain*, p. 69.

46 These later schemes suggest the architectural-only garden of La Scarzuola in Umbria, Italy. Built by Tomaso Buzzi in the twentieth century, this landscape of brick architectonic forms was created as an "ideal city" but reads more as a large-scale environmental sculpture.

47 Isamu Noguchi to Mr. Jones, 3 December 1964, in Watari, ed., *Play Mountain*, p. 51.

48 Louis I. Kahn, "Interview with Karl Linn," 14 May 1965, quoted in David B. Brownlee and David G. De Long, *Louis I. Kahn: In the Realm of Architecture*, abr. rev. ed. (New York: Universe, 1997), p. 183.

49 Brownlee and De Long, *Louis I. Kahn*, p. 133.

50 Joseph Lelyveld, "Model Play Area for Park Shown," *New York Times*, 5 February 1964.

51 Lelyveld, "Model Play Area for Park Shown."

52 Brownlee and De Long, *Louis I. Kahn*, p. 184.

53 Samuel Kaplan, "Mayor Signs Pact for Play Center," *New York Times*, 30 December 1965.

54 Elizabeth Kassler, *Modern Gardens in the Landscape* (New York: Museum of Modern Art), 1964.

55 Today, the retired emperor and empress.

56 Noguchi, *Sculptor's World*, p. 179.

57 "In 1939 Georgia O'Keeffe traveled to the Territory of Hawai'i to fulfill a commission for the advertising agency N. W. Ayer & Son. Her expenses were covered in exchange for two paintings to be used in advertisements for the Hawai'ian Pineapple Company (now Dole Food Company), an enterprise entangled with the conquest of Hawai'i." Sascha T. Scott, "Georgia O'Keeffe's Hawai'i? Decolonizing the History of American Modernism," *American Art* 34, no. 2 (Summer 2020): pp. 26–53.

58 Today, in an age of taller players and dunking, flexible hoops have become the norm, at least in most gymnasiums.

59 This information and subsequent parts of the restoration story are from Alexandra Lange, "The Story Behind Isamu Noguchi's Playscapes in Atlanta," hermanmiller.com/stories/ why-magazine/the-story-behind-isamu-noguchis-playscapes-in-atlanta/, accessed 16 March 2021.

60 Today, when soft composite surfaces, at times of recycled rubber, are available in numerous colors, one suspects Noguchi would have utilized the material for his surface covering.

61 Lange, "Noguchi's Playscapes."

62 Van Eyck, "On the Design of Play Equipment." On the playgrounds, see Anna van Lingen and Denisa Kollarova, *Aldo van Eyck: Seventeen Playgrounds, Amsterdam* (Amsterdam: Lecturis, 2016); Liane Lefaivre and Ingeborg de Roode, eds., *Aldo van Eyck: The Playgrounds and the City* (Amsterdam: Stedelijk Museum; Rotterdam: NAi, 2002); and Liane Lefaivre and Alexander Tzonis, *Aldo van Eyck: Humanist Rebel* (Rotterdam: 010, 1999).

>> CHAPTER 5

1 For a more complete telling of the UNESCO garden story see Marc Treib, *Noguchi in Paris: Isamu Noguchi and the UNESCO Garden* (San Francisco: William Stout, 2003). Portions of this chapter have been adapted from that book.

2 The constitution of the architectural advisory board guaranteed that the approved style of the new building would be modernist rather than traditional.

3 Most writers consider Breuer to be the building's principal designer, Nervi its engineer, and Zehrfuss its executive architect. Despite his position on the advisory board, Le Corbusier kept trying to secure the commission for himself during the building's design and claimed—not without some merit—that the overall concept of the Y-shaped layout derived from his ideas. Le Corbusier's proposal for Building II is recorded in a sketch now in the collection of the Canadian Centre for Architecture. His influence and intrigues are carefully traced by Barbara Shapiro in "'Tout ça est foutaise, foutaise et demi!': Le Corbusier and UNESCO," *Revue d'art canadienne/Canadian Art Review* no. 2 (1989): pp. 171–180, figs. on pp. 298–307.

4 The art advisory board included Herbert Read, Georges Salles, Shahid Subrawardy, and C. Para-Perez as chair. In the early 1960s, the well-known Brazilian landscape architect and artist Roberto Burle Marx would design the gardens for the courtyards in the building's extension.

5 The uses of the ground-floor spaces have changed over time, and today the lobby serves primarily for entry functions, circulation, shops, and exhibitions.

6 Noguchi, *Sculptor's World*, p. 167.

7 Noguchi, *Sculptor's World*, p. 167. Noguchi also wrote, "the possibility of planting was limited due to there being buildings directly below. It is for this reason that I asked for and secured the incorporation of the adjoining green area into the design." Isamu Noguchi to Ambassador Toshikazu Kase, 24 September 1956, INA.

8 Isamu Noguchi to Michel Dard, 24 September 1956, INA.

9 Noguchi to Kase, 24 September 1956. In another, undated, letter Noguchi again played on ethnic sympathy: "At the time when the prospect of this work was first broached to me by M. Marcel Breuer, he told me that my selection was determined in part at least by my (part) Japanese [the word "birth" is here overprinted with "name"]. It was realized that I was not a Japanese national but still I was someone they had confidence in working with." Undated letter, (January?) 1957; probably a draft as it contains handwritten editing, INA.

10 Toru Hagiwara to Isamu Noguchi, 15 January 1957, INA.

11 Treib, *Noguchi in Paris*, p. 53.

12 Noguchi, *Sculptor's World*, p. 167.

13 Isamu Noguchi to the Zehrfuss office, 7 March 1957, INA.

14 Noguchi, *Sculptor's World*, p. 167.

15 Duus, *Journey without Borders*, pp. 276–77.

16 The information on the collaboration of Noguchi and Mirei Shigemori derives from Christian Tschumi, *Mirei*

Shigemori, Rebel in The Garden: Modern Japanese Landscape Architecture (Basel: Birkhäuser, 2007), p. 51.

17 Duus, *Journey without Borders*, p. 283.

18 Herrera, *Listening to Stone*, p. 331.

19 Dakin Hart and Mark Dean Johnson, eds., *Changing and Unchanging Things: Noguchi and Hasegawa in Postwar Japan* (New York: Isamu Noguchi Foundation; Oakland: University of California Press, 2019).

20 Tôemon Sano, "A Work Reflecting the History of Our Friendship," in *Isamu Noguchi: Human Aspect as a Contemporary; 54 Witnesses in Japan and America*, ed. Shikoku Shimbun (Takamatsu: Shikoku Shinbun, 2002), pp. 68–70.

21 Ashton, *East and West*, p. 146.

22 Ashton, *East and West*, p. 19.

23 Sanô, for example, served as Noguchi's agent for acquiring and shipping the stones for the 1 Chase Plaza courtyard [see chapter 6].

24 Isamu Noguchi to Mr. Thomas for the Director General, 5 June 1958, INA.

25 Minutes of Headquarters Committee, 26th Session, 4–5 September 1958 (dated 9 June 1958), p. 5, UNESCO Archives.

26 UNESCO, report of the Director General on the activities of the organization in 1958, dated Paris 1959, p. 199, UNESCO Archives.

27 In a brochure issued by UNESCO, Hiroshi Naruse interprets the features of the garden and its rock groups using Japanese identification and terminology. Hiroshi Naruse, *Jardin japonais* (Paris: UNESCO, 2000).

28 In the garden for his Kagawa Prefectural offices in Takamatsu of 1958, Kenzô Tange also used stones with a strong, erect profile.

29 Isamu Noguchi, "Garden of Peace: UNESCO Gardens in Paris," *Arts and Architecture* 1 (1959), reprinted in Apostolos-Cappadona and Altshuler, eds., p. 60.

30 Noguchi, *Sculptor's World*, p. 167.

31 Friedman, *Sculpture of Space*, p. 22. Emphasis added.

32 Noguchi, *Sculptor's World*, p. 167.

33 Bruno Zevi, "The Modern Dimension of Landscape Architecture," *Journal of the Institute of Landscape Architecture* (November 1962): p. 18.

34 Gordon Bunshaft, Travel diaries, 2 May 1959, quoted in Nicholas Adams, *Gordon Bunshaft and SOM: Building Corporate Modernism* (New Haven, CT: Yale University Press, 2019), p. 175.

35 Reyner Banham, "UNESCO House," *New Statesman* (6 December 1958), reprinted in *A Critic Writes: Essays by Reyner Banham*, ed. Mary Banham et al. (Berkeley: University of California Press, 1996), p. 31.

36 Lewis Mumford, "UNESCO House: Out, Damned Cliché!" (1960), in *The Highway and the City* (New York: New American Library, 1964), p. 80.

37 Mumford, "UNESCO House," p. 92.

38 Mumford, "UNESCO House," p. 92.

39 Alison de Lima Greene, "Interview with Isamu Noguchi" (March 1986), in *Isamu Noguchi: A Sculpture for Sculpture; The Lillie and High Roy Cullen Sculpture Garden* (Houston: Museum of Fine Arts, 2006), p. 3.

40 Herrera, *Listening to Stone*, p. 324.

>> CHAPTER 6

1 Noguchi, "New Stone Gardens," 64.

2 Fukuzawa had studied American higher education at Brown University in Providence, Rhode Island. en.wikipedia.org/wiki/Keio_University.

3 Yone Noguchi, *Hiroshige and the Japanese Landscapes* (Tokyo: Japan Travel Bureau, 1954).

4 Yone Noguchi, "Japanese Art," *Calcutta Review* (December 1935): p. 51, reprinted in Edward Marx, ed., *Later Essays* ([Santa Barbara, CA]: Botchan Books, 2013).

5 Noguchi, *Sculptor's World*, p. 31.

6 See Makiko Sugiyama, *Banraisha: A Poetic Architecture by Yoshiro Taniguchi and Isamu Noguchi* (Tokyo: Kajima Institute, 2006).

7 Although no direct connection seems obvious, Noguchi recalled that the garden reminded him of Shisen-do in Kyoto. Noguchi, *Sculptor's World*, p. 127; "A Stage, Quietly Dramatic," *Kokusai Kenchiku* (November 1950); and *Shinkenchiku* (February 1952), quoted in Sugiyama, *Banraisha*, p. 69. Perhaps he was comparing the tranquility of this space for relaxation and thought to that of Shisen-do. Two other sculptures were part of the program, *Gakusei* (Student), today on a lower floor of the new building, and *Kokeshi* (Dolls), which was placed against the terracotta wall.

8 A. O. D., "Bunshaft and Noguchi: An Uneasy But Highly Productive Architect-Artist Collaboration," *AIA Journal* (October 1976): p. 52.

9 Noguchi, *Sculptor's World*, p. 160.

10 Miller, ed., *Fourteen Americans*, p. 12.

11 A. O. D., "Bunshaft and Noguchi."

12 Duus, *Journey without Borders*, p. 292.

13 A. O. D., "Bunshaft and Noguchi," p. 52.

14 Noguchi, *Sculptor's World*, p. 173.

15 Gordon Bunshaft, Travel diaries. I thank Nicholas Adams for providing me with the relevant pages.

16 Bunshaft thought the piece, now executed in metal, "looked marvelous in scale." Carol Herselle Krinsky, *Gordon Bunshaft of Skidmore, Owings & Merrill* (New York: Architectural History Foundation; Cambridge, MA: MIT Press, 1988), p. 163.

17 Charles Luckman, *Twice in a Lifetime: From Soap to Skyscrapers* (New York: W. W. Norton, 1988), p. 239.

18 As he writes in his autobiography, Luckman already had a vision for Lever House and "knew exactly what I wanted," although he had no desire to personally design the building. Luckman, *Twice in a Lifetime*, p. 241.

19 "I want pedestrians to be able to walk through open gardens on Park Avenue and into the glass-enclosed lobby of the building." Luckman, *Twice in a Lifetime*, p. 242.

20 Friedman, *Noguchi's Imaginary Landscapes*, p. 47.

21 Noguchi, *Sculptor's World*, p. 164.

22 "The Lever Brothers job fell through with a thud. I had done my best—but it was refused. Did the anguish, under which I worked, show through, or had they really run out of cash?" Noguchi, *Sculptor's World*, p. 34. His honest assessment of the design: "The distraction of too much contrasting 'interest' when seen from below (as with passing automobiles) and fully revealed when approached in the open court by foot, became difficult to reconcile to the scale and the 'interest' of the platform itself. Thus I twice failed in realizing this project." Noguchi, *Sculptor's World*, p. 164.

23 The four-story addition shares the same curtain-wall detail as the original structure.

24 Why he was not responsible for the fourth courtyard—possibly designed by SOM house landscape architect Joanna Dimon in a Noguchian manner—is not known.

25 "Insurance Sets a Pattern," *Architectural Forum* (September 1957): p. 115, quoted in Louise A. Mozingo, *Pastoral Capitalism: A History of Suburban Corporate Landscapes* (Cambridge, MA: MIT Press, 2011), p. 115. I thank Matthew Kirsch at the Noguchi Museum for noting that little documentation exists concerning the terrace and that knowledge of Noguchi's involvement with its design is spotty.

26 The transfer of the Connecticut General offices from downtown Hartford to suburban Bloomfield denied employees easy access to the everyday facilities provided by the city, like restaurants and cafes, dry cleaners, and supermarkets. To mitigate these difficulties the corporation

provided a selection of these services on-site, as well as sufficient parking for those who commuted—even a short drive requires a parking space.

27 A. O. D., "Bunshaft and Noguchi," p. 54.

28 A. O. D., "Bunshaft and Noguchi," p. 54. However, in his oral history, Bunshaft recalled the developments this way: "As we looked [for the appropriate place for the sculpture], we looked across the pond that we'd created. There was a little swell there, and Noguchi said, 'Why don't we take it over there and try it?' I've forgotten whether Noguchi said that or Frazar Wilde or I don't remember." Betty J. Blum and Gordon Bunshaft, *Oral History of Gordon Bunshaft* (Chicago: Art Institute of Chicago, 2000), p. 183.

29 A. O. D., "Bunshaft and Noguchi," p. 54.

30 A. O. D., "Bunshaft and Noguchi," p. 54.

31 Christopher Tunnard to Frazar B. Wilde, President, Connecticut General Life Insurance, 12 February 1957, Yale University Archives. On Tunnard, see Marc Treib, *Thinking a Modern Landscape Architecture, West & East: Christopher Tunnard, Sutemi Horiguchi* (Novato, CA: ORO, 2020).

32 Matthew Kirsch notes that Noguchi claimed he had been contacted by the architects years earlier and had dissuaded them from using the court for access to the lower level.

33 D. M. Hummel (SOM), Minutes of meeting with the architects and university personnel, 16 December 1960, Beinecke Rare Book and Manuscript Library Archives, Yale University.

34 Quoted in Robin Peck, "Sculpture and the Sculptural in Halifax and Vancouver," in *Vancouver Anthology: The Institutional Politics of Art*, ed. Stan Douglas (Vancouver, BC: Talonbooks, 1991), p. 208.

35 Isamu Noguchi, "The Road I Have Walked," Kyoto Prize lecture, 1986, p. 101. INA. Noguchi's stated that his ideas "started from the sand mounds often found in Japanese temples. But soon the image of the astronomical gardens in India intruded, as did the more formal paving patterns of Italy." Noguchi, *Sculptor's World*, p. 170.

36 Friedman, *Imaginary Landscapes*, p. 61.

37 Torres, *Study of Space*, p. 118.

38 David H. Hughes (SOM) to T. Hood (George A. Fuller Company), 18 August 1961, INA.

39 Noguchi, *Sculptor's World*, p. 170.

40 The torus would become a motif in his repertoire to which he returned, for example, in *Black Sun* (1969) at the Seattle Museum Art and *Downward Pulling #2* (ca. 1972).

41 Hunter, "Isamu Noguchi," p. 154.

42 Isamu Noguchi, "Explanation of the Sculpture Garden," n.d., INA.

43 Noguchi, *Sculptor's World*, p. 170.

44 Noguchi, *Sculptor's World*, pp. 170–71.

45 Noguchi, *Sculptor's World*, p. 170.

46 Noguchi, "Road I Have Walked," p. 101.

47 "After several more variants, there evolved the present concept of a garden with actual symbolical meaning, something more specific than might be read into any abstraction." Noguchi, "New Stone Gardens," p. 64.

48 Paul Goldberger, "Toward Different Ends," in *Collaboration: Artists & Architects* (New York: Whitney Library of Design, 1981), p. 63.

49 David L. Shirey, "Dubuffet Is Doing 40-Foot Sculpture for Chase Plaza," *New York Times*, 24 November 1970.

50 Shirey, "Dubuffet Is Doing 40-Foot Sculpture."

51 Noguchi, "Road I Have Walked," p. 101.

52 Bonnie Rychlak, *Zen No Zen: Aspects of Noguchi's Sculptural Vision* (New York: Isamu Noguchi Foundation, 2002), p. 22 n18.

53 Herrera, *Listening to Stone*, p. 365.

54 Rychlak, *Zen No Zen*, p. 22n18.

55 Noguchi's early vision for the courtyard including plantings and variations in water flow dependent on the seasons. "(1) In the winter it is empty excepting for very low planting such as juniper, dwarf pines, and the like. (2) Occasionally, as the season or occasion calls for it, the fountain may be used as a cascade (or as a spray), the garden mostly dry will permit the planting of flowers in the holes (such as it is), or well pruned flowering crab-apples etc. (3) The garden as a water garden in summer." Isamu Noguchi to Walter Severinghouse (SOM), 13 May 1964, INA. Thanks to Matthew Kirsch for noting the mention of using goldfish at the time of the garden's opening.

56 Noguchi, "Road I Have Walked," p. 101.

57 Gordon Bunshaft to Noguchi, 9 October 1961, INA.

58 "I had a hell of a time trying to get it back again. It had been shipped to the other end of Japan by someone who had purchased it. I used every kind of pull I had to get it back." Noguchi quoted in Friedman, *Imaginary Landscapes*, p. 61.

59 "[T]he ground around buildings, underneath buildings, into the buildings need not be merely flat space; it can be sculpted." Noguchi, *Sculptor's World*, p. 53.

60 Friedman, *Imaginary Landscapes*, p. 61.

61 Many fountains are at their worst in winter when they are dry, thereby exposing their piping. One of the triumphs of the Chase court is that no pipes are visible, even in the winter.

62 Jiro Takei and Marc P. Keane, *Sakuteiki: Visions of the Japanese Garden* (Boston: Tuttle, 2001), p. 177.

63 Takei and Keane, *Sakuteiki*, p. 188.

64 Takei and Keane, *Sakuteiki*, p. 184.

65 Isamu Noguchi, unpublished text, 1960s(?), INA.

66 Adams, *Gordon Bunshaft and SOM*, notes 130–32 to chapter 6.

67 Noguchi, *Garden Museum*, p. 168.

68 Duus, *Journey without Borders*, p. 298.

69 Noguchi, *Sculptor's World*, p. 172.

70 Friedman, *Imaginary Landscapes*, p. 66.

71 As I have found little material concerning this project, I have relied heavily on Alona Nitzan-Shifran's excellent *Seizing Jerusalem: The Architecture of Unilateral Unification* (Minneapolis: University of Minnesota Press, 2017). The Western Wall was the principal exhibition in the Israel Pavilion at the 2018 Venice Architecture Biennale, which included the model of the Noguchi proposal published here. Unfortunately, I have not been able to locate the name(s) of its maker(s).

72 The demolition followed the area established by architect Arieh Sharon; the work commenced even before the war had ended. Nitzan-Shiftan, *Seizing Jerusalem*, p. 233.

73 Nitzan-Shiftan, *Seizing Jerusalem*, p 240.

74 Rose Halprin, the landscape architect's mother, had served as the president of Hadassah, an American charitable association supporting the Zionist cause. Nitzan-Shiftan, *Seizing Jerusalem*, p. 159.

75 New York–based Robert Zion was the other landscape architect on the committee.

76 Consider, for example, the controversy that followed the proposal for the Vietnam Memorial in Washington, DC, at times focused on its use of black granite.

77 Nitzan-Shiftan describes it as "Jewish endurance throughout the ages." Nitzan-Shiftan, *Seizing Jerusalem*, p. 262.

78 Moshe Safdie, *Jerusalem: The Future of the Past* (Boston: Houghton Mifflin, 1989), quoted in Nitzan-Shiftan, *Seizing Jerusalem*, p. 263.

79 Arthur Kutcher and Shlomo Aronson, "Research for the Design for the Area of the Western Wall," Jerusalem: Ministry of Religion, 1973, Israel Museum Archives. I thank Elissa Rosenberg for translating the text of the report for me.

80 The project is neither illustrated nor mentioned in his guide to the Isamu Noguchi Museum, which includes almost all his other landscape designs.

81 Bert Winther-Tamaki, "The Ceramic Art of Isamu Noguchi: A Close Embrace of the Earth," in Louise Allison Cort and Bert Winther-Tamaki, *Isamu Noguchi and Modern Japanese Ceramics: A Close Embrace of the Earth* (Washington, DC: Smithsonian Institution, 2003), p. 68.

82 Duus, *Journey without Borders*, p. 331.

83 Juni'chi Kawamura, "Treating the Earth Itself as a Sculpture," in Shimbun, ed., *Human Aspect as a Contemporary*, p. 32. Kawamura would later be instrumental in realizing Moerenuma Park.

84 Hunter, "Isamu Noguchi," p. 190.

85 Sôfu Teshigahara, *Kadensho: The Book of Flowers*, trans. Christopher Blasdel (Tokyo: Sôgetsu Bunkajigyo, 2011), p. 41.

86 Hunter, "Isamu Noguchi," p. 190.

87 Noguchi was also searching for "a major project to provide employment for his assistant stone cutters on the island of Shikoku, where he lives in Japan." Friedman, *Imaginary Landscapes*, p. 80.

88 Sôfu Teshigahara, *The Fifty Principles of Sôgetsu* (Tokyo: Sôgetsu School of Ikebana, 2004), p. 91.

89 Teshigahara, *Kadensho*, p. 25.

90 Duus, *Journey without Borders*, p. 331.

91 Osvald Sirén, *A History of Early Chinese Art* (London: Ernest Benn, 1930), quoted in Ashton, *East and West*, p. 86.

92 Hiroshi Teshigahara, "A Growing Sense of Existence," in Shimbun, ed., *Human Aspect as a Contemporary*, pp. 88–89. Hiroshi Teshigahara's own massive bamboo installations are exceptions to this pronouncement, responding to and enveloping the space.

93 Yoshio Taniguchi, Interview with Marc Treib, Tokyo, 11 October 2005.

94 Ashton, *East and West*, p. 283.

95 Ashton, *East and West*, p. 279.

96 Ashton, *East and West*, p. 256.

97 Ashton, *East and West*, p. 283.

98 Ashton, *East and West*, p. 270.

>> CHAPTER 7

1 Brian O'Dougherty, *Inside the White Cube: The Ideology of the Gallery Space* (Santa Monica: Lapis, 1976), 1986.

2 The architectural historian David Leatherbarrow has more poetically termed this trio "clock, calendar, and chronicle." David Leatherbarrow, *Topographic Stories* (Philadelphia: University of Pennsylvania Press, 2004), p. 252.

3 Shula Eisner, "Afterword: The Prelude," *Ariel*, no. 60 (1985): p. 90.

4 Tali Tamir, "The Israel Museum: From Dream to Fulfillment, *Israel Museum Journal* (Fall 1990): p. 7.

5 Duus, *Journey without Borders*, p. 300.

6 Isamu Noguchi, quoted in Duus, *Journey without Borders*, p. 300.

7 Herrera, *Listening to Stone*, pp. 366–67.

8 Herrera, *Listening to Stone*, pp. 366–67.

9 AICF to Isamu Noguchi, Brief for the sculpture garden, 15 February 1960, p. 1, INA .

10 Brief for the sculpture garden, p. 2.

11 Brief for the sculpture garden, p. 3.

12 Isamu Noguchi, "IN Notes [handwritten] relative to Amer. Israeli Foundation Contract," 1 February 1960, p. 2, INA.

13 It is no coincidence, for example, that one of the buildings on the Technion (Israel Institute of Technology) campus in Haifa is called the Miami Building, a name reflecting financial support from that quarter.

14 While the Metabolist works gave the appearance of flexibility and change, in fact their construction in concrete normally precluded any significant modifications over time. The original form became the permanent form, evident in such buildings as Kenzô Tange's Yamanashi Communications building in Kofu and Kisho Kurokawa's celebrated Nakagin Capsule Building in Tokyo. Unlike the realized Metabolist projects, the Israel Museum has actually been expanded several times since its opening in the 1960s and is said to occupy at least five times the floor area today that it did at its time of origin.

15 In time a model of Jerusalem would be constructed below the Shrine of the Book, well within the view shed of the Billy Rose Art Garden.

16 Alfred Mansfeld to Isamu Noguchi, 9 April 1960, INA.

17 Billy Rose to Theodore Kollek, 14 April 1960, INA.

18 Isamu Noguchi, "Art Garden in Jerusalem" (typescript), dated fall 1964, INA.

19 Isamu Noguchi, Untitled statement, 19 April 1965, INA.

20 Herrera, *Listening to Stone*, p. 367.

21 Marc Treib, interview with Alfred Mansfeld, 14 November, Haifa, Israel.

22 The fill was projected at almost 17,000 cubic meters, and the boulders of Jerusalem stone used for the retaining walls estimated at 1,600 square meters. Memo [no named author; contractor Hillel Fefferman?], 3 March 1961, INA.

23 Isamu Noguchi to Alfred Mansfeld, 20 November 1962, INA.

24 Billy Rose to Hillel Fefferman, 3 December 1952, Israel Museum Archives.

25 Isamu Noguchi, "Billy Rose Art Garden—A Space for Sculpture for Jerusalem," typescript (for the Jerusalem Post), 30 April 1965, p. 2, Israel Museum Archives.

26 A. H. Witt, PDC Planning and Development Center, to Billy Rose, 9 August 1962, Israel Museum Archives.

27 Memo [no named author], 1 November 1962, Israel Museum Archives.

28 H. H. Witt, PDC Planning and Development Center, to Yonatan Beham, 7 May 1964, Israel Museum Archives.

29 Interestingly, Abraham Karavan was the father of sculptor Dani Karavan, who would also create sculptures at the scale of land art, for example in Tel Aviv and with Axe Majeur in Cergy-Pontoise, France, as well as a sculpture adjacent to Noguchi's UNESCO garden.

30 Isamu Noguchi to Hillel Fefferman, 11 March 1963, INA.

31 Isamu Noguchi to Hillel Fefferman, 25 March 1963, INA.

32 Isamu Noguchi to Billy Rose, 5 February 1963, INA.

33 Yonatan Beham to Billy Rose, 26 February 1963, Israel Museum Archives.

34 Yonatam Beham to Ralph I. Goldman, AICF, 27 July 1963, p. 1, Israel Museum Archives.

35 Beham to Goldman, 27 July 1963, p. 2

36 Beham to Goldman, 27 July 1963, p. 3

37 Isamu Noguchi to Hillel Fefferman, 7 August 1963, INA.

38 Elaine Rosenfeld, AICF, to Yonatan Beham, 13 August 1964, INA.

39 Theodore Kollek to Billy Rose, 16 March 1965. Israel Museum Archives.

40 Isamu Noguchi, memo [to unnamed recipient], 27 April 1965, INA.

41 Isamu Noguchi, memo [to Hillel Fefferman?], 13 May 1965, INA.

42 Isamu Noguchi to Yonatan Beham, 2 June 1965, INA.

43 AICF (possibly Elaine Rosenfeld) to Theodore Kollek, 15 July 1965, INA.

44 Karavan was the chief landscape architect of Tel Aviv from the 1940s to the 1960s. en.wikipedia.org/wiki/Dani_Karavan.

45 Daniel Gelmond, Israel Museum administrator, to Billy Rose, 28 July 1965, INA.

46 Daniel Gelmond to Billy Rose, 10 August 1965, INA.

47 Isamu Noguchi to Abraham Karavan, 9 August 1965, INA.

48 Billy Rose to Abraham Karavan, 3 November 1965, INA.

49 Gelmond to Billy Rose, 21 November 1965, INA.

50 Daniel Gelmond to Billy Rose, 2 September 1965, INA.

51 Isamu Noguchi to Yonatan Beham, 11 October 1965, INA.

52 Yonatan Beham to Isamu Noguchi, 17 September 1965, INA.

53 Isamu Noguchi, "An Art Garden in Jerusalem," *Ariel* (Spring 1965): p. 3.

54 Yonatan Beham to Noguchi, 21 June 1967, INA.

55 Isamu Noguchi to Daniel Gelmond, 30 April 1968, INA.

56 Noguchi, Untitled statement, 19 April 1965, INA.

57 In the video no water flows from the fountain; hopefully, this was due to the closure of the museum because of the Covid-19 pandemic. Secrets of the Art Garden with Israel Museum Director Ido Bruno, posted 26 May 2020. youtube.com/watch?v=7X-iJav6Cu4.

58 Noguchi, "Billy Rose Art Garden," p. 3.

59 This section is a condensation and reworking of my essay "A Sculpture for Sculpture," in Greene, *Sculpture for Sculpture*.

60 "The Lillie and Hugh Roy Cullen Sculpture Garden of the Museum of Fine Arts." *MFAH Bulletin* (April 1986): p. 14.

61 Greene, "Interview with Isamu Noguchi," p. 2.

62 Greene, *Sculpture for Sculpture*, p. 10. An overview of the efforts to construct a sculpture garden are reviewed in a letter from Hugo Neuhaus, Chair, Museum Building Committee, to architect (?) Christopher Egan, 18 July 1979, INA. For an overview of the museum's design and expansion until 1972, see Donnelley Erdman and Peter Papademetriou, *The Museums of Fine Arts, Houston: Fifty Years of Growth, 1922–1972*; Architecture at Rice 28 (Houston: Rice University School of Architecture, 1972).

63 For example, during the investigations for site work, the builders found a concrete slab six feet below the ground that would seriously affect the nature of the foundations for the sculpture garden's walls. Shoji Sadao to William Agee, 25 October 1979, Museum of Fine Arts, Houston Archives.

64 Isamu Noguchi to Peter Marzio, 25 April 1983, INA.

65 No visual documentation for the first scheme has been located in the archives of either the Museum of Fine Arts, Houston, or the Isamu Noguchi Foundation. Thus, my descriptions and comments can only be speculative.

66 Isamu Noguchi to Mrs. George Brown (Alice Pratt Brown), 6 January 1977, Museum of Fine Arts, Houston Archives. In Noguchi's take on the situation, the problem lay with Mrs. De Menil (Dominique de Menil) rather than Mrs. Brown. In a letter to Patrick Lannan, whose suggestion had helped secure the commission, he wrote: "As you can tell from the contents [of the enclosed letter—a copy of the one cited in this note] things have not gone well in Houston, which I think is not the fault of Mrs. Brown but of Mrs. de Menil, who in this case chose to throw her weight around to everyone's discomfort. I imagine further, and this is all imagination on my part since I am not privy to the gossip there, that they are all scared of Mrs. de Menil because of whatever she may bequeath to the Museum. She for her part must either dislike the Museum, or dislike what I do. I cannot understand why else she sabotages something which can only be good for the Museum." Isamu Noguchi to Patrick Lannan, 6 January 1977, INA.

67 Again, due to lack of visual documentation this description is speculative.

68 "Half mounding thus relates to the garden which is being raised [to separate] its level from that of the automobile, a psychological barrier. Large areas of this are in turn depressed to allow for easy handling of sculpture and to enhance third dimensionality." Noguchi to Mrs. Brown, 6 January 1977, INA.

69 Isamu Noguchi to William Agee, 6 January 1977, Museum of Fine Arts, Houston Archives.

70 William Agee to Isamu Noguchi, 3 February 1977, Museum of Fine Arts, Houston Archives. Curiously perhaps, the museum also solicited designs from the New York landscape architect M. Paul Friedberg, who submitted three schemes the following month. No document records the response to his proposals, but they do not seem to have progressed beyond that first submission. Neuhaus to Egan, 18 July 1979, INA, sheds some light on the matter: "Isamu Noguchi was engaged to prepare the first preliminary design. He presented it to the Building Committee and the Trustees, who had reservations about certain features of it. He was asked to revise the design, which he could not do until his return from a lengthy trip to Japan. Friedberg's design bore certain similarities to Noguchi's plan: a completely walled garden with elements extending across the church parking lot. It was not particularly well received and shortly thereafter Noguchi returned with his revised design. This fits the needs of the Museum, encompassed the entire frontage of Bissonet and provided a handsome, sculptural entrance facing the Brown Pavilion."

71 Joseph C. Gaf, The Cullen Foundation, to Alexander K. McLanahan, president, Museum of Fine Arts, Houston, 1 May 1978, Museum of Fine Arts, Houston Archives.

72 Especially, Agee writes, since "our method for dealing with the garden is now more streamlined and efficient." William Agee to Isamu Noguchi, 30 September 1978, Museum of Fine Arts Houston Archives.

73 Isamu Noguchi to William Agee, 27 October 1978, Museum of Fine Arts, Houston Archives.

74 Minutes of the Executive Committee, 21 February 1979. Museum of Fine Arts, Houston Archives.

75 A local architect wrote, "It has come to our attention that the funds which are provided the Museum, very graciously from the Cullen Foundation, will be used to construct a wall around the proposed sculpture Garden. Please don't." He then outlined possible solutions including Plexiglas and glass panels. Lowell Lammers to Alexander McLanahan, 12 July 1979, Museum of Fine Arts, Houston Archives.

76 Ann Holmes, "A Storm of Controversy," *Houston Chronicle*, 23 December 1979.

77 The final costs were estimated at between $3.2 and $3.6 million.

78 Minutes of the Sculpture Garden Meeting, 4 April 1983, Museum of Fine Arts, Houston Archives.

79 Minutes of the Sculpture Garden Meeting, 4 April 1983.

80 Greene, "Interview with Isamu Noguchi," p. 3.

81 Susan Chatwick, "How Does Our Garden Grow? New Cullen Sculpture Garden Leaves Much to Be Desired," *Houston Post*, 1 April 1986.

82 Patricia C. Johnson, "Quiet Conversation: Artists' Works Commune with Sculptor's Garden," *Houston Chronicle*, 3 April 1986.

83 Chatwick, "How Does Our Garden Grow?"

84 Noguchi, *Garden Museum*, p. 186.

85 Johnson, "Quiet Conversation."

86 "I recently visited my garden at UNESCO in Paris. It was my first study garden and I was assisted by Japanese gardeners. Now with UNESCO's problems nothing is being done, and the garden had overgrown with weeds, jabbering away and having a wonderful time. The trees have grown to the max, and the garden is all on its own with nobody taking care of it. I've never seen it look so beautiful. I hope that time will also play with this garden as it grows older. Of course, the walls and sculpture are impervious to the transient seasons, but all gardens change. . . . I cannot imagine a landscape or a sculpture that is mute." Greene, "Interview with Isamu Noguchi," p. 3.

>> CHAPTER 8

1 Noguchi's longtime collaborator Masatoshi Izumi stated, "Stone in nature is the thing which undergoes the least change, and water the most change—because of this contrast they belong together." Ashton, *East and West*, p. 256.

2 Toshitsuna (attrib.), *Sakuteiki*, p. 177.

3 He also mentions a collaborative mural project for a union building with Philip Guston and Paul Goodman that did not materialize. Noguchi, *Sculptor's World*, p. 24.

4 On my last visits, in 2017, the fountain was still dry.

5 The statue was removed in response to racial concerns raised by the community and a rethinking of the status of Confederate Army and governmental personnel in today's America. en.wikipedia.org/wiki/Robert_E._Lee_Monument_(New_Orleans).

6 Noguchi, *Sculptor's World*, p. 169.

7 Perhaps it is only a coincidence that New Orleans is known as the Crescent City.

8 Isamu Noguchi, quoted in Makoto Suzuki, "Fountain and Sculpture," *Japan Architect* (May–June 1970): p. 162.

9 Noguchi, *Garden Museum*, p. 174.

10 Makoto Suzuki, like Takasi Sasaki, an assistant on the project, claimed, "Twelve fountains in nine varieties [were] placed in the three artificial lakes running east and west at right angles to and on the north side of the Festival Plaza." Makoto Suzuki, "Sculpture," *Japan Architect* (May–June 1970): p. 162.

11 The Osaka fountains share certain characteristics with sculptures by Susumu Shingu and kinetic works driven by the wind or the sun, as well as parallels with kinetic pieces by Alexander Calder and George Rickey.

12 This section is an expansion and revision of Marc Treib, "The Fountain as Urban Oasis," in *Fountain: Splash and Spectacle: Water and Design from the Renaissance to the Present*, ed. Marilyn Symmes (New York: Rizzoli, 1998), pp. 160–82.

13 Friedman, *Sculpture of Space*, p. 29.

14 Friedman, *Sculpture of Space*, p. 29.

15 "Noguchi's solution allowed the salvaged subterranean space to be used for a road, parking areas, a restaurant, access to theater and ice-skating areas and, of course, commodious areas for ethnic celebrations." Friedman, *Imaginary Landscapes*, p. 80.

16 Isamu Noguchi to Horace E. Dodge Fountain Selection Committee, 25 August 1971, INA. "There was a large parking lot by the river for which a plan had been made by the architects. But, realizing this to be inappropriate to the fountain concept, I was asked by the chairman of that firm, Robert Hastings, to do the entire plaza as well." Isamu Noguchi to Ada Louise Huxtable, 25 April 1979, INA.

17 "Design for Detroit Civic Center Plaza Focuses on Fountain of Jetting Water," *AIA Journal* (August 1973).

18 Neil Genzlinger, "Architect Turned Concepts of 2 Visionaries into Reality," *New York Times*, 18 November 2019.

19 "Architects Would Come to Him," p. 101.

20 "Architects Would Come to Him," p. 101.

21 "Architects Would Come to Him," p. 101.

22 Shoji Sadao, "The Sculptor's Genius Sparks at 'Aluminum,'" in Shikoku Shimbun, ed., *Human Aspect as a Contemporary*, pp. 141–42.

23 The design of the 1925 James Scott Memorial Fountain was a collaboration between architect Cass Gilbert and sculptor Herbert Adams.

24 Friedman, *Imaginary Landscapes*, p. 80.

25 "Noguchi: The Fountain and the Artist Deserve Better of the City," *Detroit Free Press*, 23 April 1979.

26 Nolan Finley, "City Pulls Plug on Bugs in Dodge Fountain Flow," *Detroit News*, May 1980. Noguchi himself acknowledged the engineer's role during a visit to the troubled fountain in 1979: "The sole reason the fountain does as well as it does . . . is because Louis Klei, the city engineer, has been so passionately committed to it." Polk Laffoon IV, "Fountain Flaws Anger Artist," *Detroit Free Press*, 20 April 1979.

27 N. Scott Vance, "A Fresh 'Doughnut,' At Last," *Detroit News*, 3 July 1987. In an article published the previous month Vance had noted that an additional $800,000 would be spent "to put the spray and sparkle back into the Hart Plaza's troubled Dodge Fountain." N. Scott Vance, "Hart Fountain May Be Fixed," *Detroit News*, 16 June 1987.

28 Noguchi to [Plaza Design Committee], 16 February 1973, INA. Noguchi would continue to lament the city's reluctance to install the vegetation as specified.

29 Noguchi to Horace E. Dodge Fountain Selection Committee, 25 August 1971.

30 Noguchi to Horace E. Dodge Fountain Selection Committee, 25 August 1971. The fountain consultants were Beamer/Wilkinson & Associates, Oakland, California. "Splashy Fountain Bejewels Motor City Plaza," *Engineering News Record* (6 October 1977).

31 Noguchi to Horace E. Dodge Fountain Selection Committee, 25 August 1971. In a memo to the committee, William H. Kessler summarized the suggestions for plaza activities solicited from civic leaders. John D. Ryan of the J. Walter Thomson Co. emphasized that the plaza should be destined for "ongoing activities as opposed to single events." General Motors' Charles Hagle suggested that "Activity should not encourage 'hippy haven' or 'protestor center' [but should] truly be a place where people can sit and enjoy a view of the river." He added parenthetically that the "Information Center [should be] accessible by auto," INA.

32 Noguchi tended to keep a close watch on his projects even after completion, and this was no exception. In 1979 he wrote the mayor's office, troubled by lighting standards and kiosks that had been added without his consultation and offered alternatives. Isamu Noguchi to Mayor Coleman Young, 22 August 1979, INA. In 1988, on the eve of a major renovation, Noguchi wrote the Central Business District Association President, reminding him of his central role and longstanding involvement with the project: "As you must know I am the one who worked on what there is there starting in 1971, over a period of about seven years. The design is mine in the smallest detail. The Pylon was my free gift to get things going." Now, the integrity of the design was being undermined by additions: "It would be nice and appropriate if the designer's work could be respected when changes and 'improvements' are made by others. I was not informed." Isamu Noguchi to Diane J. Edgecomb, 8 July 1988, INA.

33 *Slide Mantra* was first installed outside the American Pavilion at the Venice Biennale in 1986 as part of Noguchi's solo exhibition there. In 1991 it was permanently installed in Miami in Bayfront Park, as a part of his design. *Black Slide Mantra*, made of black granite, was installed in Odori Park in Sapporo, Japan, in 1992.

34 Pepper Fountain folder, no date, INA; cited in Alexandra Eve Kirby, "Reassessing the Public Spaces of Isamu Noguchi" (Master's thesis, Columbia University, 2013), p. 49.

35 Kirby, "Reassessing the Public Spaces," p. 50.

36 Dore Ashton, "Space as Sculpture," *Landscape Architecture* (special issue, "The Landscapes of Isamu Noguchi") (April 1998): p. 43.

37 A related work is *The Well* (*Variations on a Tsukubai*) (1982), on display in the garden of the Isamu Noguchi Garden Museum.

38 For a more detailed discussion of *yûgen*, see chapter 10.

>> CHAPTER 9

1 Henry Segerstrom, Interview with Marc Treib in the Segerstrom office, Costa Mesa, California, 18 August 2004.

2 The dairy farms were sold at the start of World War II.

3 Segerstrom, Interview.

4 Segerstrom, Interview.

5 Karl Klokke was the project architect.

6 Tamara Thomas was a respected art consultant based in Los Angeles. She studied art history at the University of California, Berkeley, and thereafter spent five years in Europe "increasing her knowledge and background in the arts," and then founding Fine Arts Services, Inc. in 1970. Fine Arts Services, Inc., "Description of Firm and Staff," no date, INA.

7 Tamara Thomas to Isamu Noguchi, 13 November 1979, INA.

8 This attitude may have derived from, or was intensified by, Noguchi's experience with the developers while creating the lobby and fountain for 666 Fifth Avenue in Manhattan today extensively gutted, although it may also have been a philosophical or ethical stance.

9 Cathy Curtis, "Interview of Henry T. Segerstrom," *Los Angeles Times*, 15 January 1989, reprinted in part in Jenny Dixon, *California Scenario: The Courage of Imagination*, exh. brochure (Long Island City: Isamu Noguchi Museum, 2010).

10 Stanford University had already approached Noguchi about creating a sculpture for the campus, if not a major spatial work.

11 Henry Segerstrom to Isamu Noguchi, 3 December 1979, INA.

12 Isamu Noguchi to Tamara Thomas, 7 January 1980, INA.

13 Tamara Thomas to Isamu Noguchi, 17 January 1980, INA.

14 Tamara Thomas to Isamu Noguchi, 13 February 1980, INA.

15 This information, as well as what follows, derives from my conversation with Ken Kammeyer on-site at *California Scenario* on 17 August 2004. I am most grateful for his time, knowledge, and insights regarding the project.

16 Segerstrom, Interview. Other estimates have proposed nearly five million dollars as more accurate, given the adjustments and changes made at Noguchi's request during the course of design and construction.

17 Henry Segerstrom to Isamu Noguchi, 2 September 1980, INA.

18 Tamara Thomas to Henry Segerstrom, 10 July 1980, pp. 1–2, INA.

19 Henry Segerstrom to Isamu Noguchi, e December 1979, INA.

20 Segerstrom, Interview. The lithograph derived from a photograph of the piece by Toren Segerstrom taken in Takamatsu before the sculpture was shipped.

21 Of course, this assumption is open to question. Ken Kammeyer, Interview with Marc Treib, on-site at *California Scenario*, 17 August 2004.

22 Ken Kammeyer, Interview with Marc Treib.

23 Curtis, "Segerstrom Interview."

24 Curtis, "Segerstrom Interview."

25 Ken Kammeyer to Isamu Noguchi, 30 July 1980, INA.

26 Isamu Noguchi to Rick Anderson, 1 August 1980, INA.

27 Rick Anderson to Isamu Noguchi, 14 August 1980, INA.

28 Kammeyer, Interview. *A Sense of Place*, a video by Michael Rich made in 1982, shows Noguchi supervising the setting of the stones. youtube.com/watch?v=N8IG-zclH2xY&t=6s.

29 Henry Segerstrom to Isamu Noguchi, 2 September 1980, INA.

30 C. L. Peck, Minutes of the meeting, 20 October 1980, INA. By November the weight estimated by Noguchi now stood at 80,000 pounds. Segerstrom to all those receiving copies of the minutes, 21 November 1980, INA.

31 C. L. Peck, Minutes of the meeting 4 November 1980, INA .

32 C. L. Peck, Minutes of the meeting of the general and masonry contractors, 7 November 1980, on-site at Two Town Center, Isamu Noguchi Foundation. Stone paving such as that proposed may have been influenced by seismic issues in California and the soft quality of the soil on the site.

33 Ken Kammeyer to Isamu Noguchi and Fuller & Sadao, 12 November 1980, INA. At some point Noguchi, Kammeyer, Segerstrom, and his son Toren made an excursion to the Huntington Gardens in San Marino to look at plants in its celebrated desert garden. Curtis, "Segerstrom Interview."

34 Ken Kammeyer to Isamu Noguchi, 2 April 1981, INA.

35 Kammeyer, Interview.

36 Henry Segerstrom to Noguchi, 6 June 1981, INA.

37 "California Scenario: A Noguchi Celebration," Preview of Events, 24 March 1982, INA.

38 Henry Segerstrom to Hisashi Yamada, Urasenke school of tea, 31 December 1981, INA.

39 Henry Segerstrom to Isamu Noguchi, 25 January 1982, INA.

40 Isamu Noguchi to Segerstrom, 2 April 1982, INA.

41 Noguchi to Segerstrom, 2 April 1982.

42 During our interview, Henry Segerstrom told me that the cost was probably around $1.2 million, which was the same figure mentioned in early correspondence. Given the changes in materials, delays in construction costs, fees for landscape architect and consultants, and the artist's own increase fee, I suspect the figure was far higher.

43 Segerstrom, Interview.

44 Isamu Noguchi to Henry Segerstrom, 3 December 1981, INA.

45 See Matthew Kirsch, "Noguchi and the Jantar Mantars of Northern India," in *Looking Up: Skyviewing Sculptures of Isamu Noguchi*, ed. Hafthor Yngvason (Lewes, UK: D. Giles; Bellingham: Western Washington University, 2022), pp. 24–41; and Dominika Glogowski, "Isamu Noguchi's Geometric Landscape Model: A Scientific Encounter with the Observatories of India," in *Gartenkunst und Wissenschaft, Transformation seit dem Beginn der Frühmoderne*, ed. Julia Burbulla and Ana-Stanca Tabarasi-Hoffmann (Bern: Peter Lang, 2011), pp. 231–69. I thank Matthew Kirsch for providing me with a copy of this essay.

46 The water falling down the chute recalls the Indian *chadar*, an inclined arrangement of stones that disrupts the smooth fall of water from one level to the next, aerating and animating as it falls—while providing an acoustic as well as visually cooling effect.

47 Isamu Noguchi, quoted in Deborah A. Goldberg, *Isamu Noguchi, Patent Holder: Designing the World of Tomorrow* (New York: St. John's University, 2015), p. 29 n125.

48 Segerstrom, Interview.

49 Given its scale and peri-urban site, Moerenuma Park may be the sole exception to the pattern.

50 Isamu Noguchi to Ken Kammeyer, 16 July 1981, INA.

51 See *A Sense of Place*.

52 Noguchi to Segerstrom, 3 December 1981.

53 Compare the resolution of drainage at *California Scenario* with that at Teardrop Park in New York, designed by Michael Van Valkenburgh Associates and opened in 2006. Along the base of a wall of cyclopean rocks by Ann Hamilton extends a linear drain that all but destroys the effect of the wall's massive stonework. Noguchi further exploited the mystery and magic of disappearing water in his series of *tsukubai*, for example *Water Stone* at the Metropolitan Museum of Art in New York, installed in 1986 [see 8-32].

54 Ken Kammeyer to Marc Treib, 8 January 2003.

55 Henry Segerstrom to Isamu Noguchi, 14 June 1981, INA.

56 Kammeyer, Interview.

57 Kammeyer, Interview.

58 Kammeyer recalls that it was an engineer from Disney who came up with the idea. Kammeyer, Interview.

59 Shoji Sadao to Tom Piller, C. L. Peck, Contractors, 14 August 1981, INA.

60 Judith Neumann, "Jumping to Conclusions: 'California Scenario' Visitors Were Anything but Neutral. They Called It amazing. Important. Even Alienating." *Register* (9 May 1982).

61 Curtis, "Segerstrom Interview."

62 Isamu Noguchi to Paul J. Ruffing, 23 July 1984, INA.

63 Noguchi to Ruffing, 23 July 1984.

64 Segerstrom, Interview.

65 Byron de Arakal, "Wake Up, Mr. Anderson, the Oompa Loompas Have Gone," *Pilot*, 23 May 2001.

66 Karen Graham, Interview with Marc Treib, on-site at *California Scenario*, 17 August 2004.

67 In 2004, the garden was being maintained by Terra Pacific.

>> CHAPTER 10

1 Italo Calvino, *Invisible Cities*, trans. William Weaver (New York: Harcourt Brace Jovanovich, 1974), p. 17.

2 Arata Isozaki, *Japan-ness in Architecture*, trans. Sabu Kohso (Cambridge, MA: MIT Press, 2011).

3 Marc Treib, "Evocative Parallels: Japan and Postwar America Landscape Design," *Consultants in Landscape Architecture Journal* (in Japanese) (January 2002), English translation in Marc Treib, *Settings and Stray Paths: Writings on Landscapes and Gardens* (London: Routledge, 2005).

4 Lao Tzu, *Tao Te Ching* (Book of Tao), trans. John Minford (London: Penguin Random House, 2019). For a psychoanalytical view of learning and artistic practice, see Lawrence S. Kubie, *Neurotic Distortion of the Creative Process* (New York: Farrar, Straus, and Giroux, 1961).

5 See Harold Bloom, *The Anxiety of Influence: A Theory of Poetry* (New York: Oxford University Press, 1973).

6 Teiji Itoh, quoted by Donald Richie, *A Tractate on Japanese Aesthetics* (Berkeley, CA: Stone Bridge, 2007), p. 11.

7 Arata Isozaki, *MA Space-Time in Japan*. New York: Cooper-Hewitt, 2001; Sigfried Gideon, *Space, Time, and Architecture* (Cambridge, MA: Harvard University Press, 1941).

8 Teshigahara, *Fifty Principles of Sôgetsu*, pp. 6, 8.

9 *Jimi* "usually is translated as 'good taste,' though it does have a pejorative edge." In contrast, while *hade* may translate as "loud," it has no negative connotations. Richie, *Tractate*, p. 41.

10 Donald Richie quotes aesthete Sôsetsu Yanagi: "[Shibui] is not a beauty displayed before the viewer by its creator . . . viewers must seek out the beauty for themselves. As our taste grows more refined we will necessarily arrive at the beauty that is shibui." *Tractate*, p. 40.

11 Richie, *Tractate*, p. 44.

12 That over the centuries the practice became ritualized as a ceremony and taught by factionalized schools is another story.

13 Kakuzô Okakura, *The Book of Tea* (1905; repr. Rutland, VT: Tuttle, 1956).

14 Richie, *Tractate*, p. 47.

15 Makoto Ueda, *Literary and Art Theories in Japan* (Cleveland, OH: Case Western Reserve University Press, 1967), p. 63.

16 Marc Treib, "Reduction, Elaboration, and Yûgen: The Garden of Saiho-ji," *Journal of Garden History* (April–June 1989): 95–101, reprinted in Treib, *Settings and Stray Paths*.

17 Teshigahara, *Kadensho*, p. 6.

18 Teshigahara, *Kadensho*, p. 6.

>> CHAPTER 11

1 This chapter is a revised and expanded version of a text first published as Marc Treib, "Sculptur[ed] Park," *Landscape Architecture Magazine* (May 2006).

2 Jun'ichi Kawamura, Interview with Marc Treib, Architect 5 office, Tokyo, 11 August 2005.

3 Despite this initial denial, Noguchi created *Black Slide Mantra* (1992), installed in Ôdori Park in central Sapporo.

4 welcome.city.spapporo.jp/moerenuma/im-e.html, accessed 1 October 2006. Architect 5 had prepared the master plan for the university. Kawamura, Interview.

5 Jun'ichi Kawamura, "Treating the Earth Itself as a Sculpture," in Shimbun, ed., *Human Aspect as a Contemporary*, p. 32.

6 A complete timeline is found in Ec[illegible]en Toshiya, *Timeless Landscapes: Isamu Noguchi, Moerenuma Park* (Tokyo: Millegraph, 2020), pp. 68–69.

7 Noguchi, *Sculptor's World*, p. 16[illegible].

8 *Isamu Noguchi: The Exhibition Celebrated the Grand Opening of the Moerenuma Park* (Sapporo, Japan: Museum of Contemporary Art, 200[illegible]).

9 For the Sapporo project, however, Architect 5 would be responsible for the construction drawings and specifications.

10 Tange had assigned Kawamura to Noguchi when working on *Tengoku* for the lobby of the Sôgetsu building in Tokyo. Architect 5 was formed in 19[illegible] by three alumni of the Tange office: Kawamura, Hidetsugu Horikoshi, and Takeo Matsuoka. japan-architect.jimdofree.com/japanese-architects/architect-5-partnership/.

11 welcome.city.sapporo.jp/moerenuma/im-e.html.

>> CHAPTER 12

1 "Masatoshi Izumi: Seeing the Soul of the Stone," *Articulate* with Jim Cotter, Nine PBS, St. Louis, 2018. Most subsequent biographical information concerning Masatoshi Izumi derives from this video.

2 "From 1967 until Noguchi's death, in 1988, Izumi worked alongside the artist to create works including Supreme Court Building Fountains, Energy Void, Time and Space, Tokobashira and Tengoku, Landscape of Time, Momo Taro, The Spirit of the Lima Bean, Constellation, Water Garden, and others." Noor Brara, "This Artist and Master Stone Carver Was Isamu Noguchi's Collaborator for Decades. Why Do So Few People Know Who Masatoshi Izumi Is?" *artnet*, 11 November 2022. news.artnet.com/art-world/masatoshi-izumi-isamu-noguchi-2032214

3 Teshigahara, *Kadensho*, p. 6.

4 "Masatoshi Izumi."

5 Masatoshi Izumi, "Utada Hikaru's Pilgrimage to the Isamu Noguchi Garden Museum," *Casa Brutus* (special issue, "Century of Isamu Noguchi") (2005): p. 93.

6 The bands of small stones today found at the base of these slopes were not original, but were later added to facilitate drainage during times of heavy rainfall.

7 The remaining half of his ashes would be deposited in New York at the Noguchi Museum in Long Island City, New York.

8 Noguchi, *Garden Museum*, p. 204.

9 Masao Hayakawa, *The Garden Art of Japan* (Tokyo: Heibonsha, 1974), p. 10.

10 Bashô, *The Narrow Road to the Deep North and Other Travel Sketches*, trans. Nobuyuki Yuasa (Baltimore: Penguin, 1968), p. 97.

11 Toru Takemitsu, "Isamu Noguchi—A Traveler," in *Play Mountain: Isamu Noguchi + Louis Kahn*, ed. Marumo Planning (Tokyo: Watarium, 1996), p. 125.

12 For example, Pablo Picasso's Pink, Blue, Synthetic, and Analytic Cubist periods.

13 "Isamu Noguchi Neither an Artist Nor a Sculptor, but a Curator of Time and Space," *Latin America Daily Post* (Brazil), 1981.

14 Noguchi, "Sculptor and the Architect," p. 54.

15 Bourriaud, *Relational Aesthetics*, p. 11.

16 Ferdinand de Saussure, *Course in General Linguistics*, trans. Wade Baskin, ed. Charles Bally and Albert Sechehaye (New York: McGraw Hill, 1966).

17 Among other viewpoints are those expressed in John Dewey, *Art as Experience* (1934; repr., New York: Penguin, 2005) and Richard Rorty, *Consequences of Pragmatism (Essays 1972–1980)* (Minneapolis: University of Minnesota Press, 1982).

18 Noguchi, *Garden Museum*, endpaper.

>> BIBLIOGRAPHY

>> ARCHIVES

Beinecke Rare Book and Manuscript Library Archives, Yale University, New Haven, CT.

Isamu Noguchi Archive, Noguchi Museum, Long Island City, NY.

Israel Museum Archives, Jerusalem.

Museum of Fine Arts, Houston Archives.

UNESCO Archives, Paris.

>> INTERVIEWS

Treib, Marc. Interview with Karen Graham, 17 August 2004, Costa Mesa, California.

———. Interview with Masatoshi Izumi, 5 November 2015, Mure-cho, Japan.

———. Interview with Ken Kammeyer, 17 August 2004, Costa Mesa, California.

———. Interview with Jun'ichi Kawamura, 11 August 2005, Tokyo.

———. Interview with Alfred Mansfeld, 14 November 1993, Haifa, Israel.

———. Interview with Henry T. Segerstrom, 18 August 2004, Costa Mesa, California.

———. Interview with Yoshio Taniguchi, 11 October 2005, Tokyo.

>> TEXTS BY ISAMU NOGUCHI

Noguchi, Isamu. "The 'Arts' Called 'Primitive.'" *ARTnews* 56 (March 1957).

———. "Garden of Peace: UNESCO Gardens in Paris." *Arts and Architecture*, no. 1 (1959).

———. "A Garden That Is Sculpture." *Jerusalem Post*, May 1965.

———. "Guggenheim Proposal." 1927.

———. *The Isamu Noguchi Garden Museum*. New York: Harry N. Abrams, 1987.

———. "Meanings in Modern Sculpture." *ARTnews* (March 1949).

———. "New Stone Gardens." *Art in America* (June 1964).

———. "Noguchi on Brancusi." *Craft Horizons* 36, no. 4 (August 1976).

———. "On Louis Kahn." *Architecture + Urbanism* (1975).

———. "Road I Have Walked." Kyoto Prize lecture, 1986.

———. Foreword. Teiji Itoh. *The Roots of Japanese Architecture: A Photographic Quest by Yukio Futagawa*. New York: Harper & Row, 1963.

———. *A Sculptor's World*. New York: Harper & Row, 1968.

———. "A Sculpture Garden in Jerusalem." *Ariel*, (Spring 1965).

———. "A Stage, Quietly Dramatic." *Kokusai Kenchiku*, November 1950.

———. "The Sculptor and the Architect." *Studio International* 176, (July–August 1968).

———. "The Sculpture of Space." In Martin Friedman, ed. *Isamu Noguchi: The Sculpture of Space*. New York: Whitney Museum of American Art, 1980.

———. "Towards a Reintegration of the Arts." *College Art Journal* (Autumn 1949).

———. "Tribute to Martha Graham" (audiotape), 20 November 1973, Performing Arts Library, New York.

———. "Trouble among Japanese Americans." *New Republic*, 1 February 1943.

———. Untitled. *UNESCO Courier* (November 1958).

———. "What's the Matter with Sculpture?" *Art Front* 16 (September–October 1936).

>> TEXTS BY OTHER AUTHORS

"Architects Would Come to Him . . . and He Would Redesign the Architecture: Interview with Shoji Sadao." *Casa Brutus* (special issue "A Century of Isamu Noguchi") (2005).

A. O. D. "Bunshaft and Noguchi: An Uneasy but Highly Productive Architect-Artist Collaboration." *AIA Journal* (October 1976).

Adams, Celeste Marie. "The Sculpture Garden: A Conversation with Isamu Noguchi." *MFAH Bulletin* (Summer 1986).

Adams, Nicholas. *Gordon Bunshaft and SOM: Building Corporate Modernism*. New Haven, CT: Yale University Press, 2019.

———. *Skidmore, Owings & Merrill: The Experiment since 1936*. Milan: Electa, 2006.

Lady Allen of Harwood (Marjory Allen). *Planning for Play*. London: Thames & Hudson, 1968.

———, and Mary Nicholson. *Memoirs of an Uneducated Lady: Lady Allen of Hurtwood*. London: Thames & Hudson, 1975

Altshuler, Bruce. *Isamu Noguchi: Early Abstraction*. New York: Whitney Museum of American Art, 1994.

———. *Noguchi*. New York: Abbeville, 1994.

Apostolos-Cappadona, Diane, and Bruce Altshuler, eds. *Isamu Noguchi: Essays and Conversations*. New York: Harry N. Abrams, 1994.

Arakal, Byron de. "Wake Up, Mr. Anderson the Oompa Loompas Have Gone." *Pilot*, May 2001.

Asbury, Edith Evans. "Billy Rose's Will Is Upheld Here." *New York Times*, 26 July 1967.

Ashton, Dore. *Noguchi: East and West*. New York: Alfred A. Knopf, 1992.

———. "Space as Sculpture." *Landscape Architecture Magazine* (special issue) (April 1998).

Bach, Friedrich Teja, Margit Rowell, and Ann Temkin, *Constantin Brancusi, 1876–1957*. Philadelphia: Philadelphia Museum of Art, 1995.

Bailey, Paul. *City in the Sun: The Japanese Concentration Camp at Poston, Arizona*. Los Angeles: Westernlore, 1971.

Banham, Mary, et al. *A Critic Writes: Essays by Reyner Banham*. Berkeley: University of California Press, 1996.

Bashô. *The Narrow Road to the Deep North and Other Travel Sketches*. Translated by Nobuyuki Yuasa. Baltimore: Penguin, 1968.

Beardsley, John. "The Machine Becomes a Poem." *Landscape Architecture Magazine* (special issue) (April 1998).

The Billy Rose Sculpture Garden. Jerusalem: Israel Museum, 1982.

"Billy Rose's Two Sisters Lose Fight for His $50 Million Estate." *New York Post*, 15 January 1967.

Birks, Kimberlie. *Design for Children: Play, Ride, Learn, Eat, Create, Sit, Sleep*. London: Phaidon, 2018.

Bourriaud, Nicolas. *Relational Aesthetics*. Translated by Simon Pleasance and Fronza Woods. Dijon: Les Presses du Réel, 2002.

Brara, Noor. "This Artist and Master Stone Carver Was Isamu Noguchi's Collaborator for Decades. Why Do So Few People Know Who Masatoshi Izumi Is?" *artnet*, 11 November 2022. news.artnet.com/art-world/masatoshi-izumi-isamu-noguchi-2032214.

Brooks, H. Allen. "Frank Lloyd Wright and the Destruction of the Box." *Journal of the Society of Architectural Historians* (March 1979).

Brosterman, Norman. *Inventing Kindergarten*. New York: Harry N. Abrams, 1997.

Brownlee, David B., and David G. De Long. *Louis I. Kahn: In the Realm of Architecture*, abbrev. ed. New York: Universe, 1997.

Burbulla, Julia, and Ana-Stanca Tabarasi-Hoffmann, eds. *Gartenkunst und Wissenschaft, Transformation seit dem Beginn der Frühmoderne*. Bern: Peter Lang, 2011.

Calvino, Italo. *Invisible Cities*. Translated by William Weaver. New York: Harcourt Brace Jovanovich, 1974.

Caplan, Frank, and Theresa Caplan. *The Power of Play*. Garden City, NY: Anchor, 1973.

Caro, Robert. *The Power Broker: Robert Moses and the Fall of New York*. New York: Alfred A. Knopf, 1974.

Casa Brutus (special issue, "A Century of Isamu Noguchi") (2005).

Cho, Hyunjung. "Hiroshima Peace Memorial Park and the Making of Japanese Postwar Architecture." *Journal of Architectural Education* 66, no. 1 (2012).

"Cities Inquire after Details of Playground," *Virginia Pilot* (Norfolk), 17 April 1952.

Clothier, Peter. "Isamu Noguchi, South Coast Town Center." *Artforum* (April 1982).

Cooper, David E. *A Philosophy of Gardens*. Oxford: Oxford University Press 2006.

Cort, Louise Allison, and Bert Winther-Tamaki. *Isamu Noguchi and Modern Japanese Ceramics: A Close Embrace of the Earth*. Washington, DC: Smithsonian Institution, 2003.

Cummings, Paul. *Artists in Their Own Words*. New York: St. Martin's Press, 1979.

Curtis, Cathy. "Interview of Henry T. Segerstrom." *Los Angeles Times*, 15 January 1989.

Danz, Ernst. *Architecture of Skidmore, Owings & Merrill, 1950–1962*. London: Architectural Press, 1962.

Dear Heartfelt Friend, Isamu Noguchi: The Exhibition in Celebration of the 90th Birthday of Kenichiro Inokuma. Marugame, Japan: Genichiro Inokuma Museum of Contemporary Art, 1992.

Dewey, John. *Art as Experience*. 1934; reprint, New York: Penguin, 2005.

Dixon, Jenny. *"California Scenario": The Courage of Imagination*. Exhibition brochure. Long Island City, NY: Noguchi Museum, 2010.

Duus, Masayo. *The Life of Isamu Noguchi: Journey without Borders*. Translated by Peter Duus. Princeton, NJ: Princeton University Press, 2003.

Eisenstein, Sergei. *Film Form: Essays in Film Theory*. Translated and edited by Jay Leyda. New York: Harcourt, Brace & World, 1949.

Eisner, Shula. "Afterword: The Prelude." *Ariel*, no. 60 (1985).

Ewing, Robert. "The Artistic Age: Noguchi and Pacific Mutual Spark New Interest in Orange County Outdoor Art." *Orange Coast*, November 1982.

Fabre, Gladys, and Doris Wintgens Hütte, eds. *Van Doesburg and the International Avant- Garde: Constructing a New World. London: Tate Modern, 2010.*

Friedberg, M. Paul, and Ellen Perry Berkeley. *Play and Interplay: A Manifesto for New Design in Urban Recreational Environment*. New York: Macmillan, 1970.

Friedman, Martin. *Noguchi's Imaginary Landscapes*. Minneapolis: Walker Art Center, 1978.

———, ed. *Isamu Noguchi: The Sculpture of Space*. New York: Whitney Museum of American Art, 1980. Includes an essay of that same title by Noguchi.

Frost, Joe. L. "Play Environments for Young Children in the USA: 1800–1990." *Children's Environments Quarterly* 6, no. 4 (Winter 1989).

Genzlinger, Neil. "Architect Turned Concepts of 2 Visionaries into Reality." *New York Times*, 18 November, 2019.

Gideon, Sigfried. *Space, Time, and Architecture*. Cambridge, MA: Harvard University Press, 1941.

Glogowski, Dominika. "Isamu Noguchi's Geometric Landscape Model: A Scientific Encounter with the Observatories of India." In Julia Burbulla and Ana-Stanca Tabarasi-Hoffmann, eds. *Gartenkunst und Wissenschaft, Transformation seit dem Beginn der Frühmoderne*. Bern: Peter Lang, 2011.

Goldberg, Deborah A. *Isamu Noguchi, Patent Holder: Designing the World of Tomorrow*. New York: St. John's University, 2015.

Goldberger, Paul. "Toward Different Ends." In Barbaralee Diamonstein-Spielvogel and Vincent Scully, eds. *Collaboration: Artists and Architects*. New York: Whitney Library of Design, 1981.

Gordon, John. *Isamu Noguchi*. New York: Whitney Museum of American Art / Frederick Praeger, 1968.

Gottehrer, Barry and Tim Hutchens. "Court Battle and Confusion Over Playground." *New York Herald Tribune*, 27 February 1965.

Green, David B. "Builder of Jerusalem: Teddy Kollek 1911–2007." *Windows on Jerusalem* (Winter 2007).

Greene, Alison de Lima, ed. *Isamu Noguchi. A Sculpture for Sculpture; The Lillie and High Roy Cullen Sculpture Garden*. Houston: Museum of Fine Arts, 2006.

Grounds for Play: The Movement that Built Playgrounds for the People of New York. New York: Urban Center, no date (late 1980s?).

Grove, Nancy. *Isamu Noguchi: A Study of the Sculpture*. New York: Garland, 1985.

———. *Isamu Noguchi: Portrait Sculpture*. Washington, DC: Smithsonian Institution Press for the National Portrait Gallery, 1989.

Gruen, John. "The Artist Speaks: Isamu Noguchi." *Art in America* (March–April 1968).

Hart, Craig H. *Children on Playgrounds: Research Perspectives and Applications*. Albany: State University of New York Press, 1993.

Hart, Dakin. *Isamu Noguchi: Archaic / Modern*. Washington, DC: Smithsonian American Art Museum, 2016.

Hart, Dakin and Mark Dean, eds. *Changing and Unchanging Things: Noguchi and Hasegawa in Postwar Japan*. New York: Isamu Noguchi Foundation; Oakland: University of California Press, 2019.

Hayakawa, Masao. *The Garden Art of Japan*. Tokyo: Heibonsha, 1974.

Helfrich, Kurt, and William Whitaker, eds. *Crafting a Modern World: The Architecture and Design of Antonin and Noémi Raymond*. New York: Princeton Architectural Press, 2006.

Herrera, Hayden. *Listening to Stone: The Art and Life of Isamu Noguchi*. New York. Farrar, Straus and Giroux, 2015.

Herrington, Susan. *Cornelia Hahn Oberlander: Making the Modern Landscape*. Charlottesville: University of Virginia Press, 2013.

Heseltine, Peter, and John Holborn. *Playgrounds: The Planning, Design and Construction of Play Environments*. New York: Nichols, 1987.

Hess, Thomas. "Playgrounds." *ARTnews* (April 1952).

Holt, John. *How Children Fail*. New York: Dell, 1964.

Huizinga, Johan. *Homo Ludens: A Study of the Play Element in Culture*. Boston: Beacon, 1955.

Hunter, Sam. *Isamu Noguchi*. New York: Abbeville Press, 1978.

Ikeda, Yikihiro, et al. *Architectural Space as Memory: Isamu Noguchi, Yoshiro Taniguchi, and Keio University*. Tokyo: Keio University Research Center for the Arts and Arts Administration, 2005.

The Interlocking Sculptures of Isamu Noguchi. New York: PaceWildenstein, 2003.

Isamu Noguchi and Qi Baishi: Beijing 1930. Long Island City, NY: Isamu Noguchi Foundation, 2013.

Isamu Noguchi at Gemini 1982–1983. Los Angeles: Gemini G.E.L, 1983. Essay by Michael McClure.

Isamu Noguchi: Bronze and Iron Sculpture. New York: Pace Gallery, 1988. Essay by Dore Ashton, "Isamu Noguchi: Bronze and Iron Sculpture."

Isamu Noguchi Exhibition in Glass Pyramid. Sapporo, Japan: Moerenuma Park, 2003.

Isamu Noguchi Play Equipment: Playing with Isamu Noguchi. Mure, Japan: Isamu Noguchi Foundation of Japan, 2004.

Isamu Noguchi: Stones and Water. New York: PaceWildenstein, 1998. Essay by Jeremy Strick, "Stories of Stone."

Isamu Noguchi: The Exhibition Celebrated the Grand Opening of the Moerenuma Park. Sapporo, Japan: Museum of Contemporary Art, 2005.

Isamu Noguchi: Variations. New York: Pace Gallery 2015.

Isamu Noguchi: We Are the Landscape of All We Know. Portland, OR: Portland Japanese Garden, 2013.

Isozaki, Arata. *Japan-ness in Architecture*. Translated by Sabu Kohso. Cambridge, MA: MIT Press, 2011.

———. *MA Space-Time in Japan*. New York: Cooper-Hewitt, 1979.

Jakob, Michael. *Faux Mountains*. Novato, CA: ORO, 2022.

James, Philip, ed. *Henry Moore on Henry Moore*. London: Macdonald, 1966.

Kaplan, Samuel. "Mayor Signs Pact for Play Center." *New York Times*, 30 December 1965.

Kawamura, Jun'ichi, and Nobuo Katsura. "Moerenuma Park: A Sculpture Engraved Upon the Earth by Isamu Noguchi." *Approach* (Autumn 2004).

Kirby, Alexandra Eve. "Reassessing the Public Spaces of Isamu Noguchi." Master's thesis, Columbia University, 2013.

Kirsch, Matthew. "Noguchi and the Jantar Mantars of Northern India." In Hafthor Yngvason, ed. *Looking Up: Skyviewing Sculptures of Isamu Noguchi*. Lewes, UK: D. Giles; Bellingham: Western Washington University, 2022.

Kogawa, Joy. *Obasan*. Toronto: Penguin, 1981

Krinsky, Carol Herselle. *Gordon Bunshaft of Skidmore, Owings & Merrill*. New York: Architectural History Foundation; Cambridge, MA: MIT Press, 1988.

Kroc, Ray. *Grinding It Out: The Making of McDonald's*. Chicago: H. Regnery, 1977.

Kubie, Lawrence S. *Neurotic Distortion of the Creative Process*. New York: Farrar, Straus and Giroux, 1961.

Kuh, Katherine. *The Artist's Voice*. New York: Harper & Row, 1962.

Kutcher, Arthur. *The New Jerusalem: Planning and Politics*. London: Thames & Hudson, 1973.

"The Landscapes of Isamu Noguchi." *Landscape Architecture Magazine* (special issue) (April 1998).

Lange, Alexandra. "The Story Behind Isamu Noguchi's Playscapes in Atlanta." hermanmiller.com/stories/why-magazine/the-story-behind-isamu-noguchis-play-scapes-in-atlanta/.

Lao Tzû. *Tao Te Ching* (Book of Tao). Translated by John Minford. London: Penguin Random House, 2019.

Larrivee, Shaina D. "Playscapes: Isamu Noguchi's Designs for Play." *Public Art Dialogue* 1, (March 2011). Reprinted in *Isamu Noguchi: Parques / Playscapes*. Mexico City: Museo Tamayo, 2016.

Le Corbusier. *Towards a New Architecture*. 1922. Translated by Frederick Etchells. 1933; reprint, New York: Dover, 1986.

Ledermann, Alfred, and Alfred Trachsel, *Creative Playgrounds and Recreation Centers*. New York: Frederick Praeger, 1959.

Lefaivre, Liane, and Ingeborg de Roode, eds. *Aldo van Eyck: The Playgrounds and the City*. Amsterdam: Stedelijk Museum; Rotterdam: NAi, 2002.

Lefaivre, Liane, and Alexander Tzonis. *Aldo van Eyck: Humanist Rebel*. Rotterdam: 010, 1999.

Lelyveld, Joseph. "Model Play Area for Park Shown." *New York Times*, 5 February 1964.

Ligtelijn, Vincent, and Francis Strauven, eds., *Aldo van Eyck Writings*, Volume 2. Amsterdam: Sun, 2008.

Lyford, Amy. *Isamu Noguchi's Modernism: Negotiating Race, Labor, and Nation, 1930–1950*. Berkeley: University of California Press, 2013.

———. "Noguchi, Sculptural Abstraction, and the Politics of Japanese American Internment." *Art Bulletin* (March 2003).

Maeda, Robert J. "Isamu Noguchi: 5-7-A, Poston, Arizona." *Asiamerica Journal* 20, no. 2 (1994).

Markino, Yoshio. *A Japanese Artist in London*. London: Chatto & Windus, 1912.

Marx, Edward. *Leonie Gilmour: When East Weds West*. [Santa Barbara, CA]: Botchan, 2013.

———. *Yone Noguchi: The Stream of Fate*, Volume 1, *The Western Sea*. Santa Barbara, CA: Botchan, 2019.

Massara, Kathleen. "The Japanese-American Artists Who Went to the Camps to Help." *New Yorker*, 31 January 2017.

McLeod, Mary. "Modernism." In Iain Borden, Murray Fraser, and Barbara Penner, eds. *Forty Ways to Think About Architecture: Architectural History and Theory Today*. Chichester, UK: Wiley, 2014.

Miller, Dorothy C., ed. *Fourteen Americans*. New York: Museum of Modern Art, 1946.

Miller, Mara. *The Garden as Art*. Albany: State University of New York Press, 1994.

Moere Fan Club. *Access Moere Park: Message Sculpted in the Earth*. Sapporo, Japan: Moere Fan Club, 2008.

Moyao, Arely Ramírez, and Mara Garbuno, eds. *Isamu Noguchi: Parques / Playscapes*. Mexico City: Museo Tamayo, 2016.

Mumford, Lewis. "UNESCO House: Out, Damned Cliché!" 1960. In *The Highway and the City*. New York: New American Library, 1964.

Naruse, Hiroshi. *Jardin japonais*. Paris: UNESCO, 2000.

Neumann, Judith. "Jumping to Conclusions: 'California Scenario' Visitors Were Anything but Neutral. They Called It Amazing. Important. Even Alienating." *Register* (9 May 1982).

Nitzan-Shiftan, Alona. *Seizing Jerusalem: The Architecture of Unilateral Unification*. Minneapolis: University of Minnesota Press, 2017.

Noguchi. Kamakura, Japan: Museum of Modern Art, 1952.

Noguchi, Yoneshirô. *The American Diary of a Japanese Girl*. New York: Frederick Stokes, 1902. Reprint. Edward Marx and Laura E. Franey, eds., *The American Diary of a Japanese Girl*. Philadelphia: Temple University Press, 2007.

———. *Hiroshige and the Japanese Landscapes*. Tokyo: Japan Travel Bureau, 1954.

———. *Later Essays*. Edited by Edward Marx. [Santa Barbara, CA]: Botchan, 2013.

Ogata, Amy. *Designing the Creative Child: Playthings and Places in Midcentury America*. Minneapolis: University of Minnesota Press, 2013.

Okakura, Kakuzô. *The Book of Tea*. 1906; reprint, Rutland, VT: Tuttle, 1956.

Peck, Robin. "Sculpture and the Sculptural in Halifax and Vancouver." In Stan Douglas, ed. *Vancouver Anthology: The Institutional Politics of Art*. Vancouver, BC: Talonbooks, 1991.

Pellerin, Ananda, ed. *Noguchi and Greece, Greece and Noguchi*. Los Angeles: Atelier Éditions / Noguchi Museum, 2022.

"Playground for the United Nations." *Interiors* (April 1952).

Raymond, Antonin. *An Autobiography*. Rutland, VT: Charles E. Tuttle, 1973.

Richie, Donald. *A Tractate on Japanese Aesthetics*. Berkeley, CA: Stone Bridge, 2007.

Roberts, Brady M. "The European Roots of Regionalism: Grant Wood's Stylistic Synthesis." In *Grant Wood: An American Master Revealed*. Davenport Museum of Art, IA; Rohnert Park, CA: Pomegranate Artbooks, 1995.

Ronen, Meir. "Rose + Noguchi = Unique Centre of Sculpture." Source unknown (*Jerusalem Post*?), early 1960s.

Rorty, Richard. *Consequences of Pragmatism (Essays 1972–1980)*. Minneapolis: University of Minnesota Press, 1982.

Rose, Billy. *Wine, Women and Words*. New York: Pocket Books, 1950.

Ross, Stephanie. *What Gardens Mean*. Chicago: University of Chicago Press, 1998.

Russell, John. "Castles in the Sand." *New York Times*, 28 April 1968.

Rychlak, Bonnie. *Relocated: Twenty Sculptures by Isamu Noguchi from Japan*. Long Island City, NY: Isamu Noguchi Foundation, 2001.

———. *Zen No Zen: Aspects of Noguchi's Sculptural Vision*. Long Island City, NY: Isamu Noguchi Foundation, 2002.

———, et al. *Noguchi and Graham: Selected Works for Dance*. Long Island City, NY: Isamu Noguchi Foundation, 2004.

Ryo, Niimi. "The Modern Primitive: Discourses of the Visual Arts in Japan in the 1950s." In Ryu Nimi et al. *Isamu Noguchi—Rosanjin Kitaoji*. Tokyo: Sezon Museum of Art, 1996.

Sadao, Shoji. *Noguchi: Sculpture and Nature*. Long Island City, NY: Isamu Noguchi Foundation, 2002.

Sanô, Tuemon. "A Work Reflecting the History of Our Friendship." In Shikoku Shimbun, ed. *Isamu Noguchi: Human Aspect as a Contemporary; 54 Witnesses in Japan and America*. Takamatsu, Japan: Shikoku Shimbun, 2002.

Sandseter, Ellen Beate Hansen. "Characteristics of Risky Play." *Journal of Adventure Education and Outdoor Learning* 9, no. 1 (2009).

Saussure, Ferdinand de. *Course in General Linguistics*. Translated by Wade Baskin and edited by Charles Bally and Albert Sechehaye. New York: McGraw Hill, 1966.

Schaffner, Ingrid, and Lisa Jacobs. *Julien Levy: Portrait of an Art Gallery*. Cambridge, MA: MIT Press, 1998.

"Sculptor Works with Rocks and Trees to Make Beauty at New HQ." *UNESCO House News*, 18 (October 1957).

Scott, Sascha T. "Georgia O'Keeffe's Hawai'i? Decolonizing the History of American Modernism." *American Art* 34, no. 2 (Summer 2020).

Shanes, Eric. *Constantin Brancusi*. New York: Abbeville, 1989.

Shapiro, Barbara E. "'Tout ça est foutaise, foutaise et demi!': Le Corbusier and UNESCO." *Revue d'art canadienne / Canadian Art Review* 16, no. 2 (1989).

Shigemori, Mirei. *Selected Arrangements of Moribana and Heikwa*. Volume 2. New York, Boston, and Chicago: Yamanaka & Co. Mitsuharu Hashizume, 1934.

Shikoku Shimbun, ed. *Isamu Noguchi: Human Aspect as a Contemporary, 54 Witnesses in Japan and America*. Takamatsu, Japan: Shikoku Shimbun, 2002.

Shirey, David L. "Dubuffet Is Doing 40-Floor Sculpture for Chase Plaza." *New York Times*, 24 November 1970.

Sofu Teshigahara in the Postwar Avant-Garde Era. Tokyo: Setagaya Art Museum, 2001.

Solomon, Deborah. "Striving to Become Israel's Louvre." *New York Times*, 24 October 1999.

Solomon, Susan G. *American Playgrounds: Revitalizing Community Space*. Hanover, NH: University Press of New England, 2005.

Soseki, Musô. "Poem on Dry Mountain." In *Sun at Midnight: Musô Soseki, Poems and Sermons*. Translated by W. S. Merwin and Sôiku Shigematsu. San Francisco: North Point Press, 1980.

"*Spirit of the Lima Bean* Unveiled at the SC Plaza," *Costa Mesa News*, 11 March 1981.

Sugiyama, Makiko. *Banraisha: A Poetic Architecture by Yoshiro Taniguchi and Isamu Noguchi* (in Japanese). Tokyo: Kajima Institute, 2006.

Suzuki, Makoto. "Fountain and Sculpture." *Japan Architect* (May–June 1970).

———. "Sculpture," *Japan Architect* (May–June 1970).

Symmes, Marilyn, ed. *Fountain: Splash and Spectacle: Water and Design from the Renaissance to the Present*. New York: Rizzoli, 1998

Takahashi, Koji, et al., eds. *Isamu Noguchi Retrospective 1992*. Translated by Stanley N. Anderson. Tokyo: National Museum of Modern Art, 1992.

Takei, Jirô, and Marc P. Keane. *Sakuteiki: Visions of the Japanese Garden*. Boston: Tuttle, 2001.

Takemitsu, Toru. "Isamu Noguchi—A Traveller." In Shizuko Watari, ed. *Play Mountain: Isamu Noguchi + Louis Kahn*. Tokyo: Watarium, 1996.

Tamir, Tali. "The Israel Museum: From Dream to Fulfillment." *Israel Museum Journal* (Fall 1990).

Tange, Kenzô, and Noboru Kawazoe. *Ise: Prototype of Japanese Architecture*. New Haven, CT: Yale University Press, 1965.

Temko, Alan. "Noguchi's California Parable." *San Francisco Chronicle*, 26 September 1982.

Teshigahara, Sôfu. *The Fifty Principles of Sôgetsu*. Tokyo: Sôgetsu School of Ikebana, 2012.

———. *Kadensho: The Book of Flowers*. Translated by Christopher Blasdel. Tokyo: Sôgetsu Bunkajigyo, 2011.

Threlfall, Tim. *Isamu Noguchi: Aspects of a Sculptor's Practice; A Continuity with Life*. Sussex, England: Seagull, 1992.

Torres, Ana Maria. *Isamu Noguchi: The Structure of Space*. New York: Monacelli, 2000.

Toshiya, Echizen. *Timeless Landscapes: Isamu Noguchi; Moerenuma Park* (in Japanese). Tokyo: Millegraph, 2020.

Tracy, Robert. *Spaces of the Mind: Isamu Noguchi's Dance Designs*. New York: Limelight, 2000.

Treib, Marc. "Elaboration, Reduction, and Yûgen." *Journal of Garden History*, (April–June 1989). Reprinted in Marc Treib, *Settings and Stray Paths: Writings on Landscapes and Gardens*. London: Routledge, 2005.

———. "Evocative Parallels: Japan and Postwar America Landscape Design." *Consultants in Landscape Architecture Journal* (in Japanese) (January 2002). Reprinted in Marc Treib, *Settings and Stray Paths*.

———. "The Fountain as Urban Oasis." In Marilyn Symmes, ed. *Fountain: Splash and Spectacle: Water and Design from the Renaissance to the Present*. New York: Rizzoli, 1998.

———. "Modes of Complexity: The Distilled Complexity of Japanese Design." *Landscape Journal* (Spring 1993).

———. *Noguchi in Paris: Isamu Noguchi and the UNESCO Garden*. San Francisco: William Stout; Paris: UNESCO, 2003.

———. "Noguchi's Landscapes: The Garden as Sculpture." *Ptah*, no. 8 (Finland) (2009).

———. *"Noguchi's Spiritual Quest." Landscape Design (England) (April 1998).*

———. "On Plans." *Utblick Landskap*, no. 4 (1998). Reprinted in Marc Treib, ed., *Representing Landscape Architecture*. London: Taylor & Francis, 2008.

———. "A Sculpting of Space." *Landscape Design* (England) (February 1998).

———. "Sculptur[ed] Park." *Landscape Architecture Magazine* (May 2006).

———. "A Sculpture for Sculpture." In Alison de Lima Greene, ed. *Isamu Noguchi: A Sculpture for Sculpture; The Lillie and High Roy Cullen Sculpture Garden*. Houston: Museum of Fine Arts, 2006.

———. *Settings and Stray Paths: Writings on Landscapes and Gardens*. London: Routledge, 2005.

———, ed. *Meaning in Landscape Architecture and Gardens*. London: Routledge, 2011.

———, ed. *Modern Landscape Architecture: A Critical Review*. Cambridge, MA: MIT Press, 1993.

Tschumi, Christian. *Mirei Shigemori, Rebel in The Garden: Modern Japanese Landscape Architecture*. Basel: Birkhäuser, 2007.

Tsubaki, Andrew T. "Zeami and the Transition of the Concept of Yûgen: A Note on Japanese Aesthetics." *Journal of Aesthetics and Art Criticism* (Autumn 1971).

Two Buildings in San Francisco. San Francisco: San Francisco Museum of Art, 1959.

Tyson, Rae. "As New Ground Is Broken, Plow Is Dying Out." *USA Today*, 23 May 1994.

Ueda, Makoto. *Literary and Art Theories in Japan.* Cleveland, OH: Case Western Reserve University Press, 1967.

Uematsu, Yuka. *Arizona: Isamu Noguchi, Issey Miyake.* Marugame, Japan: Genichiro Inokuma Museum of Contemporary Art, 1997.

Van Doesburg, Theo. *Principles of Neo-Plastic Art.* 1925. English translation. London: Lund Humphries, 1966.

Van Lingen, Anna, and Denisa Kollarova. *Aldo van Eyck: Seventeen Playgrounds.* Amsterdam. Amsterdam: Lecturis, 2016.

Walker, Peter. "A Levitation of Stones." *Landscape Architecture Magazine* (special issue) (April 1998).

———, and Melanie Simo. *Invisible Gardens: The Search for Modernism in the American Landscape.* Cambridge MA: MIT Press, 1994.

Watari, Shizuko, ed. *Play Mountain: Isamu Noguchi + Louis Kahn.* Tokyo: Watarium, 1996.

Wilkinson, Alan, ed. *Henry Moore: Writings and Conversations.* Berkeley: University of California Press, 2002.

Williams, Tod, and Billie Tsien. *Quiet Light: An Installation of Isamu Noguchi's Akari Light Sculptures.* New York: Gallery at Takashimaya, 1994.

Winther-Tamaki, Bert. "The Ceramic Art of Isamu Noguchi: A Close Embrace of the Earth." In Louise Allison Cort and Bert Winther-Tamaki. *Isamu Noguchi and Modern Japanese Ceramics: A Close Embrace of the Earth.* Washington, DC: Smithsonian Institution, 2003.

Wolf, Amy. *On Becoming an Artist: Isamu Noguchi and His Contemporaries, 1922–1960.* Long Island City, NY: Isamu Noguchi Foundation and Garden Museum, 2010.

Wong, Herman. "Sculptor Salutes Plaza's Past." *Los Angeles Times*, 11 March 1981.

Wright, Frank Lloyd. *An Autobiography.* New York: Duell, Sloane & Pearce, 1943.

Wyver, Shirley, et al. "Ten Ways to Restrict Children's Freedom to Play: The Problem of Surplus Safety." *Contemporary Issues in Early Childhood*, no. 3 (2010).

Yamamoto, Hitishi. "Isamu Noguchi and Sapporo." *Japan Landscape*, no. 30 (1994).

Yashiro, Katsuhiko. "The Message Isamu Noguchi Left to the Moerenuma Park." In *Isamu Noguchi: The Exhibition Celebrated the Grand Opening of the Moerenuma Park.* Sapporo: Museum of Contemporary Art, 2005.

Yau, John. "Rethinking Noguchi's Greatness." In *Isamu Noguchi: Variations.* New York: Pace Gallery, 2015.

Zevi, Bruno. "The Modern Dimension of Landscape Architecture." *Journal of the Institute of Landscape Architecture* (November 1962).

Zwigenberg, Ran. "The Most Modern City in the World: Isamu Noguchi's Cenotaph Controversy and Hiroshima's City of Peace." *Critical Military Studies*, no. 2 (2015).

>> VIDEOS

Rich, Michael, dir. *A Sense of Place.* 1982. youtube.com/watch?v=N8IGzclH2xY&t=6s.

Secrets of the Art Garden with Israel Museum Director Ido Bruno. 2020 youtube.com/watch?v=7X-iJav6Cu4.

>> POSTFACE AND ACKNOWLEDGMENTS

The seeds of this book were planted long ago in the mid-1980s on a visit to *California Scenario* in Costa Mesa, California. As described in chapter 9 that visit provoked strong reactions, most of which were hardly positive, yet it led to a lifelong interest in the sculpture and gardens of Isamu Noguchi. Granted a Fulbright Senior Fellowship in 1993–94, I was based in Paris with research focused on the emergence of modern landscape architecture in several Western European countries. After my first visit to UNESCO House, however, I became curious about Noguchi's so-called *Jardin japanais* and began research on the project using the agency's archives. That archival work, and the opportunity to experience the garden through the seasons, eventually led to the book *Noguchi in Paris: Isamu Noguchi and the UNESCO Garden*, copublished by William Stout Publishers in San Francisco and UNESCO in Paris in 2003. For his support on this project and for years of friendship, I must acknowledge Bill Stout, who graciously agreed to publish the book before UNESCO joined in the venture, and who questioned only aspects of the book's design rather than its content.

One always embarks on projects such as these building on foundations established by other scholars, and this project was certainly no different. I am grateful to many people who supported that work, among them the late Dore Ashton, who at the time I began my research had recently published a comprehensive biography of the artist and shared insights into Noguchi's work, elusive factual information, criticism, and encouragement in my efforts. Markku Järvinen, the UNESCO archivist at that time, helped me sort through the masses of reports and materials in the archives, in which mention of the garden project and its protagonists was sadly quite sparce. Throughout the project Dorothée Imbert, today Director of the Knowlton School of Architecture at The Ohio State University, offered encouragement and criticism on a daily basis, both of great benefit. Architect Ana Maria Torres kindly allowed the use of several images drawn from her own excellent study of Noguchi's spatial works. Also in 1993, a short-term Fulbright Lectureship to Israel administered by the United States–Israel Educational Foundation supported my sole visit to the Billy Rose Art Garden in Jerusalem as well as archival research in the Israel Museum. The late Alfred Mansfeld, the architect responsible for the museum's design, graciously shared his stories about the project along with his recollections of Noguchi's concepts and working method. In writing the chapter on the garden in Jerusalem almost three decades later, this material still proved valuable. In New York, Bruce Altshuler, at the time the director of the Isamu Noguchi Foundation and Garden Museum, who had already published his own book on Noguchi, could not have been more encouraging—as was former curator Bonnie Rychlak, who provided several fruitful readings of Noguchi's thinking and spatial undertakings. Perhaps the strongest supporter of my efforts in those early years was the foundation's long-term Director of Administration and External Affairs, Amy Howe, who helped me understand and navigate the museum's collection and archives, and who kindly established contacts for me in the United States and Japan. I owe her a substantial debt of gratitude.

I pursued the subject of Noguchi and his landscapes off and on in the intervening decades, although admittedly far more off than on. Invitations to lecture at several universities, and especially the Portland Japanese Garden, sustained my efforts to reevaluate the research materials that had been collecting, and coaxed their organization into some kind of comprehensible order. As I traveled, should I be in the vicinity of a Noguchi site or collection, I tried to visit, and when successful took numerous photographs. Over the years, I published several articles that tested the waters in journals including the British *Landscape Design* and the Finnish architectural journal *Ptah*, working with their editors—whom I respectively thank—the late Ken Fieldhouse and Esa Laaksonen. A request to contribute to a book on the Museum of Fine Arts, Houston's sculpture garden catalyzed deeper research into its landscape, a condensation and reworking of which appears in this book. For that invitation and for her insights, I must wholeheartedly thank Alison de Lima Greene, Curator of Modern and Contemporary Art. Former Cooper-Hewitt Museum Curator Marilyn Symmes's kind invitation to contribute an essay on urban fountains to her exhibition and book on the topic led to a more detailed study of the Dodge Fountain in Detroit.

As I periodically inched toward producing a book I worked with no fewer than three directors of the Isamu Noguchi Foundation and Garden Museum, each of whom has been extremely helpful: Bruce Altshuler, already mentioned; then Jenny Dixon; and, most recently, Brett Littman. At the Isamu Noguchi Garden Museum in Mure, Japan, I warmly thank Administrative Director Fumi Ikeda for facilitating my visits to the Noguchi house, studios, and landscape, and for sharing her knowledge and experience garnered from her long association with the site. On my several visits there, the late Masatoshi Izumi was generous in sharing his thoughts and recollections of working with Noguchi in conversations that accompanied several pleasant afternoon teas at his house.

A research fellowship at the Henry Moore Institute in Leeds, England, allowed access to materials on sculpture otherwise unavailable to me, as well as the time and setting for considering why and when we might consider a landscape as art. Discussions with Jon Wood, Research Curator, and former director Lisa Le Feuvre were particularly fruitful, and enjoyable.

In Japan friends, colleagues, and others facilitated access to sites and materials, and graciously lent their time for discussions. These include Tokyo Institute of Technology Emeritus Professor David Stewart; Tokyo University of Agriculture Emeritus Professor Makoto Suzuki; Kyoto University of the Arts Emeritus Professor Yoji Sasaki and Professor Ken Kawai; architects Jun'ichi Kawamura of Architect 5 and Yoshio Taniguchi; and University of Washington Professor Ken Oshima. I also thank Architect 5 for the use of several photographs of Moerenuma Park.

In the United States, I thank Professor Nicholas Adams for sharing his vast knowledge of the life and architecture of Gordon Bunshaft, who commissioned many of Noguchi's key landscapes; I also appreciate his review of the relevant chapter with his usual critical eye and good humor. With landscape architect Ken Kammeyer I visited *California Scenario*, where he shared his exhaustive knowledge of the garden, whose success owed so much to his own contributions. There, I also interviewed the late Henry T. Segerstrom, who instigated the project and who believed so much in Noguchi's participation that he devoted considerable time and effort to successfully woo the artist into accepting and completing the commission. While on-site I met with Karen Graham, who told me of Commonwealth Properties' belief in the significance of the landscape and their efforts to maintain Noguchi's original vision for the garden. For providing important documents, I need acknowledge William Whitaker at the University of Pennsylvania Architectural Archives and Catherine Wallack at the University of Arkansas Library's Special Collections. Thanks also to both University of British Columbia Professor of Landscape Architecture Susan Herrington, who directed me to key readings on the subject of play, and Professor Elissa Rosenberg, who translated materials on the Western Wall from Hebrew. Most recently, as the sequestering forced by Covid-19 coerced me to return to writing and the eventual completion of the book, current staff members of the Isamu Noguchi Foundation and Museum have been exceptionally helpful, supporting my use of their archival holdings and reviewing an earlier draft of the book. The access to the Noguchi archives and use of their materials has been critical. Sincere thanks are due Head of Archives Janine Biunno, who made extensive efforts to locate and process the images from the Noguchi Museum presented in this book. I am also grateful to Curator of Research Matt Kirsch, and former Senior Curator Dakin Hart for the time spent with me and for sharing their knowledge and understanding of Noguchi the artist, his ideas, and his work. And although in the end I am working with another publisher, I would like to acknowledge the initial interest and support of Katherine Boller, Editorial Director of Art and Architecture books at Yale University Press.

Once again I need heartily thank those at the the Hubbard Edcational Trust for their generous funding toward the publication of this book. As on other of my book projects, the trust's support has been crucial.

At ORO Editions Gordon Goff has actively supported this book and helped bring it to light; copy editor Jane Friedman made sense of garbled prose and applied judicious pruning where needed; as on all our earlier collaborations, Jake Anderson has been the model production manager, cheerleader, and troubleshooter. t is a pleasure to work with people upon whom I have relied so substantially.

Finally, let me acknowledge those friends and professional colleagues who have helped shape my thinking about landscapes in general, if not always Isamu Noguchi's landscapes in particular: landscape architects, longtime friends, and travel buddies, Thorbjörn Andersson, and Benetton Foundation Director Luigi Latini. Over many years University of Sheffield Senior Lecturer Emerita Catherine Dee provided knowledge on landscape architecture and the arts with an understandably English perspective, always with good cheer. It was my great friend, the late landscape architect Ron Herman, who initially encouraged me to visit *California Scenario* almost forty years ago, a consequential visit that eventually led to this book's appearance decades later. A big heap o' thanks goes to my Canadian pal Alyssa Schwann for all the informative conversations, reference recommendations, encouragement, criticism, and smiling tolerance that have all contributed to finally getting this thing done.

And lastly, to those who have helped, encouraged, or critiqued my efforts over the decades, but whose names I have omitted due to memory lapses, I offer both my gratitude and apologies—it's been a very long process, and the mind forgets more than it remembers.

Marc Treib
Berkeley, July 2023

>> INDEX